Human Rights NGOs in East Africa

Political and Normative Tensions

Edited by Makau Mutua

PENN

University of Pennsylvania Press

Philadelphia

Copyright © 2009 University of Pennsylvania Press

Published by
University of Pennsylvania Press
Philadelphia, Pennsylvania 19104-4112

Printed in the United States of America on acid-free paper
10 9 8 7 6 5 4 3 2 1

Library of Congress Cataloging-in-Publication Data

Human rights NGOs in East Africa : political and normative tensions / edited by Makau Mutua.
       p. cm.—(Pennsylvania studies in human rights)
    Includes bibliographical references and index.
    ISBN 978-0-8122-4112-9 (alk. paper)
  1. Africa, Eastern—Politics and government—1960–   2. Human rights—Africa, Eastern.
  3. Democratization—Africa, Eastern.   4. Non-governmental organizations—Africa,
  Eastern.   5. Civil society—Africa, Eastern.   6. Democracy—Africa, Eastern.   I. Mutua,
  Makau.
JQ2945.A91H88   2008
323.06'0676—dc22   2008025562

CONTENTS

PART V
NGO Institutional Case Studies

PART VI
South/South and North/South NGO Relations

Introduction

Makau Mutua

THE PHENOMENON OF the modern civil society is a recent development in East Africa. The emergence of the modern civil society in the region is directly traceable to the imposition of the colonial state in the nineteenth century.[1] But this modern phenomenon is to be distinguished from the civil society that existed in precolonial Africa.[2] Originally, civil society in Europe traditionally referred to *societas civilis*, and was coterminous with the state.[3] In this tradition, which stretched back to ancient Greece, "to be a member of civil society was to be a citizen—a member of the state—and, thus, obligated to act in accordance with its laws and without engaging in acts harmful to other citizens."[4] In contrast to the contemporary usage of the term, civil society denoted the complete obedience, dependence, union, and fealty to the state. It was not until the early nineteenth century that civil society and the state became distinctly different spheres.[5] It is an irony of history that this distinction would develop on the cusp of the colonial conquest of Africa by European imperial powers.

Within the African colonial state, only the colons enjoyed the full rights of citizenship because they were recognized as the sole members of civil society. As Mahmood Mamdani correctly notes, in this order Africans were not citizens but subjects without basic freedoms.[6] It is precisely the exclusion, exploitation, and degradation of Africans by the colonial state that led to the anticolonial struggle. A key motive of the anticolonial struggle was the deracialization of civil society. Simply put, Africans sought the full gamut of citizenship rights enjoyed by the white settler classes. Mamdani writes that the "anti-colonial struggle was at the same time a struggle of the embryonic middle and working classes, the native strata in limbo, for entry into civil society."[7] Paradoxically, Africans had to struggle against the state to become a part of it. But the deracialization of civil society and the colonial state—through its replacement by the postcolonial state—did not result in a free society. Throughout Africa, the postcolonial state has remained a fundamentally illiberal institution. Since decolonization, the African state has primarily been a predator, an instrumentality bent on the destruction of civil society.[8]

The tortured history of the African postcolonial state is the unavoidable lens through which civil society on the continent must be viewed. Reminiscent of the anticolonial struggle—which sought to abolish race as a qualification for citizenship—the current political upheavals in Africa aim to reform the state through the medium of democratization.[9] As before, the struggle is focused on the redefinition of the nature of civil society and its role within the state. An educated and urbanized African middle and professional class, a large part of it connected to the so-called international civil society, has been at the forefront of this reformist wave. Since the late 1980s, this class has organized itself either in opposition political parties or in nongovernmental organizations to demand change. It seeks a rule of law state bounded by constitutionalism and incubated in a political democracy. By 2000, as a result of these political pressures, all but several of Africa's fifty-four states had acquiesced to some form of democratic transition.[10] The ironclad one party and military dictatorships of the postcolonial state are largely gone. In large measure, this change is a tribute to the resilience of the civil society, pro-democracy movement in Africa.

Except for North Africa and a handful of blatantly autocratic regimes in sub-Saharan Africa, more open political space has been created. Even so, one should not exaggerate the transformative nature of these political transitions. In some cases, such as Benin and Zambia, open electoral politics and democratic freedoms are being routinized. But there have also been serious setbacks in Niger, Gambia, and Sierra Leone, among others, where elected governments have been overturned.[11] Elsewhere, such as Kenya, electoral politics have ushered in regime change but failed to uproot institutional corruption or entrench meaningful reforms.[12] Kleptocracies and predatory elites continue to rule under the cloak of democracy in many African states. The one-party mandarins and military rulers of yesteryear have quickly adapted themselves to some forms of electoral politics to retain their stranglehold on power. The consequence has been a failure to transform the undemocratic, and often illiberal, nature of the state. That is why most Africans remain at the margins of society, if not worse. Citizenship in the state exists only as a formal matter, and offers little meaning or protection.

The Second Liberation—the post-Cold War wave of democratization—has brought some relief but largely failed to defang the African postcolonial state.[13] Internally, these failures have been blamed on a number of factors including imperial cartography, the legacy of colonialism, the ethnic cleavages of the African state, an unforgiving international order, and the bankruptcy of African

ruling elites.[14] Evidence now suggests that electoral politics alone are not a panacea for the African malaise.[15] What is required is the reconstruction of the African state from the ground up. At the center of the dysfunction of the African
state is how power ought to be organized, shared, and executed. The overriding
project should aim to legitimize the state so that its power becomes a force for
progressive change. The challenge of the African postcolonial state is therefore
singular: how to create viable, legitimate, and democratic societies. Simply put,
African states must effectively address the deficit of democracy and give each
citizen a reason to identify with political society. Otherwise, the gains of the
most recent wave of political liberalization will stagnate the state and revert it to
either naked despotism or catastrophic collapse.

The African democratic renaissance will not be possible unless several bottlenecks are addressed boldly. First, political parties, the vehicles through which
the state is ruled in a democracy, must become receptacles of the national interest. Unfortunately, African political parties have not generally been a force for
democratization, even though they have used the open ballot to ascend to
power. Parties are rarely incubated in a coherent ideology or philosophy. Instead, they are empty vehicles for tribal barons or cabals of kleptocrats without
a committed vision for reform. As a general rule, African political parties in the
age of multipartyism lack sound ideological direction and rarely mobilize the
population on genuinely important social or economic questions. That is why
they have been unable to deepen democracy or incubate a culture of reformist
politics. In Kenya, for example, political parties are seen as instruments of conve-
nience for individual politicians.[16] In such a state, political parties are captive to
all manner of corrosive identity politics—divisive ethnic demagoguery and religious exceptionalism. Rather than help forge a national consciousness, political
parties heighten identity consciousness and drive the state to further fractional-
ization.

Since political parties have not been able to lead in the reconstitution of the
political order, civil society remains as the only other viable sector capable of
reforming state power. Civil society has long been recognized as the difference
between democracy and state tyranny.[17] The traditional role of civil society in
established democracies has been to keep the state honest and accountable. In a
word, civil society plays a civilizing role in a democracy. Without doubt, this is
a role that African civil society must play. However, it must do more simply
because it operates in conditions that are vastly different. In addition to acting
as the cartilage between the state and society and checking the arbitrariness of
state power, civil society must act to create the conditions for democracy. Put
differently, civil society in Africa must be a key agent for democratization. John
Harbeson, a leading scholar on African politics, has argued that an effective and

viable civil society is the condition precedent to democracy in Africa. Even if all the other variables necessary for democracy are realized, African renaissance will not be possible without a strong civil society:

> civil society is a hitherto missing key to sustained political reform, legitimate states and governments, improved governance, viable state-society and state-economy relationships, and prevention of the kind of political decay that undermined new African governments a generation ago.[18]

This is the conclusion reached by a number of leading thinkers and practitioners of African politics. In countries as diverse as South Africa, Kenya, and Nigeria, civil societies have played key roles in the fundamental reconstruction of politics. As Michael Bratton has written, in some cases, the control of politics has shifted from state elites—those connected with government and political parties—to more popular forces precisely because strong civil societies have opened up more political space.[19] Generally, where civil society is weaker, the pace and depth of democratic reforms have been slow or nonexistent. In countries where the state has suffocated civil society, such as Egypt or Ethiopia, state elites are more able to easily manipulate and manage change to their advantage. Unchallenged authority by the state is the sine qua non for autocracy, the form of government that the existence of a viable civil society cannot permit. While it is too early to assert that African civil societies have turned the corner, it is not outlandish to argue that they are now a permanent feature of the political landscape. What is arguable is the depth, effectiveness, and independence of civil societies, not their de facto existence and import.

Even though civil societies are critically important to Africa's democratic development, there has been a dearth of scholarship on the subject. This has been particularly the case with regard to scholarship by Africans themselves about their own political realities. There seems to be more attention on civil society in Africa by Africanists in Europe and North America. There are several explanations for this disparity. Western academics have placed a lot of emphasis on the role of civil society in the African democratization process.[20] According to Mamdani, "In the late 1980s, the theme of a society-state struggle reverberated through Africanist circles in North America and became the new prismatic lens through which to gauge the significance of events in Africa."[21] Needless to say, the subject has dominated the Africanist academy ever since. Over the last two decades, Western donor agencies and charities in Africa have reflected this bias towards civil society.[22] Grants and other forms of support have been pumped into the nascent civil society, making it one of the largest recipients of

Western assistance.[23] But the dearth of scholarship on civil society by Africans is largely a result of the atrophied state of the university on the continent. As in almost every other area, in the last several decades, scholarship in Africa has suffered greatly because of the challenges facing the African university. Political interference, the legacy of colonialism in education, underdevelopment, state failure, and the lack of resources have combined to rob the African university of its promise.[24] Even worse, a culture of anti-intellectualism among ruling elites has marginalized the academy. Under these conditions, African scholars have been hard put to effectively engage in the free pursuit of knowledge and the unencumbered study of emergent ideas and institutions.

This book addresses the multiple challenges to civil society in East Africa while at the same time critically reflecting on the nature of nongovernmental organizations and their role in the politics of the individual countries in the region. The contributors pay special attention to human rights NGOs in the region, easily the most visible civil society quotient. This sector of civil society has grown rapidly in the last two decades and accounts for the most critical voices against the state. As such, it has played the leading role in the struggle to open up political space.[25] Even so, it is a sector that has existed at the peril of its leaders. The East African states have historically adopted hostile—even coercive—policies against human rights NGOs. In Kenya, for example, the state under the Kenyatta, Moi, and Kibaki regimes viewed NGOs with suspicion, if not outright dread. As a result, Kenya has historically pursued repressive policies towards NGOs, although the Kibaki regime appeared to adopt a less abusive approach. Both Tanzania and Uganda have closely regulated NGOs and sought to either co-opt or muzzle them. In spite of these hurdles, the nascent civil society movement in East Africa continues to grow. It is the potential for civil society to act as a socially transformative agent in the region that inspired this work.

This volume deals with the most critical themes and challenges that face civil society in East Africa. In Part I, Makau Mutua and Betty Murungi define and explore the main challenges to civil society in the region. Mutua critically analyzes the anatomy of civil society in postcolonial East Africa. He argues that the rise of civil society in the region directly corresponded to the dysfunction and despotism of the postcolonial state.[26] But he links the explosion of human rights NGOs in the region to the rise of the dominant Western-based human rights movement, an association that foretells the deficit of ideological and conceptual originality in African human rights groups.[27] Mutua decries the thin social base of human rights NGOs and challenges them to exercise more independence from Western donors and cultivate local moral and financial support.

Rather than focus solely on the norms of a liberal democratic state, Mutua pushes African NGOs to pay particular attention to economic, social, and cultural rights and issues—the central questions that cry out for urgent attention on the continent. This calls for a thinking human rights movement that he believes is only possible if human rights groups draw from universities, analysts, and think-tanks in the region. It is only such a reorientation of human rights NGOs in the region that will avoid a paralyzing crisis of legitimacy. He questions the need for emphasis on so-called internal democracy within NGOs, and calls instead for accountability and transparency in decision making and execution of policies. Finally, he advocates for a politically astute relationship between civil society and the state: NGOs must remain fiercely independent, but retain flexibility to selectively collaborate with the state where necessary.

Murungi focuses attention on Kenya. Like Mutua, she expresses dismay over the alienation of NGOs from the grassroots. She attacks the elitist, aristocratic nature of NGO leaderships. Using the Kenya Human Rights Commission and FIDA-Kenya among others as examples, she demonstrates how strong and effective NGOs can be created, but warns against the dangers of alienation and overdependence on foreign donors. Murungi sees legitimacy as a multifaceted concept that encompasses morality, knowledge, performance, and politics, and argues that human rights NGOs need to cultivate legitimacy in all these contexts; they are legitimized by whom they represent and what they do. Murungi's central concerns have increasingly become the subject of serious discussion by human rights scholar-activists.[28] In a region with an emergent human rights movement, it is important to sidestep the deficits of the global movement in crafting institutions geared to the local African context.

Part II addresses perhaps the most important problem facing NGOs: mandate and vision.[29] It isolates three of the most charged questions in contemporary politics and human rights discourse and articulates approaches that are germane to East Africa. Common to the chapters are a lament of NGOs' failure to fully and robustly engage certain thematic matters and proposals on how to imagine a more relevant NGO community. In Chapter 3, Sylvia Tamale takes local NGOs to task for their failure to address the complex intersection between law, sexuality, and gender. Because of the socially conservative nature of politics in the region, and the domination of the public space by a patriarchy in tradition and the Abrahamic faiths, NGOs have been reluctant to explore the disempowerment of women and girls through the lens of sexuality. Even though women are disproportionately ravaged by HIV/AIDs, civil society has been unwilling to link the crisis to marginalization and abuse of women because of their gender. Only an open interrogation of the subordination of women and demonization of public discourses on gender, sexual orientation, patriarchy, and misogyny can start the process of the full liberation of women, gays, lesbians, transgender, and transsexual persons from the tyranny of culture, religion, heteropatriarchy, and tradition.[30] Tamale challenges women's and human rights groups in particular to take on these debilitating conditions directly.

In Chapter 5, Willy Mutunga, revered as a father of the human rights movement in Kenya, takes the conversation on gender and sexual politics to an emerging area that East Africans and Africans in general are now only starting to address. He explores the phenomenon of feminist masculinity, characterized by men who are committed to organize themselves in the struggle for gender equality and women's rights and devote resources and organizational skills to fight against the conditions that reproduce the patriarchy and its social ills.[31] This male-driven movement realizes that misogyny and the exploitation of women hurt both women and men, and aims to free both men and women from the clutches of the patriarchy. He analyzes the nascent feminist masculinity movement in South Africa, Kenya, Namibia, and Malawi that has been inspired and incubated by the African Women's Development and Communitarian Network (FEMNET), the continental network of women's rights NGOs. He urges feminist masculinity NGOs to mobilize committed constituencies of men if they are to become an effective voice in the struggle for the rights of women.

In Chapter 6, Jacinta Muteshi uses the Kenya constitution-making process to showcase the great potential to advance women's rights when women practice coalitionary politics.She details the strategies and politics that enabled four NGOs—FIDA-Kenya, Kenya Human Rights Commission, Institute for Education in Democracy, and League of Kenya Women Voters—to mount a campaign to engender the 2004 Kenya draft constitution; it lobbied delegates, publicized key gender issues, and prevailed upon the drafters to mainstream gender in the draft constitution. According to Muteshi, the key to the success of the exercise was the group's ability to mobilize enough resources, its expertise in women's rights and capacity to lobby delegates and offer advice and language, and its leaders' access to key players in the constitution-making process. It is a vindication of how the normative character of a national document can be transformed by the advocacy of a committed group of women.[32]

Joe Oloka-Onyango in Chapter 4 critically analyzes the rights at the base of most manifestations of powerlessness: economic, social, and cultural rights.[33] He exposes the gap in the international human rights movement between these and civil and political rights, and explores why leading human rights groups have failed to center them in the struggle against powerlessness. Oloka-Onyango explodes the myth that one can draw watertight distinctions between the two normative sets of rights and blames the gap on the Cold War, globalization, and the politics of liberalism that emphasize markets over human welfare. He dismisses excuses such as justiciability that are frequently offered to blunt the push for economic and social rights, and demonstrates how courts can be a front in this struggle. Oloka-Onyango pegs the legitimacy of the global human rights movement, its East African iteration in particular, to a full engagement with economic and social rights. But he warns that these rights will remain at the margins unless human rights NGOs in East Africa radically reform their mandates to truly reflect—in theory and practice—the importance of this long-despised corpus.

Part III examines the problematic relationships between local NGOs and external funders. Virtually all East African human rights NGOs are almost wholly funded by external, usually Western, charities, governments, and institutions.[34] Needless to say, such near-total dependence on foreign funds is sure to distort the ideological vision of civil society and alienate it from the people on whose behalf it is supposed to struggle. As put by Chidi Odinkalu, African "human rights groups exist to please the international agencies that fund and support them."[35] In Chapter 7, Connie Ngondi-Houghton explores the detrimental effects of the dependency syndrome and concludes that local human rights NGOs must end this reliance on foreign support if they are to serve legitimate East African ends. In Chapter 8, Karuti Kanyinga argues that because of lopsided Western support, local NGOs have generally pursued neoliberal values over socioeconomic issues that matter most to East Africans. He urges NGOs to assert more independence both from external donors and the state to play a transformative role in the lives of citizens in the region.

A key problem that has burdened civil society since its origin is its relationship with the state.[36] In the two country case studies in Part IV, Livingstone Sewanyana and Wanjiku Miano demonstrate how civil society has attempted to open up political space working both against and with states that were suspicious of it. In Chapter 9, Sewanyana shows the balancing act that human rights NGOs must execute when operating in an illiberal state like Uganda. Even so, he argues that NGOs must be insightful enough to retain their autonomy while cooperating with the state. Only internally strong and viable NGOs can play a meaningful role in such challenging circumstances. In Chapter 10, Miano sketches the impressive contributions of civil society as the engine of change in the struggle for a new democratic constitution in Kenya. But she also argues that NGOs have a critical role in pushing for reforms during political transitions from a more authoritarian past, as was the case after the 2002 elections. She cautions civil society to remain independent of the political class because of the short-term vision of electoral politics.

In Part V, L. Muthoni Wanyeki and Dani Nabudere bring their activist experiences to two institutional case studies. In Chapter 11, Wanyeki uses her vantage point as executive director of FEMNET to illustrate how networking among women's human rights groups in Africa is fraught with challenges that involve barriers of communication, identity, vision, politics, and structure. Yet the network has clearly created a pan-African forum to continentalize women's issues. She leaves little doubt of the need for such a vital network in spite of the many obstacles. In Chapter 12, Nabudere, a scholar-activist who has gone back to the grassroots, argues that human rights can only become a true fabric of a society if they are not imposed from above or outside. Using studies of several small rural NGOs in Uganda, he demonstrates a stunning learning curve in which "victims" become their own liberators, in a deep transformation within the community. Implicit is a rejection of the popular human rights tourism favored by donors and practiced by city-based African NGOs. These cases indicate the real probability of creating a socially organic, people-driven human rights NGO culture—the type Odinkalu has argued is so elusive.[37]

Part VI explores the tensions and benefits of South-South and South-North NGO relations. The relationships between NGOs, particularly those from regions with huge asymmetries of power and resources, have long been a matter of serious scholarship and debate.[38] In Chapter 13, Margaret Burnham makes a case for transnational advocacy to combat the death penalty, showing how activists and lawyers—both South-South and South-North—have coordinated and enriched international jurisprudence on the practice. She argues that East Africans should internationalize their efforts to maximize pressure and increase expertise. In Chapter 14, Shaila Gupta and Alycia Kellman write about the lessons the Institute for a Democratic Alternative for South Africa (IDASA) may offer NGOs in East Africa in political transitions. Gupta and Kellman wrote this chapter with the input of Paul Graham and Ivor Jenkins, executive director of the Cape Town Democracy Centre and manager of IDASA respectively. Graham presented the paper on which the article is based at the Nairobi Conference in October 2004. IDASA was a vital NGO in fostering the climate for dialogue that led to the birth of a post-apartheid state.

Finally, Chris Maina Peter takes stock of the history of NGOs in East Africa and concludes that they have become a permanent feature of society. Even so, he cautions that they must remain skeptical of the intentions of donors and wary of the state. He calls on NGOs to develop ethical, democratic institutions that demonstrate adherence to the values of democracy and social justice. He decries an NGO culture that elevates the interests of NGOs above the communities they serve. An authentic human rights movement for East Africa must be incubated in communities and seek to advance their welfare above all else. To do so, NGOs must cultivate a culture of autonomy, effectiveness, and an anchor in ethical and noble goals and motives.

PART I

Defining Challenges to Civil Society in East Africa

CHAPTER ONE

Human Rights NGOs in East Africa: Defining the Challenges

Makau Mutua

IT IS NOT possible today to imagine a vibrant, democratic, and modern society in which the state is not policed by an active, independent, and effective civil society.[1] While this appears to be a universal truth, the rise of civil society in much of Africa seems to directly correspond to the dysfunction and despotism of the postcolonial state.[2] Nowhere has this conclusion been truer than in East Africa, a region whose misfortunes have included misrule by maniacal dictators, autocratic states, and irresponsible political elites. In its roughly two decades of existence, civil society in East Africa has played significant, and even pivotal roles, in reversing social decay, rolling back the dictatorial state, and advancing individual liberties. It is almost certain that the region's downward spiral—particularly in Kenya—would have pushed society to the edge of anarchy had civil society not filled the vacuum left by an increasingly illegitimate state. Yet, civil society is a complex phenomenon, one that is fraught with contradictions, some of them perhaps detrimental to the nation. It is this paradox that requires serious interrogation if civil society in East Africa will meet the challenges of the democratic project and respond to the nuanced threats posed by globalization while it sheds its opacity and enhances its independence and effectiveness.

The complexity of civil society largely emanates from its origins and the changing nature of the relationship between the state and those under its rule. Historically, the term civil society is part of a longstanding European tradition, and was, until the middle of the eighteenth century, used to "describe a type of political association which places its members under the influence of its laws and thereby ensures peaceful order and good government."[3] Used in this sense, the term "civil society was conterminous with the state."[4] But in the latter half of the eighteenth century, the term civil society started to implode, giving rise to the distinction between the state or government on the one hand and an independent civil society on the other. The antistatist impulse in the rupturing of the term civil society—drawing a rigid distinction between the state and civil society—grows from the opposition to the despotic state and the push for limited, constitutional government. Although it ebbed and flowed, the conception of civil society became a permanent feature of Western democracies.

But civil society is a very broad term. According to John Keane's interpretation of G. W. F. Hegel, civil society is a large cartilage that is positioned "between the simple world of the patriarchal household and the universal state."[5] As Keane notes, civil society includes "the market economy, social classes, corporations and institutions concerned with the administration of 'welfare' and civil law." It is a "mosaic of private individuals, classes, groups and institutions whose transactions are regulated by civil law and, as such, are not directly dependent upon the political state itself." Both Hegel and Alexis de Tocqueville agreed that civil society was one of the major achievements of the modern world.[6] In fact, "a civil society that is self-organized and independent from the state is necessary for the consolidation of democracy."[7] Thus "civil society is the 'independent eye of society,' made of a plurality of self-organized and vigilant civil associations."[8] Without civil society, "those in power can turn into despots."

But the vibrancy and centrality of civil society has been uneven in the last century. Most recently, it was not until the 1980s that the term civil society once again acquired new currency with the rapid wave of democratic renaissance in previously closed, military, one-party, authoritarian, and totalitarian states within the Soviet bloc, Asia, Africa, and Latin America. In the African context, the failure of the postcolonial state and the end of the Cold War focused attention on an emergent civil society across the continent. It was the illegitimacy of the centralized state that necessitated the emergence of non-state actors, the phenomenon that Michael Bratton described as "public political activity that occurs in the realm between the state and the family."[9] In order for human potential to be maximized, the breadth and width of civil society in Africa—which includes all civil non-state actors—will have to grow and vigorously engage both the state and society.

While I recognize the importance of all actors in the civil society world, it is outside the scope of this book to address them. I am specifically interested in the increasingly important category of civil society organizations referred to as nongovernmental organizations, or NGOs. But even in this category, I am more discriminatory because my paper only deals with the subsector of NGOs known as human rights NGOs. NGOs form a special category because they differ in principles, membership, organization, and goals from other civil society groups, or even other ascriptive entities. Thus, NGOs do not involve themselves directly in the market and are distinct from government or quasi-government institutions although they interact with the state. According to Claude Welch, human rights NGOs occupy an even more rarefied plane: they

> seek to benefit society, or at least a significant portion of it, without necessary direct benefit to themselves. They constitute both a precondition for, and a supplement to, the constitutionally defined political process and the formal political bodies of the democratic state. As voluntary organizations in large measure, they often pursue idealistic causes. But these causes are crucial to the functioning of a modern society.[10]

Since the 1980s, an NGO revolution has swept the globe. East Africa has not been an exception to this development. What is clear, in the context of East Africa, is the fact that civil society, or the NGO movement, as understood in the modern sense, is a very recent phenomenon. Even more recent is the presence of human rights NGOs, a specialized sector of civil society. By definition, authoritarian or dictatorial states seek to choke off and oust civil society, particularly human rights NGOs. As such, throughout East Africa, whose brush with political democracy has been halting and ambivalent, human rights NGOs were largely nonexistent until the 1980s, although germs of such organizations have existed since the 1970s. But it simply was not possible to establish full-fledged human rights groups until the late 1980s, and in most cases, the 1990s.

Even then, the relationships between human rights groups and states in East Africa have at best been contentious. In many cases human rights groups have operated at the risk of their generally small, but dedicated, staffs. The point is that the human rights movement in East Africa is so young that it is faced with a multiplicity of challenges. Clearly, the state remains one of the major challenges facing the human rights movement in the region. Although generally there have been political openings in East Africa, particularly in the 1990s, the terrain still remains uncertain, and many human rights groups are still finding their footing. For their part, states are unsure what to make of human rights NGOs and how to relate to them. In the three East African states, the spectrum goes from suppression to co-optation and independence. It seems fair to conclude that a settled culture of state-civil society relations remains experimental.

But the relationship between the state and civil society is just one of the many challenges that face human rights NGOs. The other major, and perhaps more serious, problem is internal to the human rights movement in the region. These internal challenges are conceptual, ideological, structural, and logistical. They revolve around questions of the identity of the human rights movement in the region, its social bases, the quality of its cadres, normative questions about its mandate, and its professionalization.[11] In other words, is the basic character of the movement fashioned to respond to the identities of those on whose behalf it purports to speak, its constituencies? Who are the human rights scholars and advocates that define and drive the movement in the region? How are they connected to their constituencies? Is the movement largely an urban phenomenon, and if so, what can be done to change this identity?

On the question of mandates, what is the movement designed to do, and what exactly does it do? How many components of the movement can be identified, and how complementary—or contradictory—are those components? For example, are there activist and intellectual components, or are the two indistinguishable? If they are different, how do they relate to, and feed into each other? Or does intellectual direction come from external sources, such as outside the region, or from the donor community? In this respect, does the human rights NGO movement in the region need think tanks from where intellectual direction and policy analyses can be developed?

In terms of human resources, how does the movement replenish its ranks? How are its foot soldiers and leaders produced? Who produces them, and for what purposes are they trained? Is the human rights movement in the region professionalized? If so, what are the benefits and drawbacks? Is there inertia among the ranks, and how is it addressed? Does the movement have an internal ethical and professional code, and if not, what can be done to develop one? How is democracy within the local NGOs cultivated and enhanced?

On normativity, one needs to ask not only whether human rights NGOs in the region effectively participate in advocacy, but also whether they contribute to the development of human rights standards at the national, regional, continental, and universal levels. Is there any evidence that human rights groups in the region have exerted any discernable impact on norm development? If not, why? Does the movement in East Africa produce ideas? If so, what kind of ideas does it produce, and what kind of impact have those ideas had in the region, and beyond? What, in normative terms, have NGOs in the region added to the human rights corpus? In the underdeveloped areas of gender, transitional justice, terrorism and human rights, regional (such as the African Union), and universal processes, trade and human rights, sexual orientation, economic, social, and cultural rights, and even on the right to development, have groups in East Africa simply mimicked boilerplate approaches elsewhere or have they been innovative?

Another critical area for exploration is external, and concerns the relationships between human rights NGOs in East Africa and the outside universe, including donors. But donors include those who have offices in the region. What is the nature of these relationships, and how do they impact the work, development, and sustainability of human rights NGOs in the region? Do these relationships encourage creativity, independence, and growth? Or do set universal or institutional criteria, cultures, and interests predetermine them? In other words, how do donor-donee relationships affect the mandates of NGOs, their foci, and development? What are the legitimate—if any—areas of encroachment by donors? Have such questions been addressed openly in East Africa? If not, why?

The last important area of external concern is the relationship between local NGOs and international NGOs or INGOs, the large multinational human rights groups such as Amnesty International and Human Rights Watch, which are based in the cultural and political capitals of the West. Are there any discernable areas of cooperation or competition between the two? Or is the relationship asymmetrical, with INGOs playing the leading role, both locally and internationally, in terms of mandate and norm development and the creation of an international human rights agenda? Are local groups simply consumers of the proceeds of INGOs, or do INGOs exploit local NGOs? Is there any reality to the notion of an international civil society, or what others call partnerships, as far as local NGOs are concerned?

Rooting Human Rights NGOs in East Africa

According to Paul Tiyambe Zeleza, at the "beginning of 1990, all but five of Africa's fifty-four countries were dictatorships, either civilian or military."[12] Consequently, most of the African publics were excluded from political participation and competition, a fact that made sure that citizens could neither elect their leaders nor influence public policy. Shockingly, as Zeleza notes, prior to 1990 no African leader had left office through electoral defeat; while three— Leopold Senghor of Senegal, Ahmadou Ahidjo of Cameroon, and Julius Nyerere of Tanzania—had voluntarily stepped down and handed over power to their handpicked successors. By 2004, however, most African states had either introduced, or succumbed to, varying degrees of political, social, and economic reforms. That intense period of rapid political liberalization—even if it has been characterized by serious and notable reversals—has witnessed the mushrooming of human rights NGOs.

Even in Tanzania, whose history of the state and civil society is complicated by nuance, the human rights NGO sector in East Africa was true to the Africa norm and did not enjoy much political space before the introduction of multipartyism in the early 1990s.[13] In his seminal work, Chris M. Peter demonstrated that Tanzania, despite the absence of overtly repressive state machinery, nevertheless tightly controlled civil society and denied important basic human rights.[14] In Uganda, the post-Amin, post-Obote states—the period under Yoweri Museveni starting in 1986—has been characterized by the countervailing impulses of openness, conflict, and repression. [15] Kenya, a state adept at repression under the cloak of the law, largely prevented the emergence of a vibrant civil society until 1992 when multipartyism forced it to permit independent citizen activity.[16]

In short, it was not until the 1990s that civil society, and in particular human rights NGOs, became a serious feature of the political landscape in East Africa. Not surprisingly, the emergence of human rights NGOs in the region was part of a continental—and indeed universal—revolution in which civil society groups have come to exert an unprecedented influence on states and intergovernmental institutions around the globe.[17] I have made this argument elsewhere:

> Most Sub-Saharan human rights groups arose in the late 1980s as despotic states started to lose support of their benefactors in the North. A number of factors contributed to this phenomenon, including the end of the Cold War and the withdrawal of economic and military support by the East and the West, the utter inefficiency of one-party authoritarian states (both civil and military) agitation by forces promising democratic reform, and defeat in contested elections to pro-democracy activists. The whittling away of absolute state power by all these factors opened the political space necessary for the establishment of human rights groups.[18]

The political crucible in which the human rights NGO movement in East Africa was born has largely determined its identity, although it is important to remember that there was nothing original in its template. The human rights movement in the region is a rump extension of the so-called international human rights movement, which originated and is headquartered in the industrial democracies of the West. The relationship between the international human rights NGOs and domestic NGOs rhymes in conception, mandate, methods of work, and funding. Even though domestic human rights groups in the region have started to exert some originality in some of these areas, I believe that the genetic fingerprint of the "parent" human rights organizations, such as Amnesty

International or Human Rights Watch in the North, remains dominant. This is true of many groups in the region, including the Kenya Human Rights Commission, of which I am a cofounder. Others, such as FIDA-Kenya or the local sections of the ICJ, are the literal offspring of an actual parent organization. Again, I have made this contention in another forum:

> Many of the new groups [domestic human rights NGOs] were orchestrated, funded, and supported or at the very least deeply influenced individuals, human rights organizations, and foundations from the North. It is little wonder that most African human rights organizations echo AI, HRW, and ICJ in mandate, structure, and methods of work. They monitor, document, and publicize human rights conditions a la AI and HRW. But they also train paralegals and carry out educational and rights awareness campaigns such as those promoted by the ICJ. Many of them are miniature replicas of their more powerful counterparts in the North: they are funded by the same sources; they are organized similarly with almost identical mandates and use similar tactics and strategies of advocacy and work.[19]

Like their counterparts in the industrial democracies of the West, human rights groups in East Africa have largely been lawyer-led and driven. Leading groups such as AI, HRW, ICJ, Human Rights First (formerly the Lawyers Committee for Human Rights), and Global Rights (formerly the International Human Rights Law Group) have been dominated by lawyers. In East Africa, Kituo Cha Sheria, or the Legal Advice Center, one of the first human rights NGOs in the region, and other leading NGOs in Kenya, Uganda, and Tanzania, including Zanzibar, have largely been led by persons with legal training as well. The reason for this myopia in leadership is the association of human rights with the law and the discourse of rights, a medium and language that are perceived to be the most effective tools of confronting state despotism. Furthermore, human rights groups have generally equated the containment of despotism with the attainment of human dignity, an assumption that reflects their bias for civil and political rights rather than economic, social, and cultural rights.

Human rights NGOs in East Africa are therefore a response to state despotism in the region, and an inspiration from the international human rights movement. These two factors have largely defined the scope, mandate, philosophies, structures, and relationships that NGOs in the region have cultivated. In a sense, human rights NGOs in East Africa have a script, a blueprint that is determined by their parentage. While it is true that many NGOs have necessarily been influenced by local conditions, it is undeniable that on the whole they replicate well-known templates. Although the "copycat" identity of East African NGOs clearly has its drawbacks, it imports models that have been tested over time and that work. But rather than the problem of originality, the questions that vex NGOs in the region are those of innovation, legitimacy, sustainability, self-reliance, and independence.

Mandate: Situating NGOs in the Liberal Paradigm

The political histories of the three East African states—and others beyond the region—demonstrate beyond a shadow of a doubt an emerging consensus among political, intellectual, and civil society elites. Not surprisingly, that consensus concentrates on the possibilities of constructing a liberal democratic state. After flirting with various models—including the Marxian variety—elites in the region appear to have settled on political democracy as the system of choice. The weight of the evidence suggests that by and large East African elites are rhetorically committed to the construction of states where political parties openly contest for power within the rubric of the liberal state. In this respect, political parties are seen as a vanguard for political reform in the reclamation of the illiberal, one-party, authoritarian, or opaque state that for long has dominated the landscape in East Africa.

Political democracy, as understood in its rudimentary forms, calls for a state bounded by law and the ethos of constitutionalism.[20] In its bare bones, constitutionalism refers to the typology of state that broadly carries the following features, to a greater or lesser degree. The first of these is the notion of popular sovereignty in which the constitution guarantees the accountability of the state to the populace through a series of techniques and institutions, the key and most important one being the requirement of open, contested, periodic, and genuine elections in a multiparty system. This is the fundamental facet of a liberal state. Secondly, the notion of constitutionalism, consistent with the liberal tradition, requires that the constitution control and limit the powers of the government in a number of ways, including the system of checks and balances through the separation of powers doctrine that must include an independent judiciary.[21]

It is this model of the state—the liberal democratic state—which has driven civil society elites in East Africa to form human rights NGOs. My contention is that it is impossible to understand the mandates of human rights NGOs in East Africa without situating them within the liberal paradigm. The parent international nongovernmental human rights organizations (INGOs), such as AI, HRW, and ICJ, the models that inspired domestic NGOs elsewhere in the world, are firmly rooted in liberal thought and philosophy. As Steiner has written, INGOs are "committed to traditional Western liberal values associated with the human rights movement."[22] In fact, the international human rights project seeks to universalize liberal Western values.[23] Much of the human rights regime is derived from bodies of domestic jurisprudence developed over many centuries in the West.[24] No less an authority than Antonio Cassese, the distinguished Italian jurist, has categorically stated that the West "imposed" its own philosophy of human rights on the rest of the world.[25] In any case, the two basic human rights texts on which the movement is founded—the Universal Declaration of Human Rights and the International Covenant on Civil and Political Rights— read like a manifesto of Western liberal values.[26] Suffice it to note that liberalism, political democracy, and human rights are intrinsically part of the same historical and philosophical tradition. Hence the argument that East African human rights NGOs are part of the liberal tradition.

A cursory review of human rights NGOs in East Africa places them squarely in the struggle for the liberal democratic state. Although formally nonpartisan—in the sense that as a rule virtually all human rights groups in East Africa have not officially declared their political preferences—there is no secret that their mandates work to support the emergence of a political democracy.[27] In other words, the main human rights NGOs in East Africa have sought to promote basic civil and political rights, and especially political participation rights, such as the rights to assemble, speak, publish, and organize, due process protections, equal protection rights, and antidiscrimination norms. These rights are central to an open democratic process, in particular a free and fair election, which is the essential cornerstone of a political democracy. Human rights groups in the region have therefore been basic materiel in the battle for the liberal democratic state. Ian Martin, the former secretary general of Amnesty International, recognized in a memorable passage the fallacy of the rigid distinction that AI had drawn between human rights and political democracy:

> The determination to establish impartiality in the face of human rights violations under different political systems led Amnesty International to shun the rhetorical identification of human rights and democracy. But in fact the struggle against violations, committed mostly by undemocratic authoritarian governments, was closely bound up with the struggle for democracy. Thousands of prisoners of conscience for whom Amnesty International worked in its first three decades were political activists challenging the denial of their rights to freedom of expression and association.[28]

But the traditional human rights NGO mandate has come at a cost for local NGOs. To be sure, the mandate of a civil society group should not be largely a product of external factors. For an example, traditional human rights groups in the West, which are known as civil rights or civil liberties organizations, such as the American Civil Liberties Union (ACLU) or the National Association for the Advancement of Colored People (NAACP), arose from material conditions in the United States. While it is true that human rights groups in East Africa have been a response to the violations of basic individual rights by the state, a focus that mirrored reporting and advocacy in the region by INGOs, actual human rights atrocities have had a more complex identity and composition. In Kenya, for example, the murder and mayhem of the so-called ethnic clashes in the 1990s were inextricably bound up with the land question in the country, and the exploitation of that issue to suppress political dissent and outlaw opposition to the hegemony enjoyed in the state by the Kenya African National Union.[29] An overlooked component of those abominations was the extreme suffering of women solely on account of the economic and social disadvantages they bear because of their gender. Yet, human rights reporting largely focused on grim statistics—the so-called body count—cataloguing the violations of civil and political rights without analyzing the context, or addressing seriously the violations of economic, social and cultural rights. This was both a mandate problem as well one of the conceptual limitations of the narrow specialization of NGOs. Similarly, the near collapse of the Kenyan State after the disputed elections in December 2007 was a result of deep-seated economic and social grievances that manifested themselves in genocidal ethnic violence.

Traditionally, parent INGOs have had very narrow mandates, focused until recently almost exclusively on the violations of what are called "core rights," defined as breaches of bodily integrity such as torture, and key civil and political rights, particularly due process protections and expressive rights. The mandates of INGOs such as HRW or AI read as though they are lifted, almost directly, from the bills of rights of the industrial democracies of the West. HRW, for example, asserts that it "defends freedom of thought and expression, due process and equal protection of the law, and a vigorous civil society; we document and denounce murders, disappearances, torture, arbitrary imprisonment, discrimination, and other abuses of internationally recognized human rights."[30] Similarly AI traditionally has had a narrow mandate, focusing on an almost identical set of rights.[31] These two leaders of the human rights movement remained hostile to economic, social, and cultural rights, reflecting the political biases of the West during the Cold War. In the late 1990s, however, HRW cautiously abandoned its formal opposition to economic, social, and cultural rights, although it has continued to treat them as second-rate and peripheral to its human rights work.[32] AI, arguably the most influential INGO, has only in the last couple of years started to explore how it might begin to address economic, social, and cultural rights. Much of the change in AI is attributable to the leadership of Irene Khan, the AI secretary general, who is the first woman, Muslim, and Asian to lead the organization.

Historically, there simply was no major INGO that took seriously the International Covenant on Economic, Social and Cultural rights. The one possibility was the New York-based Center for Economic and Social Rights, although it thus far has been unable to acquire the prestige and support of an AI or HRW. Although United Nations doctrine maintains that all rights—civil and political rights, and economic, social, and cultural rights—are indivisible, interdependent, and interrelated, the assertion has not been more than hot air.[33] Clearly, economic, social, and cultural rights were a casualty of the Cold War, and in particular, of the fear by the West that the redistributive logic in them was at odds with the dominant understanding and practice of liberalism and the free market culture. The collapse of the Soviet Union and communism has dimmed some of these fears, but the welfare state in the industrial democracies has been in retreat ever since—a fact that makes advocacy for these rights still Herculean. The liberal bias against economic, social, and cultural rights is philosophical and the triumph of right or center-right political parties in the West will continue that tradition. As Jack Donnelly has argued, conceptions of individual rights against the state, the pivot of the human rights regime, trump the more "radical" strand of liberalism, which limits individual rights, stresses a more social vision, and is the source of the welfare state.[34] Unfortunately, human rights groups have fallen prey to this devastating dichotomization of human rights.

I am afraid that most human rights groups in East Africa have rather blindly copied the models of AI and HRW with respect to the question of their mandates, although the majority of East Africans live a meager existence defined by the most blatant, brutal, and unimaginable denials of the most basic economic, social, and cultural rights. This certainly has been the script of the most visible and prestigious human rights NGOs in the region. Clearly, state despotism has been the central threat to the realization of human dignity in the region. But state repression—defined by naked brutality—has been inseparable from grand corruption, cultural dispossession, and the destruction of the social fiber. Often, violations of civil and political rights are committed to buttress economic, social, and cultural abominations, and vice versa. East African NGOs have been slow, even unwilling or unable, to see human rights violations as a matrix that combines both sets of rights. Apart from the KHRC, whose work on land and labor rights is well-known, the other prominent exceptions have been Mazingira Institute and the Green Belt Movement, both of which address environmental issues, with Mazingira also focusing on housing rights.[35]

There are, obviously, other structural and conceptual bottlenecks that impede East African NGOs from imagining a more robust mandate. They are clearly hamstrung by the problem of originalism; that, in effect, they are cultural transplants that mimic their counterparts in the West both institutionally and conceptually. Second, they are youthful organizations operating under extremely adverse conditions. These facts are undeniable. But, frankly, NGOs in the region have been neither interested in, nor able to reflect on their work and interrogate themselves on human rights. In other words, NGOs do not really have a conceptual understanding of human rights or their complexity. Few human rights activists have any serious training in human rights, beyond the dry recitation of some provisions in the major human rights treaties. Nor do many human rights executives and senior staff treat their organizations as living, "thinking organisms." When was the last time, for instance, that a local human rights NGO organized a seminar or meeting to interrogate, as a matter of scholarship, the philosophy of human rights? Yet, there is no paucity of retreats on "bonding," strategic planning, fund-raising, networking, and so on. These are important pursuits but they pale in comparison to time spent understanding the human rights universe. This point was poignantly brought home to me when in 2003 I conducted two highly successful "thinking sessions" for the Kenya National Commission on Human Rights and the senior executives of NGOs in Kenya.

The poverty of knowledge on human rights both as doctrine and discourse in the NGO world in East Africa is compounded by the reluctance of NGO executives to create more organic relationships with academics. Granted that universities in the region have been in decline and anemia may pervade many departments. But there are a number of serious academics and other thinkers in the professions who could be integrated into the NGO world for their expertise and knowledge. Such individuals would form a thinking corps for the human rights movement in the region. A logical place for thinkers would be on the boards of NGOs or even as consultants for particular projects. It is this nexus between thought or theory and action that could lead to more imaginative mandates for NGOs. There is no reason why NGOs in the region should continue to be the mere recipients of ideas, as opposed to being producers of ideas. The uniqueness of the challenges that face NGOs in the region gives them a wonderful opportunity to make significant contributions to the jurisprudence of universal human rights.

I will suggest a number of concrete ideas that could jump-start serious scholarship and thinking within the NGO sector in the region. First, it is essential that time be regularly blocked out for reflection, discussion, or argument on a question of human rights within each organization. The simplest and most cost-effective way to fire up the imagination of staff and broaden their horizons is by tapping resources within the organization. Usually, each organization has one or two individuals who have at least some formal basic training in human rights as a discipline, generally from a doctrinal point of view. Such persons should initiate regular sessions by staff to discuss readings, host a local speaker from the academy or a think tank, or debate a human rights issue. Such meetings would make NGOs not just forums for implementing human rights norms, but also springboards for thought and self-education. Besides, an opportunity exists here to conduct serious research into questions of human rights and universality through the prism of the rich African cultural heritage and values in the region. Otherwise, the region is condemned to believe that it has nothing valuable or original to contribute to human rights.

Second, NGOs should cultivate links with universities in the region. In addition to putting academics on boards of directors where they could help develop the vision, mandate, and policies of the organization, scholars in the region could create synergies between the academy and the NGO movement. Some academics in the region have done this well, but the numbers are still very low, and the gulf between them and civil society remains large.[36] It is not difficult to imagine the NGO community either collaborating with, or even inspiring the establishment of, human rights programs at local universities. For example, the relationships between universities and NGOs, particularly in the human and civil rights fields, have been critical for their vibrancy in the United States.[37] Some of the most renowned human rights scholars in the United States either sit on the boards of leading NGOs or are regularly consulted by them.[38] These relationships between the academy and civil society are critical because they provide the human rights movement with intellectual leadership, help it define its goals, which are often complicated, and assist in unpacking the complex normative edifice of the human rights corpus. A human rights movement without intellectual direction and guidance is rudderless and will ultimately be of very limited utility to the region.

But even with an in-house capacity to think about human rights, NGOs still need standing institutions, such as think tanks and human rights institutes, to create a more sustained intellectual life for the movement. The Kenya Human Rights Commission, for example, has recognized the importance of such a center, and has established a human rights institute. The Kenya Human Rights Institute acts like an academic center on human rights. It has a speaker series and regular workshops, conducts research, and plans to publish a scholarly journal, conduct a "summer school" with visiting academics from universities around the world, and teach and train activists in human rights. The KHRC hopes that through the Kenya Human Rights Institute the NGO sector will have a forum to explore a multiplicity of human rights questions and keep up with emerging issues, scholarship, and jurisprudence in other institutions and regions of the world. Currently, Kituo Cha Katiba,[39] the Kampala-based regional think tank, is the only such structure in the region. It needs to be strengthened and complemented by similar institutions in the region.

Ultimately, one cannot overstress the importance for the region of a human rights movement that is intellectually alert, because it is essential to the defining and refining of NGO mandates. It was sensible initially to mimic the scripts of INGOs when the movement in the region was at its infancy. But more than a decade later, NGOs in the region should be locally conceptualized to address conditions germane to the region.[40] The KHRC, for instance, has constantly reviewed its mandate and added new campaigns, including those on the horticultural industry, export processing zones, land rights, and labor conditions at Del Monte, among others.[41] Some of these programs went beyond the traditional, classical human rights mandate favored by leading INGOs. In any case, INGOs are external to the region, and were not inspired by conditions particular to East Africa. In fact, INGOs were by design meant to investigate human rights violations in the Third World.[42] Since they are not resident in the region, INGOs engage in human rights tourism and use a standard approach in all countries. As such, their mandates are crafted as a boilerplate, a blueprint that could be applied anywhere. In contrast, domestic NGOs should be driven by local demands and conditions. That is why NGOs in East Africa should reexamine their mandates to make sure that they are not trapped in biases that are external to the region.

The Crisis of Legitimacy

The legitimacy of any civil society organization is a result of several interrelated factors. These include, but are not limited to, effectiveness, representativeness, sustainability, institutionalization, indigenousness, and responsiveness. Each one of these elements, which are complex and difficult to unpack, takes long periods to cultivate and consolidate. But legitimacy is particularly important to human rights NGOs because moral capital is their most important asset. Human rights NGOs in East Africa, however, are so youthful that even the most established ones are still struggling to develop these essential dimensions and attain a certain degree of maturity, both individually and collectively as a social phenomenon. The picture is certainly a mixed one: the verdict for now is that much work remains to be done to transform a collection of NGOs in the region to a genuine human rights movement.

Ten years ago I wrote—a fact I still believe to be true—that it was "premature to talk of a human rights community in the traditional sense" in most African countries.[43] I meant that human rights groups in individual countries—

and the continent at large—could not be properly called a human rights movement. The word movement entails a certain degree of cogency—irrevocability, irreversibility, and permanence. In turn, each of these terms implies a high degree of embeddedness and the singularity of identity, characteristics that, save possibly for South Africa, I think the rest of the continent is lacking. This conclusion should come as no surprise, given the paucity of civil society organizations across the continent just a decade ago.

The codification of human rights is a recent phenomenon in world history. It literally started with the UN Charter in 1945, was quickly followed by the adoption of the UDHR, the ICCPR, and International Covenant on Economic, Social and Cultural Rights before the UN unleashed a torrent of norms in thematic treaties on race, women, children, and torture, among others.[44] It was not until the 1970s, however, that human rights started to capture the public imagination, especially through the work of Amnesty International. For many Africans, the work of AI—as a foreign and distant voice decrying the violations of civil and political rights by African states—was their first contact with the nascent international human rights movement. In East Africa, as elsewhere in sub-Saharan Africa, the seeds of the current human rights NGO sector were planted in the 1970s by the most activist segments of the bar and the law schools. Back then the term "human rights" was considered subversive, alien, seditious, and unpatriotic by most African governments, and rights activists dared not use it to describe either their work or organizations. Ten years ago, I captured these tenuous origins of the human rights NGO sector in Africa, including East Africa, in the following passage.

> A handful of lawyers would initially provide legal aid and then create a human rights organization, usually on the model of AI, where conditions allowed or compelled. Legal aid does not directly threaten the state unless political prisoners are represented, and therefore provided cover for the nascent movement. Usually originating or connected to the low key, non-confrontational provision of legal services to the poor, organizations such as the Nigerian Civil Liberties Organization (CLO), the Lagos-based Constitutional Rights Project (CRP), and the Zimbabwe Catholic Commission for Justice and Peace, the Kenya Human Rights Commission (KHRC), and the Zairian League for Human Rights have arisen to document abuses and challenge repressive policies and the violations of human rights.[45]

In Kenya, for instance, Willy Mutunga, a former law lecturer, was instrumental in the development of Kituo Cha Sheria and later cofounded the KHRC.

In Tanzania, Joseph Kanywanyi, Issa Shivji, and Chris Peter, among others, have inspired and led the legal aid and human rights agenda in Tanzania. In Uganda, Joe Oloka-Onyango and Fred Jjuuko were instrumental in the creation of a human rights program at Makerere University. In short, the human rights enterprise in East Africa is largely a product of activist lawyers and law teachers, many of whom started with an interest in legal aid. As such, the East African human rights NGO sector is still, in a sense, in its first generation. Although there has been a multiplication of human rights groups in the region in the last decade, only a handful are well established and can claim institutional stability. The vast majority is marginal, badly managed, poorly resourced, ill staffed, and teeter on the brink of extinction. The high public visibility of the few vocal NGOs deceptively gives the impression of a well-established, ubiquitous, and formidable human rights movement. Nothing could be further from the truth.

The class identity of those who have originated and lead human rights NGOs in the region conceptually limits the reach and vision of the sector and objectively undercuts its legitimacy. Both states and civil societies the world over are led by elites. While that phenomenon is a universal one, it could have seriously adverse consequences in countries with narrow classes of elites and limited middle classes. Leaders of human rights NGOs in East Africa are drawn from the law and other highly elitist professions. Even worse, the leadership of NGOs by elites can create destructive pathologies where such elites are highly concentrated in a few large urban centers. In East Africa, the major NGOs are concentrated in the capital cities of Kampala, Dar es Salaam, and Nairobi. These groups may have a few satellite, skeleton offices in a couple of larger urban areas such as Mombasa or Kisumu. In a departure from this tradition, the KHRC has through Vision 2012 started processes to directly engage communities.[46] But not only are most groups detached and alienated from rural folk, where the majority of East Africans live, they also view victims from an "us-and-them" lens, which is essentially an "othering" approach. Odinkalu has bitterly denounced the alienation of human rights groups from their constituencies:

> The current human rights movement in Africa—with the possible exception of the women's rights and faith-based social justice initiatives—appears almost by design to exclude the participation of the people whose welfare it purports to advance. Most human rights organizations are modeled after Northern watchdog organizations, located in an urban area, run by a core management without a membership base (unlike Amnesty International), and dependent solely on overseas funding. . . . With media-driven visibility and a lifestyle to match, the

leaderships of these initiatives enjoy privilege and comfort, and progressively grow distant from a life of struggle.[47]

Human rights groups cannot be legitimate unless they resolve the problem of alienation and disconnection from the people they serve, their constituencies. The indigenousness of these groups, which is critical for their effectiveness and relevance, must be undergirded by moral, political, material, and ideological support from their constituents. There is no alternative to opening real and effective offices in rural areas with the staff and leadership drawn from those communities. Where such staff and leadership do not exist, it is incumbent upon the NGO to train them. Another, and perhaps more viable approach, might be for the bigger local NGOs to identify existing community human rights groups and forge mutually beneficial relationships with them. I hesitate to call them "equal partnerships," a term the KHRC favors, because I think the term belies the power imbalances inherent in the relationships.[48] Alienation from both potential and actual victims cannot be the basis for the creation of a viable human rights movement in the region. As I have asked, "how can an organization advocate on behalf of strangers?"[49] Although it may have its drawbacks, the problem of alienation could be addressed through the transformation of human rights NGOs into membership organizations. But criteria for membership must be strict and narrow. Otherwise, tribalists, chauvinists, misogynists, demagogues, and anti-democrats could hijack human rights NGOs. Odinkalu correctly thinks that a membership base could go a long way in curing NGOs of their aloof elitism. Members have the potential to make groups more accountable to their constituents.

> In the absence of a membership base, there is no constituency-driven obligation or framework for popularizing the language or objectives of the group beyond the community of inward-looking professionals or careerists who run it. Instead of being the currency for social justice or conscience-driven movement, "human rights" has increasingly become the specialized language of a select professional cadre with its own rites of passage and methods of certification. Far from being a badge of honor, human rights activism is, in some places I have observed it, increasingly a certificate of privilege.[50]

A critical gap in the credibility and legitimacy of NGOs is their heavy, virtually exclusive reliance on external support. Although largely financial, such debilitating dependence extends to matters of intellectual and ideological direction, moral support, and political orientation. I am not opposed to transnational

NGO networks, but I firmly believe that such relationships should not come at the cost of the independence, sustainability, and legitimacy of African NGOs. After all, as Larry Cox, a long-time human rights activist now head of AI-USA and a former Ford Foundation program officer, has noted, "groups in the North, of course, also retain access to powerful external forces that can be an important part of an overall strategy, such as wealthy governments, multinational institutions, and citizen action groups that can effectively organize boycotts and other forms of consumer pressure."[51] Paradoxically, it is the imbalance and asymmetry of power and resources that exists between African NGOs and Western-based INGOs that makes the notion of the so-called "international civil society" a mockery.[52] Nor should the deployment of terms, such as partnership, used by INGOs to describe their relationships with national NGOs, fool anyone. In East Africa, NGOs should be alert to these unequal, exploitative relationships in which they become nothing more than conduits, conveyors, or legitimizers of the agenda of the INGOs and other external actors at the expense of their constituents. Often, local NGOs are sucked into external agendas and fail to make their own priorities based on the needs of their constituents and the confluence of local conditions. Even worse, the dice, as Cox points out, is objectively loaded against local NGOs.

> The possibility for groups outside Western Europe and the United States either to set the international agenda for human rights or even to influence, as equal partners, the strategies set by international groups for their countries is very limited. To change this would take a much deeper commitment than currently exists on the part of either donors or NGOs to invest in travel, discussions, and the alteration of old patterns.[53]

But the unhealthy reliance on external, donor funding from the West is the biggest threat to the NGO sector in East Africa. Not only does it encourage the most destructive pathologies on the part of the donor and donee alike, it also attacks the heart of one of the basic norms of the human rights corpus: self-determination. African human rights NGOs, a sector of society that should be committed to good government, the delivery of services, and political empowerment, cannot encourage dependency and replicate the client status of African states. A core norm of the human rights movement, captured in Common Article 1 of both the ICCPR and ICESCR, is that self-determination is at the heart of the entire human rights corpus. How can human rights NGOs encourage and court practices and relationships that seek to gut such a fundamental principle of the human rights movement? Such dependence ultimately negates the very values NGOs seek to inculcate in society. There is no doubt those human rights groups in East Africa would not have survived without donor support and at times protection from donor states. However, both NGOs and donors should work to alleviate dependence, not encourage it. Experience indicates that excessive donor support for human rights NGOs distorts their vision, plays havoc with their loyalty, retards creativity, confuses lines of accountability, and encourages the development of a "fat cat" mentality among NGO executives. These characteristics—which foundations, charities, philanthropies, and other donors objectively cultivate—only harden the elitist posture of human rights NGOs.

> With overseas donors as sources of reference and accountability, the only obligations local human rights groups have are reporting requirements arising under grant contracts where they exist. The raison d'etre of the African human rights movement is primarily to fulfill such contracts rather than to service a social obligation or constituency. Local human rights groups exist to please the international agencies that fund or support them. Local problems are only defined as potential pots of project cash, not as human rights experiences to be resolved in just terms, thereby delegitimizing human rights language and robbing its ideals of popular appeal.[54]

There is no doubt that pathological donor-donee relationships distort NGO mandates, confuse priorities, and undermine the creation of a viable, legitimate human rights movement. What human rights NGOs in East Africa must realize is that donors exist to vindicate their own agendas, many of which may be incongruent with the needs of the region. What is needed, first and foremost, is a new ethics in donor-donee relationships. But such ethics are not possible unless the parties engage in systematic, open, regular, and candid conversations devoid of hypocrisy on either side. Each party also needs to be self-critical, and carry out independent evaluations and audits of its methods of work with the other party. Donors could progressively wean organizations from their support. Donors could also help NGOs establish endowments or purchase office space, a major expense for NGOs. There are, however, some encouraging signs. Some local NGOs are starting to assert their autonomy, and some donors have now on their staffs Africans in responsible positions. Some of these developments may help alleviate barriers associated with colonial legacies and racism. However, the larger responsibility lies with local NGOs to assert their autonomy, expand their support base, and diversify their sources of income. It is unfortunate that the elite human rights organizations in East Africa have grown too fat and complacent because they can always count on donor support and funding. It is absolutely imperative that NGOs start immediately to cultivate local sources of financial and material support. Graduated membership drives—where dues are pegged to different categories of memberships—is one of the most effective ways to draw local support. Targets ought to include professionals, businesspersons, politicians, ordinary citizens, and companies. In 2003, FIDA-Kenya had a highly successful "friends-of-FIDA night" in which substantial pledges were made.[55] There is no reason why organizations cannot employ similar and other creative methods of fund-raising from local sources. These could include "award nights" at which individuals who have made a difference are recognized by guests who "buy a table," a euphemism for a large donation. I have also argued elsewhere that NGOs ought to explore the possibility of an NGO-controlled fund that the state would finance. While risky, it could work if conceptualized well and run professionally.[56] But perhaps the most effective and innovative way of reducing financial dependence on all donors—whether local or foreign—is by venturing into the profit-making world. There is no reason why local human rights NGOs cannot set up businesses—restaurants, publishing houses, and real estate, among others—to generate income for their programs. Such businesses could be run by trusts accountable to the NGOs.

NGO Deficits: Institutionalization, Transparency, and Democracy

Human rights NGOs—whether national or international—are first and foremost pressure groups against governments, intergovernmental institutions and, increasingly, corporations or business enterprises. Human rights groups are change agents and the only measure of their success is effectiveness in vindicating their core mandates. As a matter of the logic for these NGOs, every other consideration is largely secondary. Welch captures the justification for human rights NGOs by identifying their primary missions.

> As advocacy organizations, human rights NGOs have traditionally concentrated their efforts on a few crucial areas: working with (or against) governments in developing agendas for action; in standard setting (that is, establishing international norms for state behavior, set forth in legally binding treaties that have been negotiated and ratified by governments); in preparing and providing information about abuses based on research; in lobbying officials and media; and in providing direct assistance to victims of human rights abuses.[57]

The legitimacy of human rights NGOs results partially from their ability to fulfill these missions. To be sure, an NGO that is unable to deliver on its core mandate cannot properly lay a claim on legitimacy. The suggestion here is that effectiveness on the core mandate of the organization-and not the degree of institutionalization, transparency, or internal democratization—is the key to its viability. But effectiveness presupposes that the organization is not only responsive to the needs of its constituents, but also is not alienated from them. This is critical because domestic human rights NGOs always present themselves as the voice of the people—the "masses"—at the national level. They present themselves as the conscience of the people, fighting against the state, the behemoth and ogre that they depict as bent on the consumption of humans.[58] NGOs see themselves as the saviors who work at the intersection of power and powerlessness, on behalf of the poor and powerless, and against the powerful who are allied to the state, and to whom the state belongs. By appropriating a seemingly unassailable high moral ground, human rights NGOs acquire the aura of nobility and righteousness—they are beyond reproach. In this contest, they are "good" while the state is "evil." One of the most shocking developments of the last two decades is that states, intergovernmental organizations, and citizens the world over have indeed ceded to the view that human rights NGOs occupy a hallowed, if not sacred, plane as the conscience of society. But is this what human rights NGOs really are, or do they misrepresent themselves?

Even when human rights NGOs are legitimate and effective voices for the poor and the powerless, they are nevertheless generally defined by a number of deficits. The most important of these deficits are those of institutionalization, democracy, and transparency. The majority of NGOs, even the most established in East Africa, are relatively small organizations with strong management but weak oversight structures. In plain English, most human rights NGOs in East Africa have powerful executive directors, largely compliant staffs, and weak or dysfunctional boards of directors. Internally, most NGOs are not adequately institutionalized. For instance, in the absence of the executive director, an operational vacuum usually develops, and program staff is frequently paralyzed for fear of making key decisions or proceeding without the express authorization of the executive director. In other areas, such as disciplinary measures, procurement, personnel matters, and other key questions, quite often too much power is concentrated in the executive director, even where internal administrative structures exist to address them.

In East Africa, the boards of directors, the policy-making organs of NGOs, are generally ineffective, or in some cases only interested in the capital that comes with membership. Such perks may include sitting allowances, the prestige associated with membership, consultancies within the organization, or even overseas junkets on behalf of the organization. Few board members help craft policy, raise funds, perform in-kind, voluntary work at the organization, or mentor program staff. Clearly, board members are extremely busy people, but they must perform once they take on the obligation. In the event, ineffective boards normally look the other way as long as the executive director does not infringe on their "benefits." The consequences of disconnection between the boards and the secretariat of NGOs include inertia, lack of direction, inability to be innovative and responsive to urgent matters, organizational malaise and decay, cruelty against junior staff by senior staff, including sexual harassment, and ultimately lack of effectiveness. Unfortunately, except for donors, there are no other mechanisms for accountability and transparency within NGOs. That is why self-policing—through strong and ethical boards of directors—is essential. Donors must also seek audits of internal management structures and procedures and initiate real and meaningful dialogue with donees.

In other cases, where human rights NGOs are highly functional and professional, they still remain elitist. That is because human rights NGOs are generally not democratic institutions. Nor should they be. What is important is that both accountability and transparency are watchwords. It bears reminding that human rights NGOs in East Africa are self-appointed, unelected, usually individual-driven, and run by an individual or an elitist group that determines the agenda and priorities of the organization. These are not in themselves necessarily deleterious characteristics. What is important is that those groups, or the elites running them, be responsive to their constituents and have internally coherent, efficient, and humane administrative structures and procedures. It is also important that the board of directors exercises real oversight over the management so that transparency and accountability are not compromised. In membership NGOs, modes of accountability ought to be created without turning the NGO over to its members. In any case, both the staff and boards of directors ought to be governed by clear terms of service with reasonable, defensible limitations.

Significantly, transparency and accountability for civil society ought not to be conflated with democracy. Human rights NGOs must be both accountable and transparent, but their full democratization would spell a death knell. In fact, it is precisely because it is not constrained by the dictates of democracy that civil society—and in particular human rights groups—can be effective as pressure groups. Democracy is slow, cumbersome, and prone to gridlock. In contrast, nondemocratic pressure groups, such as human rights groups, are nimble and can react quickly without the paralyzing fetters of the democratic process. How effective would a human rights NGO be if it had to wait for its staff, the board, and its membership to vote on an operational question? In that case, virtually no NGOs would have any impact on human rights conditions. NGOs in East Africa should seek to be accountable and transparent without necessarily being democratic. Such accountability should be to their constituents by showing fidelity to their core mandate—and their understanding of human rights. Ken Anderson has captured this distinction well.

> Civil society is not conceived of as being a substitute for the democratic processes, let alone conveying democratic legitimacy. On the contrary, the glory of civil society is precisely that it is something different from democracy and democratic processes. . . . Put bluntly, the glory of organizations of civil society is not democratic legitimacy, but the ability to be a pressure group.[59]

State-Civil Society Relations: An Age-Old Conundrum

Historically, the relationship between the state and civil society is one of uneasy coexistence. In established democracies, civil society organizations are a fact of life. In fact, it is not possible to imagine a democracy in the absence of civil society. States remain, at least for now, the repositories of sovereignty and the key actors within national borders. Civil society organizations have not contested this central role by the state, except they have insisted on the receptivity of the state to the popular wishes of the people, which they claim to represent. In East Africa, unlike the in Western world, the relationship between the state and civil society is a matter of bitter contestation primarily because the state in the region is not really democratic, even in Kenya and Tanzania, where a formal democracy has been declared. The other problem clearly is the infancy of civil society: it is no more than two decades old in most of the region. Between independence in the 1960s and the 1980s, most of the so-called civil society organizations in the region—women's groups, bar associations, trade groups, and other nonstate actors—were tethered to the state through the ruling party or the cooptation of their leaders. In reality, therefore, genuine civil society in East Africa has only emerged over the last two decades.

The infancy of civil society combined with the halting democratization of states in the region makes the relationship between the two fluid, uncertain, and experimental. Human rights groups in the region have adopted either of three strategies in their relationship with the state: confrontation, collaboration, or a combination of both given the issue and circumstances. These are universal and paradigmatic NGO approaches to states and not unique to East Africa. NGOs put difference emphasis on their relationship with the state given its political orientation. In Kenya, for example, virtually all human rights NGOs opposed the policies of the Moi-KANU state, which was ousted by Mwai Kibaki and the National Rainbow Coalition in 2002. Many human rights groups initially supported NARC policies, and a number of NGO luminaries joined the government in human rights or reform-related positions.[60] For the first time in Kenya's history, a number of human rights NGOs were engaged in collaborative projects with the government, although some pulled back as NARC reneged on key reforms.[61]

Throughout the entire region, human rights NGOs remain relatively few and concentrated in large urban areas. They lack a popular base and are therefore vulnerable to the state. But equally important is the fact that NGOs have played a major role—most visibly in Kenya—in creating space for the democratic process. In Kenya and Tanzania, civil society should adopt a nuanced and strategic approach to the state and exploit the space created by formal democracy. This is essential to deepen and enlarge the state's commitment to basic human rights. In these states, the primary role of civil society should be that of a watchdog: to critique, expose, and chastise the state. Its main mission must remain confrontation with the state. In Uganda, where political liberalization lags behind, civil society must assume a highly vocal and heightened activist strategy. Support for Ugandan civil society from its counterparts in Kenya and Tanzania would buoy its prospects.

Conclusion

Today, the struggle for human rights is a universal enterprise. What happens within the borders of one state is no longer just the business of that state; it is the responsibility of the entirety of mankind. Even so, the actual vindication of the rights regime remains an essentially national effort. That is why states themselves are the basic obligors—and the targets—of the human rights corpus. But since 1948, when the UDHR was adopted, it has become clear that when left to themselves, states do not generally create internal processes and institutions to protect human rights. If anything, history has taught us that none of these rights would be protected without a vigilant and vibrant civil society.

That is why the fledgling human rights NGO sector in East Africa is critical if the march in the region toward more open, responsive, and humane societies is to continue. Clearly, the weak NGO sector must take the lead in addressing its pathologies and deficits, in particular those of legitimacy, transparency, and accountability. Importantly, NGOs in the region must relentlessly seek sustainability, even if it means pioneering new models for NGOs. But it is a fallacy to believe that NGOs will attain self-reliance and end their full dependence on external support any time soon. Hence there is a need to work with donors to create a viable human rights movement in the region. Such collaboration must candidly explore all the pitfalls of the relationship and address the negative and destructive legacies of the past.

CHAPTER TWO

To Whom, for What, and About What?
The Legitimacy of Human Rights NGOs in Kenya

Betty K. Murungi

> *The age of blind faith in institutions is over. We have entered the age of "accountability" processes by which institutions are made responsible to external audiences and constituencies are now the subject of intense and ongoing attention.*
> —Kumi Naidoo

LONG BEFORE THE *Economist* published the famous September 2000 article questioning the credibility of nongovernmental organizations, the Kenyan ruling political elite had already challenged the legitimacy of civil society in direct attacks.[1] The Kenyan state, which was corrupt, inept, and undemocratic, was suffering a severe crisis of confidence. Opposition parties and groups that worked closely with civil society organizations and social movements had established themselves as important and influential actors in the political arena. As a result, disillusioned citizens placed their trust in civil society organizations. In response, the state responded by raising questions about the legitimacy and accountability of pro-democracy and human rights NGOs. It declared often that NGOs were an unelected nuisance or the agents of foreign interests or powers. The attacks were meant to minimize the influence of NGOs.

Questions about the legitimacy, accountability, and transparency of NGOs are valid and must be addressed openly. In this chapter, I argue that it is preferable that the NGO human rights sector ask these questions and seek solutions to the challenges, rather than allow others, including governments and donors, to do it.[2] Self-criticism by NGOs will build their effectiveness and credibility. This is important if NGOs are to create a self-sustaining nongovernmental sector. This chapter explores the question of legitimacy for human rights organizations in Kenya. It poses questions and offers suggestions for NGOs to consider in creating a legitimate, accountable, and viable civil society culture. It looks at the ways in which NGOs can enhance their legitimacy with the multiple constituencies to which they must be accountable.

This chapter does not purport to examine each and every organization that styles itself a human rights NGO in Kenya. Rather, it takes a broad view and utilizes specific examples that illustrate and advance the arguments it makes with respect to legitimacy and accountability. It uses the term "human rights organization" liberally to include groups engaged in the pro-democracy movement.

The Human Rights Sector

To its credit, the human rights NGO sector in Africa has in the recent past engaged in an exercise of self-criticism and in-depth examination. Serious debates have ensued on the questions of legitimacy, accountability, and sustainability. These discussions have been continuous and focused. Very often, they have resulted in resolutions that relate to the value of being accountable to, but independent of, foreign donors. In short, there is self-induced momentum on the challenges that face human rights NGOs in the region.

Chidi Odinkalu, a leading Nigerian scholar-activist, has written about the elite nature of human rights organizations on the African continent.[3] Odinkalu has argued that most African human rights organizations are modeled after northern watchdog groups. He identifies several characteristics of the majority of African NGOs: they are located in urban areas; most are run by secretariats with governing boards that set policy; most lack a membership base; and almost all are dependent solely on foreign funding. There is little doubt that some of these questions raise serious problems. How, then, have they been addressed?

Odinkalu argues that even the most successful human rights NGOs only manage to achieve the equivalent status of public policy think tanks, research institutes, or specialized publishing houses. He writes that instead of being the currency of a social justice or conscience-driven movement, "human rights" have increasingly become the specialized language of a select professional cadre with its own rites of passage and methods of certification: "Far from being a badge of honour, human rights activism is, increasingly a certificate of privilege."[4] Kayode Fayemi, another Nigerian scholar and civil society leader argues that there is nothing wrong with NGO specialization if it is done well and that the existence of a liberal civil society "aristocracy" does not mean that there are no grassroots organizations engaged in similar pursuits.[5] Another feature of the more successful human rights organizations is the self-appointing and self-perpetuating nature of their governing boards.[6] The failure by the founders of these organizations and of civil society leadership to build a successor cadre directly affects their sustainability upon the death or departure of the leaders. That is why transitions and successions in NGOs in Africa have often been difficult and trying processes.

The Influence of Human Rights NGOs

Before the pogroms of the December 2007 post-election violence, the period between 1970 and 1997 had witnessed the most egregious violations of human rights in Kenya. Torture, political murders, political repression, detention without trial, corruption, and theft of state resources were conducted with impunity. This period saw the establishment of important human rights organizations, pressure groups, citizens groups, and community based organizations—all with a mission to promote and protect the rights of Kenyans and lobby for a democratic and plural society. The oldest human rights organization in Kenya is Kituo Cha Sheria, set up in 1973. Kituo is a membership organization with a mandate to provide legal aid and raise awareness among the population about their legal rights.

In 1985, the Federation of Women Lawyers in Kenya (FIDA-Kenya) was established as a membership organization as a result of the women's conference in Nairobi that year.[7] Its initial mandate was the modest mission of providing legal aid to indigent women. Since then, it has evolved into an important organization that monitors the status of the human rights of women nationally. It is engaged in public interest litigation and monitors government compliance to reporting standards on international conventions. It has a deep influence on law reform and works closely with government ministries involved in the administration of justice. FIDA has three national offices and a countrywide network of trained human rights monitors.

The Law Society of Kenya (LSK) is a professional bar association that has been in existence since 1949.[8] The LSK, a conservative institution for most of its life, embraced the activism and language of human rights starting in the late 1980s. The effectiveness of the LSK as a watchdog largely depended on the officials sitting on its governing council.[9] For a period of about ten years—starting in the late 1980s—the LSK became the voice of pro-democratic forces. Its reach and influence were felt countrywide. It was no longer just a professional society. It joined hands with opposition forces within the country to push for a new constitution and, for the first time in its history, partnered with other civil society organizations in efforts to expand the democratic space for citizens. An elite organization, the LSK quickly rose in prominence and was perceived by Kenyans as the "conscience of the people."

The Kenya Human Rights Commission (KHRC) exploded onto the scene in 1992, and with it a new style of leadership of the human rights movement in Kenya.[10] Whereas other groups were registered under existing laws, the KHRC was initially denied registration for close to two years. Its style of advocacy was aggressive—it was confrontational and pulled no punches. In its first two years, it published a bevy of hard-hitting reports on topics including academic freedom in public universities, state-instigated violence during the 1992 general elections, torture of and the denial of health care to political detainees, and on Amos Wako, the attorney general, in a critically biting piece titled "The Fallen Angel."[11] Human rights in Kenya became synonymous with the KHRC. Led by respected and highly reputable individuals, the legitimacy of the KHRC was unquestioned in civil society and within its wider constituencies, including among donors.

The KHRC was formed in the United States in 1991 by Kenyan exiles and academicsspecifically to lobby for the respect of human rights and promotion of democratization, accountability, and good governance in Kenya.[12] The people who ran it were steeped in human rights law and practiced in advocacy. They were extremely well organized and tooled the KHRC into a formidable advocate for the people and against despotism and dictatorship. This organization took human rights advocacy to a new level, and made it possible for other groups to emerge and join the struggle for social justice and change.

The KHRC set an important precedent by hosting and giving legal cover to human rights groups that had been denied registration by the Kenya government. These groups included the Release Political Prisoners pressure group (RPP), the Legal Resources Foundation (LRF), the Citizens Coalition for Constitutional Change (4Cs), Muslims for Human Rights (MUHURI), and the Kenya Pastoralist Forum (KPF). Quite apart from providing legal cover, this collaboration expanded knowledge and impact on the struggle for the respect for human rights and democratization in Kenya. The KHRC has taken its work to communities and has proposed an ambitious plan to empower communities to lead in promoting and protecting their own human rights. In this approach, communities become the agents and not the objects of social change.

It is not in question that human rights NGOs have provided the intellectual leadership in the campaign for a new constitution in Kenya.[13] In an ambitious project aimed at reconstructing the state through constitution making, the 4Cs took leadership of the project for constitutional change and incorporated into its coalition women's organizations, youth groups, church groups, and trade unions. The 4Cs brought together many groups, including the Law Society of Kenya, the International Commission of Jurists, FIDA-Kenya, the National Convention Assembly (NCA), and National Convention Executive Council (NCEC), to form a social movement for constitutional reform. This movement was instrumental in the formation of the Ufungamano Initiative, a civil society citizen effort for a new constitution that was eventually taken over by religious groups.[14] There is no doubt that these groups risked life and limb in the 1980s and 1990s to campaign against torture, corruption, impunity, and lack of academic freedom and democratic governance.

The Green Belt Movement, a citizens' environmental justice group with over 100,000 members, expanded its advocacy and embraced a broad area of rights.[15] It has worked with mothers of political prisoners to lobby for their release and, together with the political opposition, lobbied for an end to forest excision and land grabbing by politically connected and corrupt individuals.[16] This movement worked with the Public Law Institute (PLI), another public interest group, to bring a case against KANU, the ruling party, and the government, to cease the irregular acquisition of public land to erect party headquarters in historic Uhuru Park. Like Greenbelt, the Mazingira Institute and its "Operation Firimbi" campaign clearly advocated not just for environmental protection and social economic rights, but also against corruption and impunity.[17] Mazingira became involved in the campaign for a new constitution and Davinder Lamba, its executive director, was the coconvener of the NCEC.

Many civil society actors in Kenya have decided to locate their work within a human rights framework. They worked extremely well across issues and were able to network effectively. In a very real sense, these groups were the voice of the people with a crucial role to play in raising questions about governance and influencing policy and constitutional change. Only the state questioned their legitimacy. In retrospect, any failures that the pro-democracy movement experienced during the period described here were due in large part to an inability to successfully work across movements, including established political movements.

In the December 2002 general election campaigns, many civil society groups threw their energies and resources behind what they perceived to have been the democratic alternative to KANU and openly supported the opposition forces.[18] These NGOs and other unregistered citizens' groups had acquired legitimacy as leaders of the pro-democracy movement working to oust KANU and president Daniel arap Moi from power. They held the high moral ground because they sought to reestablish structures of good governance and restore a culture of constitutionalism and respect for the rule of law. They correctly gave up the pretense of nonpartisanship.

Defining Legitimacy

Michael Edwards has written that "legitimacy is generally understood as the right to be and do something in society—a sense that an organization is lawful, admissible, and justified in its chosen course of action."[19] There are at least four categories of legitimacy for civil society that have been identified by researchers in the field: legal, moral, knowledge/expertise/performance, and political.[20]

Legal Legitimacy

Legal legitimacy refers to an organization's compliance with legal requirements such as constitutions and bylaws. This base of legitimacy means that civil society organizations comply with statutory requirements such as establishing boards of directors and adhering to auditing and reporting procedures. Governments, particularly oppressive ones, are very keen on this type of legitimacy and often raise questions of compliance. But this base of legitimacy does not necessarily establish legitimacy with most stakeholders and often creates disturbing excuses for criticism by detractors of citizen participation in governance. This is the least important of the four bases of legitimacy.

There are many types of NGOs in civil society. Some of the disreputable ones include business organization NGOs (BONGOs), political NGOs (PONGOs), briefcase NGOs (BRINGOs), donor NGOs (DONGOs), government NGOs (GONGOs), First Lady NGOs, family-owned NGOs (FANGOs), and a host of others. These NGOs do not represent any popular constituencies and are therefore accountable only to those who fund them. They do not make public any reports of their internal operations. Many often hire family members or cronies as staff. Their offices are usually located in their own homes or at fictitious Yahoo or Hotmail e-mail addresses and cellular phone numbers that are unreachable.

Unfortunately, many of the dubious NGOs are dangerous because they are very sophisticated. The First Lady NGOs, for instance, are well run and highly resourced initiatives.[21] Others have perfected the art of proposal writing, program design, and reporting. Many speak the language of human rights but are only accountable to a family, political party, or the government. For these types of NGOs, there is only one level of accountability that counts—vertical and to their donors.

Although these questionable NGOs have legal legitimacy, many lack basic knowledge and expertise in human rights, and therefore cannot be effective advocates. The organizations lack internal democracy and do not even respect human rights. They do not acknowledge or practice any of the known mechanisms of accountability except those that relate to accountability to donors. Conversely, organizations that claim other important bases of legitimacy are careless about legal processes. They do not file returns with the NGO Council, refuse to pay annual dues or undertake annual financial audits, and even fail to report on time to donors. This may put them on watch lists from where they could be denied funds, their political and moral legitimacy notwithstanding.

Repressive regimes often deploy the law to undermine the operations of NGOs they deem hostile. Groups with other important bases of legitimacy often fail to obtain legal legitimacy and only operate under cover through being "housed" by registered groups. In Kenya, the denial of registration was used to exclude groups that challenged the corrupt and authoritarian nature of the state.

Moral Legitimacy

Claims of moral legitimacy are based on a group's ability to speak for the "people" and to effectively represent their values.[22] NGOs can ground their claims to legitimacy in "transcendent moral values that have overwhelming force in the circumstances."[23] For example, the campaigns to halt the politically instigated massacres prior to the 1992 and 1997 general elections in Kenya were the moral responsibility of every human rights organization. Groups that campaign to end genital mutilation of six-year-old girls appeal to legitimacy in morality. So do groups that campaign against hunger and famine. This is also true for groups working in the areas of refugee rights and health. The groups need to make a compelling case for moral legitimacy within critical constituencies that have a similar moral code. Anticorruption groups such as Transparency International can also claim this base of legitimacy in societies where values of good governance have been internalized.

Knowledge/Expertise/Performance Legitimacy

It is not possible to claim legitimacy in human rights advocacy without the requisite knowledge, expertise, and performance. Among others, students and professors of human rights law are entitled to claim legitimacy on this basis. Donors are particularly fixated on this base of legitimacy. They want to know that the NGO has the expertise to undertake the proposed program work. An indication of the donor shift in favor of technical or performance legitimacy has been the propensity to support human rights NGOs led by academics and lawyers. This assures the donor that it will receive a useful and competent report at the end of the reporting period. This base of legitimacy applies to policy think tanks and research institutions.

Knowledge and expertise is an important base of legitimacy for all human rights NGOs—one should not operate a human rights organization without an adequate understanding of the normative and institutional issues in the field. In particular, a theoretical grounding in human rights is critically important. This together with a personal commitment to promote and protect human rights makes for an ideal combination for advocacy. Individuals who are unethical in their own lives, like wife beaters, for example, have no business running a human rights NGO.

Political Legitimacy

An analysis of the legitimacy of NGOs must acknowledge certain political realities. Where the state is nonexistent, has failed, or is illegitimate, then civil society organizations involved in governance and human rights must increasingly fill the void left by the state. Citizens will confer political legitimacy on groups that perform tasks that the state is either unable or unwilling to undertake.[24] Other forms of political legitimacy arise from the internal processes of participation of the membership of NGOs and the extent to which the groups are transparent and accountable to the people whom they represent. Political legitimacy is the most important base of legitimacy—organizations with this type of legitimacy are often the credible NGOs in society.

NGOs should seriously consider their bases of legitimacy in relation to their mission and strategic direction. This will allow them to determine the extent of the influence and impact they can achieve among multiple stakeholders. To do so, there should be a systematic process of identifying weaknesses and strengths. This applies to both emergent and established groups. With others, L. David Brown has proposed a set of model steps to address this question:[25] step 1—identifying organizational visions, missions, and strategies; step 2—mapping stakeholders critical to the implementation of strategies; step 3—articulating grounds for legitimacy with key stakeholders; step 4—resolving legitimacy questions with key stakeholders; step 5—meeting legitimacy standards in implementing programs, including knowledge, expertise, and performance.

In this region we recognize different aspects of the above model in certain stages of strategic planning that most organizations undertake religiously every three or five years. We tend to pay more attention to the stages that do not involve stakeholder consultation and monitoring programs for impact.

Context and Legitimacy

Context is important in the definition of legitimacy. It is important to realize that human rights organizations operate under varying political, economic, and social contexts. Since the so-called third wave of democratization in the 1980s, the NGO global context has seen movement away from autocracy. However, this is being replaced by a context of rising militarism, antiterrorism, and failed transitions. It is a context in which human rights, particularly rights of women, have suffered a major backlash. Civil rights have been suspended as the U.S.-led war on terror ascends to new and frightening levels. An example is the proposed antiterrorism legislation that targets particular communities and negates their human rights.[26]

Since 2003, Kenya has been in a failing political transition. This was confirmed by the near collapse of the state following the disputed December 2007 elections. The opposing political parties—Raila Odinga's Orange Democratic Movement (ODM) and Mwai Kibaki's Party of National Unity (PNU)—engaged in a highly tribalized campaign. When Kibaki was reelected president in an election marred by rigging and fraud, Odinga refused to concede defeat. In the aftermath, ODM supporters attacked those of PNU along tribal lines. More than 1,000 were killed and more than 300,000 internally displaced. Civil society organizations found themselves on the defensive as both sides accused them of being disloyal to ethnic agendas. The further tribalization of politics has exposed civil society to greater risks, with the potential for sharply curtailing its influence. In Uganda, perhaps the term "transition" cannot be used in the same sentence with "context" because the government has kept a tight rein on political activity. But Tanzania has made a smooth transition from single party rule to open political pluralism. These different contexts in each country have affected the influence of NGOs in the political process. In East Africa, Kenyan NGOs have exerted the most influence in the political process over the past decade.

Donors and the Sustainability of NGOs

Donors play a key role in sustaining the human rights movement in Kenya. Unfortunately, an increasing number of organizations design programs to suit donor agendas that may have very little to do with building or supporting the movement. Mahmood Mamdani sees involvement of donors as a shift from one type of clientelism to another, resulting in a retrogression of civil society.[27] This negative shift disables civil society from making the critical link between the struggle for rights and the struggle for justice. Even after more than fifteen years of foreign funding, local organizations are not ready to raise funds locally. In Mamdani's opinion, African civil society has turned into clients of international donors. Issa Shivji has even harsher criticism of NGO leadership in Africa. He argues that part of the problem is that "African intellectuals are busy writing grant proposals, reports, accounts, and so on, and under these circumstances they have no time for intellectual work or even critical reflection or analysis."[28] Shivji also contends that East African universities ceased being centers of critical reflection in the 1970s.

The challenges being posed are those of ownership. Who owns the agenda and ideas of NGOs? This patron-client relationship is particularly disturbing when it implicates intellectuals in the region. Since intellectuals provide the backbone of the human rights movement in our region, it is a matter of great concern when two of the most celebrated thinkers in East Africa hold such a dim view. Without freedom to think, there can be no creativity. NGOs have had the mettle to oppose both the public and governments to advance the cause of human rights. It would be tragic if donors held them hostage.

In 2004 the Ford Foundation committed $7 million to the emerging human rights movement in the United States.[29] What are the implications for funding in Africa when the Ford Foundation allocates such a large amount of money to its "domestic" movement? A recent survey by the Ford Foundation concluded that most funders thought of human rights as "international"—to be funded abroad, not within the United States.[30] However, after September 11, funders started to make linkages between international and domestic human and civil rights funding. But as Larry Cox, formerly with the Ford Foundation, observed in *Close to Home*, this "integrated approach" was still the exception rather than the rule within the funding community.[31] Competition for resources is bound to become stiff as groups in the West, particularly in the United States, embrace a human rights framework for their work. This shift relates to the changing global context for human rights advocacy.

The Challenges of Accountability

Closely tied to legitimacy and sustainability is the question of accountability—the obligation to report on a group's activities to a set of legitimate authorities. In this regard, the following questions present the most immediate challenges. What responsibility do NGOs take to sustain their work? How do NGOs deal with the deficit of good governance? What steps have been taken to ensure accountability within NGOs and how does such accountability affect the society as a whole? How do NGOs measure their impact and effect—for themselves, their constituencies, and donors? Who benefits from specific accountability mechanisms? What is the nature of relationship within the NGO sector itself? How accountable are NGOs to their grassroots constituents? What constitutes "accountable" behavior? Are there minimum standards of transparency and internal democracy? What field of accountability should be strengthened to protect and expand the political space within which human rights NGOs operate?

Conclusion

NGOs are legitimized not by whom they represent, but by what they do. NGOs and their networks are legitimized by the validity of their ideas, the values they promote, and by the issues they care about.[32] NGOs need to pay attention to the following matters. In participation, NGOs should make greater efforts to involve the stakeholders that will be affected by their programs. NGO activism should be more about the participation of the ordinary citizen and less about representation. There is a need to strengthen accountability to constituencies and peers—downward and horizontal accountability for greater effectiveness.

NGOs should more effectively manage intersectorial tensions and respect diversity. The civil society should be ethical, transparent, and the epitome of good governance. It should have people of unquestioned integrity in leadership positions. Finally, NGOs should reduce dependence on external donors. Raising funds locally can do this. There are enough resources in the region to match donor funds and possibly make external funding unnecessary.

PART II

Interrogating NGO Mandates:
Gender, Sexuality, and ESC Rights

CHAPTER THREE

Law, Sexuality, and Politics in Uganda: Challenges for Women's Human Rights NGOs

Sylvia Tamale

WOMEN'S MOVEMENTS ON the African continent have been the most orga- nized and vibrant sectors of civil society.[1] Women's rights groups have made impressive gains in their quest to obtain political, legal, economic, and social equality between African men and women. The women's movements in the East African nations of Kenya, Uganda, and Tanzania have many formidable activists that have consistently stood up to challenge all forms of patriarchal dominance. No doubt, significant successes have been recorded. Despite this, the majority of women in the subregion are yet to enjoy the substance of equal- ity, citizenship, and human rights. One significant issue that has remained on the back burner of the African women's movements is sexuality.[2] Indeed, sexual- ity continues to be cloaked in a heavy shroud of secrecy, shame, taboos, and silence.[3] This is so despite the recognition by many African feminist scholars of the intersection between the human body, gender, and politics.[4] Indeed, there is a direct link between women's sexuality and their subordinate status.

Of course there are certain aspects of women's sexuality that are consistently highlighted within the women's movement. Movement activists have been ex- tremely vocal in opposing sexual violence, that is, rape, defilement, and genital mutilation, and in advocating for women's reproductive health on matters of contraception, safe motherhood, and maternal mortality. There are several non- governmental organizations with programs that address these issues. But very few organizations have gone beyond the violence/maternity agenda when dealing with women's sexuality. Not much has been done to mobilize around issues of women's sexual rights—the rights to sexual fulfillment and freedom, abortion, voluntary sex work, the dignity of unmarried women, single mothers, widows, women living with HIV/AIDS, alternative sexual orientations, and intersexuality. The tendency is to leave what the law, culture, and religion say about women's bodies and sexuality uncontested. Rarely do we conceptualize the significant link between women's bodies and sexuality to their oppression, subordination, and exploitation.[5]

The seventh regional conference on Beijing + 10 held in Addis Ababa is a good illustration of this point. The NGO forum at the conference was extremely reluctant to adopt language that would unequivocally reject the discrimination of African women on grounds of lesbianism.[6] It was disturbing that women's rights NGOs from around the continent dragged their feet on this issue in the wake of the brutal sexual assault and violent murder of a Sierra Leonean woman who had been actively engaged in the struggle of the rights of lesbians and other sexual minorities locally and regionally.[7]

In this chapter, I shall argue that sexuality lies at the heart of African women's oppression and that the patriarchal state has a vested interest in keeping a tight leash on women's bodies and/or their sexuality. Using the Ugandan legal regime as a case study, I shall illustrate how the law is used as a tool to institutionalize the control of women's bodies and their sexuality and link it directly to male dominance and women's subordination. I shall attempt to explore the reasons why, despite its centrality, mainstream women's rights NGOs do not pay much attention to the pivotal issue of sexuality as a right. Why are African NGOs willing to compromise when it comes to women's sexual rights and freedom? If the ultimate goal is women's full empowerment, to break the chains that keep them in bondage, then why is it that NGOs do not attack the problem at full throttle? Indeed, it is ironic that the ideological base upon which most women's rights NGOs develop their work plans facilitates the construction, rather than the deconstruction, of the hierarchies and traditional social structures based on gender and power.

In September 2004, I conducted in-depth interviews with activists from fourteen NGOs, all of which dealt with the rights of women and/or children as shown in Appendix 1. The discussions gave me some insights into the external and internal challenges that such groups grapple with in their day-to-day activities, as well as the extent to which they deal with issues of sexuality. Both the directory of the National Association of Women Organizations in Uganda (NAWOU) and the Web site of the Women's Organizations in Uganda Network (WOUGNET) were extremely valuable in providing further detailed profiles of other women's NGOs and grassroots organizations.[8] This information was useful in throwing more light on the general focus of issues that the Ugandan women's movement tackles.

My analysis will begin with a demonstration of how patriarchy uses the law, both statutory and customary, to regulate women's sexuality and their reproductive role as a self-sustaining tool to maintain the sex/gender hierarchy. In the third section, I analyze the extent to which women's rights NGOs in Uganda address the issue of sexuality and consider some of the reasons behind their apparent reticence to wage a full-scale war against patriarchal control of women's sexuality. In this section, I quote quite extensively from the interview notes. However, for purposes of confidentiality, I am careful not to link such material to the participants. The chapter ends with a conclusion and suggestions for the way forward.

Focus on Sexuality: A Conceptual Justification

Sexuality holds positive and empowering possibilities, but it also represents considerable constraints for the emancipation of women in Africa. In many African contexts, the relationship of women to their own bodies is often different from the disembodied, negative relations rooted in the legacy of colonialism. Precolonial societies in Africa were not immune to manipulating culture to oppress women. Likewise, the Judeo-Christian and Arabic-Islamic cultures imposed a particular sexuality on African women as "hyperdeveloped" and in need of control.[9] This cultural construction facilitated the consolidation of the patriarchal colonial state.[10] In a postcolonial context, the legacies of these two sociopolitical formations impose a variety of gendered constructs on the African woman.

Patriarchy and capitalism have many tools at their disposal to create and maintain gender roles and relations in African societies. Women's bodies constitute one of the most formidable tools for this purpose. If one imagines the body to be a tabula rasa (blank slate) at the time of birth, culture then proceeds to inscribe rules, images, symbols, and even hierarchies that give shape and character to that body. Although the texts that culture inscribes on African women's bodies remain invisible to the uncritical eye, it is in fact a crucial medium for effecting social control. The nibs of culture, religion, the law, the media, and especially the systems of education are all instrumental in constructing African women's sexuality and desire through the inscriptions they engrave on their bodies. Through the reproductive and sexual control of African women's bodies, their subordination and continued exploitation is guaranteed.

If women's sexual autonomy is taken to be part of the human rights corpus, then it must be recognized that such a right is universal, indivisible, and interdependent. For example, a woman who is forced to carry an unwanted pregnancy, whether resulting from rape, incest, failure of a contraceptive method, or economic hardship to term, will obviously be affected in her ability to enjoy other basic rights such as personal liberty, human dignity, work, civic participation, and education, among others.

The need to control women's sexuality and fertility is crucial in patriarchal societies at two levels. First, it is for purely economic reasons. Male domination under patriarchy generally depends on men's control of resources and their relative economic power over women. These economic relations are reflected within the family where the man, as head of the household, exercises control over the lives of women and children, who are virtually treated as his property. It is essential that the man's acquired property and wealth be passed on to his male offspring in order to sustain the patriarchy. Hence, it becomes important to control women's sexuality in order to guarantee the *legitimacy* of children when bequeathing property.[11] To this end, the monogamy of women is required without necessarily disturbing men's polygamous sexuality.

Second, it is important for market patriarchal societies to separate the "public" sphere from the "private" realm. The two spheres, which are artificially created to serve patriarchy, are highly gendered with the former representing men and the locus of socially valued activities such as politics and wage labor, while the latter is representative of unremunerated domestic activities performed by women.[12] This necessitates the domestication of women's bodies and their relegation to the private sphere where they provide the necessities of productive and reproductive social life *gratuitously*, thus subsidizing capital,[13] while they are economically dependent on their male partners.

Regulating and controlling women's sexuality is therefore essential for the survival of patriarchy and capitalism. It represents a vital and necessary way of instituting and maintaining the domesticity of African women. It works to delineate gender roles and to systematically disenfranchise women from accessing and controlling resources. Laws are used by patriarchal states as a mechanism of regulation and control. The examples below of sexual laws from the Ugandan legal regime demonstrate the political and legislative strictures that undermine women's autonomy through the social control of their bodies and their sexuality.

Criminal and Penal Laws

Criminal Adultery

Under the Ugandan penal code, a wife is guilty of criminal adultery if she engages in sexual intercourse with *any* other man except her husband. A husband, on the other hand, will only be guilty of the same offense if he has sex with a married woman. Here, the law blatantly imposes double standards on sexual norms. It essentially endorses male sexual promiscuity, as long as he is not playing around with the "property" of another man, while imposing strict controls on women's sexuality. This is further proven by the fact that under the penal code a convicted adulterer must pay compensation for "damaged goods" to the husband of the adulteress. Such a law is clearly in line with the ideology of lineage rights in property alluded to earlier that guarantees the legitimacy of a man's children.

Rape

The law of rape in Uganda, which is gender-specific, is constructed to protect women's chastity, but also men's "property" in women's sexuality as daughters and wives. The fact that the crime of rape is listed under "Offenses Against Morality" is telling.[14] By constructing rape within the discourse of morality, the penal code places emphasis on a subjective ethical notion while pushing the violent aspects of the crime to the margins.

The insignificance of the assault aspects of the crime of rape can further be seen in the basic legal ingredients that make up the offense: penile-vaginal penetration and lack of consent. The phallocratic culture in which the crime is constructed fails to imagine sexual assaults beyond the narrow confines of the penile-vaginal penetration.[15] To limit the "acts" that constitute rape to nonconsensual penile-vaginal penetration is to ignore a range of sexual assaults that may even be more traumatic than penile-vaginal penetration such as forced oral sex, anal penetration, or penetration with an object.

Moreover, the woman's consent becomes irrelevant in marital relationships. Thus rape is "legal" between husbands and wives. In other words, marital rape is an exception in many African legal systems, including Kenya, Uganda and Tanzania. Justification for the husbands' exemption from the crime of rape stems from an archaic English Common Law rule that held that a wife's irrevocable consent was given at marriage.[16] However, the simple reality is that patriarchal law considers a wife's body as her husband's property that he is at liberty to use as he pleases.

Sexual Harassment

Perhaps the most efficient way of maintaining gender politics in African societies is through the mechanism of sexual harassment. Sexual harassment is especially rampant at the workplace and in educational institutions. Through sexual harassment, men objectify women's bodies as a means of maintaining their power and control over them. Women's bodies are also assaulted as a way of silencing them and imposing compliance.

Very few African countries have a national policy or law on sexual harassment.[17] Here, the law enforces gender norms through an omission; by not criminalizing sexual harassment, the law maintains that sense of entitlement for men—sustaining the illusion that the "public sphere" is exclusively a male domain. By omitting to legislate against sexual harassment, African states overtly condone the practice.

Prostitution

In 2003, the minister of health of the Buganda Kingdom announced that he was going to campaign for a law that rewards all Baganda brides who are virgins.[18] This was an attempt to curb prostitution and underage sex among Baganda women. Virginity and women's chastity provide ready patriarchal tools for male control of women's bodies.

Prostitution is illegal and subject to a penalty in Ugandan criminal law.[19] Although the law was amended in 1990 to define a prostitute in gender-neutral terms, womanhood continues to be firmly ingrained on the body of a Ugandan prostitute today. The focus of the legislation against prostitution focuses on the "immorality" of women who engage in promiscuous sex. Prostitution endorses polyandry or women taking on multiple sexual partners, something that runs against patriarchal and bourgeois morality. Moreover, it conflicts with the role of domesticity and "mothering" that society has constructed for women. And because it is counter to "normal" femininity, it represents a threat to the patriarchy.

Like rape, prostitution is listed under "Offenses Against Morality" in the Ugandan penal code. The important element of prostitution is the indiscriminate character of the intercourse, otherwise seen as women having greater control of their sexuality. This regime is based on the belief that effective law enforcement and repression can and should reduce prostitution. The fact that the law equates female sexual promiscuity with prostitution is evidence of its determination to control female sexuality and maintain male control over women's bodies.[20] Further proof is the fact that the penal code limits culpability of this offense to the sellers of sex, the majority of who are women, and not to the buyers, who are mostly men.

For the majority of women, prostitution is not about sex or morality. It is purely an economic matter. Commercial sex is about economic survival, and it is emancipatory because it allows women who engage in the profession to support their families.[21] By criminalizing it, not only does society narrow the employment opportunities available to women, but it also increases the vulnerability of those women that engage in the trade.[22] In Senegal, a country whose population is over 90 percent Muslim, prostitution has been recognized as legitimate work since 1966. In that country, a sex worker may ply her trade as long as she is registered, has regular medical check-ups, and is discreet in her trade activities. Prostitutes are also required to pay taxes like any other worker, thus boosting the country's economy. Today, Senegal is one of the countries on the continent with the lowest rates of HIV/AIDS infection, thus exploding the common myth that prostitution fuels the spread of the disease.

Abortion

Abortion is prohibited in Uganda with the only exception being to save the life of the pregnant woman.[23] Criminalization of abortion signifies the forceful and violent control of women's bodies by the patriarchal state; it amounts to the nationalization of women's wombs. It represents a deliberate attempt by the state to force women into motherhood without any promise of help with the child. The fact that it is illegal has never stopped women with unwanted pregnancies from seeking abortions as they consciously take the decision to control their bodies and fertility. Unsafe illegal abortions account for millions of female deaths in Africa.[24] Criminalizing the practice is nothing less than institutionalized violence against women.

Imposing forced motherhood on women, coercing them into bearing and rearing children, fits perfectly with the gender roles that society has constructed for women, that is, childcare and homecare. It leaves little time and room for women to pursue goals outside the confines of domesticity. Thus, the status quo of "private/domestic" women and the "public/political" men is safely entrenched in African societies.

Homosexuality

The assumptions that underlie gender relations in patriarchal societies foreground heteronormativity, that is, heterosexuality, as the norm. The prefix "hetero-," derived from the Greek term meaning "different" or "other," means that human sexual relations are "normatively" expected to take place between members of the opposite sex. Precisely, it assumes a "natural" hierarchy in sexual relations between a dominant *male* partner and a subordinate *female* mate.[25] These assumptions are communicated through various means including religion, culture, education, the law, and the media. Women (and men) who resist heterosexuality and subvert dominant culture are subjected to strict punitive laws and discriminatory social discourses.

Compulsory heterosexuality in Africa is legitimized and secured by penal laws that prescribe very strict sanctions against same-sex erotics, usually referred to as "sex against the order of nature." Homosexuality is criminalized in the majority of African countries through legislation or religious laws such as Shari'a. In some countries, such as Uganda, the offense carries a maximum life sentence.[26] In a phallocratic culture, what is considered to be "natural" is penile-vaginal intercourse between a male and a female. By portraying homosexuality as "unnatural," the law maintains the hierarchical sexual conditions of a controlling male and a subordinated female.

A persistent argument against homosexuality from politicians, religious leaders, scholars, and the media is that homosexuality is "un-African." It is further portrayed as a perversion resulting from Western sexual decadence. But the fact is that there is a long history of diverse African peoples engaging in same-sex relations. Anthropological and historical studies point to the presence of homosexuality in a variety of forms in precolonial times in at least fifty-five African cultures.[27] In Uganda, for example, among the Langi of northern Uganda, *mudoko dako* "males" were treated as women and could marry men.[28] Homosexuality was also acknowledged among the Iteso, Bahima, Banyoro, and Baganda.[29] It was an open secret in Royal Buganda that the Kabaka, King Mwanga, was gay.[30] Hence, trends both in the present and the past reveal that it is time for Africans to bury the tired myth that homosexuality is "un-African." Ironically, it is the dominant Judeo-Christian and Arabic religions that most African anti-homosexuality proponents rely on to buttress their attacks on the practice as a foreign import alien to the African continent.[31]

The gendered dimensions of sexuality are very clear when one considers the implicit erasure of lesbian identity in African societies. Somehow, the dominant phallocentric culture maintains the stereotype of women as the passive recipients of penetrative male pleasure; sex that is not penetrative does not count as "real" sex. In fact, African women's sexuality is often reduced to their conventional mothering role and conflated with their reproductive capacities.[32] What is therefore particularly threatening to patriarchy is the idea of intimate same-sex relationships where a dominating male is absent and where women's sexuality cannot be defined without reference to reproduction. Power, the main factor in the patriarchal equation, is missing. So is the preservation of gender hierarchy.

The mainstream aversion to same-sex relations consequently reflects a larger fear. Homosexuality threatens to undermine male power bases in the African "private" sphere at the level of interpersonal relationships and conventional definitions of the "family" as well as in public discourses where myths abound about what it means to be a man or a woman. Homosexuality presents a challenge to the deep-seated masculine power within African sexual relations and disrupts the very core of the heterosexist social order.[33]

Customary Laws

Patrilineality and Patrilocality

The combined traditions of patrilineality and patrilocality[34] in most African communities collectively entrenches the patriarchy that is mediated through the female body. Historical and anthropological studies on African cultures have confirmed Frederick Engel's theory by revealing that many present-day patrilineal African societies were once matrilineal.[35] It was through several historical interventions such as private property, the state, and religion that successive generations reshaped descent practices to meet the needs of the patriarchy. With the gradual shift from the female line of descent to patrilineality came the tighter control of women's sexuality to ensure purity and the certainty of paternity.

When matrilineality was overthrown, it was not replaced with bilateral descent but by patrilineality.[36] Historical evidence suggests, for instance, that the monarchical Baganda in Uganda used to be a matrilineal society. Vestiges of matrilineality can still be found in the fact that the Kabaka belongs to his mother's clan. Indeed, tracing descent through women makes logical sense given their role in reproduction. In fact, patrilineality and patrilocality are essential for patriarchal rule. Suppressing and erasing women's lineage, as well as insisting that the postmarital residence is with the man's family, work to assure male dominance. Although women in matrilineal African societies enjoy a relative degree of autonomy, no matriarchal society exists on the continent. Matrilineality exists within an entrenched patriarchal context. This means that for all practical purposes, women are subordinated to men even in matrilineal societies, the only difference being that inheritance and authority passes through women to the male line.

The Institution of Bridewealth

The term that Western outsiders attached to the African customary rituals preceding a wedding ceremony is pregnant with signs of their inherent and misconceived biases.[37] The term "wealth" had connotations of accumulation and possession, values that were not traditionally associated with this African institution. Indeed, all communities on the continent used a specific term for the marriage gift transaction distinct from that used for the payment of goods. Examples are lobola, bogadi, and bohali.[38] A woman was free to, and often did, walk out of an abusive marriage and return to her parents and relatives. Within these family/clan arrangements men and women jointly made decisions that governed the norms and ethos of their cultural, political, and juridical lives. Driberg epitomized the precolonial idea behind bridewealth thus:

> It is one side of a legal contract, providing for the filiation of the children and their lawful inheritance: it supplies a religious and ritual sanction, invoking the benevolent regard and interest of the ancestors, from whom the cattle were inherited: it stands as a security for the good treatment of the wife in her new home and serves as a social and political link between the clans of the contracting parties.[39]

The (in)famous 1917 East African case of *R. v. Amkeyo* successfully illuminates the misreading of the values behind bridewealth that was typical during the colonial era. In this case, a British judge referred to bridewealth as "wife-purchasing" in total ignorance of its cultural value. He stated:

> Women so obtained by a native man commonly spoken of, for want of a more precise term, as "wives" and as "married women," but having regard to the vital difference in the relationship of the parties to a union by native custom from that of the parties to a legal marriage, I do not think it can be said that the native custom approximates in any way the legal idea of marriage.[40]

In many African countries, colonial law attempted to abolish and later standardize bridewealth, changes that led to conceptualizing it as a purchase deal, in the process denigrating the institution with the concomitant denigration of women's status. Such degrading commodification of African women's bodies was a far cry from the reality behind the institution of bridewealth. Traditional marriage was *not* a commercial transaction and the parties involved were largely free partners within the context of societies that emphasized communitarian ideals in contrast to individual autonomy.

Sadly, this reconceptualization of bridewealth has persisted. Over the years, African male patriarchs have themselves embraced it to consolidate their power and control over their wives. As a result, lobola has been commercialized and women's bodies commodified with no trace of the traditional values that were associated with it. Whatever values originally existed in the African institution of bridewealth, there is no doubt that today it has evolved into a kind of stamp duty imprinted on women's bodies to indicate that she is the property of her husband. In a 1995 nationwide study conducted by a Ugandan NGO on "Gender and Inheritance," the link between patrilineality, patrilocality, and dowry-payment to women's oppression and disinheritance was brought into bold relief. Study findings showed that infused within inheritance practices was the common notion that wives were part of the inheritable estate. Bridewealth, which today is construed as "payment" by the groom's family to the bride's family, was largely responsible for shaping such mentality. The remark of one male respondent in Kumi district was very telling. When asked for his views about women's right to inheritance, his brief retort was: "How can property own property?"[41]

Dowry payment has also legitimated domestic violence in Ugandan society. The ever-increasing dowry demands have progressively led to the commercialization of the institution of bridewealth that in turn has amplified the commodification of women's bodies. Perceiving a wife as "the property of their husbands," on the one hand, and the husband as "the head of the family" on the other, leaves a lot of latitude for women's oppression within the family.

Female Genital Mutilation

Perhaps the severest form of controlling and manipulating women's bodies and sexuality is through the cultural practice of female genital mutilation (FGM).[42] In Africa, various forms of the practice are prevalent in approximately thirty countries. Among the communities that practice FGM, the culture is associated with "women's purity" and its proponents argue that it makes women more virtuous by reducing their sexual desires.[43] Whatever spirited defenses have been put up to justify female genital mutilation, the bottom line is that FGM coerces women to accept male authority through patriarchal control of their bodies and sexuality. The mutilation of women's genitals through FGM not only violates their bodily integrity, but also their human rights, that include sexual and reproductive rights.

Today, open discussion of sexual matters is taboo in most African traditions. Masturbation is also considered a taboo. Such taboos work to repress and deny women knowledge about their own sexuality. For example, not many African women are aware that they possess a sexual organ—the clitoris—that is nothing but a bundle of nerves and twice as erotic and sensitive as the male penis.[44]

Thus, by amputating the clitoris, whether partially or wholly through the FGM ritual, women are denied their right to sexual pleasure, not to mention the physical and psychological trauma that they routinely suffer. Thus, women's sexual autonomy is curtailed and their sexuality appended and subjugated to that of their husbands.

Traditional Sexual Initiation Rites: The Ssenga Among the Baganda

The institution of Ssenga among the Baganda is one of the most powerful cultural inscribers of women's bodies.[45] It is the role of a paternal aunt or Ssenga to provide sex education to young Baganda women. Traditionally, such education was comprehensive, covering a wide range of topics from the fundamentals of male/female anatomy to sexual etiquette, premenarche practices, to tips and tricks of bringing pleasure to oneself and one's partner.

Tutelage would begin at puberty just before a girl starts menstruating, when she would "visit the bush" under the tutelage of her Ssenga. "Visiting the bush" involves a procedure of stretching or elongating the labia minora of a woman. Traditionally, among the Baganda, the meaning attached to this cultural practice was a tightly kept secret that was associated with enhanced female arousal in foreplay. The purported and commonly touted meaning of the elongated labia was that it enhanced the erotic pleasure of a man who came into sexual contact with it. Of course this practice was viewed through a completely different light by the imperialists who came across it. They perceived it as a barbaric mutilation of the female genitals and today it has been condemned and classified as "Type IV FGM."[46]

With the consolidation of patriarchy and entrenchment of a masculinist sexual hegemony in Buganda, the sexual curricula became slanted with the primary emphasis shifting to the teaching of young brides how to bring maximum pleasure to their husbands during sexual intercourse. Significantly, no similar coaching exists for young grooms. Under the recent liberalization of the Ugandan economy, the institution of Ssenga has become commercialized whereby young women can "hire" the services of an advertised Ssenga.[47] However, today this cultural institution has generally been reduced to teaching women how to colonize their bodies to their male partners. Elsewhere, I show how young Baganda women are challenging this sexual ideology and demanding that men also receive training in how to please their female partners.[48]

Sexuality and Women's Rights NGOs

Women's rights NGOs within the Ugandan mainstream women's movement hardly ever deal with women's sexual rights. Instead, a small and relatively nascent group of women whose sexual rights have variously and persistently been trampled upon have attempted to organize themselves at the fringes of the women's movement. Examples of such groups include the Single Mothers' Association, the National Community of Women Living with HIV/AIDS in Uganda (NACWOLA), the Association of Ugandan Prostitutes, Lady Mermaid Bureau (sex workers), the Freedom and Roam (FAR—a lesbian group), Sexual Minorities in Uganda (SMUG), the National Union of Women with Disabilities in Uganda (NUWODU), and the Slum Aid Project.

To their credit, some mainstream NGOs like the Uganda Association of Women Lawyers (FIDA) and Action for Development (ACFODE) have run some programs on HIV/AIDS prevention, education, counseling, and capacity building. However, not much has been done to challenge the complex inequalities of gender and sexuality that facilitate and reinforce the transmission of HIV. Recently, ACFODE and the Forum for African Women Educationalists (FAWE) have embarked on tackling the issue of sexual harassment.[49]

In June 2003, in a meeting organized by the Uganda Women's Network (UWONET) to discuss the Domestic Relations Bill, the issue of the rights of women in situations of cohabitation was raised.[50] The majority of activists argued that the women's movement must not be seen to promote immorality within Ugandan communities. After listening to all the moralistic arguments, one physically handicapped woman raised her hand and submitted that by not recognizing the rights of female cohabitees, the meeting was excluding women with disabilities because they are the ones that mainly fall in this category. She argued that few men were willing to enter into a legal marriage with them. She ended by asking the meeting: "What happened to choice anyway, what if I don't want to get married?" A long silence followed the woman's submission, indicating that she had raised issues that the meeting had hitherto not deemed important.[51] The lingering ambivalence within the women's movement to take on issues of sexuality was expressed in various ways. Below are some excerpts from additional interviews that I conducted with various women:

> We would like to bring sexuality to the fore and do policy work around it but at the same time we are aware that it will set us on a collision course with both our detractors and our constituency. . . . Quite honestly, our constituency thinks that sexuality is not a priority; we can't just "home" it. But in the last two or three years we're gaining more confidence because there is greater willingness to engage with these issues especially in the context of conflict and HIV/AIDS.

> We would like to deal with sexuality issues more comprehensively but we lack the expertise and the space. . . . We decided to omit it out of

our programs and leave it to other organizations that specialize in sexuality. But then which ones are these?

America and Europe can discuss abortion and homosexuality as they're more developed than we are. But our people here are still struggling with the basics; the most critical is hard to come by. . . . If we jump onto the global trends such as abortion, we'll leave gaps because the basic "normal" ones have to be dealt with first.

No, we don't deal with sexuality issues here. But I feel that we need to take a more holistic view of the issue of women's rights. A major component of this discourse is sexuality and how patriarchy has impacted on it.

As far as sexuality goes, our organization has kept within a 'safe range' of activities . . . can't even remember what we've done . . . rape and defilement mostly. We've shied away from abortion, prostitution, and homosexuality. And why? I think that going beyond that is stepping into [laughs].

Many of us, gender activists, are apologists who think that the women's movement owes allegiance to the president. We worry about rocking the boat. This leads to a failure to conceptualize issues as sexual rights. . . . Because of the diversity within the women's movement, the language and approach that we use is also different. For example, some women demand for their rights while others request politely.

What do you mean? Why do you ask? Sexuality may have an indirect effect on our clients but they don't look at it as a big problem, therefore it is not something that we have taken on board. . . . We ourselves have not internalized the issue of sexuality, thus our clients would not appreciate it; they think it is elitist.

We mostly work on sexual violence, rape and defilement. There is too much work to be done. During the 16 days of activism we don't get a moment's rest.[52] We've found that the law enforcement agencies like the police, judicial officers, still hold stereotypic beliefs about women and men; there's a serious need for sensitization.

Despite the general reticence and reluctance to confront women's sexual rights on the part of mainstream NGOs, the study detected a turning of the trend. Most of the signals for this development seemed to lie in the impact of the HIV/AIDS pandemic in Uganda. It is quite evident that the equation of gender/power relations has been rendered more complex by the HIV/AIDS pandemic, with significant impacts on women's activism. While the pandemic has had a debilitating effect on virtually every household, it has also spurred a new kind of political consciousness and self-organization for Ugandan women. HIV/AIDS has forced what have been considered fixed and accepted norms around issues of sexuality, gender, identity, and rights to shift in ways that provide serious challenges and opportunities for women's diverse work. Put another way, HIV/AIDS has indeed begun, albeit in measured ways, to deconstruct hierarchies and traditional social structures based on gender and power.

Analyzing the Limitations

The preceding analysis shows how statutory and customary law, with the firm support of imported religions, work as a surveillance tool to regulate and control women's sexuality. Equally worse, women's sexuality is largely omitted from the ambit of the human rights framework. This issue draws scant attention from the women's rights NGOs, a fact that demonstrates an insufficient appreciation of its strategic importance in the struggle for the emancipation of African women. Somehow, women's freedom to bodily integrity—the right to inhabit and control one's body—is written out of the conceptualization of rights. By imposing a sexual morality that is sexist in nature, the patriarchal state institutionalizes women's subordination. The significance of sexuality is basically lost on women's rights groups in Uganda because "gender activism" has largely been ripped of its political element. Time and again, Ugandan NGOs have openly declared that they are "nonpolitical." They distance themselves from formal politics because they do not want to be tarred with its brush. But how can we avoid politics when women's subordination and oppression are political issues? How can they engage the patriarchy without confronting politics? There are many additional factors that have contributed to the apparent spilling of the wind from the sail of the Ugandan women's movement. Below I discuss a few of them.

The Gap Between Theory and Practice

The theoretical grounding of the activism of women's rights NGOs leaves a lot to be desired. Undertheorized activism has implications for the remedial strategies that are adopted for engendering social change. Paulo Freire has argued that it is through praxis that transformation can be brought about.[53] He underscores the necessity of theory to "illuminate" praxis.[54] My observation is that social activism on the continent remains largely undertheorized. It is extremely important for the women's movements to enhance their research capacities and engage vigorously in producing homegrown feminist theory. They must reconceptualize the important linkages between theory and practice. This is the only way of pursuing goals with clarity and inspired action. I believe that the clouded understanding of the significant linkages between sexuality and Ugandan women's oppression, for example, is largely on account of this deficiency. Activists have yet to fully appreciate the link between "pleasure," "choice," "power," and women's oppression.

Feminists in the Ugandan academy and activist practitioners on the ground tend to operate in separate cocoons. Gender equality and women's rights rhetoric barely spread beyond the legal landscape. Yet, theory leads to informed activism. Theory is about understanding the "what," "why," and "how" questions about Ugandan women's oppression, about power. When feminist theory does not speak to gender activism and when the latter does not inform the former, the unfortunate result is a half-baked and truncated feminism. Undertheorized praxis is comparable to groping in the dark in search of a coffee bean. To use President Museveni's favorite word, it leads to "obscurantism," hindering clear vision, knowledge, progress, and enlightenment. Social transformation can hardly be achieved under such conditions.

Focus on Careerism

As a general observation, there was a genuine commitment to the cause of women's rights when struggle in Uganda was spearheaded through community-based organizations and prior to the boom of nongovernmental organizations. Women (and a few men), volunteered and sacrificed their time and resources with the fervor of guerrilla freedom fighters. However, because of the sheer size of the work that has to be done by feminists, the fact that most of them work double, or even triple, shifts inside and outside the home, the fact that women's work is underresourced, they were forced to turn to the development industry. Today, the culture of donor-driven NGOs has overtaken the struggle.

This, coupled with government's tight control of NGO work, has depoliticized the women's movement. Presently, many of women are in "the business of women's rights" not as political activists but mainly to advance their own personal interests. They sit and strategize not on how to genuinely transform society but on how their positions will bring in more cash, help them win scholarships or a trip abroad. "Careerism" has eaten so deeply into the Ugandan women's movement that many women activists do not even practice the feminist principles they preach.

External Influences and Co-Optation

Although some scholars have hailed the Ugandan women's movement as being relatively autonomous, I personally believe that the majority of mainstream women's NGOs are in many ways beholden to either the state or to donors.[55] The National Resistance Movement (NRM) government itself adopts an extremely paternalistic attitude toward the women's movement in Uganda. This is on account of the various ways that the administration has promoted women's leadership and constitutional rights, at least on paper, which are an obligation and not a favor that is expected of every government.[56] The women's movement must also vigilantly guard against the risks of co-optation by the state and multilateral initiatives. President Museveni has often referred to himself as "the driver of the vehicle of the women's movement." In a very paternalistic fashion, he has requested women to leave him, as driver, to control the speed of women's emancipation.[57] I have commented elsewhere on the paternalistic "where-would-you-be-without-us" attitude within the NRM leadership to women's emancipation.[58] In a sense, there is no fundamental difference between the NRM and the pre-1986 regimes in showing real commitment to women's issues. The problem is that many activists within the women's movement have fallen into the trap of complacency, feeling that with the NRM "we have arrived."

We should guard against being used as pawns in a jigsaw puzzle. How many activists have been "bought off" by the government by offering them leadership positions in bureaucratic organizations and in government? The state has grossly abused affirmative action by co-opting talented women into the ranks of political elites without challenging fundamental structural characteristics of the political economy. The top-down, co-optive fashion in which government has involved civil society in the Poverty Eradication Action Plan (PEAP) does not speak well of this relationship. "Gender mainstreaming" is the latest form of co-optation that is bound to compromise the feminist transformative agenda.

Moreover, as part of civil society, women's rights NGOs are subject to strict government scrutiny and regulation. The legislation governing the operations of NGOs was recently amended with the aim of tightening the stranglehold on any type of activism that the state deems unpalatable to its own values and philosophy.[59] The NGO community has decried the spirit of "restriction" and "control" that runs through the amended law, which requires security agencies such as the Internal Security Organization (ISO) and the External Security Organization (ESO) to have permanent seats on the NGO board.[60]

In short, it is not in the interests of the patriarchal state, with the NRM at its helm, to dismantle the male tributaries of power. Clearly, the NRM policies are symbolic and tokenistic, completely detached from the reality of the lives of the majority of Ugandans. It will only tolerate limited reforms, sufficient to win over the women's constituency but not enough to rock the boat. That is why the appeals of "don't push the vehicle too fast" are made. The fate of women in the political agenda of the NRM government thus remains vulnerable to "the shifting needs of different regimes for legitimacy."[61]

Reformist and Issue-Based Approach

There is a tendency in women's struggles to lay too much emphasis on the reform of both the received and customary laws as a panacea to the woes of Ugandan women. Reformist strategies or other silver bullet approaches are essentially limited in that they leave the oppressive system intact. Reformist strategies usually overlook the underlying power relations and structures that create imbalances and inequities between Ugandan men and women. The struggle must move away from the episodic, single-focused character such as the struggle over land rights, from the "crisis approach" to a more sustained and holistic one. It must pursue strategies that will keep issues of gender and equity constantly visible in the society. There consequently is an urgent need to develop a radical theoretical framework with the potential to radicalize reformist strategies.

Shrinking Resources

One reality that is catching up with those engaged in NGO work and other institutional contexts is that financial and material resources that were readily available five years ago are dwindling fast. The dominant development approaches in the globalized world have led to a major shift in the operations of the donor community. For example, recently the UN Development Fund for Women (UNIFEM) suffered a serious setback when the Dutch government—its biggest financial source—made a decision to cut a substantial amount to its programs. Doubtless, this is going to have a debilitating and ripple effect on thousands of UNIFEM-funded projects run by women's rights groups in Uganda and the rest of Africa.

Today, donors are very reluctant to fund advocacy work because it is not easily quantified. Donors are more interested in quantitative, rather than qualitative, indicators. They also shy away from funding long-term strategic work. The traditional monitoring and evaluation tools used by donors are limited in scope, capturing only short-term quantitative indicators. Thus, advocacy, law reform, and other long-term oriented work, most of which is qualitative and incremental by nature (such as following up and evaluating a domestic violence survivor who walked out of an abusive relationship five years ago), will generally not attract much funding.

Women's rights NGOs in Uganda have expressed great frustration with the high levels of donor dependency within the community. According to an interview conducted by the author with a staff member of a Ugandan women's rights NGO, this frustration was poignantly expressed in the excerpt below:

> Much of our work is donor-driven; many times we have to tailor the programmes to fit their "flavour-of-the-year" projects. This makes it difficult to work on issues that you find most pressing. . . . All NGOs work without knowing how the next funding cycle will go. . . . A quarter of our time is spent fund-raising, competing for donor forms, having to conform to the number of words that you must fit in each section. . . . We need to emulate South East Asia where NGOs have developed indigenous self-sustaining funding.

The tendency today is for multilateral and bilateral donors to shift their support from nongovernmental organizations to the sector-based approach (SWAP) or "basket" funding within government ministries that is linked to poverty reduction strategies.[62] The male-designed poverty reduction strategy papers (PRSPs) are typically gender-insensitive—largely ignoring the qualitative dimensions of poverty that stem from inequality, powerlessness, "voicelessness," vulnerability, dependency and lack of choice.

Extremism and Fundamentalism

All fundamentalisms—whether cultural fundamentalism, such as the revival of virginity tests, or religious fundamentalism, such as hailing women's subordination to men, economic fundamentalism, such as neoliberal structural adjustment policies, or legal fundamentalism, such as criminalizing issues of women's sexual autonomy—pose a serious threat to the feminist agenda. Women need to carefully analyze and understand the capitalist social structures that go hand in hand with the resurgence of all types of fundamentalisms and their totalizing discourses. They threaten to erase all the work that women have achieved thus far and to silence them into total patriarchal submission.

Conclusion

The lines drawn between a full-fledged war against the control of women's sexuality and the agendas of mainstream women's rights NGOs are mainly religious and political. A limited conceptualization of sexuality further blurs women's understanding of the link between their sexuality and subordinate status. This chapter has attempted to analyze the sociolegal factors that have shaped and influenced the sexuality of Ugandan women, thereby exposing its oppressive and disempowering dimensions. A case was made for the transformative potential in empowering women's sexuality, hence the clarion call for the women's movement to take a united and firm stand on this issue.

There is great need for more research and theorizing around the issue of African women's sexuality. It is through a clearer understanding of the bodies of African women and sexuality that a concerted struggle to resist patriarchal control and regulation can be launched. In precolonial times, women used their sexuality to resist male and colonial domination, as happened during the famous "Women's War" in Nigeria or the 1958/59 women's rebellion in Cameroon known as Anlu.[63] Some recent examples of resistance through violating patriarchal sexual codes include women's social protest against big oil companies in the Nigerian oil delta; Kenyan mothers rising against the illegal political imprisonment of their sons; Kenya's sixty-seven-year-old politician Wambui Otieno, who in 2003 defied custom and married a man forty-two years her junior.

It is very important to openly discuss women's sexuality at this time when increased cultural, religious, and political fundamentalisms are finding new ways of safeguarding male power and privileges in East Africa. The "mystery veil" must be removed from the face of sexuality and its true agenda exposed. There is need to talk about women's sexual rights outside the reproduction-violence-morality framework. A big part of the emancipation of African women shall inevitably involve freedom from the cultural taboos that prevent them from comfortably discussing sexuality. African women must recognize that issues of sexuality and eroticism have political implications; power and pleasure are definitely interlinked. Sexual freedom is fundamental to their liberation.

Considering the diversity and pluralism among African women, there is no claim in this chapter for a universal sexuality among this social group. The differences between and among women in Uganda, for instance, are based on race, ethnicity, religion, spirituality, age, educational level, social class, physical ability, geographical location, and so forth. Indeed, there is a danger in essential-izing an "African sexuality" and ignoring the various forces that impinge on particular cultures and societies. However, some shared experiences, such as colonialism, neocolonialism, racism, and patriarchy provide a common base from which one can draw some generalizations about African female sexuality.[64] Hence, the concept of "African sexuality" is used loosely here to acknowledge common legacies without necessarily obscuring the diversities among and be-tween African women.

The Way Forward

The first thing that we as African women must do is to set aside our apathetic reluctance and engage the political structures, systems, and institutions of public governance. We must recognize that women's oppression is a political issue and see gender equity as one of the major pillars of democracy today. Gender equity would ripen Uganda's democracy in its truest sense. All women's organizations involved in the struggle for women's rights should, therefore, explicitly declare their political agendas. Furthermore, we should engage in a mass, large-scale human rights education that raises the awareness of the public on the crucial issues of gender inequality, development, and human rights. Experience has proved that women's rights are a gateway to the protection and realization of human rights generally.

Second, it is vital for African women to theorize their work. I cannot over-emphasize the need for African women to enhance their research capacities and vigorously engage in the production of homegrown feminist theory. It is crucial that they link patriarchal control of their bodies to the subordinate status they hold in society. Take the patriarchal discourses on HIV/AIDS spearheaded by the male dominated Uganda AIDS Commission. Most of its programs and conferences singularly proclaim HIV/AIDS as a disease, while they completely disregard its gender dimensions. If the UAC had seriously adopted a gender approach to HIV/AIDS, the pandemic would be almost wiped out by now. It is important to understand that sexuality has a whole lot to do with women's oppression. It is invoked to challenge women who seek political office, women who wish to further their education/training, abortion laws, sex workers, erotica, the way sexuality is conflated with reproduction, and the stigmatization of child-less women, among others This means that attempts to liberate women must address this crucial issue.

Third, women must guard against all the "isms" in our struggles, including sexism, ageism, elitism, tribalism, and racism. Space should be created for all people who believe in equity and justice to actively participate. Women must forge alliances and build coalitions with other marginalized groups of society. These include people with disabilities, minority ethnic groups, environmental activists, and lesbian, gay, transsexual, bisexual, and intersexed people (LGTBI) groups. Enlightened progressive men should be welcomed to join the struggle of the feminist movement but they must allow women to own and direct feminism. No man can pretend to have a *daily* personal understanding of what it means to be subjugated and subordinated on the basis of gender. As people heaped with power and privileges under the patriarchal set up, men—even the most enlightened of them—will have the tendency to "take over" feminism, in a paternalistic and offending fashion. Because feminists are working in an environment that is still pervaded with patriarchy, men's presence becomes problematic at times. Women must also create strategic links and networks with sympathetic elements within parliament, academia, the media, grassroots organizations, as well as regional and international women's movements. By so doing, the political agenda of their struggle shall not be lost.

Fourth, women in the struggle must be brave enough to tread where others have not dared enter. Many times women are intimidated into avoiding controversial paths; their work is discredited and delegitimized by the dominant patriarchal forces. They are made to feel lonely, isolated, and unsupported, like social outcasts. Hence, it is important to form their own support mechanisms, to be there for each other, to keep the fire burning, to be perpetually drunk on their objectives, not to lose track of their cause. They should not be ashamed to associate themselves with stigmatizing terms such as "militant" and "radical" that are used to describe them, for it will only take radical and revolutionary foundations to overthrow the patriarchy. Patriarchy uses the age-old trick of divide and rule. With their collective efforts, women can in fact achieve the impossible. Who, for example, ever dreamed that the tiny African country of Rwanda would achieve the unimaginable of having 48.8 percent female representation in their parliament? Who would have dreamed that they would beat countries that have had a long history of feminism and democracy like Sweden, Finland, and Denmark, which had dominated the top statistics in this area for decades?

Fifth, women should embrace radical strategies in their struggles. They must reject the arguments that Kenya, Uganda, or Tanzania is not ready for radical feminism. What such arguments are saying in essence is that Africa is not ready for *transformation*. In fact, the majority of people that espouse the "women-should-take-it-nice-and-slow" line are those that have never directly experienced gender discrimination. Slave owners made a similar argument in the nineteenth century in a bid to preserve that immoral and barbaric institution. Colonialists also made similar arguments in the middle of the twentieth century. Most recently, the language of the pro-apartheid defenders in South Africa used the same lame logic. It must be remembered that their oppressors once labeled great figures such as the abolitionist Frederick Douglass, Mahatma Gandhi, and Nelson Mandela "radicals." No one learning about the struggles of these men today through history books would think for one minute that their demands were too radical. But the oppressors did. African traditionalists should say when they think conditions will be right for Africa to adopt a radical approach on women's issues. Radical feminism is a movement intent on social change of rather revolutionary proportions. It questions why women must adopt certain roles based on their biology, just as it questions why men adopt certain other roles based on theirs. It attempts to draw lines between biologically determined behavior and culturally determined behavior in order to free both men and women as much as possible from their previous narrow gender roles.

"Feminism" is not a well-liked term in our society, but this is not surprising given the fact that it represents a goal that challenges dominant hegemony. A similar "ism" that is equally unpopular in Uganda is "multipartyism." East Africans need to make sure that multipartyism in this region leads to genuine pluralism and that it does not minimize or defeat the gains that have already made in the last two decades. Furthermore, Africans must realize that the enemy of the women's movement is not "men" but rather "patriarchy" and that dismantling the patriarchy will benefit both men and women.

Donor partners should be more flexible in funding advocacy work and other qualitatively oriented feminist work. They should explore the potential of creating endowments for women's rights NGOs for specific long-term programs that focus on gender equity.

Finally, even as some embrace radical feminism, they must not completely discard the mainstream moderate methods that have dominated the struggle. Indeed, history teaches that all successful social movements adopted a range of approaches in dismantling the structures of oppression that they were fighting. The abolitionist movement in the United States that ended slavery used strategies that ranged from moral persuasion to boycotts to the endorsement of violent rebellion. The undeniable benefit of the aggressive, radical method of advocating for women's rights in Africa is that it has strengthened the bargaining position of moderate feminists. The radicals provide a militant edge against which moderate strategies and demands are regarded as "reasonable." Furthermore, radicals can create "crises" that are resolved to the advantage of the moderates. Radical feminism was *the* cutting edge of feminist theory and if we are to build and strengthen African feminist theory, it is the inevitable breeding ground.

Appendix: List of NGOs interviewed (September 2004)

1. Isis-Wicce
2. Akina Mama wa Afrika
3. Association of Uganda Women Lawyers (FIDA-Uganda)
4. Uganda Women's Network (UWONET)
5. Action for Development (ACFODE)
6. Eastern African Sub-Regional Support Initiative for the Advancement of Women (EASSI)
7. Sexual Minorities in Uganda (SMUG)
8. Association of Ugandan Women Medical Doctors
9. Hope After Rape (HAR)
10. Uganda Youth Development Link
11. Forum for Women in Democracy (FOWODE)
12. Center for Domestic Violence Prevention
13. National Association of Women Organizations in Uganda (NAWOU)
14. Lady Mermaid Bureau

CHAPTER FOUR

NGO Struggles for Economic, Social, and Cultural Rights in UTAKE: A Ugandan Perspective

Joe Oloka-Onyango

CONFUSION AND CONFLICT over the recognition, implementation, and enforcement of economic, social, and cultural rights (ESCRs) is an issue of historic dimensions that engaged scholars and activists even before the two principal international human rights covenants were adopted in 1966. The International Covenant on Civil and Political Rights (ICCPR) is well known for the articulation of rights governing the protection of speech, freedom of association, the prohibition of slavery and forced labor, and freedom from torture. Although adopted at the same time, the International Covenant on Economic, Social and Cultural Rights (ICESCR) for many years remained on the back burner of international human rights attention and advocacy. To top it all, the manner in which rights issues were approached led to the erection of a "Chinese Wall" between the two categories of human rights.

For many years, very little connection was seen to exist between the realization of one category of rights (the civil and political) versus the other (the economic, social, and cultural). This partially explains why the most prominent international human rights advocacy organizations—Amnesty International, Human Rights Watch, Global Rights (formerly the International Human Rights Law Group), the International Commission of Jurists, and Human Rights First (formerly Lawyers' Committee for Human Rights)—only recently began to pay attention to ESCRs and their realization.[1] While this new attention to ESCRs may at first sight appear to be a welcome development, one of the main objectives of this chapter is to ask whether it is the kind of attention that this arena of struggle really needs.

Each of the countries of East Africa—named in this chapter as UTAKE for Uganda, Tanzania, and Kenya—have fairly elaborate constitutional instruments of governance. Tanzania introduced a bill of rights into its constitution in 1985. Both Kenya and Uganda have had more recent extensive discussions on constitutional reform, resulting, for the latter, in a new constitution promulgated in 1995. On its part, Kenya is still searching for a democratic constitution after a contested draft was defeated in a national referendum in November 2005. There is little doubt that the Kenyan process will probably go down in history as the most protracted constitutional review ever undertaken. Uganda returned to the drawing board and passed several amendments to the constitution in 2005, including the controversial lifting of term limits on the presidential tenure of office. In sum, there is a great deal of activity on the front of constitutional and human rights development in the region. Unfortunately, that activity has generated considerably more heat than it has light.

Looking farther back in history, none of the independence constitutions took ESCRs into account in any elaborate fashion. Indeed, aside from the issue of land and property rights—which in many respects belongs in a quite distinct category—and general concerns about employment, very little has been said or done about this category of rights in UTAKE. Why is this so? How is it that a region of the world facing severe constraints in meeting the goals of social and economic progress is not engaged in serious deliberations over how best to achieve these objectives through the constitution? Do the governments feel that existing mechanisms are sufficient? Are ESCRs of no concern to the general citizenry or to civil society? What of the phenomenon of globalization a double-edged sword that has the ability to both empower and to marginalize individuals, communities, and even whole countries? Finally, what has been done to protect languages in danger of extinction, or to ensure that minorities and indigenous peoples are secure in their livelihoods and cultural practices? Are not these rights, to paraphrase Jeremy Bentham, simply "nonsense upon stilts"?

Part of the answer to the above questions relates to the very issue of how ESCRs are conceptualized. Much confusion surrounds what exactly ESCRs entail: can governments be sued for failing to provide clean, drinkable, and accessible water in the same way that they can be brought to book for the practice of torture? What does a *right* to food actually entail? Who is responsible for enforcing the right to education: is it the state, educational institutions such as schools and universities, or is it teachers and parents? How, in the first instance, is such a right violated? Moreover, by focusing on the issue of poverty in its various manifestations, have these governments actually addressed ESCRs in a more fundamental and sustainable manner? Delving into these debates is one of the primary objectives of this chapter. Understanding the conceptual dimensions of the struggle for the realization of economic, social, and cultural rights, and distinguishing, or relating this to the overall quest for economic development is the other. A third, but intricately related objective of the chapter, is to understand the struggle for the realization of ESCRs as ultimately and intrinsically a political struggle. In the words of Professor Frederick Ssempebwa, Chairman of Uganda's Constitutional Review Commission (CRC), which submitted its report to government in late 2003,

The Commission's consultation gatherings have been very well attended. Whereas the people's respond (sic!) to the Commission guidelines or constitutional issues, the more spontaneous and passionate contributions are about welfare issues. Everywhere in the rural areas, talk is about poverty, inability to market produce and the burden of taxation. In summary, the state of the economy, the absence of growth and development are of primary concern raising questions about the relevance of constitution making. . . . We have concentrated on the constitutional infrastructure for political liberalisation. What is needed is added emphasis on how the infrastructure can improve people's welfare.[2]

Such views make it abundantly clear that any examination of why ESCRs remain marginalized in East Africa must be linked to the broader issues of globalization and economic reform in which the three countries have been embroiled since the early 1980s. This will illustrate that at the end of the day the question of the realization of ESCRs is intricately connected to questions of political economy. Put another way, to what extent can ESCRs be realized within a context of unbridled market liberalization, wide-scale privatization, and the unmitigated promotion of international trade and foreign direct investment (FDI)? If the political will necessary to ensure that ESCRs are given constitutional recognition and enforcement is lacking, how can these rights be realized on a sustainable basis? Finally, how do we confront the various issues of discrimination—gender, social class, and ethnicity—in the realization of ESCRs unless there is a firm constitutional foundation on which they are constructed? Given all these factors, it is necessary not to fall prey to the assertion that because these are economic interventions they must follow a different, largely technocratic logic insulated from considerations of a noneconomic or political or social nature. In other words, such issues must be understood in terms of their manifestly *political* frameworks of operation.

To offer some response to these varied questions, this chapter begins with a brief overview of the influence of the forces of globalization on contemporary human rights struggles, beginning with a survey of the economic policy framework. The chapter then examines the question of how ESCRs remain far from effective enforcement at both the international and the regional level. This comparative tour is coupled with an examination of the situation in Uganda prior to the enactment of the 1995 constitution. Uganda is selected for particular attention principally because ESCRs have been incorporated to a greater extent within its constitutional framework than is the case with either of its two East African counterparts. Building on this analysis, the chapter specifically focuses on the fashion in which ESCRs are approached in the 1995 constitution with illustrations drawn from the rights to health, food, and education. This allows us to revisit the vexed question of the justiciability and enforcement of ESCRs, specifically in a situation in which resource constraints are a major factor in the debate. Finally, the chapter concludes by offering some suggestions on what human rights organizations (HROs) in UTAKE need to do in order to end the marginalization of ESCRs in the region.

Globalization and Human Rights Struggles

The Economic Policy Framework

To fully comprehend the context in which ESCRs are sought in UTAKE, it is essential to first analyze the overall framework within which economic policy is designed and implemented. For both Uganda and Tanzania, the defining element in that policy since the early 1980s has been structural adjustment as dictated mainly by the country's donors, especially the World Bank and the International Monetary Fund (IMF). Structural Adjustment Programs (SAPs) emerged out of concern that the decades of the 1970s and 1980s had effectively been "lost" because the countries of sub-Saharan Africa had failed to emerge from abject poverty and marginalization, and to fully benefit from decolonization. Under President Daniel arap Moi, Kenya was relegated to pariah status within the international community. Consequently, while it pursued many of the same policies as its counterparts in the region, it was basically starved of donor assistance until Moi departed the scene in 2002. The consequences of this action—a point to which the chapter shall return—are of considerable significance to this analysis.

SAPs were primarily concerned with the structural and institutional impediments retarding effective development. Among these were foreign exchange controls, tariff and trade barriers, and high rates of inflation, inefficient and bloated state bureaucracies, and parastatal corporations that excelled in losing money. Known as the "Washington Consensus," the package of reforms was designed as a kind of shock therapy intended to jump-start African economies.[3] In response to this situation, SAPs included an emphasis on market forces rather than on state intervention, a promotion of the role of private capital rather than public expenditure, and the stimulation of export-led production versus import substitution. SAPs dictated that the state should be confined to the promulgation of policy frameworks that facilitated investment, trade, and manufacture, rather than directly involving itself in any of these activities. In sum, SAPs favored macro- versus microeconomic interventions.

The logical consequences of this ideology have been the privatization of previously state-owned and managed enterprises, cost-sharing in public educational and health institutions, and the liberalization of state controls over trade and investment. Tanzania has generally led the way in this regard, with Uganda following, while Kenya still has a fairly large parastatal sector. Needless to say, the benefits of these measures can be the subject of extensive debate. Human rights principles place an emphasis on the situation of the individual, and on the principles of nondiscrimination, equity, and access. From this perspective, it is questionable whether SAPs have actually effected an overall improvement in the observation and protection of human rights, especially of the economic, social, and cultural variety.

More recently, the economic policy framework has shifted, at least at the rhetorical level, to an emphasis on poverty alleviation, reduction, or eradication, as part of the process of securing debt relief for countries that have a debt service burden considered unsustainable. That shift comes in the wake of the realization that debt levels after the many years of shock therapy were not sustainable. Thus, the World Bank and the IMF began to speak the language of "poverty reduction," and in 1996 linked it to the introduction of the Highly Indebted Poor Countries (HIPC) initiative. HIPC—which came on the heels of criticism from civil society—represented the first time that a concerted effort was made to include multi-lateral institutions (MLIs) in the search for a comprehensive debt-relief program for developing countries.[4] In quantitative terms, HIPC could be considered fairly impressive, registering an easing of some of the burden of the debt stock of several African countries. Qualitatively, however, HIPC did not go far enough, and indeed, specifically in the case of both Uganda and Tanzania, debt repayment burdens remain heavy.[5]

The emphasis on poverty and its consequences came after the failure of SAPs to substantially reduce the incidence of poverty. To address this failure, a 1995 World Bank report urged an improvement of the investment incentive regime, export facilitation, and support for nontraditional agricultural exports as the key to poverty reduction in the medium to long run.[6] The emphasis on poverty has been sustained through the adoption in Uganda of the Poverty Eradication Action Plan (PEAP) that has been the blueprint for the Poverty Reduction Strategy Papers (PRSPs) deployed worldwide.[7] However, there is a thread of continuity between the old policy stipulations and the new, in that the "fundamentals," including liberalization of the economy, rapid privatization, and deregulation have remained intact. Against this background, the problems of the poverty approach in relation to the improved observation and protection of human rights is captured in the following message of the Uganda Human Rights Commission on Constitutional Day:

> Poverty, which has been and still is one of the major problems in this country, continues to rise or increase in areas where there is insecurity or instability. As a result, many people cannot afford the basic necessities for leading a decent life. However, in areas where there is stability, poverty levels have greatly reduced and people can afford to live fairly decent lives. This in itself contradicts the constitutional provision of equality among the citizens.[8]

Recent analyses of poverty in fact demonstrate that at least with respect to the case of Uganda, it is on the increase despite what has been described as spectacular levels of growth.[9] The country has also had problems in matching levels of GDP growth with the improvement of its overall human development—the latter illustrating the more qualitative dimensions of economic change in a country.[10] To crown it all, a recent study of PRSPs and their impact has illustrated that there is little in the way of poverty alleviation that this new program has introduced.[11] But for both Uganda and Tanzania, the levels of donor influence over economic policy and direction are quite frightening, as is illustrated in Table 1.

The table clearly demonstrates that growth in both Tanzania and Uganda has been robust in comparison to Kenya. However, it is important to ask a number of *qualitative* questions: who has benefited from this growth? Is it a sustainable model of growth? What consequences does this model of economic growth have for the realization of ESCRs? What becomes clear is that with respect to the realization of ESCRs, significant questions of a global nature come into play. In other words, the phenomenon of globalization and its related consequences need to be given full consideration. Among the major issues of concern are the role and place of institutions such as the World Bank and the IMF in the arena of economic policy and its ramifications in the social sphere.

TABLE I. REGIONAL COMPARISION OF ACTUAL REVENUE SOURCES, 2003/2004

	Kenya		Tanzania		Uganda	
Source	US$ mill	%	US$ mill	%	US$ mill	%
Internal revenue	4,631	93.8	1,345	55.7	856	48.2
External aid	308	6.2	1,071	44.3	920	51.8
Total revenue	4,939	100.0	2,416	100.0	1,776	100.0
GDP growth rate (%)	1.8		5.6		6	

Source: Richard Ndungu, "Focus and Clarity in Budget Speeches!" *msafari* 48 (2004): 31.

Indeed, as John Pender has pointed out, the World Bank has seized the moral high ground as a result of its poverty "reorientation." It has thus "Gained legitimacy for greater regulatory interventions in poor country society than even during the now discredited regimes of structural adjustment."[12] But rather than pursuing development as a goal, the lowest common denominator has become the alleviation of poverty, which is effectively a downscaling of the horizons from which African progress is viewed. Likewise, the WTO agreements in areas such as agriculture, intellectual property rights (IPRs), and the provision of services have serious implications for ESCRs.

Gender, Age, and Minority Status

It is a trite observation that despite the uniformity of the application of human rights principles, some groups have faced more historical marginalization in the observation and realization of their human rights. Among these are women, the youth, especially children, older people, ethnic minorities, and indigenous peoples. With particular respect to ESCRs, there is still much that needs to be done to ensure that such marginalization is brought to an end. Whatever category of economic, social, or cultural rights that can be selected—for example the rights to food, health, and education—the situation of these groups tends to be worse than those of men who dominate the political arena. In this respect, all the countries of East Africa have tried to introduce programs of affirmative action in order to address this imbalance. For example, Uganda's 1995 constitution recognized the specific situation of these groups. Provisions in the constitution cover equality and nondiscrimination (Article 21), the rights of the family (Article 31), affirmative action (Article 32), the rights of women (Article 33), children (Article 34), people with disabilities (Article 35), and of minorities (Article 36). Older persons are not mentioned in the Bill of Rights, although Principle VII stipulates that the state shall make reasonable provision for the welfare and maintenance of the aged. Clearly, a number of ESCRs are contained in this list and in doing work on women's and children's rights especially, most HROs are effectively engaging this category of rights.

However, aside from children, virtually none of these groups have either legislation or designated institutional mechanisms that specifically address the many issues they face, least of all the ESCRs that are of most concern to them. In part, this is on account of the manner in which the state prioritizes those issues it considers most important. However, there is also the fact that conditions of discrimination and marginalization are difficult to remove, largely on account of vested interests and resilient institutions such as patriarchy. The fate of Uganda's domestic relations legislation is illustrative of this fact. Although attempts at reforming the structure of the family have been underway since independence, legislation to address this issue is yet to be passed. The debate over the Domestic Relations Bill raised many of the traditional bogeymen (in terms of religion and culture) and eventually was shelved by the government in the wake of elections in early 2006. It is unlikely that the bill will be revived given the emotions it stirred and the lack of political will to push it through. Further still, communities that are a minority by virtue of ethnicity, such as the Batwa in Uganda, the Ogiek in Kenya, and the Maasai in Tanzania face serious problems of marginalization, especially with regard to their rights to food, land, culture, health, shelter, and education.[13] In Kenya, the recent protest by the Maasai over the issue of colonial land thefts demonstrates the varied dimensions of this issue. Likewise, Tanzania confronts similar problems, particularly against the continuing attempts to secure more land for private investment and the promotion of tourism.[14]

Needless to say, considerable problems remain with respect to the institutional framework for the realization of the ESCRs. For example, the institutional mechanism in Uganda that was envisaged under the 1995 constitution to specifically address this issue—the Equal Opportunities Commission (EOC)—is the only constitutional body that has not yet been established.[15] This is a telling demonstration of the manner in which the rights of these groups are perceived by the state and other dominant members of society. In many respects, Tanzania has buried its head in the sand over the issue of minorities—a legacy of Mwalimu Nyerere's emphasis on nationalism as opposed to ethnic particularity.[16] Needless to say, despite the greater cohesion of Tanzanian society, there are serious minority questions that remain unaddressed. Kenya also lacks any public institution directed toward these issues. Quite clearly, any strategy for the enhanced promotion and protection of ESCRs will seriously have to review the institutional mechanisms that exist or are designed to address their situation.

Globalization and the Role of Human Rights NGOs (HROs)

The issue of how effectively ESCRs are implemented depends on the concern of the society at large. To what extent can ESCRs be *politicized* so that they are not just the grist for the mill of government rhetoric, but have resonance as rights in the populace? There is little doubt that HROs have played an important and critical role in ensuring the progressive realization of ESCRs around the world.[17] But on more critical reflection on East Africa, what does the evidence show? In each of the countries of UTAKE, the predominant focus of HROs has been civil and political rights for the more than two decades they have been in existence. The three most prominent human rights HROs in UTAKE—the Foundation for Human Rights Initiative (FHRI) in Uganda, the Kenya Human Rights Commission (KHRC) in Kenya, and the Legal and Human Rights Centre (LHRC) in Tanzania—consider civil and political rights issues as their bread and butter. Of the three, the LHRC appears to have devoted more attention to ESCRs, publishing studies on privatization, workers rights, and the environment. KHRC did some impressive work on the situation of workers in the flower industry, while FHRI conducted a study on Uganda's Universal Primary Education (UPE) program.[18] There does not appear to have been a sustained follow-up on these specific areas, nor do the groups appear to have charted new paths in the area of ESCRs.

Each of these groups is successful in its own right. However, their strategies and methods are largely a clone of Western groups such as Amnesty International, Human Rights Watch, and the International Commission of Jurists (ICJ).[19] In contrast, however, a reorientation in the focus and strategies of international NGOs (INGOs) has already taken place, with one commentator observing that the shift has been "impressive."[20] Thus, INGOs like Human Rights First have began work on the accountability of transnational corporations. Others are tracking the human rights obligations of the Bretton Woods institutions, and yet others are targeting the ramifications of the WTO trade liberalization agenda.

But one would be remiss not to question the modus operandi and effectiveness of local HROs, especially given the fact that much of their energies are expended on hosting workshops and carrying out civic education—strategies that would more appropriately be left to academic institutions. Indeed, in a recent report on HROs in Uganda entitled *Beyond Workshops*, views were expressed that such groups have adopted nonconfrontational, even complacent, attitudes toward the state, and focus primarily on peripheral issues to such an extent that the state takes scant notice of their activities.[21] In the case of Uganda, to the extent that HROs have been instrumental in pursuing the realization of

ESCRs, unfortunately, this has been from a predominantly *welfarist* perspective. Indeed, religious and charity-based groups have been prominent in providing health, educational, and nutritional services in Uganda for decades.[22] The same can be said of Kenya and Tanzania, albeit to a lesser extent given the much greater emphasis on state intervention in the case of Tanzania. But in all three countries, there is a reemergence of civil society. Two factors that are responsible for this are the growing inability of the state to provide basic services, while the second comes from the lacuna in employment: the NGO sector is a large employer. Susan Dicklitch also points to the Bretton Woods New Policy Agenda (NPA) whereby the recent emergence of NGOs is "Reflective of international trends which embrace the dominant discourse of neoliberal economics, as well as domestic responses to the withdrawal of the state from basic service provision."[23] A survey of Ugandan human rights and development organizations published in 2002 catalogued 245 organizations, of which 56 assert that they are working on human rights, ranging from those that work with prisoners, to those that deal with the rights of persons with disabilities.[24] Of that number, fewer than ten can be said to focus on ESCRs in any serious and consistent manner. Similarly, Professor Samuel Mushi has noted that despite the recent proliferation of civic groups in Tanzania, their capacity to deliver even basic services is seriously impaired by a number of factors.[25]

This analysis implies that there is a critical need for the reorientation of the manner in which HROs have approached the realization of ESCRs. They must shift from a predominantly welfarist to an activist stance. Thus, for example, the dearth of cases on ESCRs both before the Uganda Commission on Human Rights and in respect of the courts of law of all three countries is partly explicable by the fact that HROs do not bring suits on these matters. It is certainly not because there are no violations on which to sue. This is whether one considers the health and food rights of IDPs, the employment rights of women workers in flower farms, and other high-labor industries, or in relation to government plans on the privatization of essential services such as water, public housing, or tertiary education. In sum, HROs in UTAKE need to demonstrate that the poverty alleviation they claim to be actively involved in is not simply directed internally to their own personnel. In this respect, a leaf can be taken from the examples of HROs like the Treatment Action Campaign (TAC) in South Africa, or the Social and Economic Rights Action Centre (SERAC) in Nigeria. Both have been active in the pursuit of ESCRs in their respective countries and have utilized different methods to achieve this objective. Finally, a note must be made on the need for international action, whether at the regional level or beyond. HROs in the region need to consider how to pursue the realization of ESCRs in institutions like the African Commission on Human and Peoples' Rights, as well as within the framework of the United Nations.

A Global and Regional Perspective on ESCRs

It is one of the great paradoxes of international human rights law that although attention to ESCRs preceded global concern with political and civil rights, the latter overtook the former as a primary focus of attention.[26] Thus, one of the most prominent and earliest human rights given legal articulation—the rights of working people—was in fact an economic right that witnessed few conceptual obstacles to its recognition. The establishment of the International Labor Organization (ILO) in 1919 saw the right to work become a well-established human right by 1948 when the Universal Declaration of Human Rights was adopted and well before the United Nations was formed. In his widely quoted 1941 Four Freedoms speech, U.S. President Franklin Delano Roosevelt included freedom from want among those essential conditions for the existence of humankind, alongside freedom of speech and worship, and freedom from fear. However, as the Cold War set in to dominate international relations and politics, ESCRs were a major victim of superpower struggles. Principally because the United States and its Western allies considered such rights to be "communist" in inspiration and content, sharp resistance was leveled against attempts to foster their increased realization. A telling example of such resistance was the strengthening of the ICCPR with a protocol for individual complaints while the ICESCR was left without one.[27]

The International and Regional Context

Against the preceding backdrop, what has been achieved on the international scene concerning the realization of ESCRs? Aside from the promulgation of the ICESCR in 1966 and its eventual entry into force a decade later, ESCRs made little headway in the intervening years. However, in the wake of the Vienna Conference and Declaration of 1993, heightened attention has been paid to this category of human rights. Several reasons explain this development. First, in recognition of the marginalization of the latter category of rights, the declaration stated that civil and political rights on the one hand, and economic, social, and cultural rights on the other, were *indivisible, interdependent, interrelated,* and *interconnected.* Second, the Committee, designated with the task of supervising the implementation of the ICESCR, began to progressively reconceptualize its function.[28] Through the issuance of "general comments" on the provisions of the Covenant, the Committee began to provide conceptual clarity and focus on how states should meet their obligations in a more comprehensive fashion.

Finally, the rise of the phenomenon of globalization, market and trade liberalization, and the operations of the international financial and trade institutions—the IMF, the World Bank and more recently, the WTO—have projected concerns about enforcing ESCRs to a new level. Civil society actors have also been prominent in developing standards on ESCRs. The 1987 Limburg Principles on the Implementation of the International Covenant on Economic, Social and Cultural Rights and the 1998 Maastricht Guidelines on Violations of Economic, Social and Cultural Rights are particularly important in this regard.[29] At the present time, an optional protocol to allow for individual complaints on ESCRs is under consideration in the UN human rights mechanisms. Entering the new millennium, views about ESCRs have undergone a remarkable shift, spurred on in part by concern with the negative consequences of globalization. Former UN High Commissioner for Human Rights Mary Robinson pushed the organization to become more actively engaged in ESCRs. Institutions like the World Bank and the IMF—previously reluctant to be drawn in on the debate—also lay claim to a renewed commitment to the promotion and protection of human rights, especially those of an economic, social, and cultural character.

In the African context, the struggle for ESCRs assumed a more prominent form through the promulgation of the African Charter on Human and Peoples' Rights in 1981. According to Chidi Odinkalu, the African Charter "Represents a significantly new and challenging normative framework for the implementation of economic, social and cultural rights, placing the implementing institutions of the Charter and human rights advocates working in or on Africa in a position to pioneer imaginative approaches to the realization of these rights."[30] Breaking new conceptual ground, the Charter brought ESCRs to the fore by including them in a single instrument.[31] Through the articulation of so-called "third generation" rights such as the right to a healthy environment and the right to development, the Charter raised the international profile of these rights.[32]

For many years, the Commission responsible for enforcing ESCR rights could only have been described as lackluster.[33] Recently the Commission has paid more attention to this category of rights.[34] The matter was brought to a head in a decision on the plight of the Ogoni peoples of the Niger Delta region of Nigeria.[35] In that instance, the Commission made several observations concerning the despoliation of the environment and a score of violations of ESCRs by the Nigerian government together with several multinational corporations in the exploitation of the rich oil reserves of the region.[36] The African Commission strongly argued that it had the capacity to deal with any of the rights enshrined in the Charter regardless of categorization.[37] The Commission found that the Nigerian government together with several multinationals had violated, among others, the rights to life, housing, food, health, and the environment.[38] As the issue of governmental abuse of ESCRs is a major one in Africa, the *Ogoni* decision should be regarded as a landmark ruling. The decision is also important because of the fashion in which the Commission demonstrated how and why it is essential to analyze these rights in their interconnection.

What of the realization of ESCRs in the context of individual countries? Outside Africa, the decisions of the Indian Supreme Court have attracted most attention in terms of ensuring that ESCRs are actually enforced.[39] The Indian context is particularly important in relation to the issue of whether courts can enforce ESCRs. That is, whether they are *justiciable*.[40] Secondly, it is important to comprehend that the protection of ESCRs is not necessarily, or even primarily, an issue of resources. Finally, it points to the critical role of nonstate actors in pushing the frontiers of civic and social change. Among African countries, postapartheid South Africa has ironically blazed the trail to ensure that ESCRs are actually enforceable.[41] I use the word "ironic" because one of the recurring themes about the failure of most African governments to protect and promote ESCRs is the use of poverty as a defense. While South Africa cannot be categorized as poor, the distortions in the distribution of income between black and white in effect mean that South Africa is really two countries in one—the white affluent society and an extremely poor black majority.[42] Substantively, many parts of South Africa are thus little different from the other low-income countries around the continent. What the South African case illustrates is that half of the problem relates to whether or not a government has the political will to give ESCRs the priority they deserve. The other half of the problem is the extent to which civil and popular society are willing to push their governments to ensure that these rights are given protection. In this respect, the manner in which South African civil society has approached the realization of ESCRs and the response of government is of great importance to the current discussion.

Postapartheid South Africa has approached ESCRs in several unique ways.[43] First, it has incorporated several of those rights that are normally confined to the section of the constitution on national objectives within the constitution itself. The argument about justiciability was thus immediately dealt with because the introductory provision of the bill of rights states: "This Bill of Rights is a cornerstone of democracy in South Africa. It enshrines the rights of all people in our country and affirms the democratic values of human dignity, equality and freedom."[44] Rights to housing, health care, food, water, social security, and education[45] are incorporated in the bill of rights together with those on the freedom of expression and political rights. It thus became impossible to claim that a different mode of enforcement from the rest of the rights should be employed.

More importantly, the Constitution of South Africa places an obligation on the state to "respect, protect, promote and fulfil the rights in the Bill of Rights."[46] These obligations imply different degrees or levels of enforcement and a lot will depend on the right in question and the level of violation complained of.[47] In cases ranging from whether a person had a right to kidney dialysis treatment to what the state is obliged to do with regard to access to housing, the South African Constitutional Court has demonstrated that ESCRs can indeed be made justiciable.[48] This is irrespective of whether or not a state has resources.[49] In each of the judgments they have given on this category of human rights, the courts have made clear that issues such as the resources of the country, the practical enforceability of the right in question, and the implications of doing so are given full consideration in rendering their decision. This extends to a test of the reasonableness of the demand made by the litigant. Thus, the South African situation offers an important example of the way in which ESCRs can be effectively promoted and protected within an East African context.

An Overview of ESCRs in East Africa

The advent of independence in the early 1960s came against the backdrop of a colonial experience in which the state had paid attention to ESCRs largely by default.[50] Take for example the rights within the context of work or employment. Colonial rule commenced on the basis of the extraction of forced labor as an institutional practice, illustrating that the notion of workers in a colony having rights was alien. Labor unions in UTAKE were a post-World War II phenomenon, and even then, severe restrictions were imposed on activities that were considered central to effective working class organization and expression.[51] Thus, the right to strike was severely proscribed. As a consequence, labor rights activists were routinely subjected to punitive and even criminal sanctions, extending from fines to internal exile and even deportation.[52]

Makhan Singh and Tom Mboya in Kenya, Bibi Titi Mohammed in Tanzania and James Miti and Ignatius Musaazi in Uganda were prominent advocates of the rights of workers. With respect to the provision of economic and social services in the broader sense, colonial policy never recognized that this was a fundamental obligation of the state. Rather, the services that were provided came from the largesse of the Crown, as part of the overall mission of bringing "civilization" to the blighted poor natives of the colony. From the imposition of foreign languages to the desecration of indigenous artifacts, sacred practices, and religions, the colonial state paid scant attention to cultural rights.

Even more importantly, there was never the acknowledgment that the colonized had any rights to free expression regarding their ESCRs. There is little doubt that the colonial economy performed well in general terms and in respect of ensuring that overall access to social services such as hospitals, schools, and housing improved over time. However, there was a glaring disparity—grounded primarily in considerations of race—affecting the distribution of these resources. A reading of both the legal regimes as well as a critical consideration of the manner of resource expenditure of the peoples of the colonies will evince distinctly disproportionate expenditures based on social categorization. In sum, the colonial era was marked by a legal and factual apartheid.

It is no surprise that none of the independence constitutions made any mention of ESCRs.[53] With the lone exception of the right to property, the bill of rights sections of the Kenyan and Ugandan constitutions focused almost exclusively on civil and political rights.[54] Nothing was said about education, health, shelter, or even about an adequate standard of living, despite the fact that the inspiration for the new constitutional dispensation came from the international human rights instruments. Moreover, the manner in which property rights were articulated was clearly not intended to cover those most in need—the socially marginalized and disenfranchised groups and communities. Rather, it was inserted in the constitutions in order to protect the property of the nationals of the departing colonial power, and to ensure that in the event of expropriation, prompt and adequate compensation would be guaranteed. Especially with respect to Kenya—given the expropriation that had taken place in the so-called White Highlands—the protection of private property interests was an issue of special concern to the departing colonial power. Tanganyika and Zanzibar were exceptions, with TANU, the leading anticolonial party, objecting to the inclusion of a bill of rights in its constitution. The 1964 revolution in Zanzibar did away with the bill of the rights there. This omission was only corrected two decades later.[55]

Both the 1966 and 1967 Ugandan constitutions contained formulations similar to that in the independence instrument, although the latter is better known for the numerous additional restraints it imposed on the exercise of fundamental rights and freedoms, particularly those of assembly, association, expression, and movement.[56] Again, it is important to point out that it was the government of the Uganda People's Congress (UPC) that was responsible for these instruments. This is because soon after enacting them, the UPC was to make a turn to the

"left" in a bid to "capture" the commanding heights of the economy and transform it primarily into a state-run enterprise. It is thus rather surprising that
ESCRs did not feature in the later instruments. Indeed, a careful inspection of
the manner in which the UPC government dealt with the rights of workers
illustrates regression rather than improvement. This was from a government
asserting a socialist orientation. In Kenya, although the rather strange claim was
made that "African Socialism was to be the guiding ideology of the Kenyatta
government," neither the legal regime nor the practice of the government reflected such a philosophy. While Tanzania's version—embodied in the philosophy of *ujamaa*—was certainly more socialist in orientation, it was much more
state-centered: top down, rather than from the grassroots up.

However, the more important reason for failure to include ESCRs must be
viewed against the backdrop of the international context. That context did not
give pride of place to ESCRs. Moreover, it was a context in which the conceptualization of this category of rights was underdeveloped. To cap it all, there were
few examples from elsewhere on the continent or in relation to countries of a
similar situation in Asia or South America where ESCRs had been given priority.
Even as a subject of academic attention, ESCRs were clearly considered of secondary importance to the protection of civil and political rights. The dearth of
court cases and political agitation on ESCRs, with the possible exception of the
rights of workers, illustrates that public concern with ESCRs assumed secondary
importance. Again, it is also part of the strategy of governance not to encourage
the notion that ESCRs were indeed rights because in a class-stratified society,
considerations of equity are given short shrift. Has the third phase of African
constitution making been any different?

ESCRs and UTAKE's Constitutional Order

Enacting ESCRs: Comparing Uganda and Kenya

A quick examination of the 1995 constitution of Uganda reveals several important facts. First, several new rights derive their source and inspiration from the
international categorization of ESCRs. These include the rights to education,
employment, and a clean and healthy environment.[57] There is an extensive re-
formulation of the clauses on equality and nondiscrimination that are expanded
beyond the category of persons protected, and deal with different forms of treatment. With particular respect to the situation of women—a social category that
suffers most acutely from the deprivation of ESCRs—the 1995 constitution
broke many conceptual and practical barriers.[58] The constitution pays special

attention to the rights of the family (inheritance, marriage, and parental duties), the rights of children, the rights of persons with disabilities, and the protection of minorities.[59] In Kenya, the 2004 draft constitution produced by the National Constitutional Conference contains a host of new ESCR provisions. These include the rights to social security, health, education, housing, food, water, sanitation, and consumer protection.[60] An entire chapter is devoted to culture, surely the most elaborate development of the subject in any constitutional instrument.[61] Although the document still retains the traditional hierarchy by starting with civil and political rights, the content of the ESCRs in the document and the attempt to deal with many of the criticisms about justiciability and resources provides a solid foundation on which activism in the area can be built.[62]

The 1988 Uganda Constitutional Commission (UCC) preceded the enactment of the country's 1995 constitution. Among other issues addressed was how to incorporate new rights and how to improve on the old ones. In 1993, the Commission reaffirmed the need to ensure that the bill of rights gave effect to the basic needs and rights of the people.[63] After criticizing the failure of earlier instruments and governments, the Commission argued that not all rights were amenable to enforcement or judicial review. That is why it called for general principles to guide the implementation of the constitution.[64] Therefore, the discussion on economic and social rights was relegated to the section on National Objectives and Directive Principles of State Policy. The specific examples the UCC gave related to cultural, social, and economic rights. Of these, the Commission concluded that "it is also clear that these cannot all be realized and given full effect immediately."[65] The only other category of economic and social rights that were given extensive attention in the report was the rights of workers.[66] Thus, ESCRs were relegated to the chapter on principles and objectives of socioeconomic development, attended by the often repeated caution that such rights were not enforceable and would only be used as a yardstick to measure governmental performance in improving overall development.[67]

Consequently, though the Commission argued that its recommendations went further than those in India, Nigeria, Sri Lanka, Bangladesh, and Papua New Guinea, and were a "liberating innovation," it stipulated that these principles and objectives would only "provide direction." They were, in the submission of the Commission, unenforceable and nonbinding on the state.[68] In the opinion of the Commission, only the following ESCRs were enforceable and merited inclusion in the fundamental rights of individuals and groups: the rights of farmers and workers to join or form economic or trade associations to protect their economic rights and interests, including farmers' associations and trade unions; the right to strike or withhold labor; the right of children to be protected from exploitation and dangerous occupations; and the right to equal treatment between women and men in employment, remuneration, economic opportunities, and social advancement.[69]

The list of ESCRs excluded from the Bill was much longer and covered, among others, the right to a decent standard of living including adequate food, water, clothing, housing, and medical care.[70] With respect to the Constituent Assembly (CA)—the body elected to debate the draft constitution—only a few delegates spoke of human rights in terms broader than the well-known civil and political rights. Of course, employment rights featured most prominently. Not only were these rights given fairly extensive coverage both in the report and in the draft constitution, but also the labor movement was also able to effectively organize and strategize on the further articulation and promotion of these rights in the CA. Thus, in contrast to many of the other ESCRs in the draft, the provisions on workers rights attracted considerable debate—both those in favor and those opposed.[71]

To illustrate the situation since the enactment of the 1995 constitution, this analysis focuses on the rights to health, food, and education. This is because when seen in combination, these rights cut to the core of an understanding of why it is important to improve the enforcement of ESCRs. With respect to the first two, both appear in the National Objectives and Directive Principles of State Policy, while the right to education is enshrined in the bill of rights of the constitution.[72] Needless to say, the issue of health is a critical matter in contemporary Uganda given the HIV/AIDS pandemic and its impact on human life. To what extent has the government adopted a rights-sensitive approach to the realization of this human right? The right to food is selected for consideration on account of the fact that Uganda is predominantly an agricultural economy and is largely regarded to be food secure. To what extent would an approach to food as a human right change the fashion in which it is approached today? Finally, we consider the right to education, both because it is the only other social right enshrined in the constitution, but also on account of the policy of Universal Primary Education (UPE) that was adopted shortly after the enactment of the 1995 constitution. That policy has had significant ramifications on the realization of this right.[73] Finally, each of these rights resonates within the specific situations of Kenya and Tanzania for a variety of reasons. Both face a similar HIV/AIDS crisis, and at the present time Kenya is not only emerging from a serious bout of drought, but famine continues to afflict many parts of the country. Kenya has also recently introduced a program on UPE.

Whither the Right to Health?

The right to health (RTH) is protected in both the UDHR as well as the ICESCR. Under the 1995 Ugandan constitution, health issues, with the exception of the right to a healthy environment in Article 39, are covered in the National Objectives and Principles of State Policy. These include Principle VII (protection of the aged), XV (recognition of the role of women in society), and XVI (on persons with disabilities). Principle XX stipulates that the state shall take all practical measures to ensure the provision of basic medical services to the population. There is no explicit provision on the right to health in the bill of rights section of the constitution. In this respect, Uganda is similar to most other countries that do not recognize the right at all, or simply confines it to the "non-justiciable" section of the constitution. A few countries, most notable among them South Africa, have nevertheless included the right within the main body of their constitutions. It is also important to recall that several additional rights—the right to life, freedom from torture, and the protection of bodily integrity—are also of relevance to the protection of the right to life.

There is little need to emphasize how critical the right to health is, particularly in an underdeveloped context such as Uganda. In the observation of Richard Ssewakiryanga, ill-health and disease are the most frequently cited causes of poverty: "Time lost, when sick and, for women especially, time spent taking care of the sick, reduces productivity while the cost of care uses up savings and leads to the sale of assets."[74] However, there continues to be much contention over the exact meaning and content of the right and over the nature of the obligations that flow therefrom.[75] Health, in the rights conceptualization, does not merely imply the absence of disease. Rather, it entails a state of complete physical, mental, and social well-being.[76] Against this background, the right to health must be interpreted as the enjoyment of a variety of essential facilities, goods, services, and conditions necessary for the attainment of the highest level of health—mental and physical.

The conditions necessary to ensure that the right to health is progressively realized translate into what have been termed the "4As"—Availability, Accessibility, Acceptability, and Appropriateness (Quality). A*vailability* entails the existence of functioning public health care facilities, goods, services, and programs. *Accessibility* encompasses nondiscrimination, physical access, and economic and informational equity. *Acceptability* relates to the cultural and religious dimensions of health care, whose design should not offend these sensibilities. Lastly, the issue of *Appropriateness* (*Quality*) covers the protection of health care users, in relation to drugs, mechanisms of oversight of health sector institutions and actors, and the response to the pressure of international actors such as pharmaceutical companies. When the right to health is viewed through the poverty paradigm, it becomes clear that poor people should not be disproportionately burdened with health expenses in comparison to those who are better off and more able to meet them.[77]

In the case of Uganda, there are several dimensions relating to the RTH that are critical in the debate when viewed against the backdrop of the economic policies since the early 1980s. Public health facilities in Uganda suffer greatly from inadequate and poorly remunerated health personnel—both medical and support. To make matters worse, the facilities are run-down, outdated, and inappropriate. The absence of sufficient drugs and other medical necessities has become chronic in many hospitals, particularly those outside a very narrow radius of the capital city.[78] Moreover, both on account of the expenses involved in securing formal health care, as well as cultural and other beliefs, nonformal or traditional avenues of health care have grown. While traditional health care methods may in fact be superior to those of the formal sector in several respects, the problem is the lack of oversight and regulation, effectively compounding the problem of quality. This combination of factors makes for a situation in which the realization of the RTH has for the vast majority of the population in Uganda become a chimera.

The most critical issue in terms of the RTH in Uganda relates to the scourge of HIV/AIDS. On the one hand, there can be little doubt that Uganda has made tremendous strides in both profiling the dangers of the disease as well as in the creation of the framework for its treatment and in addressing sufferers and their dependents.[79] For this reason Uganda is so often cited as a trailblazer not simply on the African continent, but around the world. Organizations such as The Aids Support Organization (TASO) have provided templates for the operation of community-based organizations and have been duplicated by CSOs in numerous other countries. The rates of infection are believed to have reached a plateau and new infections are falling.

But there is a certain degree of ambivalence about the state and some its main functionaries, such as President Museveni, with respect to the disease. George Muwanguzi has conducted an extensive study of the degree to which the policies of the Ugandan government match the international guidelines on the response to the disease. The study has demonstrated that there is some degree of inconsistency and even contradiction with respect to Uganda's policies on the treatment of persons with HIV/AIDS.[80] For example, there is still no comprehensive legislation specifically addressing the rights of people living with HIV/AIDS (PLWHAs). Discrimination in the workplace and at institutions such as schools is not uncommon. There are still problems in terms of accessing essential drugs, especially in relation to cost, although a great deal has been done to effect a reduction. Although President Museveni is often praised for highlighting the manner in which the disease has ravaged Uganda, during the presidential election campaigns of 2001, he made the claim that Kizza Besigye, his main opponent, was afflicted by AIDS. The remark appeared intended to discredit Besigye.

The predominant approach by HIV/AIDs civil society groups to the issues raised by the pandemic is either humanitarian/welfarist or medical/public health. A short-lived coalition of groups that came together around the issue of access to essential drugs collapsed when U.S. president George Bush set up an international fund to provide free drugs to the worst affected countries. However, serious issues remain, not least of which was the conditionality that the Bush government imposed on the use of the fund monies, including restricting drug purchases to U.S. companies. Domestically, there are still several rights issues that require attention, but little has been done to focus on this dimension of the issue. Traditional HROs do not appear interested in the issue. How much better is the situation with respect to a related right, the right to food?

The Right Food in the Ugandan Context

Article 11 of the ICESCR lays down the specific elements of the right to food (RTF). General Comment 12 of the Committee on Economic, Social and Cultural Rights has also laid down the key components of the right and the steps necessary to achieve its progressive realization. However, discussions on the right to food in Uganda suffer from the same conceptual problems as those regarding the right to health but with the added dimension that most people believe that such a right means the right to be fed![81] In addition, discussions on the RTF are also affected by the belief that Uganda is a food secure country, leading to the view that the state should play no role in ensuring that individuals have a right to food because it is only the lazy who are unable to provide for themselves. In the Constituent Assembly, both these perspectives were apparent. The 1995 constitution covers several aspects of the right to food, albeit, as in the case of the right to health, only in the National Objectives section of the instrument. Indeed, Objectives XIII (Protection of Natural Resources), XXI (Clean and Safe Water), and XXII (Food Security and Nutrition) cover various aspects of the RTF.

A considerable amount of work has been done at the governmental level to articulate a national policy in this area. In July 2003, the Ministries of Agriculture, Animal Industries, and Fisheries (MAAIF), and Health published the Uganda Food and Nutrition Policy. The document covers a number of subjects from food supply to accessibility to research and includes topics such as external food trade, food standards and quality control, and gender, food, and nutrition. The policy takes off from the approach of General Comment No. 12 and the various dimensions of food and nutrition outlined in the 1995 constitution. It also identifies the basic problems that the country has encountered in ensuring that all people are free from hunger, malnutrition, and famine. A special focus of the policy is the situation of marginalized groups of persons who may not be fully enabled to realize their right to food.

From a rights perspective, problems nevertheless still persist with both government policy and practice on the right to food. Among them is the failure to incorporate the right in the bill of rights. This is so despite the assertion by Human Rights Commissioner Aliro Omara that its inclusion in the National Objectives is "a powerful constitutional reminder that the government has an obligation to be mindful of that right."[82] Aside from the issue of the legal positioning of the right, as Apollo Makubuya has stated, despite Uganda's abundant rainfall and bountiful food production, there are cases of food scarcity and famine.[83] Over half the population lacks access to safe drinking water and adequate sanitation. While Uganda has been engaged in a long-standing debate over the issue of land tenure rights, neither the 1995 constitution nor the Land Act of 1998 have resolved many of the tensions on the struggle over property rights. Moreover, proposals by the cabinet seeking to increase the power of appropriation of land to the state are a sure recipe for further dispossession and marginalization, with dire implications for the right to food. The situation of internally displaced persons (IDPs) in the northern and northeastern parts of the country has assumed a humanitarian crisis of immense proportions. All of these problems are compounded by the fact that the legal framework and the institutional mechanisms designed to ensure that the right to food is either outmoded or functionally deficient.

The nexus between the forces of globalization and the realization of the RTF has assumed prominence with respect to two issues that affect the debate in the case of Uganda.[84] The first is the development of genetically modified organisms (GMOs), especially foods, while the other is the privatization of water services, and thus its relationship to the right to water (RTW)—an intrinsic aspect of the RTF. Due to his faith in trade liberalization, President Museveni thinks that the exploitation of GMOs would help to boost Uganda's productive capacity and its ability to compete in the export market. He has encouraged further experimentation with GMOs. He also has not offered any resistance to external offers of assistance from countries such as the United States that are heavily dependent on GMOs and want to "help" Uganda. However, the national policy on the issue of GMOs is very clear. National policy is mindful of the dangers of imported substandard and expired foods and of their risk of introducing foreign diseases. It states: "At the same time, genetically-modified (GM) food, seeds or livestock, which are still controversial, should be discouraged because of their unknown effects on agriculture, health and the environment."[85] President Museveni's actions in this regard are in direct contra-distinction to government policy.

There is considerable pressure, especially from the United States, for countries like Uganda to adopt this technology, and also to be a more ready market for the goods of food and agro multinationals like Monsanto and Nestlé.[86] However, there is worldwide resistance to the increased adoption of this technology, not least of which comes from the countries of the European Union. There are dangers in the increased use of GM crops both in terms of food security and food dependency. Moreover, a country like Uganda has considerable potential in developing an industry based on organically produced goods, which, although specialized, has a growing and profitable market. That market ensures that environmental considerations are taken into account. It is also less technology dependent and more in tune with traditional methodologies of food production in the country.

Uganda has not fully internalized the threat that the development of GM technology has for food security in the country and that HROs are yet to develop a coherent approach to the issue. In the heat of the debate about GMOs, Opiyo Oloya wrote an article urging the introduction of legislation that would, inter alia, spell out how indigenous organic seeds that have been cultivated by generations of Ugandan farmers will be protected from contamination by the new technology; outlining measures to safeguard traditional farmers who use organic seeds from undue pressure to switch to GMO seeds; and dealing specifically with the problem of farmers who choose to buy GMO seeds one season but later save some harvest to plant in the next season.[87]

The government has yet to address the issue further, leading to a fairly stark lacuna in the protection of food rights. The debate about GMOs very clearly illustrates the nexus between the two categories of rights—the civil and political, and the economic and social. The position of the Ugandan government on these issues is greatly affected by the manner in which it positions itself in the global economy. The forces of globalization—especially as represented in the WTO—are exerting pressures that will have significant consequences on the right to food. Among these forces are those pushing for the privatization of water services, increased food exportation, and the diversification of food production, with a focus on the so-called nontraditional industries such as horticulture, essential oils, vanilla, and seeds. While such policies may boost incomes in the short and medium term, the long-run implications for overall food security and the improvement of standards of human development are poor. In virtually every country where water services have been privatized, problems of access by the poor have been compounded, as the case of Tanzania illustrated.

Education as a Human Right

The centrality of education to humankind today cannot be underestimated. Countries that have invested in education are more likely than not to witness improved levels of human development and overall social progress. This implies that they are better empowered to exercise their fundamental rights, whether of a civic and political nature or with respect to the economic, social, and the cultural fields. Furthermore, a more enlightened population will ultimately be less of a burden to the state, whether in terms of social welfare, or in relation to physical mobility and their prospects for employment. In the age of globalization and the information revolution, it is quite clear that those societies best equipped to cope are those that have invested in educating their people.[88] While there is considerable debate about the most appropriate or "developmental" forms of education, there is little doubt that education today is a central component of a holistic existence. The linkages between education and the two preceding rights reviewed here—health and food—have also been established very clearly. The better educated a population, the better equipped it is to feed itself and to remain healthy.

It is in this regard that the story of the education sector in Uganda must be reviewed. In many respects, there is a fairly typical correlation between the education sector and the political development of the country. Thus, it was grossly affected by the political and economic instability of the 1970s and 1980s. When the NRM came to power in 1986, the government view was that the education sector was not a priority, especially when placed against the critical issues the new government confronted at the time, including security, rehabilitation of the economy, and reconstruction of basic infrastructure. At the time, the number of government-aided primary schools was a little under 8,000, the number of teachers nearly 73,000 while student enrolment stood at 2.31 million.[89] This meant that the student/teacher ratio was 32:1. Following the introduction of the policy of UPE in 1997, there was a dramatic alteration in the figures: 10,000 schools; 98,700 teachers, and 5.3 million students.[90] The student/teacher ratio rose to 54:1. In 2002, the number of students had risen to 7.4 million, and although the number of teachers had risen to above 130,000, the student/teacher ratio remained at 54:1, demonstrating the sector was faced by a serious crisis.[91]

There can be little doubt that UPE has dramatically increased the number of primary school student enrollments, with respect to the "4As" test articulated with respect to ESCRs. UPE has greatly boosted both the availability and accessibility to education.[92] The more intricate question, and the one that is certainly of greater relevance from a human rights perspective, is the *qualitative* impact of the policy.[93] In other words, what is the acceptability and the quality of the education services that have been made available as a result of these changes? Furthermore, while the issues of availability and accessibility might have been addressed fairly comprehensively at the primary level,[94] post-primary educational facilities were placed under tremendous stress once the first UPE graduates moved on in 2004. It is clear that the secondary school sector is ill equipped to handle the influx of qualified student numbers. The implications of this fact are quite stark, not only in terms of the UPE policy itself, but also in relation to overall human development. In February 2007, President Museveni introduced Universal Secondary Education (USE). This development—coupled with the pressure from UPE—is bound to place considerable stress on the sector.

Dramatic developments have also take place at the tertiary level. In 1986, Makerere University was the only publicly funded university. Conditions were so dire that strikes of both students and staff were commonplace.[95] It is illustrative that the strikes were principally linked to issues of welfare; in the case of staff, the demand for a "living wage," and on the part of students, resistance to the imposition of cost sharing measures. Since then, university education has changed dramatically principally through the introduction of private schemes for university entrance and the liberalization of the sector to allow for alternative private actors to offer university education. Both measures have boosted student enrollments, with Makerere jumping from less than 5,000 students at the turn of the decade to over 30,000 in 2006. The impact of these developments has been highly mixed. Pressure on classroom and library facilities, plagiarism and staff "burn-out" on account of high numbers are just a few of the most obvious consequences of the policy of liberalization.

Virtually on a daily basis, complaints about the state of Makerere find their way into the daily papers. The implications on academic freedom are manifest, especially as moonlighting and consultancies have become the preferred modus for university personnel, leaving little time for active engagement with social issues. This is related to the shift in international aid to the funding of basic education, thereby starving universities of public funds. Simultaneous to this development was "the transfer of education from public law and its redefinition from a public good to a freely traded commodity."[96] As Katarina Tomasevski succinctly points out,

> Distribution of public funds within education is seen as—by necessity rather than choice—a zero-sum game. It pits beneficiaries of public funding for education against each other. This makes concerted strategies for halting the decrease of public funding for education even more

difficult. There is always too little funding available for all levels and types of education, everywhere. Increased allocations to primary education deplete higher levels of education of public funding, increasing direct costs for students and their families. An acquired right to free university education is criticized as depriving young children of access to any education whatsoever. However, where university students are paying the full cost of their education there is no evidence that primary school children benefit.[97]

Against this postulation, it is important to note that donor funding in Uganda has been central to the development of the education sector and particularly to UPE since the policy was introduced. Indeed, the Poverty Action Fund (PAF) that was launched in June 1998 as an initiative to mobilizing resources for the social sector including education, health, roads, water, and sanitation is largely donor-driven.[98] Although there can be no doubt about the dramatic quantitative improvements in the provision of primary education since the introduction of UPE, there are several issues of a qualitative nature that require further attention. As Gariyo points out, access to education is still "biased in favor of the rich, of males and towards urban areas."[99] Additionally, there is a lack of sufficient classroom space, trained teachers, scholastic materials, and teaching aids.

Finally, it is important to point out that the scourge of corruption has greatly affected the degree to which government and other resources actually reach their intended beneficiaries. Aside from the large scandals in the Ministry of Defense and the Uganda Revenue Authority (URA), the misappropriation of finances at the local level, and especially funding for education, can only be described as criminal. From shoddy classroom construction to the padding of salary schedules with "ghost" teachers, the extent of financial vice at the district level directly affects the realization of the right to education.

The bigger picture is the overall dependency on external funding from which Uganda suffers. In a study of this issue, Tomasevski, the United Nations Special Rapporteur on the right to education, found that "the priority attached to debt repayment can jeopardize investment in human rights."[100] She points out that in a situation where internally generated revenues are "insufficient for both debt repayment and implementation of human rights obligations, the priority for debt repayment undermines investment in human rights."[101] Tomasevski goes on to say that it is erroneous to make the equation between the policies of international financial institutions like the World Bank and the IMF, and poverty eradication:

defining education solely as an instrument for poverty reduction and or economic growth does not conform to the definition of the right to education in international human rights law. Investment in education therefore does not necessarily facilitate effective recognition of the right to education and the impact of such investment ought to be carefully assessed.[102]

There are additional issues that relate to the entrenchment of the right to education in Uganda. Despite its inclusion in the constitution, the right has not been translated into legislation. This means that even the much-touted UPE policy has no legislative underpinning. It also means that the specific rights of students in the education process are not comprehensively articulated. This is important because UPE is highly donor-supported. If that support is either reduced or terminated, what is the binding obligation on the state not to deviate from the policy? Second, a legislative framework would stipulate the parameters of nondiscrimination, equity, and access that all Ugandans would be entitled to as of right. As it is, such provisions remain at the level of policy that is not enforceable in the same manner as legislation.

With respect to ESCRs, examining the policy framework helps to come to grips with the degree to which rhetoric matches or departs from reality. As Manisuli Ssenyonjo has argued, while it is important to consider what legislative and other measures have been adopted, there is a need to look further.[103] In the absence of such specific legislation, policies such as UPE remain in place at the pleasure of the state, and are viewed not as an obligation, but as a gift. Furthermore, issues such as gender or other forms of discrimination are not grounded within a framework that ensures that they cannot be tampered with. It is interesting that even though the RTE is embodied in the bill of rights, no HRO has devoted significant attention to any of the issues recounted here.

Justiciability, Implementation, and Enforcement: A Critical Inquiry

Arguments about the justiciability of ESCRs have affected discourse over these rights virtually since they were codified in international instruments. Unfortunately, the arguments have been collapsed into unresearched claims about the cost of realizing the rights to health and education. Urging for a critical rethinking of the exercise, Edward Ssempebwa of the CRC reported that the exercise of collecting people's views on the subject demonstrated a deficit in the constitutional reform process. According to him, "We have concentrated on the constitutional infrastructure for political liberalisation. What is needed is added

emphasis on how the infrastructure can improve people's welfare."[104] Ssempebwa's argument is clear: unless a different approach is taken toward the enforcement of human rights, the majority of people will remain marginalized. In sum,
how can the constitution address the enforcement and protection of ESCRs
since Uganda's 1995 constitution fell short on this very same issue?

Revisiting the Debate on Justiciability

In Uganda, the issue of justiciability proved to be the major impediment to a
more holistic approach to the recognition of ESCRs, and to their inclusion in
the body of the constitution, rather than in the section on National Objectives.
CA delegates largely took their cue from the Constitutional Commission report
that was reflective of a long-held position among legal scholars and practitioners.
In the flowery words of Nigerian author, Toriola Oyewo, such objectives and
principles

> are responsibilities enumerated without sanction as far as the funda-
> mental obligations of the Government are concerned and to us they
> look like sterile law notwithstanding the fact that it places observance
> and conformity of its provisions on all organs of government, with all
> authorities and persons, exercising legislative, executive or judicial
> powers.[105]

However, other jurisdictions with national principles or objectives similar
to those in the 1995 constitution have given them considerable weight. For example, in the case of *Société United Docks v. Government of Mauritius*,[106] the
Mauritius Supreme Court and the Privy Council stated that the initial declara-
tory section of the constitution was not a mere preamble or introduction. The
Indian Supreme Court has made famous an approach to National Objectives
that has seen the enforcement of numerous rights that are only covered in this
introductory, ostensibly "non-justiciable" section of the instrument.[107] Following the same spirit, the Papua New Guinea Supreme Court has stated, "Although they are said to be non-justiciable, the National Goals and Directive
Principles must be given effect wherever it is fairly possible to do so without
violating the meaning of the words used."[108] In Uganda, Justice Egonda-Ntende
stated in the famous case of *Tinyefuza v. Attorney General* that the principles
and objectives outlined in the constitution "ought to be our first canon of construction of this constitution. It provides an immediate break or departure with
past rules of constitutional construction."[109]

These judicial opinions point to the fact that the section on National Objectives in a constitution can indeed be made justiciable. This entails a less rigid approach to the issue of justiciability than has previously been in practice among courts. Secondly, these principles should be seen as linked to the justiciable rights embodied within the constitution. This would allow for both a broader construction of the constitution as well as for the development of a symbiotic relationship between the two parts of the instrument. As the court in the South African *Grootboom* case stated,

> There can be no doubt that human dignity, freedom and equality, the fundamental values of our society, are denied to those who have no food, clothing or shelter. Affording socioeconomic rights to all people therefore enables them to enjoy the other rights enshrined in Chapter Two (the Bill of Rights).[110]

ESCRs can indeed be made a justiciable part of the constitution. The most important question is how? To answer this question, one must do a more critical examination of the instrumentalities in a constitution that are supposed to oversee the enforcement of these rights.

Enforcement Mechanisms: Courts and State Commissions

Generally speaking, the institutional mechanisms for the enforcement of human rights under the 1995 constitution are fairly developed and mark a significant development on the 1967 constitution, especially in terms of access and available options such as courts, commissions, and civil action. Among these mechanisms are the regular judiciary, the Uganda Human Rights Commission (UHRC), the Electoral Commission, the National Planning Authority, the Service Commissions (on health and education), and the Inspectorate of Government. Moreover, to the extent that the doctrine of *locus standi* has been largely negative by the provisions of Article 50, the scope for the enforcement of rights is very wide. This means that an action for the enforcement of rights within a court or other similar body does not have to go through the previous rigorous test of ensuring that the litigant had a direct interest in the matter. The new formulation enshrined in Article 50 means that any person, even the proverbial busybody, could bring an action either on their own or on the behalf of another.

Take the Uganda Human Rights Commission and its application of ESCRs. The UHRC began operations in 1997. Since then, it has largely been preoccupied with civil and political rights. Its flagship magazine *Your Rights* mainly carries articles on these rights and even has on occasion featured some articles on of people with disabilities.[111] The UHRC has issued at least eight annual reports, the essence of which has been to act as a mechanism of reportage to Parliament on the activities of the Commission. The quality of the reports has improved over time, and demonstrates a growing ability to bring to light human rights violations of varying kinds. At the same time, the extent to which these reports have made an impact on the body to which the report is made is questionable. Indeed, a practice that has become almost a ritual is for the chairperson of the Commission to request Parliament to implement the recommendations of previous reports.

What has been the approach of the Commission to ESCRs? What is almost immediately apparent is that ESCRs do not enjoy a place of prominence in the reports, with the initial 1997 report paying "much less attention," in the words of Apolo Makubuya, to ESCRs than it does to civil and political rights.[112] According to Makubuya, the report "states in generic fashion that the challenges of realizing economic and social rights are "very grave" without substantiating the point. Such a position on these fundamental rights is quite disheartening and unacceptable." Moreover, there initially appeared to be a conceptual problem with understanding the character of these rights. That misconception is partly reflected by the statement in the 1998 report claiming that the enjoyment of ESCRs "are mainly dependent on resources and the state of the economy,"[113] a contention that is basically incorrect.[114] There was marginal improvement in the 2000–2001 report that devoted a scant six pages out of eighty to ESCRs.[115] A section on the state of vulnerable groups in society that covers refugees, women, children, and persons with disabilities (PWDs) considered the rights of these groups broadly.[116] A second chapter was devoted to rights at work and dealt with a number of economic and social issues in this regard.[117] The report of 2001–2002 adopted a different approach to the rights—they were spliced throughout the document.

The Commission's annual reports may not be fully reflective of the amount of attention given to problems associated with the realization of ESCRs. Among the many issues before the Commission includes the case of children, who may petition the body with a variety of matters that require adjudication, including abandonment, ill treatment, and the violation of their educational rights. In this respect, however, the Commission runs the danger of overlapping with the operations of other bodies, among them the National Council on Children which has the statutory brief to oversee the implementation of the Children's Statute and by implication, the Convention on the Rights of the Child. There is also an overlap with the Family and Children's courts, and in order to avoid a conflict, the Commission as much as possible attempts to invoke mechanisms of alternative dispute resolution (ADR) such as mediation and conciliation between the parties.

With respect to worker's rights, the Commission faces the same problem. While its operational guidelines stipulate that the Commission should not handle matters of a contractual nature, it often finds itself dealing with matters related to employment. Its preference is to refer most of these matters to the courts or to the labor department and to only handle small claims, issues of discrimination, and sexual harassment. However, once mediation has failed, there is a problem of the evidentiary proof required to support the claims. While the rules of procedure in the Commission are less stringent than those in court, petitioners still find problems in collecting sufficient evidence to support their claims.

More recently, the UHRC has avidly adopted and promoted the Rights Based Approach (RBA) to development. According to the Commission that approach

seeks to add value to the work of the lawyers and economists by providing an entry point for duty bearers and right holders to work together in a consistent and sustaining manner. This is possible because a human rights based approach is hinged on principles of legal obligations, participation, accountability and specific identification of who is vulnerable in a specific target so that they are given priority in the planning process. The rights-based approach is effective because it makes development an obligation of States and not charity dependent on the goodwill of the government in power.[118]

Emphasis on the RBA has led the Commission to some new areas of activity in the field of ESCRs, most prominent among which is the right to food. A seminar held in 2003 brought together stakeholders with an interest in the area and developed a strategic framework through which the right was discussed. The seminar reviewed the policy and legal framework on the right to food and made several recommendations on the way forward. One positive outcome of the seminar was the involvement of the Commission in the formulation of the government food and nutrition policy.[119] It is hoped that the Commission will be involved in the process of drafting legislation specifically relating to food.

One of the functions of the UHRC that has come to prominence since the enactment of the 1995 constitution is its power of adjudication on claims that rights have been violated. While the Commission tends to encourage Alternative Dispute Resolution over the more adversarial contestation common in the courts, at times it does adjudicate matters. But the number of cases it has handled that touch on ESCRs is rather low. The two decisions that have been made on ESCRs illustrate the approach of the Commission to these rights. In *Emmanuel Mpondi v. The Chairman, Board of Governors Nganwa High School et al.*,[120] the Commission dealt with the right to education. Mpondi was a student in the defendant's school where he was severely punished by two teachers, leading to his hospitalization. Following his treatment and return to school, he was sent home to collect school fees. His sponsor, however, refused to pay his school fees until the school administration had either punished the two teachers or clearly indicated the specific action it would take against them. As a consequence, Mpondi was forced to leave school for good. In dealing with the issue of the claimant's right to education, the tribunal made the following remarks:

> In our view the evidence shows that Mpondi's education at Nganwa High School was interfered with. We hold the respondents responsible for this interference. We find on a balance of probabilities that the respondents violated Mpondi's right to education.[121]

The *Mpondi* case is of interest for several reasons. In the first instance, the Commission viewed the violation as simply a tortuous or negligent wrong. Secondly, it awarded damages for the specific violation of the complainant's right to education in addition to the award it made relating to cruel and inhuman treatment. On the other hand, the case tackles the right to education in a rudimentary fashion. No reference is even made to the specific constitutional provision on which the decision was based. Furthermore, there is no elaboration of the reasons on which the Commission based its findings. For both jurisprudential and practical reasons the case is not very important because it has limited precedential value.

The conceptual failings in the *Mpondi* case were nevertheless addressed in the later decision of *Kalyango Mutesasira v. Kunsa Kiwanuka et al.*,[122] a case involving a claim against the government that was erroneously filed against the officers of the Ministry of Public Service for the payment of pensions. First, the case clearly laid down the legal basis on which the UHRC derived its power to investigate human rights violations and to award remedies in the event of a violation. That provision is Article 53(2)(c) of the 1995 constitution and does not make a distinction between civil and political rights and ESCRs on the question of enforceability. Secondly, the Commission stated that the provisions of the constitution, specifically article 254, plainly and categorically establish the *right to pensions*. In the considered opinion of the Commission:

> This provision of the constitution establishes a right to receive pensions to persons who *retire* from the public service. It does this in plain

language to the effect that a person who retires from the public service or is retired from the public service must be paid pension calculated according to his or her rank, salary and length of service. This Article is expressed in mandatory terms such that pension must be paid to a public servant who qualifies. . . . In my view Article 254 is expressed in terms which make pensions an entitlement. It becomes property. Persons who qualify for it can claim it as a right. I therefore conclude that refusal, neglect or delay in the payment of pension is a violation of human rights.[123]

A review of the *Mutesasira* decision demonstrates how far the Commission has come in articulating the enforceability of ESCRs and whether or not they are enshrined in the bill of rights of the constitution. In the first instance, the decision points out that although the constitution does not provide social security, Clause VII of the National Objectives and Directive Principles calls upon the state to make reasonable provision for the welfare of the aged. The decision cited Uganda's international obligations under the ICESCR, among which is the right of everyone to social security, including social insurance: "Pension, being a social security is therefore a human right under international law. Refusal or non-payment of pensions to those who qualify under the law would therefore violate the right to social security which is recognized as a right by Uganda."[124] The judgment is not only of importance to the jurisprudence of the Commission but it could even offer a framework of guidance for the courts.

Against this performance, one important question is whether there is a need for a Commission when it would be most appropriate to seek the enforcement of ESCRs through the courts of law and other mechanisms such as the National Children's Council and the Industrial dispute system. This is an issue that is continuously raised with respect to the Commission. There is certainly a need to clarify the roles and functions of the constitutional bodies and the other instruments and mechanisms that the 1995 constitution put in place to give effect to the rights enshrined therein. Strategic alliances among these bodies are required because they perform necessary functions, even if there is some overlap and duplication. That process would involve a clarification of the roles of the bodies to reduce costs and create well-demarcated spheres of operation. It is also important to take into account issues of access to these bodies in terms of cost, delay, and legal representation.

The state of the litigation of ESCRs in the courts of law has been discouraging and inadequate. A survey of constitutional litigation since the enactment of the 1995 constitution reveals a scanty record with the possible exception of litigation relating to the right to property[125] and the right to a healthy environment.[126]

Thus, for example, in the case of *The Environmental Action Network (TEAN) v. National Environmental Management Authority (NEMA)*,[127] Justice Ntabgoba made a declaration to the effect that smoking in a public place constitutes a violation of rights of the nonsmoking members of the public because they were denied the right to a clean and healthy environment in terms of Article 39 of the 1995 constitution.[128]

In the case of *Joyce Nakacwa v. AG et al.*,[129] among the issues was the infringement of Article 33(3) of the constitution because the second respondent, the Kampala City Council or KCC, had failed to provide medical and/or maternity care for the petitioner who was a resident in their charge. The article in question stipulates that the state "shall protect women and their rights, taking into account their unique status and natural maternal functions in society." The constitution invokes a social right specific to the maternal function of women. The petition also alleged contravention of the Public Health Act in that the minister of health was under a duty to make rules for the proper control of clinics, and specifically "for the welfare and care of children or the care of expectant or nursing mothers," and had failed to do so.[130] The specific case was concerned only with the preliminary matters raised in objection to the suit by the AG. Fortunately, the Constitutional Court overruled the preliminary objections, setting the stage for a substantive hearing on the merits of the case. Once again, fate intervened against the petitioner who died before the case could resume in a substantive manner before the Court.[131]

The case of *Dimanche Sharon et al. v. Makerere University*[132] saw the Court consider aspects of the right to education, although the issues principally related to freedom of expression and religion. The case concerned an action by Seventh Day Adventist students who averred that Makerere University was violating their rights by holding classes and other academic activities, including tests and examinations, on Saturday or the Sabbath. In dismissing the action, Lady Justice Kikonyogo, in the lead judgment of the Court made the following observation:

> I wish to emphasize that, the provisions of Article 30 notwithstanding, University education is not compulsory and is not obtainable only from the respondent. The petitioners had an option to join other Universities and other tertiary institutions. With regard to the alleged unconstitutional burden, the respondent's policy did not prohibit the petitioners or hinder them from practising, or believing or participating in any religious activities. The policy did not hinder any promotion of their creed or religion in Community with others under Article 37.[133]

In short, the claim that the rights of the claimants had been violated was given short shrift. Unfortunately, the judgment does not elaborate on what the right to education in the constitution actually means. This was an opportunity lost for the Court to give content to a right that is very broad and general as articulated in the constitution.

Conclusion

Recognize, respect, protect, promote, and fulfill. The conclusion of this chapter is that a strategy to invigorate ESCRs needs to use the following five elements as a basic operational framework. First, there is a need to recognize ESCRs as rights, and to incorporate them in the bill of rights section of the constitution. Of the three countries of UTAKE only Kenya has comprehensively attempted to do so in the contested draft constitution that was revised and eventually rejected in 2005. Uganda has made a half-hearted attempt while Tanzania needs to have a full-scale constitutional *baraza*, a public conclave, on the issue. Uganda needs to put the ESCRs in the National Objectives and Principles of State Policy in the bill of rights of the constitution. Aside from the rights to health and food examined here, there is the right to clean and safe water. Rights not included in the section but that have also gained international recognition include the right to shelter or housing and the right to an adequate standard of living including social security. The first course of action in Uganda must thus be to redraft the bill of rights section of the constitution to incorporate ESCRs. For all three countries, policy is of utmost importance because it provides an indication of the general parameters within which governmental activity is conceptualized and executed. This is the first opportunity that HROs should seize. HROs need to engage in work on ESCRs by investing in well-grounded multidisciplinary research, including human rights impact assessments (HRIAs) rather than post-mortem analyses of situations gone awry. By so doing, HROs can insert themselves directly into the policy debate to critically influence public debate.

In recognizing and incorporating ESCRs in an amended constitution for Uganda and Tanzania, the South African example can serve as inspiration, as can the now moot Kenyan draft constitution. This regards the formulation and articulation rights and the nature of the obligation of states. Transferring the rights from the National Objectives section of the constitution is not simply symbolic; it represents a recognition that these rights stand on the same level as those civil and political rights that have long been accorded enforceable status. At the same time, there needs to be a serious review of the notion that rights enshrined in the National Objectives section of a constitution are not justiciable. This can be done in two ways. The courts can do this by invoking the section whenever they are faced by a question of interpretation. Secondly, HROs should use these principles to articulate the case for comprehensive enforcement. Thus, recognition and the continuous reference and use of the rights will develop into their continuous respect, guaranteeing that all institutions and individuals give fidelity to their enforcement. Needless to say, the objective of recognition needs to apply to the other side of the table—to the activists in civil society, many of whom still do not regard ESCRs as essential to the human rights struggle. Consequently, research must be deployed in advocacy.

The obligation to protect implies an active role on the part of the state and its institutions to ensure that all policies and actions taken to effect government programs are done in conformity with the obligations undertaken with respect to ESCRs. Here, the official human rights commissions of the three countries can play a more active role in providing human rights impact assessments of government policies and legislation while still in draft form. This would minimize the negative consequences of such policies, ensuring that the damage does not come after the fact by addressing them before implementation.[134] In the absence of such action, it is imperative for HROs to institute a kind of "ESCR-watch." This would be a system of oversight of all governmental agencies that on a regular annual or biannual basis reviews the operations of all state organs on the steps they have taken to enforce ESCRs. Here, Kenyan HROs are certainly better placed than their two counterparts, in part because the agenda of economic liberalization has not extended as far as it has in Uganda and Tanzania. As Table 1 above demonstrates, Kenya survived, albeit with some bruises, without the IFIs. It needs to carefully consider how to reengage with them. Dependency and engagement with these institutions in Kenya does not have to be on the scale that was pursued in the other two countries. Furthermore, Kenya has more resources than either of the two countries on which it can build a stronger foundation for reform.

The protection of ESCRs is largely a state duty. However, it is obvious that such a role cannot be effectively carried out unless the violations are brought to the attention of the state or to the agencies given the function to protect rights under the constitution. This calls for a renewed emphasis on the role of advocacy by HROs in relation to the protection of ESCRs. Logically, it is civil society that must play this role. Not only must organizations involved in traditional human rights work take on more activities in the economic, social, and cultural arena, they must also forge a linkage between their traditional activities with regard to civil and political rights and the struggle to ensure that ESCRs are better protected. Aside from increasing litigation, such organizations should engage more directly in processes such as the PRSPs and in the debate about budgetary allocations in order to ensure that government is involved in the progressive improvement and realization of these rights rather than in their deterioration. In the final analysis, unless the vigilance over ESCRs matches the oversight of civil and political rights they will remain relegated to the margins. The pursuit of this objective must include the incorporation of ESCRs into the work of groups that see themselves primarily in the area of civil and political rights such as prison reform, nondiscrimination, and questions of access.[135] HROs need to extend the struggle for human rights to other sectors of civil society and not exert a monopoly over knowledge and strategy. In particular, it is necessary to work with organizations in the area of development and community outreach, not only to sensitize them to rights issues, but also to infect their work with an approach that does not simply take the context for granted.

CHAPTER FIVE

Feminist Masculinity: Advocacy for Gender Equality and Equity

Willy Mutunga

THIS CHAPTER SEEKS to introduce gender, women's human rights, and the social justice movement—questions that have not received much analytical attention in East Africa—into the human rights debate in East Africa. Feminist masculinity[1] is invariably described as men for gender equality, men for the equality of women and men, masculine partisans of women's liberation, male friends of the women's human rights and social justice movement, women's rights men, male friends of feminist movements, male feminists, pro-feminist men, and self-proclaimed feminists. Some of these categorizations are cynical, skeptical, and hostile in a struggle in which women insist on taking the leadership of their liberation. Men have, however, been involved either under the direction of women or on their own accord.

The chapter begins by giving a conceptual framework of feminism as a social movement. The specific area that is examined in this movement is gender inequality and inequity. The role that men play in feminism is discussed and the various debates analyzed. It then locates human rights and social justice discourses within feminism as a background to whatever practical interventions have been made.

The practical interventions that are discussed are African in general and one East African in particular. They are interventions by human rights and social justice organizations that claim to be part of the emerging movement of men for gender equality.

Feminism as a Movement

Feminism is a social movement that owes its history, intellectual ideology, and political existence to women.[2] The basis of feminism is the exploitation and oppression of women by the family, state, and market.[3] The conceptualizers and activists of this social movement have first and foremost been women. Whether this social movement is termed radical feminism, socialist feminism, materialist feminism, or postmodern feminists,[4] its main vision, notwithstanding the various iterations of the movement, has been to put an end to the exploitation and oppression of women. History is replete with the movement's successes, limitations, and challenges.

In the exploitation and oppression of women in the family by the state and the market, the man occupies a critical position.[5] Whether the analysis is of male dominance, the "body," men as beneficiaries of patriarchy, the intensification of violence against women—the pillar on which wage-slavery of men by capital is built[6]—men's contribution to the exploitation and oppression of women remains pivotal. This realization has been reflected in many feminist projects that address gender based violence, HIV/AIDs, men for gender equality, rites of passage, taboos, stereotypes, traditions, culture, education, research, media, human sexuality,[7] gender inequalities, and women's liberation.

Gender Inequality

Amartya Sen's discussion of what he calls the "distinct faces of gender inequality" falls under survival inequality, natal inequality, unequal facilities, ownership inequality, unequal sharing of household benefits and chores, and domestic violence and physical victimization.[8] To clarify these respective headings, he writes of high mortality rates for women, parental choice of boys rather than girls (a preference internalized in male-dominated societies) more opportunity for educating boys than girls, the exclusion of women from politics and commerce, the ownership of property as classic category of social inequality,[9] men's ownership of most household assets, and physical violence against women as a brutal feature of gender inequality. These categories and headings are not meant to be exhaustive or closed. There is, for example, a growing consensus among scholars and experts that gender inequality and inequity are the driving forces of the HIV/AIDS epidemic. Human sexuality reflects gender inequality in different ways.

Elizabeth Orchardson-Mazrui argues, "Language and cultural perceptions or attitudes can either liberate or dominate women. Language and imagery can be effectively used to perpetuate cultural and ideological values, or, more insidiously, domination."[10] Orchardson-Mazrui discusses visual images that depict women negatively, most notably those found in the electronic and print media, and in oral and written literature. She argues that politics has for a long time been viewed as the domain of men. She discusses the issue of the internalization of leadership as a male preserve in many communities to perpetuate patriarchal practices. For example, communities bestow leadership or eldership on male political leaders by giving them "walking sticks, knobkerries, beaded or feathered headdresses, and traditional attire."[11] Cultural stigmas are also attached to women who cannot bear children and those who are stepmothers. And when it comes to infidelity, women suffer more than men while culturally men are held blameless.[12] Orchardson-Mazrui also discusses stereotypes and myths that express gender inequality: "The notion that African girls are not scientifically and technologically able is not borne out by traditional craft practices in many parts of Africa."[13]

In the area of socialization, she argues that "in many Kenyan communities girls are socialized from early age to be subservient to men."[14] Orchardson-Mazrui makes an important point about the struggles to abolish female genital cutting (FGC). She argues that while that struggle is important, women's rights and social justice activists must pay attention to male circumcision rites. She contends that male circumcision rites create and recreate structures of power and control by men over women. This is done both overtly and subtly through education, rituals, and mentorship. She observes that "women, especially grandmothers, aunts, mothers and sisters, are the ones who prepare and serve special food for their boys during this period."[15] This observation denotes that the participation of women in socializing boys as warriors, those who do not cry and those who are protectors of women, cannot be doubted.

There is no doubt that socialization is a complex process. But what must be rejected is the argument, mainly advanced by men, that women are solely to blame for this socialization. Women are not free agents when they participate in these circumcision rituals. They do not operate freely from their domination and suppression by family, the state, and the market. Socialization is neither static nor frozen in time. It is a dynamic and evolving process. It changes from one generation to the next. Tracking changes in socialization and its impact on the changing status quo is important to understanding of what has to be done to continue the struggle for gender equality and equity.

In the context of gender inequality and women's rights in the Great Lakes, Elizabeth Orchardson-Mazrui and Kimani Njogu have posed the question, "Can culture contribute to women's empowerment?"[16] Their answer is to question the assumption that African cultures are essentially negative vis-à-vis women's rights and to claim that culture can, in fact, be an ally of women's empowerment.[17] The authors give many examples from various communities in Africa and urge more research into positive aspects of traditional African culture. The authors also revisit matrilineal societies and analyze aspects of traditional culture that can be recreated to aid women's empowerment. What needs to be understood is that the recreation of cultures is itself a struggle because there are vested interests against it. The forces that extinguished these positive aspects of traditional cultures need to be historicized and problematized. The feminist social movement, as well as feminist masculinity, will have to undertake the required research and the attendant political and ideological challenges that must be encountered.

Many reflections on gender inequality touch on underresearched sources. Jael Silliman brings attention to the impact of the Internet revolution on what may be called market violence on men and women.[18] The intrusive collection of data on people's tastes and preferences for corporate marketing strategies should be seen as a surveillance problem. There is no doubt that this revolution has resulted in more objectification of women's bodies in areas of Internet pornography and advertising. Silliman also warns about how cloning and other technologies could impact issues of equality:

> Emerging reproductive technologies, such as cloning, have the potential to blur the distinctions between genetically distinct and genetically determined individuals. This raises ethical questions regarding who would count as fully human with the attendant civil rights and liberties. Valerie Hartouni points to how standards of humanity get "partialized" (making some less human than others) in this process. She fears that, in the current social context, such technologies will be used to manage and contain diversity and the proliferation of difference.[19]

Gender inequalities have to be located in the new world disorder. International feminism is a movement that analyzes the inequalities in the world, the root causes of those inequalities, and how the world disorder affects women's struggles for rights and social justice. If a new world order is possible, is it also possible for women? What will it look like in terms of gender equality? International feminism has to keep asking these questions. The questions, of course, hearken back to discourses of reform or revolution that still plague human rights and social justice movements as well as feminism.

Women's liberation is a reformist and revolutionary clarion call that seeks to end women's exploitation and oppression. While dealing with "household slavery" at the family level, it also targets the state and the market. Market fundamentalism is what is now called globalization, although this is the baptismal name of what radicals call imperialism. While national and regional feminist movements have their specific role to play in demystifying, resisting, and combating globalization, international feminism has its role also. It is part of the movement for a new world, a global movement for justice, human rights, social justice, reproductive justice, global peace, and a clean environment. Silvia Federici has commented on this role:

> If international feminism and "global sisterhood" are to be possible, it is indispensable that women in the first world make their own struggle that the third world women are carrying on against structural adjustment, the payment of external debt, the introduction of intellectual property laws, which are means by which the new international division of labor is being organized, and the strongest evidence that capitalism is unsustainable for the majority of world population.[20]

One of the critical questions for feminist masculinity is whether gender inequality hurts men and in what way men can benefit from gender equality. The argument here is that the rejection of the current status quo will benefit African societies. Consequently, if societies benefit, then men must benefit. The basis of this argument is that inequity and inequality do not benefit society. Women who fight for gender equity are fighting for a better society for themselves and for men. Masculinity is about dominance and dominators distort their humanity as people.[21] Men as human beings are hurt in this regard. Men are also restricted to limited and stifled roles under male dominance. They fail to develop their full human potential, a condition that must hurt men. As argued in this chapter, dominance does not exist in a vacuum. It is intertwined and reinforced by other systems of domination, oppression, and exploitation. A clear connection has been made between women's unpaid labor and oppression by men, and the exploitation of male workers.

As class analyses of virtually all societies have demonstrated, men are not homogeneous. Poor men need liberation from rich men as both types of men are members of different social groups. The feminist movement has had to deal with the issue of class as well.[22] Gender inequality hurts man in his struggle to liberate himself from himself, from other men, and from a societal system that oppresses and exploits him. Man's transformation has to undertake this transformative path if man can be a committed ally in the struggle to end gender inequality and inequity. Man's transformation will, of course, remain an area of theoretical and practical inquiry. Such inquiry is difficult and will be resisted by various vested interests, including men themselves.

Feminist Masculinity

The role that men should play in feminist movements has been a source of continuing heated debates.[23] Are men meddlers in affairs of feminist movements since they are not directly and primarily involved? Are they paternalistic and self-proclaimed feminists meddling in women's affairs because men think women are not capable of dealing with their own concerns? Are men seeking to control these movements for fear that the results of the movements will go against them? Are men stating that their place in any movement, including the feminist movement, is in front? Is there really a difference between men who claim to be friends of the feminist movement and those who are declared enemies of the feminist movement? How do the friends deal with the backlash occasioned to the feminist movement by the enemies? What does it mean when men say they are helping women? Are men allowing women to speak?

There is no shortage of pertinent questions. Are men who have not abandoned their privileges accorded by the family, state, and the market committed soldiers of the feminist movement? Are men who are opposed to "conversion" to become a new type of man who understands women's liberation in its theoretical and practical sense a hindrance to feminist movements? What does the transformation of men entail? What is the content of the education that is to be given to men?[24] Are there definite criteria upon which this transformation can be discerned?[25] Is the focus on men replacing the focus on women? Are men ready to accept the leadership of women in feminist movements and not subvert them?[26]

More inquiries are necessary. Why are male dominated organizations and social movements not seriously incorporating gender perspectives and analyses in their work? Are these male dominated organizations and social movements that struggle for gender equality taking on board the issue of disempowered men as critical to men's transformation?[27] Why is there no reflection on why after almost thirty-five years into the feminist movement there is now an outreach to men? Is the involvement of men narrowly confined to specific developmental issues such as reproductive health and rights and not to the expansive approach that allows in-depth and broader analysis of the issue? How do men, and which men are selected, respond to being the vanguard? What kinds of men are attracted to this kind of work? What are the cultural shifts that have resulted in these recent concerns?

It is a valid to question to ask how men benefit from joining in the feminist movement. How are men hurt by gender inequality and how do they stand to benefit from gender equality?[28] Are these initiatives going to create competition for limited resources and thereby impact negatively on the feminist movement?

How is this competition for funding going to be handled? What risks do men face when they do this work? Is there no wisdom in providing separate and parallel safe spaces for men and women to conduct this culturally transformative work? How are these parallel and safe spaces synergized for struggles for gender equality and equity? What would be the ground rules for such synergy? Are men being problematically incorporated in development projects that help further the dominant development paradigms that have potential dangers for women because such paradigms never engage with issues of power and difference? Is there a vision of what feminist masculinity looks like?[29]

It is also a valid question to ask how men deal with the issue of diversity in masculinity. There have been arguments in East Africa, religiously framed as "human rights and morality," for example, that posit that issues of homophobia and sexual orientation are outside the purview of human rights and social justice work! Human rights and social justice activists have rightly taken the position that human rights and social justice work cannot afford to be selective. Even so, human rights and social justice activists have defended (lesbian, gay, bisexual, transgender, and intersex (LBGTI) organizing in East Africa.[30] Needless to say, these issues remain controversial and the men for gender equality movement must take them on board.

Finally, there is the question of the integration of the struggle for gender equality with the broad struggles for social transformation in all societies. The struggle for gender equality is not only a fight among sexes but also a critical battle in the just war for better societies the world over.

Some of these questions are being asked of women's rights and social justice organizations that have undertaken projects that involve men. Njoki Wainaina, a consultant with FEMNET, expresses her experience as follows:

> There are many women today who feel that working with men and boys is diluting, diverting and trivializing our struggle. Many hold the view that because men and boys are the beneficiaries of male privilege and discrimination against women and girls, they can never understand our struggle. Many doubt that men and boys can commit to changes that would mean them losing the privileges they now enjoy. But, as understandings of gender, its social construction, masculinities, femininities and their impact on all deepen, it becomes clear that males have reasons to want to change as well and that gender equality would also benefit them. Work with men and boys for gender equality is only one of the many strategies that must be combined to tackle the ever-growing problems of inequality, injustice and oppression.[31]

African Rights, another human rights group, has confronted this question in its work on empowerment and gender equity in Rwanda.[32] The fighters against genocide were both men and women. In 1994, women largely undertook the demands of the post-genocide era and war reconstruction. With most men either dead or in prison, women found themselves undertaking roles that were traditionally taboo for women. The government's commitment to gender equity and affirmative action, which were written into the new constitution, gave women an enhanced status in political participation.

African Rights conducts research on the ground and seeks to find out the role men have played in the struggle for gender empowerment and equity. It has found that men work alongside women in gender promotion; women give credit to men in positions of authority for supporting their cause for gender equity; women are convinced that men need gender education which can be given directly to men and in other cases to men and women jointly; gender education to the youth (both women and men) is critical in struggles for gender equity; priority in gender education for men has to be given to men in rural areas where there is pronounced hostility to gender education; gender education for men must focus on what men stand to gain if there is gender equity in society (the dominant idea is still that gender education is antimen, destroys harmony between men and women and within the family, and challenges dominant cultures on inheritance and women's "province" in society); and women must consolidate the gains they have acquired from the family, state, and market.

The IDS bulletin that compiles articles that interrogate and problematize this debate suggests that the issue, which reflects acute personal and political considerations, presents both a risk and an opportunity in the struggles for gender equality. The bulletin suggests a way forward:

> There is clear need for more research into how men and women are in practice negotiating male involvement in GAD programs, at all levels. There is equally a need for greater clarity about what actively promoting the involvement of men in GAD might actually look like. What kinds of policies, projects and practices would such promotion entail? What kinds of changes might be needed to current strategies to enable practitioners to focus more directly on the issues of gendered power raised by many of the contributors to this bulletin? What tactics might be needed to bring about these changes? Alongside these questions lie other more practical concerns. How might practitioners deal with conflicting emotions that male involvement may evoke? How might the sensitivities involved be best handled? And what practical steps can be

taken to tackle deep-rooted attitudes, values and beliefs in ways that recognize both women and men as gendered subjects who occupy complex and multiple positions of power and powerlessness?[33]

Men who work for women's human rights and social justice organizations as coordinators of gender equality projects or those who have set up their own initiatives to address gender equality and equity must take these questions and suggestions forward. There seem to be clear entry points that men engaged in these struggles can take up. The issue of research cannot be overemphasized.[34] Accepting the direction, vision, and support of women's human rights and social justice organizations and the feminist movements, as well as conducting principled dialogues with such organizations and movements cannot be avoided. The conversion from "masculine feminist" to "feminist" is a serious struggle that has theoretical, ideological, and political implications. It is not a matter of self-proclamation. There is a need to reiterate that these struggles do not exist in a vacuum. They exist in the disordered world, sketched above, in which human rights and social justice operate. Feminist movements and their organizations, on their part, should appreciate that their power and initiatives can liberate the lives of all human beings: women, men, and children.[35]

Masculine feminists must take initiatives that will positively affect the struggle for gender equality. There is no need for men to "feel hurt and aggrieved at having been excluded from and silenced in gender arenas."[36] The reasons for exclusion are just as sound as those for inclusion. The feminist movement has expressed its fear and asked legitimate questions about male involvement in gender inequality issues. As a beginning to principled collaboration, these issues cannot be ignored. To start principled collaboration, male-dominated organizations and movements could seriously incorporate gender perspectives and analysis in their work. The organizations and movements could consequently apply the principles and analysis and the resultant values to their lives and political domain.

Men need to liberate themselves from manhood and its attendant privileges. This liberation of men cannot, and should never, be dependent on the suppression, oppression, and exploitation of women. Nor should the liberation be dependent on the suppression, oppression, and exploitation of other men. This liberation of men should never be at the expense of others in society. These historical, socioeconomic, class, and imperialistic contexts of the liberation of men and women are fundamental to any political struggles that aim to change the status quo.

Rights, Social Justice, and World Disorders: A Site for Feminist Struggles

The struggle for human rights and social justice can be traced beyond the Universal Declaration for Human Rights in 1948.[37] The struggles of slaves and serfs, the forerunners of workers as we know them today, were about rights.[38] History records many revolutions but rarely sees them as struggles for rights. One need only analyze the demands, the ideology, and politics of many social movements to realize that the discourse of rights was not very far from the surface. Human rights and social justice discourse have their limitations.[39] Human rights and social justice discourse are double-edged and can be used negatively or positively. These discourses have their usefulness as a basis of creating democratic spaces where further demands and more crucial successes can be achieved.

In the current world of disorder characterized by exploitative globalization, militarism, recolonization, increasing poverty, insecurity, and violence, the human rights and social justice crusades are critical messages of mitigation. An analysis of the history of the world after the Bolshevik Revolution of 1917 shows vested interests under attack. These vested interests adopted the discourses of the revolutionaries. John Maynard Keynes became the father of welfare capitalism, the answer to the promises of the revolutionaries to workers and peasants. This is the background to the New Deal in the United States, welfare capitalism and social democracy in the United Kingdom and in Europe. Sidney Lewis captures this point succinctly:

> Like it or not, the New Deal had a stronger impact on the American psyche than we radicals realized. Prior to Roosevelt's inauguration, writes historian David A. Shannon, "fear of a revolution was very widespread . . . and much of the politics of the period can be understood fully only by reviewing political events against the background of anxiety about violent revolt. The vigor with which the army dispersed the Bonus Expeditionary Force from Washington in the summer of 1932, for example, had its roots in revolutionary fear." But Roosevelt introduced reforms that, though inadequate by leftist standards, did mute talk of revolution. In just four or five months during the first year of the New Deal, 2.5 million unemployed were provided with jobs. . . . In due course Congress also approved such "socialistic" measures as unemployment compensation and social security.[40]

Welfare capitalism and social democracy were meant to stave off revolutionary potential in the United States and Europe. This was especially true as the revolutionary states increased after World War II with the creation of the People's Republic of China, the Soviet Union of Socialist Republics, socialist states in Eastern Europe and the undertaking of revolutionary strategies by colonial peoples struggling for self-determination and independence. As Lewis states, the "New Deal 'had put America on the road to welfare state and thereby cut the ground from under both the socialist and communist parties.'"[41] This is also a period when the ideological and political nuances of "reform" and "revolution" were pretty clear.[42] Debates on whether reforms could fulfill ultimate revolutionary goals were common.[43]

Human rights and social justice discourse after World War II take their historical and socioeconomic basis from these policies, debates, and historical events. The debates on the usefulness, limitations, and the transformative role of human rights and social justice discourses are located in these earlier debates.[44] These systems of welfare capitalism and social democracy were attacked as unworkable by neoclassical ideologues and implementers of the Reagan and Thatcher neoclassical economic arenas, while the alternative systems called socialism or communism collapsed.[45]

A new circle of unbridled exploitation and oppression began in 1989. This was done under the propaganda that no system except capitalism was viable. Markets that were previously closed to capitalism in the Soviet Union and China were opened to foreign Western capital. Gains made by independence movements, civil society, and revolutionary movements were clawed back. But this situation has given birth to human rights and social justice movements that resist the new world disorder: the World Social Forum, 50 Years is Enough, debt relief coalitions, and other movements opposed to the engines of globalization, the IMF, World Bank, and WTO.[46] Many of these movements use the discourses of human rights and social justice.

An important milestone in human rights and social justice work was the 1993 Vienna World Conference on Human Rights that gave birth to the now famous Vienna Declaration.[47] Viewed from the history of human rights since the end of World War II and the ideological battles during the Cold War over human rights, the Vienna Declaration is a crucial watershed in human rights and social justice work. Crucially important is how the demand of women's rights as human rights was central to that conference.

These discourses have taken on board the various paradigms of liberation that were buried under the rubble of the Berlin wall that collapsed in 1989. Other movements emphasize the limitations of human rights and social justice discourse.[48] It is an opportune time for these discourses to be propagated and problematized so that their potential can be examined. The discourses can resist the discernible drift to fascism of the current global disorder.[49] Like welfare capitalism, the discourses could easily mitigate the harshness of the status quo and give it a lease on life under the guise of reforms. But the discourses could also expose, demystify, and shame the status quo and open it up for overthrow. In between these possible options there is a possible movement for a better world.

As a matter of logic, human rights and social justice projects must be sites for feminist struggles. For example, the Convention on the Elimination of all Forms of Discrimination against Women (CEDAW) provides a substantive gender equality framework. Human rights and women human rights organizations have invoked and utilized this CEDAW normative framework in their struggles. Human rights and women human rights organizations need to understand the totality of feminist struggles so that all struggles reinforce and synergize each other. The overall aim of the war for gender equality and equity should be clear—the various sites of necessary battles to win the war should be constantly and consistently identified and utilized.

Selected Feminist Masculinity Interventions in Africa

There is a growing movement throughout Africa to institute feminist masculinity interventions. Some of the more interesting cases have been in South Africa, Kenya, Malawi, and Namibia. Robert Morrell has written extensively on South African case studies that include movements of men that are against gender equality.[50] He concludes that the "organizations that constitute a pro-feminist movement have attracted financial support and provide the strongest indication of a sustained capacity to contribute to goals of gender justice."[51] On the continent, FEMNET has played a leading role in encouraging such a movement.

As a human rights and social justice organization with an African continental reach, FEMNET launched the Men to Men initiative in 2001—today known as Men for Gender Equality Now—to mark the Sixteen Days of Activism Against Violence on Women. FEMNET targeted men and this marked the organization's beginning of a partnership to promote and to increase male involvement and action in combating gender-based violence. The need to involve men in struggles for gender equality has been voiced by various national, regional, and global forums and organizations. FEMNET reflected the ideas of those with growing interest in working with men to eliminate gender inequality generally and specifically in the areas of gender-based violence (GBV) and HIV/AIDs. FEMNET's justification for this intervention is that since men and boys are beneficiaries of gender discrimination, they must be convinced that a society that values gender equality benefits them. FEMNET is convinced that men and boys can be sensitized and transformed into new human beings who are committed to gender equality. FEMNET is committed to creating, nurturing, and consolidating a movement of men who will struggle for gender equality and the consequent social transformation of their societies in the African region.

In 2001, FEMNET organized a regional Men to Men consultation that brought together twenty-seven men from Kenya, Malawi, Namibia, and South Africa. This consultation resulted in the creation of a regional Network of Men Against Gender Based Violence—now called Regional Network of Men for Gender Equality—and a regional plan of action to be implemented by the national partners in the four countries. FEMNET has since coordinated and given technical support to the collaborating national partners in the regional network. FEMNET has designed a media outreach program that disseminates men to men messages and carries out critical discussions on manhood and masculinity aimed at changing male behavior and promoting gender equality.

In its Strategic Plan and Program 2003–2005, the Regional Network of Men Against Gender Based Violence is committed to working with male activists in various institutions and organizations to create a critical mass of men who support the empowerment of women and the principles of gender equality, development, and human rights. The regional network is also committed to equip men with concepts, knowledge, and skills for gender sensitization and advocacy to transform men's attitudes, behaviors, and influence among their peers and their communities. The regional network's commitment to research, including action research, the development, and production of materials to educate this critical mass of men in its work on gender equality remains a core task. Such education, for example, includes studies of men and masculinities, relationships between gender, culture, and the use of culture in struggles for gender equality.

In Malawi, FEMNET works with the Malawi Network Against Gender Based Violence (NAGBV) and the Malawi Men's Initiative for Gender Equality, a member of both the regional Network of Men Against Gender Based Violence and NAGBV. Both organizations mobilize men to join the initiative and undertake activities to all regions of Malawi. NAGBV's mandate is to bring together organizations that work to prevent gender-based violence in Malawi that undertake the support of victims and survivors of gender violence, and ensure that offenders are punished.

In South Africa, FEMNET made contacts with various organizations including Ilitha Labantu, Molo Songolo, the Gender Training and Education Network (GETNET), and South African Men for Change. FEMNET has involved Ilitha Labantu in its Men for Equality Program strategy while networking with Ilitha Labantu in its work with men in its HIV/AIDs projects. FEMNET networks with Molo Songolo because the latter undertakes a critical program with young men. This program has important lessons for other organizations in South Africa and the African region. GETNET's "vision is for a society free of oppressive gender relations, gender violence and discrimination; where equal rights of women and men become a lived reality and women are supported in overcoming past oppression to achieve personal, social and economic empowerment. GETNET program focuses on the transformation of power relations between women and men and in the empowerment of women. This is done through education, training, research, resource development and networking. Its program covers all provinces in South Africa and extends beyond, into the neighboring countries."[52]

GETNET has a masculinities program that promotes men's active participation in the struggle for gender equality through workshops: "Based on men's experiences, the workshops provide a secure and nonthreatening environment for men to reflect and discuss a range of gender issues relevant to their personal lives, work and community. The program aims at men who are transformation officers, diversity trainers, human resource managers, members of men's groups or forums and those interested in gender work."[53] GETNET has also produced a guidebook for trainers titled *Masculinities in the Making of Gendered Identities*: "The Guidebook covers a wide range of topics including concepts and tools of analysis; masculinities in organizations, workplaces and institutions; pathways for transformation; and images of masculinities."[54]

South African Men for Change owes its vision to its founder, Thulani Nksosi, who, inspired by his own transformation,[55] decided to be a role model, a change agent, an advocate for change, therefore founded an organization that would provide a forum where men would speak to each other. Among the program of the South African Men for Change is gender sensitization and training for transformation and men's marches in support of gender equality. These South African organizations have attended meetings convened by FEMNET but have not become consistent members of the Regional Network for Men for Gender Equality Now.

In Namibia, FEMNET works with Namibian Men for Change (NAMEC) in its Men for Gender Equality Now. NAMEC's objective is to sensitize men and boys on redefined manhood and against violence against women and children. In 2001, NAMEC conducted fourteen schoolboys' workshops and twelve community men's meetings under support from UNICEF. The workshops discussed the following topics: manhood, cultural and traditional norms that condone violence and other forms of abuse against women and children, men's promiscuity and HIV/AIDs infections, and harsh penal provisions against gender violence. NAMEC is a national umbrella organization with twelve affiliate men's groups countrywide.

In Kenya, FEMNET works with the Presbyterian Church of East Africa (PCEA) at Kinoo. PCEA has an existing structure called Presbyterian Christian Men's Fellowship through which members counsel one another and have fellowship on issues of their choice. The involvement of the church in the Men to Men initiative was established by Anderson Njoroge, one of the participants of the regional consultation that took place in 2001. The Rev. Dr. Timothy Njoya, the founder and CEO of Men for the Equality of Men and Women (MEW), was until his retirement the pastor at Kinoo church. FEMNET also works with the Kenya Anglican Men's Association. FEMNET is exploring possibilities of partnering with Catholic Men's Association—yet another feature in the structure of the Catholic Church in Kenya. FEMNET also works with various NGOs and CBOs in its twin niches of GBV and HIV/AIDs.

The program coordinator of the Regional Network for Men for Gender Equality Now at FEMNET is Njoki Wainaina. According to Wainaina, the network is still young. Many of the organizations that are doing similar work still lack institutional capacity. In her view, the regional men for gender equality movement is still weak. There is a need to strengthen the national movements before regional movements can be strong. FEMNET has decided to build on the strengths of the Kenyan movement. Wainaina is convinced that the mainstay of the men for gender equality movement will be the young people who have shown commitment and motivation arising out of personal experiences and concerns.

The national coordinator of the Kenyan Network for Men for Gender Equality Now is Kennedy Otina. Otina is encouraged by the progress the emerging movement has made in Kenya in areas of GBV and HIV/AIDs. The involvement of the churches has allowed FEMNET the use of their extensive infrastructure to reach out to men and carry out training. FEMNET is also alive to the role of churches in masculinities. There are opportunities and constraints since churches do maintain and sustain gender hierarchies and promote conservative roles for women.[56] Otina is convinced that the men for gender equality movement in Kenya will form a strong basis for FEMNET's work in the African region.

The movement of men for gender equality in South Africa deals with some of the burning questions raised by feminism. FEMNET, notwithstanding the difficulties of networking with the South African movement, must continue to cultivate contacts. The successes, challenges, and lessons to be learned from the South African movement will enrich the Kenyan movement. For example, the

Kenyan movement does not seem to have engaged the broader global issues that affect its work. There is still more work to be done on reflecting, evaluating, and critiquing the Kenyan movement's partnership with religious organizations. Acceptance of men as vanguard of this movement that does not problematize the criteria of the selection and transformation of such men may impact negatively on the movement. It is also crucial to cultivate networks with intellectual and other knowledge institutions that are constantly defining and redefining critical issues of discussion and reflection in the movement of men for gender equality. It is clear that FEMNET has not resolved the fundamental question of what role men ought to play in the movement vis-à-vis the feminist movement

As the only human rights and social justice organization of men that addresses issues of gender inequality in East Africa, Men for the Equality of Men and Women (MEW) was launched in 1999 when several human rights activists came together to organize The March of Men to End Violence Against Women and Girls. Angered in part by the sad story of the late Betty Kavata, the activists were convinced that men had to speak out against gender based violence. On July 31, 1998, the twenty-seven-year-old Kavata was severely battered by her husband, a traffic policeman. The injuries resulted in Kavata's loss of all her teeth, paralysis from the neck down, and eventual death on Christmas day that year. The Coalition on Violence Against Women (COVAW) took up Kavata's case and organized gender and human rights activists who successfully called for the arrest and prosecution of Felix Nthiwa Munyao, Kavata's husband. Munyao was found guilty of manslaughter—the penal code does not use the term "woman slaughter"—and sentenced to life imprisonment. The sentence was reduced to fifteeen years on appeal.

The Kavata-inspired march took place on March 28, 1999, with the support of UNIFEM and several local human rights organizations, including the Kenya Human Rights Commission. Feminist activists and their organizations met the marchers at Freedom Corner of Uhuru Park in Nairobi. The meeting at the park heard speeches condemning gender-based violence and other aspects of gender inequality. There was no immediate follow up of the march because the leader of the initiative, Reverend Timothy Njoya, continued his pastoral duties at Kinoo Presbyterian church and did not have time to organize and mobilize the anger the men reflected before and after the march. In 2004, a retired Njoya decided to resurrect this great project. He registered MEW as a trust on December 20, 2004. With funding from the Ford Foundation, Njoya was able to conduct a feasibility study for MEW's program areas, including how it could change the attitudes of men and boys toward women and girls and what infrastructural challenges he would have to resolve. The result was MEW's strategic programs for 2005–2008.

MEW is committed to equality without dominance in the belief that men and women are born equal, that inequality is the result of flawed socialization, and that MEW can do something to nurture equality by improving the socialization process in Kenyan society. MEW is committed to changing men's and boy's attitudes and behaviors by redefining manhood in the socialization process. MEW's specific aims are to end men's domination, discrimination, oppression, and violence against women and girls; to help men own up to violence and discrimination against women and girls by rectifying the imbalances of past negative socialization; and to develop and implement new conceptual frameworks for rationalizing the basis and principles of equality between men and women based on the foundations of democracy and human rights.

To achieve its specific objectives, MEW has three programs—documentation and research, training and counseling, and outreach and advocacy. The documentation and research program seeks to research, study, and compile materials for training and education on various matters of gender equality. The program uses materials that have been written and used by women's organizations. The training and counseling program seeks to facilitate public forums on ending domination, oppression, violence, and discrimination against women and girls. It also conducts workshops with boys who are undergoing initiation ceremonies to address traditional laws, customs, myths, taboos, and languages that denigrate women and promote gender inequality. The training and counseling program helps parents make domestic duties gender inclusive so as to socialize boys as protectors of gender equality. The outreach and advocacy program organizes marches and rallies in support of gender equality. It seeks to work with teachers colleges, religious organizations and the media in undertaking these tasks. The collective impact of the activities of these programs will include addressing gender inequality at the level of cultural, ethnic, and religious roots both in urban and rural areas; initiating gender dialogue to affirm both manhood and womanhood in terms of positive attitudes and behaviors; and collaborating with partners in the promotion of men for gender equality movement.

In 2006, MEW started to implement its programs. The secretariat and other structures of governance have been put in place. The infrastructure of collaboration is also operational. MEW's work will reinforce the work of the national network that is housed by FEMNET. MEW is expected to play a key role in the emerging men for gender equality movement.

MEW needs to address those issues identified as critical to FEMNET's project. MEW seems convinced that the best way to address all questions raised by the feminist movement is to confine its work to liberating men from themselves. It appears to accept that its struggle is parallel to that of the feminist movement and that its constituency is solely men. MEW, however, does not rule out areas of collaboration and synergy. It does not resist direction and guidance by the feminist movement. Indeed, it uses materials that feminist movements have produced as resource for its training, education, and transformation. Liberating men from themselves is a theoretical and practical construct that needs to be problematized. Like the concept of transformation, it raises complex questions. MEW seems to underestimate this complexity that that has the potential to derail the commitment, passion, and drive to struggle for gender equality.

Conclusion: Prospects and Challenges

Feminist masculinity in this chapter portrays men who are committed to and passionate about gender equality. They are men who oppose gender relations that exploit and oppress women. They are men who oppose and resist the exploitation and oppression of men by other men. They are men who are committed to the social transformation of the current global disorder. As human rights and social justice activists, they are men who shun selectiveness in the upholding of the rights of all, are not homophobic, are not male supremacists, and readily accept the leadership of women in the work they do. They are men who understand men's issues in the struggles for gender equality. They are men who are committed to the struggles against men resisting gender equality. Ideologically and politically, these are men who are reformers and revolutionaries.

Organizations and initiatives of men that struggle for gender equality should be accepted as important actors in the fight against powerlessness. That is why the emerging men for gender equality movement in the African region should be recognized. Similarly, the role of women's human rights and social justice movements in establishing and nurturing some of these initiatives must be encouraged. But there should be principled dialogue between all these groups.

The emerging men for gender equality movement is limited by its lack of funding, weak institutional capacities, and the lack of critical mass following of men who support gender equality. There exist crucial vested interests in the family, the state, and the market that still oppose gender equality. There is no uniform and consolidated position of the women's human rights and social justice movement and, indeed, of the broad feminist movement on how to engage the emerging men for gender equality movement. Ideological, intellectual, and political positions are reflected in debates on the role men should play in feminist movements. Questions about what constitutes men's transformation so that they can internalize and commit themselves to gender equality demand answers. These questions will always be part of the growth of the men for gender equality movement.

The major challenge of men for gender equality movement is to secure a definite, consistent, and committed constituency of men. The struggle for gender equality cannot be divorced from other struggles in society at the national, regional, and global levels. Gender equality challenges definite vested interests at all those levels. These vested interests always fight back and seek to divide the movement on various issues and co-opt its leadership. It remains a challenge for the movement to identify areas of collaboration and synergy with other movements in the struggle for global justice.

Politics play a fundamental role in issues of social transformation. The men for gender equality movement must realize that it advocates, lobbies, and struggles for the liberation of women. Liberation is a political struggle. Political struggles are about class struggles and contestations for political power. The men for gender equality movement must clarify their ideological and political positions and mobilize men on those positions. While this issue can divide or weaken the movement, there is always the potential to delineate broad common denominators of consensus. These denominators must be identified and consolidated. It is the critical mass following of men that will in part determine the direction of growth of these broad common denominators.

CHAPTER SIX

Women's Advocacy: Engendering and Reconstituting the Kenyan State

Jacinta K. Muteshi

> *Constitutions are now the lingua franca of written law, the public docu-*
> *ments by means of which nations will themselves into being. . . . They are*
> *best described . . . as threshold documents that show where the limits of*
> *power lie.*

THE DECEMBER 2002 general election in Kenya was driven by an enormous desire for a democratic state. These aspirations led to initiatives aimed at the structural transformation of political life. One such initiative was the drafting of a new constitution for Kenya, a process that was intended to fundamentally reorder the state to advance social justice, equality, and democracy. A feature of constitution making, especially in a period of political transition, is the transformative potential to create new institutional practices and societal structures. The opportunity can be seized to convey new meanings about the nature of gender relations. National constitutions have more often than not advanced different meanings for women and men. Thus women find themselves constrained by constitutions that reaffirm customary and personal legal systems that exert pressure on them to act within restrictive gender power relations, often thwarting women's rights and gender equality. It is in the field of constitutional politics that the issues of Kenyan women were placed on the national agenda by women's organizations in collaboration with those human rights organizations that sought to further women's claims to citizenship in the Kenyan state and to entrench meaningful equality before the law.

Kenyan women called into question gender discrimination in the constitution and took their demands to the constitutional review process by actively engaging the entire formal process of instituting and crafting constitutional language. Their aim was to change the impact of the law on women. Women developed vigorous advocacy, lobbying, and education campaigns to assist women delegates and gender activists in the negotiations for a new constitution. Integrating women and gender issues in both the national agenda and in the constitution making process can be attributed to the strong leadership exercised by autonomous, resilient, and vibrant Kenyan civil society organizations that defined and mobilized public concern for women's issues. As Bessie House-Midamba reminds us, the role of African women in political development has historical antecedents. She writes that "Kenyan women's involvement in the political realm is not a new phenomenon; it has been manifested through a wide variety of associational organizations since the colonial period."[1]

Gender Work and Civil Society

The growth of women's NGOs in Kenya is a part of a global phenomenon. Increasingly, women are organizing on a variety of fronts to address a complex assortment of debilitating political, social, economic, and cultural issues. Valentine Moghadam, tracing the history of the rise of women's organizations in the Middle East and North Africa, has cogently outlined the key factors that have led to the rise of women's NGOs. Her analysis of the mobilization of women's organizations is applicable to the Kenyan context. As she states, "women's organizations can be understood as indispensable to democratization."[2] Valentine Moghadam argues that the growth of women NGOs has been partly a function of multilateral funding directed at them as partners in development because of their ability to bring attention to issues of human rights and good governance. Further, "modernizing" and "educated urban women" have been well positioned to put pressure on governments for women's equality. International factors such as women's conventions and conferences bring increasing recognition to the role of NGOs as an important sector for nurturing women's struggles. Other specific factors that have impelled women's NGOs include the reduction of public spending on basic services and the state's failure to provide for legal reforms and reproductive health services for women. These deficits have forced women's NGOs to take up advocacy on these questions. Finally, repressive political climates have driven women to establish or join civil society organizations to strengthen democratic movements.[3]

The participation of Kenyan women in public life has taken on a new vibrancy since the 2002 election. Individual women and women's NGOs have prioritized gender justice, women's rights, and gender equality as critical to sustainable development. The central theme of this chapter is the revival of the struggles in the form of a coalition inclusive of women's NGOs, individual women, and human rights organizations to participate in the negotiations to review the Kenya constitution. In particular, the chapter addresses the form of organizing and coalition building undertaken by the four local civil society organizations[4] that came together in early 2003 on a campaign to Safeguard the Gains for Women in the Draft Constitution. These four organizations, referred to hereinafter as the Coalition, were composed of NGOs with both a feminist agenda and a broader human rights mandate.

The Coalition engaged political processes in Kenya through dialogue, strategic alliances, collaboration, and lobbying to campaign for gender equality. While the work of safeguarding the gains for women in the draft constitution should be chronicled, it is also equally important to reflect on the processes of the campaign and the power of building strategic alliances. The Coalition sought to reinsert women's demands for social justice and to promote new social relations. The Coalition not only directed its activism at the Kenyan state but also at other civil society groups. Entry into the public and political domains for negotiating gender equality in the constitutional review process demanded that the strategic coalition of activists and intellectuals and their organizations conceptualize the normative frame for their commitment and formulate strategies for strengthening women's capacities for engagement and participation in the process of constitution making. Such struggles can be seen, understood, and situated within the context of ongoing broader democratic struggles in Kenya.

The premise of this chapter is that strategic alliances of diverse women at particular moments in history places them powerfully "to enrich the possibilities of rethinking and actualizing democratic practice."[5] By coming together in their diversity, women are better positioned to articulate an empowering discourse that can simultaneously uncover the heterogeneity of injustice,[6] contest domination and oppression, and develop vision and political action for democratic life. Therefore, this chapter conceptualizes the ways in which gender equality advocates have sought to understand and confront gender inequality. It brings attention to the factors and conditions that reconstituted the Kenyan public space for feminist organizing, action, and democratic engagement for gender equality. In so doing, the chapter charts how women organized as a coalition around the constitution making process to safeguard and further women's interests, rights, and freedoms in the Bomas draft constitution.

Additionally, the chapter looks at the discourses and processes of the Coalition's work, the way these discourses and processes were shaped during the review process, and some of the challenges of putting the acute concerns of Kenyan women into the agenda of the constitutional review process. Finally, it traces the lessons for strategic alliances and the increased synergies and work among civil society organizations that represent women's interests. It is a reflection on the conditions that have led to the successful outcomes and losses for Kenyan women.

Conceptualizing Gender Work

Gender equality and women's rights cannot be attained without the redistribution of power and resources. Such transformation requires just and fair social, political, economic, and cultural arrangements that facilitate and secure access to freedom and human rights. Gender equality and women's rights within the state are deeply affected by policy decisions taken at global, national, and local levels. Thus, the practices and structures that cause gender inequalities are recognized when society ceaselessly asks this question: what is the gender dimension of this social, political, economic, and cultural policy? Such questioning is then further connected to a feminist analysis of power relations. For only then is it possible to understand the links between policies and institutions that produce and perpetuate inequalities[7] and the sites of power for challenging and reconfiguring those relationships.

Addressing power relations means reconstructing gender relations, transforming patriarchal institutional practices, and questioning societal structures. Feminist theorizing of gender relations lays bare the complexities in institutionalized relationships of power between women and men, clarifying the diversity of experiences of inequalities and injustices and how they are sustained. A very powerful conceptual tool for feminist analysis is intersectionality, "enabling research and a springboard for social justice action agenda."[8] What intersectional analysis has done is "recognize that women find themselves positioned at the intersection of gender and several other identities grounded in political, cultural, racial, ethnic, age, ability and class lines among other identities."[9] Thus, the convergence of different types of disadvantage that structure the positions of women are made clearer in utilizing intersectionality. Disadvantage and discrimination can also be assessed for their specificity and multiplicity and are revealed at the intersection of those multiple identities with policies and laws that might perpetuate harm, discrimination, or create vulnerabilities for particular women. It is such contextualized understandings that have helped illuminate the nature of gender oppression and privilege thereby informing human rights work for women.

Claims for women's rights and the language of rights provide the vehicle for women to speak to the demand for equality. It is also the standard by which equality can be measured to shape societal behavior toward women. In claiming rights to equality, women have also strengthened equality theory—raising concerns about the equality discourse. Although the equal rights vision guarantees equal protection of the law to all, it has meant that women would be positioned for comparison with men where equal treatment would mean similarity to men.

Feminist analysis saw the difficult questions that emerged around comparing people who were not similarly situated and whose lived experiences were so different that formulating rights claims as if no differences existed reinforced discrimination. Feminist equality discussions have thus continued to focus on identifying the disadvantages or inequities that women experience because they are women. Feminist work also undertakes to articulate and bring recognition to the multitude of inequalities experienced by women and then seeks to develop solutions that are more often than not legal and political.

Transitional periods that offer opportunities for reviewing a constitution thus become strategic moments for articulating rights claims, such as the right to equality. This is the perfect moment to pressure the state to craft and implement a constitution that can best secure the enjoyment of human rights. Governments have specific human rights duties, namely to respect, protect, and fulfill rights. These duties require that states take a variety of steps to prevent, remedy, and punish violations of human rights. However, human rights are not just legal rules and duties, they are also ethical or moral principles guiding human relations. The implications are that nonstate actors, such as women's NGOs, other civil society organizations, and individuals have to take an instrumental role to campaign, lobby, and educate society to advance gender equality.

Feminist Organizing: The Politics of the Public Space

The circumstances that led to the birth of the Coalition need to be set out in chronological order, for they illustrate the process of ensuring that women stayed on the constitutional review agenda. In late 2002, prior to the constitutional review conference, Yash Ghai, chair of the Constitution of Kenya Review Commission (CKRC), together with commissioners to the CKRC, began a series of meetings with a select group of interested individuals, scholars, legal practitioners, and human rights activists. These individuals were drawn from universities and local NGOs to review and reflect on the comments and petitions presented by the Kenyan public on the draft bill of the Constitution of Kenya.[10] This proactive strategizing was intended to provide early input into contentious issues ahead of the review conference. Its mandate was to suggest possible solutions and positions on issues of conflict. These meetings also sought to develop improvements to the provisions in the draft constitution that were not well thought through. None of the Palacina decisions were intended to be binding upon the constitution commissioners who attended these meetings. Instead, these meetings, as part of the emerging myriad of political activities across the country, can be understood within the expanding Kenyan democratic space at a time of transition. Such forums, as sites of knowledge production, were crucial not only for the meanings and knowledge they would produce around constitutionalism, but also for their catalytic effect on political expression and the idea of new avenues for political participation.

It was thus the Palacina forum under the encouragement of Yash Ghai that urged women's input into the intellectual exchanges taking place within its forum,[11] hence my entry and participation in these meetings. As a director on the board of the Kenya Human Rights Commission (KHRC), I had an interest and focus on women's rights issues.[12] My invitation from Willy Mutunga, then executive director of KHRC, to participate in the Palacina forum led me to revisit the earlier submissions on women's issues with the intention of strengthening the language of the equality and gender provisions and ensuring that the content of the equality provisions furthered women's needs and rights.

The Palacina initiative would, however, come to be seen as threatening and would eventually be challenged by several of the commissioners and some politicians as subversive, while others saw the initiative as a taking over of the constitution making process by experts. It was accused of intending to take over the CKRC and the constitutional review conference. Such fears and animosity, widely played out in the national media as well, were in keeping with the pockets of fear wrought by the possible dramatic changes within the new transitional arrangements. Under these highly charged political conditions, all the commissioners withdrew from the Palacina meetings and the initiative ended. However, these first steps would signal the evolution of a concerted, organized, and determined collective effort around women, gender, and the production of a draft constitution by civil society organizations.

It was important to put women's issues on the agenda of this closed forum. But the critical and necessary work would ultimately require moving women's issues onto the wider national agendas of Kenyan women's organizations, political parties, and other civil society organizations. Women would, however, have to be equipped to participate in the constitutional conference to secure the gains provided by its human rights and equality framework. To paraphrase Jerald Zaslove, it is only the constituted public self that can act in protecting its individual and collective rights.[13]

Subsequently, in January 2003, Koki Muli, the executive director of the Institute for Education and Democracy (IED), an expert on representation and electoral politics, introduced Athena Mutua and me to Jane Kiragu, executive director of the Federation of Kenya Women Lawyers (FIDA-Kenya).[14] This group was joined by Grace Onyango, executive director of the League of Women Voters, and later by her successor, Cecelia Kimemia. The intention was to collaborate in order to amplify women's voices during the national constitutional conference that was scheduled to begin in April 2003.

The Coalition and the Constitutional Review Process

Constitutions . . . display a tendency—constitutive rather than contingent—to remain indifferent to the plight of those peoples who live outside history, whose destinies remain, as yet and perhaps always, unnarratable.[15]

Women understood the opportunity presented by the constitutional review process as a unique political chance to alter their unequal social and political positions by narrating and initiating particular actions to make the Kenyan state more accountable in gender-based matters. For, as Bessie House-Midamba notes about the Kenyan state, "the political reality is that the state continues to exercise inordinate control and power in determining the manner in which interaction occurs between citizens and the government . . . the rules of the game are not always clear."[16] The absence of viable institutions of governance to regulate political authority, together with a historic state antagonism to the language of democracy, a discourse that would make it possible to "propose the different forms of inequality as illegitimate and anti-natural . . . to make them equivalent as forms of oppression,"[17] had been continually made visible, challenged, and articulated by civil society organizations determined to write a different possibility. And Kenyan women as political subjects within civil society organizations have been cognizant of the need for engagement with the state to "insert their concrete reality" into current political discourses, "offering not only a critical and alternate vision of the situation in the country, but also a space to disarticulate oppression"[18] given the climate of transition and a draft constitution bill to usher in a democratic framework.

FIDA-Kenya was well placed as a woman's organization to facilitate the reflections on women's issues begun at Palacina by KHRC. FIDA-Kenya enjoyed a national reputation as a leading women's rights organization. It had been in the forefront in the struggle for women's access to legal justice and had substantial experience in national, regional, and international advocacy. It had also over the years continuously engaged the government on women's issues. The KHRC, on the other hand, was the only human rights NGO in the country to develop an organizational gender policy. The implementation of the policy was underway during the period of the constitutional review process. The KHRC and IED were, however, not publicly and visibly working on national gender issues, and were not publicly recognized as pursuing a women's rights agenda. But they had deep experience and links with the global human rights movement and a history of sustained pressure on the Kenyan state to enact its human rights commitments. They could productively engage with women's issues because as "a conceptual tool gender has been extensively and fruitfully used to transform the assumptions underlying legislation and international human rights frames."[19]

A cross section of local organizations was therefore placed to understand, articulate, and organize collaborations around the history of social justice demands for Kenyan women. To further strengthen and broaden the reach of this possible partnership, FIDA suggested the inclusion of the League of Kenya Women Voters (LKWV), an NGO with outreach at the grassroots level in several local communities, to provide the Coalition with community-based constituencies.

Organized as a coalition, FIDA, KHRC, IED, and LKWV sought to articulate how the lives of both women and men are oppressively structured. They would thus speak from a position of strength on the demands for the changes required to eradicate oppression. As a coalition, its mandate responded to the need for education to show that women's roles and positions are neither natural nor inevitable and are amenable to improvement. It would represent women's views, speak to women's subordination, and work with women to identify needs and map strategies to address gender issues within the review process. This is how the campaign to Safeguard the Gains for Women in the Draft Constitution began. It drew together five women representing four civil society organizations. The Coalition envisioned two key phases to its initiative. The first phase would involve engagement with the constitution making process, an exercise that would culminate in the adoption of a new constitution. The second phase was anticipated as the provision of civic education, advocacy, and policy development for the implementation of the new constitution.

The formation of a strategic alliance among four human rights organizations was born out of a clear recognition of the need for different strengths. The history of the women's movement in Kenya showed that there were a large number of multi-issue organizations pressing for women's issues in many different ways. By working in different ways that reflected their goals, often with fragmented relationships, these human rights organizations often duplicated functions and did not always have a unity of purpose on gender issues. Such challenges in the women's movement have further led to an unawareness of existing campaigns and shared views and a concurrent disbelief that the women's movement in Kenya has relevance to the needs of ordinary Kenyan women.

At their very first meeting, the four coalition organizations argued for the formation of a three-tier working structure made up of the core and equal leadership of the four organizations with the full responsibility of decision making, implementation, and accountability for the campaign to safeguard the gains for women in the draft constitution. The second tier would be composed of civil society organizations committed to women's issues and invited to bring self-identified, specific capacities and skills to the Coalition and the campaign in order to participate. The third tier would be women's organizations with broad national reach and community constituencies and with the human resources to share and dialogue with local communities about the campaign by the Coalition. There was, however, no attempt to formalize these structures or to develop memoranda of understanding that would govern the relationships or provide for specific responsibilities. The absence of formality in the structuring of the Coalition would eventually pose challenges to the alliances.[20] The core group's alliances with each other proceeded on the understanding that they were first and foremost making a personal commitment to the campaign. The five individuals in the core group also assumed that respective organization were committed to the cause.

Early on, the core team recognized that there was strength and potential of strategic, issue-specific, and transitory partnerships among civil society organizations for successfully negotiating demands with a variety of stakeholders, including the state. However, the core team was also cognizant that the monumental task of safeguarding and strengthening the gains for women in the draft constitution would require the conceptualization of a discursive platform upon which to frame political strategies for entrenching equality for Kenyan women in the constitution. The work demanded the building of a broad coalition for a progressive transformation of politics. The Coalition thus held consultative meetings with other civil society organizations[21] to develop its tiered structure and build consensus around goals, objectives, activities, and the assignment of organizational and individual tasks. These early deliberations by the core leadership team had one crucial objective: to build a powerful coalition. Uppermost on the agenda was a need to first establish an environment, prior to the conference, of shared unity of purpose around women's equality issues. Second, there was a need to share knowledge and understanding on the substantive progressive issues within the draft for women in order to build confidence and participation. Third, it was important to share widely the principles that the core team was developing to guide the campaign, for this would clarify the vision for social justice. Fourth, the Coalition took a tentative position on ten possible controversial issues that it sought to recommend to possible partners in order to determine negotiable and nonnegotiable positions for women in the draft constitution. The immediate result of the broad consultative meeting was the establishment of five working committees that incorporated a variety of interested individuals, women's, girl-child, and human rights organizations.

The first committee was the Conference Procedure Committee whose role was to analyze the complex conference procedures and translate them into language that would be easily and quickly understood by the delegates to the conference, especially women, and thus promote their ability to use them. The second was the Technical Committee to analyze and propose amendments to the draft provisions so that they could be available to conference delegates during the review process. This committee conducted research, developed and shared positions, discussion papers, and fact sheets to educate and inform debates on the gender issues within the constitutional debates. This committee also developed the alternative language proposals or amendments to the draft bill to strengthen women's gains. Furthermore, the committee provided technical support to women delegates during the review process.

The third committee was the Lobbying and Advocacy Team whose purpose was to identify provisions that required support, develop lobbying strategies, and monitor the progress of provisions during the constitutional conference. To do this effectively, the Coalition acquired an observer status at the review conference. The fourth was the Media Committee that was charged with the public communication and dissemination of the work of the Coalition. Lastly, there was the Training Committee mandated to educate and create awareness among all delegates and parliamentarians of relevant provisions and the alternative language suggestions on women's issues.[22] This committee would also provide training to provincial delegates on conference procedures.

The Coalition also made formal submissions to several groups on its interests and rationale for involvement in the conference and the need for support around its initiative. These groups included the Parliamentary Select Committee, the Constitution of Kenya Review Commission, as well as the full Parliament sitting in Mombasa to review the draft bill. The Coalition held consultative meetings with government ministers, several party leaders, civil society organizations, and delegates to the conference to press its campaign. These meetings and consultations were continuous as a political and pragmatic strategy for addressing change and resistance. The Coalition also shared its work for the campaign with several civil society organizations. No other NGO had their input ready and available for implementation so early in the constitution review process.

Gains for Women in the Draft Constitution

What issues are important to address in a constitution in order to establish a solid framework for gender equality? Writing on promoting gender equality in South Africa, Brigitte Mabandla noted that "it is possible for the constitution to be structured to address the demands of women and yet not to impede gender equality." She also added that "its language should not be neutral, and there must be a clear reference to men and women where such distinctions are necessary."[23] The draft constitution for Kenya was progressive on many women's issues. Responding to the political, social, and economic relations that structure and sustain women's subordination, the draft bill set about concretizing new conceptions that would direct "the state to be responsible and responsive to the demands of women."[24] Constitutional equality was guaranteed to both women and men save for the qualification for the application of Islamic law to people who professed the Muslim faith. Muslim women argued for this qualification seeing it as more protective of their interests.[25] The language of the equality clauses in the draft constitution was of particular significance to the Coalition. Its advocacy and crafting of language on equality recognized these limitations and called for "equality of results" and "equality under the law" and "equal benefit of the law." Such language would also validate affirmative action.

The bill of rights recognized and prohibited discrimination on the basis of sex, thus entrenching equality between the sexes. In so doing, it provided for a much-expanded regime of political, social, economic, civil, and cultural rights that strongly affirmed women's inclusion and reiterated state obligations to ensure those rights and freedoms for women. The draft thus provided for state compliance of its international obligations in respect of human rights. Of particular significance for women were rights that envisioned reproductive health, social security, education, housing, food, water, and sanitation. The homemaking work of women was also recognized as an important contribution to national development. At the end of the formal review process, many of these gains were retained with the key exceptions of "reproductive health rights" and the "right to life" articles that saw conservative forces reiterate discrimination and criminalization against women's autonomy[26] and self-determination with respect to abortion. The right to life article had the language of its provisions altered in ways that closed off any possibility of abortion rights while reproductive health rights were deemed unacceptable because they were perceived as framing rights around abortion.[27] The dominant debates also refused to go along with incorporating the demand for women's rights to ownership of land, vindicating the campaign by conservative cultural voices resistant to women's ownership of this strategic agricultural resource.[28]

Equality starts to become visible when women have a share in political power at all levels, but what is first required is the transformation of political structures and spaces. However, "the allocation of political resources and critical decision making power, still indicate unacceptable gender power balances . . . [and] one of the notable barriers to women's participation . . . , has been the male character of the structures of political recruitment, especially (into) political parties."[29] The draft constitution was far reaching in providing for increased representation for women in both elected and appointed posts and mandated the Mixed Member Proportional Representation (MMPR) system as an electoral system for achieving more elective seats for women at national and devolved levels. The draft required the state to direct funding to political parties that meet the "at least one-third representation" requirement for women. To alter the historical marginalization of women, the draft committed the state to provide for affirmative action as a mechanism for remedying the structural oppressions faced by women.[30] The Coalition sought to strengthen the language within these provisions on representation and affirmative action by arguing for a permanent principle of at least one third with the eventual goal of gender parity and gender balance.

The Coalition strongly supported the MMPR system.[31] However, it lost the initiative when women delegates chose the district representation system as an alternative way to ensure women better representation in the future. They argued for this as a way to enforce women-only seats in each district. Both the Coalition and women delegates were in agreement on the need to increase women's representation, but they disagreed on the political strategies for achieving it. The differences between the women delegates and the Coalition's choice of systems of representation would become very divisive, and several initiatives at consensus building failed with both sides firm about their respective stands. Koki Muli observed that the delegate's preference for district seats arose from several concerns that the women delegates voiced during debates and discussions, which also suggested a lack of understanding of the MMPR system.

The MMPR system's benefits for women remained unclear to many of the women delegates. Many women delegates continued to raise challenging and legitimate questions, including the following: Who decides who goes on the party list of the MMPR system; what quality of women will represent women in MMPR; how will women negotiate patronage and connections; and how should women deal with the divisive issue of urban elite women versus rural women in representation? Finally, the male character of political parties, their lack of democracy and accountability, together with their attendant inaccessibility and invisibility of women within them were also real concerns for many women delegates. Clearly these concerns by the women delegates seem to not have been adequately addressed. Delegates also wrongly perceived MMPR as encouraging nominations rather than elections.[32] Nevertheless, the delegates did not address how district seats would translate into real representation for women in a political environment where political parties remain the route into parliamentary politics.

The definition of citizenship is important for gender equality. National laws often abandon responsibility for some of its citizens.[33] For example, inequitable relations were inscribed into constitutional definitions of citizenship. Kenyan women generally fall outside the definition of citizenship, without power to pass their citizenship on to their children or to non-Kenyan foreign-born spouses, although such was not the case for Kenyan men. Given its power to define the existence and legality of individuals, laws in collusion with the state had denied women their rights to enjoy full citizenship. One of the gains for women in the draft constitution was that it rectified and granted equal citizenship rights to women and men. However, the fragility of women's citizenship rights was apparent even during the review process. Political conversations positioned Kenyan women married to foreign spouses as outside the protection of the Kenyan state and a threat to state security.

Under the Bomas draft constitution, the recognition and prohibition of multiple and simultaneous forms of oppression and the guarantee of security from violence from both public and private actors strengthened the environment for equitable relations. Another significant remedial device was the constitutional provision for a Gender Commission, an institution that would create and promote gender equity, equality, and advancement of women.[34] However, the state legislated a Gender Commission prior to the completion of the review process.

The draft had many critical gains for women, and several were safeguarded by the final Bomas draft. Nevertheless, as Adriana Hernandez has cautioned, "the transition to a democratic political culture is not automatic. . . . Authoritarian practices and thought are strongly rooted."[35] Indeed, many of these gains for women will continue to be challenged by the powerful paternalistic and often conservative discourses of culture that are reluctant to allow women equal status and access to resources as men. Additionally, the gains for women in the draft caused concern among many religious and conservative groups whose absolutist positions sought limitations to the scope of women's rights. These drawbacks are sure to lay the ground for continued struggles around the status of women.

Constitutional Discourses for Gender Equality

> Constitutions are bodies of rules that govern the operation govern-
> ments themselves. These rules recognize the power of the state in mak-
> ing and creating reality thus we need to look at and understand the
> power and function of the state to both enable and repress.[36]

The language of the Bomas draft constitution reaffirmed a commitment to the principles of democracy, social justice, constitutionalism, and the rule of law. The draft further reiterated the need for the full participation of women in the political, social, and economic life of the country and called for affirmative action in both appointive and elective posts. Given these gains for women in the draft, the Coalition developed a campaign that clarified, strengthened, and highlighted these principles for women.

As a first step, the Coalition developed several principles to guide it to Safeguard the Gains for Women in the Draft Constitution. The objective of the principles was to ensure that the debates and final outcomes of the constitutional review process would reflect the promised changes for women in accordance with democratic principles. The Coalition sought to deepen, clarify, and highlight the principles that would guide its campaign. These principles emphasized several areas. The first was social justice constructed as a commitment to the ethics, policies, structures, and measures to bring about just and fair social arrangements for all Kenyan people. Included here was a temporary measure of affirmative action for social justice to remedy discrimination and promote equality. The second was gender equality, equity, parity, and fair representation integrated as guiding principles to ensure respect, participation, and access to institutional power, resources, and an equal voice for women in determining the way their society was governed. Finally, the principle of gender mainstreaming was included as both a principle and strategy for creating an enabling environment to make gender a central variable in designing and implementing policies in all national spheres.

The draft constitution thus encompassed democratic principles. Athena Mutua wrote that the new legal landscape for women's rights that emerged promised changes for women in three ways: "First, it provided both in principle and in scheme the increased representation of Kenyans by women and for affirmative action for women and other disadvantaged groups. Second, it called for equality among and between women and men and laid the groundwork for this equality in specific provisions. Third, it created an institution through which gender concerns would be mainstreamed."[37]

The opportunity to draft a new constitution thus created conditions that saw gender equality and women's rights emerge as principles of democracy. The reality of women's lives in the current social order also signaled that gender sensitive language within a rights framework would require an inclusive and consultative process with a variety of groups. There was broad support and agreement among women to entrench women's rights despite differences among women on the specificity and content of those rights. Given that the constitution was a written document, it was important for the delegates to the constitutional review conference to understand the content of those rights, the language of the constitution, and the conference procedures for them to effectively participate and engage with its language. This was especially so for the women delegates whom the Coalition planned to target in shaping the language and content of the draft constitution, and thus shaping new perceptions about the need for gender equality enshrined in the constitution.

The opportunity to introduce new language while safeguarding the gains in the original draft was presented at the constitutional conference. Each provision of the constitution would be negotiated line by line. Thus, an imperative Coalition strategy was to work with language and create common meanings of the words in the constitution.[38] Toward this end, a curriculum was developed and implemented by the Coalition during the provincial training of delegates prior to the start of the conference and in subsequent workshops with women delegates during the review process.

The language of democracy that was articulated by Kenyan women as political subjects through their civil society organizations, argued a different possibility by offering "not only a critical and alternate vision of the situation in the country, but also a space to disarticulate oppression."[39] Given the centrality of gender equality in the draft constitution, the Coalition sought to safeguard ten non-negotiable positions on the following issues in so far as they had consequences for women's equality. The positions identified were indeed already present in the CKRC draft, but the work of highlighting them provided an opportunity for further conceptual development and the normative basis for ending gender discrimination and inequality. These positions included principles of democracy, accountability, transparency, human rights, social justice, and respect for diversity of groups and individuals; equality and equity in form and fact; social justice policies and the one-third principle in all appointed and elective posts; the Gender Commission; the Mixed Member Proportional Representation (MMPR) and an additional 90 seats; women to occupy all new 90 additional seats in the National Assembly; requirements that all political parties be democratic, support women candidates, and that funding be tied to these requirements; maintenance of the Kadhi's Court because of social justice and equality; current devolution requirements of 50 percent of women; and the bill of rights as written in the CKRC draft with gender fairness included in the proposed changes.[40]

Support for these positions provided an opportunity to entrench the fundamental rights of Kenyan women. The government structure was also of fundamental interest to the Coalition for "the government should be structured to facilitate gender equality at national, regional and local levels."[41] Thus, the most important question for women was how to build mechanisms into the structure of the government that would guarantee a parliament that is a strong instrument of democracy and is able to ensure that women are not discriminated against.[42]

The coalition was interested in the nature of the executive because "the choice made must enhance democracy,"[43] while "the judiciary must be structured to safeguard the representation of women at all levels." Supporting positions on democracy, gender equality, and human rights was also a way to shape, and if necessary, defend women's empowerment. While hosting workshops and consultative meetings with women delegates to the conference, the Coalition worked at ensuring representation and collective input from the women delegates on these issues.[44]

In Kenya, constitution making was perceived as a process that was enhanced by the participation of all Kenyans. Consequently, the Coalition developed a wide range of activities to engender and lobby delegates in order to raise awareness and support about the nature of gender issues and questions of specific concern to women. The Coalition's strategies for implementing a women-friendly constitution included provincial training workshops for conference delegates and continued seminars in various forums to support provisions that reflected the Coalition's principles. During the review process, the Coalition provided delegates with rapid responses to the drafting of motions that dealt with women's issues by proposing alternative language to improve the language for women's rights under the draft constitution. The coalition believed that research and activism could mobilize support for change from both outside and inside the conference. The Coalition, therefore, organized and participated in radio and television programs, and wrote and published articles in the press. As part of the activist campaign, presentations were made to the government, including the Parliamentary Select Committee and members of parliament.

The Coalition mobilized women delegates to the conference, especially those representing women's organizations. Mobilizing women was an internal strategy to encourage more women to foster commitment to women's interests. The women representing women's organizations participated at the conference because the advocacy of women's civil society organizations had ensured their inclusion. At various times during the constitutional review conference, the Coalition sought to be visible and present. The Coalition produced three handbooks, a training manual[45] for the conference delegates, a delegates' handbook, a parliamentarian handbook, and brochures on language proposals to strengthen the gender provisions. All these manuals and publications would guide delegates by providing information on alternative language, the campaign's principles, nonnegotiable positions, and concept papers on a variety of topics relevant to providing education on the constitutional debates of the conference. Information and education were especially important in helping to promote change in knowledge, informing decision making, and even addressing resistance to particular positions.

The Coalition took out advertisements in the national press. It produced a bi-weekly conference newspaper publication called *Yawezekana*[46] to report on emerging gender issues during the review processes and to capture the debates and positions taken by the delegates on women's issues. Finally, at the end of the first, third, and final sittings of the conference, the Coalition produced audits of the review process to ensure that the reporting of the conference was consistent with the discussions and to capture and share the retention and expansion of gains for women at the end of the constitution review conference. These audits by the Coalition also served a wider democratic purpose, for the mandate of CKRC stipulated that the CKRC was accountable to the people of Kenya and that the outcome of the review process should reflect the wishes of the people. The Coalition audits were thus intended to supplement the conference's own reports to ensure that debates had indeed been correctly captured and the final provisions reflected those deliberations.

The Role of Women's Civil Society Organizations

There is a body of new literature and exploratory studies that address gender discourses in systems of national governance.[47] One particularly significant and recent series of comparative studies initiated and funded by INSTRAW, addresses "the means and strategies for impact on the political process and its outcomes."[48] It provides this chapter with a constructive lens for a final reflection on "how women, given the persistent structural inequalities, overcome major hindrances to their prospects for active involvement at all levels of governance."[49] My own reflections are colored by my own position in the coalition. However, I begin this process of reflection partly to open up dialogue with other women and partly to deepen my understanding of the issues and increase potential of working across differences in the Kenyan political agenda. My reflections on women organizing women to represent women's interests are divided into two parts: the transitional context and the building strategic alliances.

Organizing in a Transitional Context

Previous Kenyan governments have scored poorly on their international commitments to human rights and gender equality.[50] Laws discriminatory to women remain on the books, women continue to be underrepresented in the elected and appointed positions, and the pervasive and visible problem of sexual and domestic violence remains inadequately addressed. Additionally, the inadequacy and inequity of interventions with regard to minimum standards of social, economic, and cultural rights, and the continued absence of respect for the law have heightened the need for a democratic constitution.

The current Kenyan government, which ran on a platform of reform and openness to democracy, had ample opportunities to engage in discourses of transformation. Furthermore, civil society organizations, which had always been at the forefront of monitoring the state, have continued in their watchdog role, although some have shaped the nature of the political transition in partnership with the state. This new role for civil society organizations was especially apparent in the run-up to the 2002 national elections when, for example, women's organizations released a ten-point "Kenya Woman's Agenda for Change" that laid out the acute concerns of women and the necessary steps to address them for women voters and political parties.[51]

The formation of the Coalition grew out of this political environment, and it harnessed a strategic moment to influence the shape of the new constitution that was being crafted with the new government's commitment "to serve the people . . . and . . . create an enabling environment for its citizens."[52] This taking up of gender issues during periods of transition has been evident in other African countries, such as South Africa, where a political transition has taken place. Some researchers have argued that "if this opportunity is seized relatively early in the transition process, then the likelihood of an engendered political agenda would increase."[53]

Building Strategic Alliances

The Coalition took a public lead in bringing debates on gender equality to constitutional discourses. It called upon other women's organizations to join in elaborating a new gender-sensitive constitution. These efforts by the Coalition generated a broad awareness of gender issues at the constitutional conference. Furthermore, occasions were created by the Coalition and by international NGOs for women from political parties, women's organizations, and women and men gender activists, academics, and the media play various roles to ensure that the constitution continued to prioritize women's issues and was gender sensitive.[54]

The Coalition had a very visible profile in the gender politics of the constitutional review process. It physically set up a tent at the conference site and engaged women delegates in its campaign priorities.[55] The CKRC had already set many of the priorities for Kenyan women prior to the national conference. The Coalition was not intent on duplicating this work. Instead, it seized the moment and the enabling framework already provided by the CKRC draft constitution. The Coalition was well positioned to do so because it had brought together diverse individuals, organizations and their constituencies. The Coalition was effective because it collaborated with diverse groups and individuals that had a wide range of technical and theoretical experience, expertise, capacity, and access to funding. These resources enabled it to engage in the reform process, to intervene in gender policy debates, to initiate public consultations, to harness politicians, activists and academics, and to have access to state institutions. The unity of purpose among the four core organizations also stemmed from their own institutional commitment to the constitutional reform processes and the fact that the lead persons were women with compatible and shared interests and commitment to engendering Kenyan politics.

There is strategic value in linking women and human rights organizations because feminists are not only women and not all women are feminists. Feminist work does not have to be something that arises only from a person's experience of oppression. In working for an equal society, men must be women's allies. Otherwise, women cannot hope to prevail in public life.[56] Another important factor was the recognition of the need for different kinds of leadership appropriate to different types of work applicable to different moments in the life of the Coalition. Right at the beginning of the Coalition, this recognition was explicitly stated. Some individuals in the Coalition were intellectuals and activists positioned to collaborate in two ways. First, it was necessary to have intellectual, gender, and legal expertise to intervene authoritatively to produce research and knowledge to inform the campaign and to equip all participants to have an impact on campaign processes from a gender perspective.[57] Second, activists already had a history of consistent pressure on government to deliver on commitments and had worked at the grassroots level to provide experiential knowledge.[58] Thus, each could lend authority and creative energy to the other's voice while their combined institutional affiliations provided "organizational leverage" to move equality issues forward.

The five core leadership members of the Coalition were a multiethnic group of women, which was unprecedented given the historic divisions and fragmentation among and between women's NGOs.[59] The urban-rural divide among Kenyan women would be a cause of divisiveness among women delegates and the Coalition. The Coalition was often accused of being an urban-oriented and upper class women's initiative. This is an attack that serves to constrain the women's movement in Kenya. Valentine Moghadam resists such "debilitation or delegitimation," to insist that although "many women's NGOs are elite, professional, and middle-class . . . [it] does not mean that they do not have a wider impact." She has written that

> The very existence of women's NGOs challenges the patriarchal order in rather profound ways. To the extent that women's organizations contribute to the democratization process, the creation of a democratic society and a civic culture, and to the extent that they seek to participate in the development process and in politics, the women's organizations are important in and of themselves . . . for the articulation of more feminist demands, as well as women's perspectives.[60]

Ayesha Imam elaborates this point further and addresses the limitations presented by the various divisions among women. She observes that to help bridge these divides, women need to call attention to the fact that differences do indeed exist among women while simultaneously recognizing that they share "compatible interests as women and as citizens and in the short-medium term gender subordination and class exploitation must be fought for by all women, for all women's [gender] interests can be fought for irrespective of religion, ethnicity, caste, and culture."[61]

Conclusion

The social and political demand of feminism is to achieve equality for women. The influence of the Coalition working on a feminist agenda was felt in providing leadership, rapidly defining and articulating demands, sharing knowledge, raising awareness, successfully mobilizing resources, and exercising influence with delegates and politicians. The presence of women at the constitutional conference was a unique moment to mobilize them nationally on account of gender. In addition, there was great potential to mobilize men by merging gender concerns into the wider democratic struggles of reordering the state through constitution making.

The Coalition believed that virtually all issues on the constitutional agenda had a deep relevance for women. At first the Coalition did not focus on the entire draft constitution. Initially, it only focused on non-negotiable positions and interests in the specific provisions dealing with women. However, the whole draft constitution very rapidly became increasingly important for the Coalition's campaign as the conference advanced. Many contentions arose forcing the Coalition to develop and publish its own model proposals for the whole draft constitution.[62] This evolution for the Coalition was born out of the recognition that the structures of governance proposed in the draft would impact the lives of women. Indeed, those structures would either ensure, promote, and protect the equality interests of women, or be detrimental to them. The final draft that emerged at the end of the debates accepted many of the recommendations of the Coalition. However, some of the draft's content also represented some important losses for women. Even though Kenya now provided a transitional political environment open to democratization, the political and cultural milieu was still unfavorable to particular types of gender protections and struggles.

The Coalition had been a point of connection for women at the conference and its success at organizing women was recognized by both women and men conference delegates. This acknowledgment led to increased levels of activity on the creation of awareness and lobbying. Many delegates reached out for help from the Coalition. Even the CKRC selected Coalition members as experts to the conference. This was a clear indication that the Coalition was reaching and influencing the constitutional review process and that the presence of NGOs at such discussions was normal and accepted.

It is encouraging that the Coalition's work, which was structured around emancipatory discourses of social justice, equality, fair representation, and respect for diversity, continued after the national constitutional conference. The constitutional stalemate around contentious issues in the draft constitution gave the Coalition an opportunity to realign itself to serve new strategic ends and interventions. The Coalition was restructured to include new organizations and leave off old ones.[63] Importantly, the Coalition sustained the work of educating and lobbying members of parliament about women's issues and the work of the government in implementing its international agreements regarding women. The work of forging consultative relationships with members of parliament and parliamentary committees did not stop. Much of this work was directed at engendering national policy and continued to bring the individual core Coalition members into continued strategic alliances.[64] The Coalition therefore remained instrumental, but at decreased levels, in drawing attention to the issues of women within the law and the draft constitution. Furthermore, the Coalition's work showed that "the capacity of women's organizations is enhanced by partnerships and shared values . . . [with aligned] NGOs able to harness the resources of expertise and funding that are best able to engage with reform processes."[65]

There are, however, some discouraging signs. Some strong civil society leaders left to join the government, leaving many of these organizations struggling without well-developed institutional transition mechanisms. This situation poses new challenges to organizing around women's needs and establishing more egalitarian alliances and partnerships. Furthermore, the normative discourses deployed in the name of custom and religion to legitimize discrimination and inequality need to be continually contested and reframed if they are not to "become crystallized in international and national normative frames."[66]

Women's NGOs have had a history of combining forces at international meetings to impact on international treaties, conventions, and conferences by ensuring gender mainstreaming. These forms of coalition building have not been replicated successfully at the national level. And yet, given the fact that women's NGOs "utilize similar vocabulary to describe women's disadvantage and the desired alternatives,"[67] it behooves women's organizations to utilize the assets they each carry for combined strategic efforts to promote equality. Strategic coalitions provide women with a promising means of ensuring that states implement their international commitments to women.

However, the Coalition painfully learned that the Safeguard the Gains for Women in the Draft Constitution campaign could only succeed if individual women from different NGOs and diverse locations came together around a common concern. This emphasis on the individuals was highlighted by Marilyn Porter and Saparinah Sadli, who elucidated that the "greatest achievements within UN [negotiating] processes begin when women work primarily as individuals and not as 'representatives' of their NGOs."[68] They called attention to personal relationships that can create other linkages to incrementally build alliances.

Finally, four important lessons emerged from the Coalition processes. First, there still remains a need for greater clarity on contextualizing gender issues and articulating the questions of gender, class, and the state. Second, further analysis regarding the emerging global concerns that affect gender within the Kenyan context is required to help develop informed policies and intervention strategies.

Such endeavors, especially the intersections of the political and the theoretical, call for research within academia to benefit the women's movements in Kenya.[69] Third, it is important to have men involved in the engendering processes and men as political allies "understanding that women's liberation is a necessary part of the conditions for their own liberation."[70] This remains part of the critical and inclusive work.

Finally, the more complex lesson is that a coalition's membership will realize that at various moments in the partnership that particular issues must be worked out *collectively*. These could include, for example, what the goals of the initiative would be, what issues need to be addressed, and how to engage with those issues. *Separately and equally* its members will also find that there are areas and issues that will require the specific skills, capacities, and resources of the individual members in recognition of their differences, and the assets that they offer to the coalition. There will be periods when the work to be done requires the creation of *specific groupings* among the individual members, or even reaching out to new individuals, around specific tasks or activities. As women build coalitions to advance their rights claims they will find that their strategic needs will encompass *information, time, resources, key state contacts,* and *coordination.*

PART III

Donors and Grantees: Convergences and Divergences

CHAPTER SEVEN

Donors and Human Rights NGOs in East Africa: Challenges and Opportunities

Connie Ngondi-Houghton

THIS CHAPTER SCRUTINIZES the relationship between donors and human rights organizations in East Africa, with a special focus on Kenya. It pays special attention to what motivates funders and analyzes several elements of donor-donee relationships. It explores how those complex relationships affect the nature of human rights organizations. The chapter acknowledges that the state, donors, and the market contest access to civil society space in Africa. It contends that donors have a far greater influence on human rights organizations than should be the case. This makes African civil society too dependent on donors. This influence extends to how NGOs network, develop advocacy strategies, and form their identity and political consciousness. It also largely determines whether NGOs can become sustainable. Finally, it distorts their vision for human rights agency and social transformation.

Donors define human rights NGOs as units of civil society, determine their reality, and the outcomes of their intentions. This unequal and patronizing relationship undermines human rights work, and I explore ways of reducing its centrality in human rights work. In doing so, I attempt to take the discourse to the structural questions of trade, debt and aid, and give consideration to more innovative ways of local resource mobilization.

The chapter uses an approach that is reflective of African associational life and defines human rights organizations in broad terms to include NGOs and all other associations within communities, whether formal or informal, long or short term, organized, episodic, or sporadic, which have donor relationships with either traditional donors, the state or other NGOs. The focus, however, is primarily on foreign donors and on funding to formal organizations. It draws analogies of the identified challenges to most donor/donee relationships across the board.

Since this is not a new inquiry, the chapter builds on existing literature on donor/donee relationship, especially with reference to developing countries.[1] It also draws on research work on the relationship between donors and civil society in Africa by the International Society for Third Sector Research (ISTR) through its Africa Research Network Meetings.

The Identity and Rationale of Donors

Who are the donors? Why are they in East Africa? And why do they fund human rights NGOs in this region? These questions are rarely asked by human rights organizations. When they are posed, NGOs respond with a mixture of annoyance and even slight indignation. Humility does not come easily to organizations that usually occupy the high moral ground.[2]

It has been the policy of the bilateral development organizations of industrialized states such as the United States Agency for International Development (USAID), the Swedish International Development Agency (SIDA), and their British (DFID), Canadian (CIDA), German, Norwegian, and Danish (DANIDA) counterparts to support development and democratization. This section largely reiterates what others have already articulated: that these organizations have their own agendas. These are calculated formal interests of foreign governments that are intended to pursue human moral values only or to support NGOs and push democracy for the sake of the people of East Africa. These goals are incidental to larger objectives. The push for political democracy in East Africa is ultimately of an economic function, as is the support of civil society.

Public and private donors did not come to East Africa simply to fund civil society. If South Africa is anything to go by, donors will not always fund civil society. Donor funding is essentially the story of the historically managed development of the African state. The basic agenda of donors is to construct the nature of the African state and its institutions. Few are concerned with its citizens and the building of citizenship, although this is also an important element of democracy. Illiberalism and hostility to ethnic pluralism together with a marginal economy have led to an overextended and inept African postcolonial state. This was compounded by neoliberal reforms that distorted African political economies.[3] As a result, the state had to be shrunk and a distinction made between the public and free market spheres. Protectionist policies were to be abandoned, the civil service downsized, state-owned enterprises privatized, and barriers to trade removed. The state would then become a mere regulatory agency.[4]

After the fall of communist states in Eastern Europe in the late 1980s, the West argued that democracy would only triumph if coupled with economic reforms in the developing world. The pursuit of liberal democratic and economic reforms henceforth became the raison d'être for Western donors.[5] Their first target was the state. They now sought to reform the authoritarian state they supported during the Cold War. However, they underestimated the depth of the roots of autocracy and the tenacity of its beneficiaries. Frustrated with the obstinacy of the state against pressure from conditionality, they turned to the agency of civil society organizations, the most established of which were human rights organizations.

In Kenya, for instance, political aid conditionality began in 1990. The Americans led the way by suspending aid and tying its resumption to political and legal reforms. Denmark suspended aid on grounds of corruption and mismanagement.[6] The final blow came when the Consultative Group of donors for Kenya suspended balance-of-payment support to Kenya awaiting further progress on a select number of governance issues. This pressure broke the tyrannical rule of the Moi regime, and thereafter the government released political prisoners and repealed one-party law to allow political competition.

The split along ethnic lines of opposition parties to the KANU regime led to Moi's victories in the 1992 and 1997 multiparty presidential and legislative elections. The KANU regime maintained its autocratic political culture marked by persecution of the opposition, heightened corruption, and impunity for human rights violations. These events revealed that the constitutional reforms of 1992 had only superficially opened up the political space, but they had not instituted a democratic culture or democratic institutions. This is what led to a disintegration of purpose by democracy donors. This included even the most politically conservative donors, such as the British, who had directly used their aid power to force political reforms.

It is in the aftermath of the elections that the real character and interests of various donors become most apparent. The French and Japanese immediately delinked political reforms from aid. Other major bilateral donors, including the United States, Britain, the Netherlands, Canada, and Denmark, followed suit with the resumption of aid.[7] The Japanese had never been enthusiastic about democratic reforms and seemed unconcerned with corruption. They did not want to jeopardize their investments in Kenya. The French had vested interests in aid resumption since their principal interest was Kenya's debt servicing capability. This was because their assistance to Kenya was not in the form of grants but of supplier credits. The French needed to have budgetary assistance resumed so that Kenya could pay French creditors.

But Italians also delinked aid from political reforms. Among those who imposed conditionality, the British and the Germans turned out to be moderates. Instead of suspending aid the moderates used aid as a carrot to support projects they felt would advance certain reforms. In the early 1990s, the British had extensive economic interests to protect with investments of close to U.S.$700 million, compared to only U.S.$200 million invested by the United States. The British interest was their investment, and the opportunity to continue and perpetuate British influence and linkages.[8]

This left the United States, Sweden, Denmark, and Canada as the main conditionality donors. These donors had witnessed the pressure by local democracy forces for political reforms. Their interests in reforms seemed to dovetail neatly, almost naturally, with those of NGOs. They shifted strategy from using direct bilateral aid to pressuring the state for democratic reforms and to funding civil society organizations to lobby the state for positive change. Politics by proxy rapidly took, at least partly, the place of diplomacy.[9] As a result, aid from the pro-democracy donors decreased significantly. The United States led the way with a decrease of 74 percent within a decade.[10] In the mid-1990s, USAID became the leading civil society donor followed by SIDA and DANIDA. Donors sought to empower civil society to confront the state as a way of fostering liberal democracy.

Other significant supporters of civil society in Kenya were the German foundations and the Ford Foundation.[11] The Ford Foundation, a private American foundation, had supported advocacy organizations in East Africa since the 1980s. Civil society was then associated with so-called "community-driven development," a term that referred almost exclusively to grassroots communities.[12] Civil society was not a reference to governance or to institution building. It was the accomplice of a political project, namely, the democratization of the public space through community participation. Other funders were international development organizations such as Oxfam through NOVIB. It seems clear that donors pursue their own interests and only support particular initiatives in East Africa when there is a mutual convergence of goals. Nor are donors motivated by the grand visions of civil society groups per se, or their passionate belief in democratic ideals. Rather, donors are interested in efforts that achieve certain ends.

It is important to keep in mind that these same donors, who are essentially foreign governments, were not interested in democratization in East Africa before the 1990s. They supported tyrannical regimes throughout Africa and the developing world for decades as a means of guarding their strategic interests during the Cold War. The dynamics of the world order are fluid. The United States, the sole superpower, can no longer presume widespread legitimacy in the world because its actions have fomented anti-Americanism in most corners of the globe. It is clear, for example, that the United States is not shy to overlook democracy in its self-declared war against terror. That war is nothing but a proxy for advancing U.S. interests. In this context, Africa remains at the bottom of priorities for the United States and other donors. Even the little aid to civil society in the region could be shifted elsewhere in the world should donor interests change.

Finally, other factors affect donor funding. Until now, most activities of human rights advocacy organizations have targeted the state for political reforms. However, with the growth of the sector in the direction of economic social and cultural rights, and the focus this brings to non-state actors such as transnational corporations, multilateral organizations, and international trade agreements, donors may reconsider their support for NGOs. Advocacy on matters that touch on economic interests, such as debt relief, is a sensitive matter for donors. This is where the goals of the donors may diverge from those of civil society organizations.

Imposed Ideological Frameworks

When the Cold War ended, communism collapsed in the Soviet bloc and a wave of political democratization swept the globe. The West led a campaign to universalize liberal ideology and infuse it throughout the developing world. This democratic project coincided with local demands for "popular democracy" in Kenya that had gathered momentum since the 1980s. The political air was just right and the timing perfect. In a short time, a union of purposes was formed between the local pro-reform forces in the political class and civil society, and the pro-democracy bilateral donors. The common purpose was that of ending authoritarianism and installing democracy. The union was characterized by the dazzling appeal of money on the side of donors, the passion for democratic ideals by civil society, and the quest for power by the pro-reform faction of the political class.

The product of this tri-union of forces more than a decade later is an infantile liberal democracy. Whatever happened to the popular social democracy that Kenyans had struggled for in the 1970s? What ideological framework did the pro-reform political elite and the opposition parties pursue after 1991? What about the civil society organizations? There seems to have been a paucity of ideas about either the meaning of democracy or an inadequate articulation of the project of democratization. But the proponents of reform may also have lacked conviction and passion to defend its tenets in the face of unprecedented amounts of aid money. Wachira Maina has argued that in early 1990s, key democracy donors in Kenya shopped for "good NGOs" to support. The result was donor overfunding and civil society underconsumption.[13] The "good organizations" that were overfunded included leading human rights and rule of law groups such as the Kenya Human Rights Commission (KHRC), the Federation of Kenya Women Lawyers (FIDA-Kenya), and the Centre for Governance and Development (CGD).

Human rights and the rule of law have been the core areas of focus for USAID and SIDA, the two funders that were front-runners in the pro-democracy aid campaign. Liberal democracy, on its principles of equality and the rule of law, finds expediency in the agency of human rights, albeit very narrowly defined within its ideology, and in the authority of the rule of law with its tenets of equality and order. The focus on these organizations was strategic. Some of them had been struggling with barely enough funds to pay any staff for years before the arrival of the pro-democracy donors. It was a boom. They grew fast and in their fervor forgot to ask the right questions.

Ideologies ought to be based on particular political, social, and economic contexts. The priorities for African countries are democracy, sustainable development, and poverty reduction. East African countries have had liberal democracy imposed on them by Western countries. The results have not been entirely pleasant. The grafting was so swift and sudden that the African forces involved, including civil society, had no time to think and ask important questions. Is liberal democracy appropriate for an African country like Kenya? What is the relationship between liberal democracy and economic development? Is democracy really essential for economic development as argued by the neoliberal ideology? Can African countries achieve economic growth with other forms of democracy or indeed without democracy as happened in Asian and Latin American countries? Do African governments have the capacity to simultaneously undertake political reforms to institutionalize liberal democracy while at the same time undertaking economic reforms as prescribed by multilateral institutions and donors? Can these reforms lead to the reduction of poverty?

Liberal democracy is a political system and culture that is a product of Western civilization as now championed by the United States. The democratization crusade seeks to impose the institutionalization of liberal democracy in African countries. But as a result of complex and mixed experiences, Africa has not evolved for itself a dominant and suitable form of democracy. Most African countries have been independent for approximately four decades. They have very poor, heterogeneous populations with weak economies. Most have gone through internal conflict, have weak states, fragile institutions, and suffer deep socioeconomic and political fissures. These are the states that have been pressured into institutionalizing liberal democracy. In these circumstances, liberal democracy has been argued to be unsuitable and inappropriate for Africa.[14]

The argument here is not that democracy is unsuitable for Africa. It is important to recall that the African people have been seeking democracy for a long time.[15] They fought for it to end colonialism. They have been fighting for it since independence, when the ruling elites imposed undemocratic and oppressive rule on them. Africans want and have always wanted democracy. The question is what kind of democracy is suitable for Africa, and how it could be attained. The tenets of liberal democracy are not only unsuitable for African countries but are a negation of humanistic morality on which the integral idea of human rights is based. The core principles of human rights are *human dignity, equal worth, liberty,* and *brotherhood.* But Western nations, especially the United States, have constructed human rights discourse on market morality. This focuses on individual freedoms, such as legal and property rights. This construction has haunted the human rights project from its inception. NGOs must appreciate these tensions that underline their work and are part of donor philosophy.

The Universal Declaration of Human Rights, the movement's founding document, is illustrative of the tensions in human rights. Ideological and philosophical divisions between nations were evident during the drafting of the UDHR. The negotiators and the drafters faced at least two ideological and philosophical conundrums. One was moral pluralism. Even though all sides had been shocked by the carnage of World War II, there was no moral consensus on how to prescribe a future society. The second conundrum was that of individualism versus community, or state, that pitted Western capitalist nations in their defense of individualism against the socialist and communalist societies. Theoretical consensus was never reached on these contentious questions. Jacques Maritain, a philosopher and one of the most active members of the UNESCO committee to study the feasibility of a charter of rights, reconciled the conundrums on a practical rather than an intellectual premise. Maritain recognized that agreement among the committee members could be achieved "not on common speculative notions but on common practical notions, not on the affirmation of the same conception of the world, man and knowledge, but on the affirmation of the same set of convictions concerning action."[16]

Maritain explained that theory is incurably impersonal because anyone from any point of view should be able to examine a theory and falsify or verify it in an objective way. Recalling what had brought them all there—the horrific events of the war—he posed two questions that broke the pluralist moral logjam. Are there not some things so terrible in practice that no one will publicly approve of them? Are there not some things so good in practice that no one will want to seem opposed to them? This allowed the committee to proceed with its work. Its members could stand on principle and avoid the trap of moral indifference and relativism. The formulation distinguished between agreement in theory and agreement in practice and created a reconciliatory background against which the UDHR was formulated. The development of the principles of the universality, indivisibility, and interdependence of rights was meant to preempt the contortion or biased interpretation of rights through the use of subjective theories, ideologies, and philosophies.

Even though the UDHR was accepted by most UN member states at the time, the central contradictions between market individualism and group rights and communalist morality has persisted. The core principles that cement the integrity of human rights—universality, interdependence, and indivisibility—are still contested because of the failure to agree on a single dominant morality. These contestations continue to impede the implementation of the human rights corpus. Proponents still continue to interpret human rights documents selectively according to their own ideologies and moralities. The United States, which is the sole superpower, has complicated the matter by its vociferous opposition to the universality and indivisibility of all rights.

Theoretically, human rights should engender social justice because of the underlying morality of the project of rights. But the neoliberal conception of the human person, which now drives the United States, is extremely narrow and selective. It identifies as most fundamental the element of "liberty" of the human person, and therefore champions "freedom" as the interpretative framework for all other elements and the value on which to base a social justice theory. It is based on the core ideas of perfect individual freedom, the free market, and the integration of the world economy. This narrow conceptualization of freedom upholds the principle of equality of all citizens in law, but does not address the question of social equity. Abstractly, the rule of law assumes that all are equal before it, but the neoliberal framework does not require that people live in dignity, a core tenet of human rights. To the contrary, the theory of laissez-faire accepts such phenomena as poverty and social inequality among citizens and nations as a natural outcome of the right and freedom of the individual to choose. It anticipates and accepts social inequity.

Neoliberalism therefore generates a conception of formal rights that protects individual freedom, the free market, and globalization. In neoliberalism, human rights focus on civil and political rights, the market rights of property, order, and security. These are protected and realized within the context of the rule of law by guaranteeing equal treatment and order within the political framework of democracy and good governance. Yet for the majority of Africans that live on less than a dollar a day, equality is a dry, empty, and rhetorical figment that delivers nothing to them. They lack the means to realize a variety of rights such as access to courts, transportation, and legal representation. What use are property rights when one cannot afford a meal? Many people cannot even sell their produce or their labor, lack access to credit, and cannot compete with foreign investors. For the poor, these rights do not accord them basic human dignity, equality, or freedom.

Kenyan human rights organizations, such as the KHRC and the ICJ (K), initially worked on civil and political rights. But they have realized the limitation of formal rights in the struggle to combat poverty and inequity in the country. They broadened their conceptualization of human rights to include economic, social, and cultural rights. Politically, this is a movement towards social democracy, or what Arche Mafeje has called new democracy in which "the livelihood of citizens will not be contingent on ownership of property but on equitable access to productive resources."[17] It is a difficult task in a political and economic framework in which the principles of universality, interdependence, and indivisibility of human rights are deeply contested. These strategic changes by human rights organizations echo the views of African intellectuals in the last few years that liberal democracy per se will not work in Africa. As Mukandala Rwekaza observed,

> Even if one leaves out the extreme cases, for example Sierra Leone, Liberia, and Somalia, democratic development in many countries is on trial. No matter the yardstick or the standard that is used to measure democratic transition and consolidation, the results cannot be in doubt. . . . All in all, it is hard to escape the conclusion that liberal democracy is not faring well in Africa . . . even if liberal democracy was pushed to its logical limits . . . grave economic, social and political problems would still remain.[18]

Dependency and Limited Visions

The visions of most human rights organizations read like a manifesto for social justice. Some are radical, even revolutionary. They envision a society characterized by independence, equity, equality, peace, and justice, and where the hegemonies of the traditional oppression such as economic exploitation, dominant culture, class, and sexism are neutralized. Some call for a total transformation of the economic, social, and political orders in society. They recognize that many of these oppressive orders thrive on entrenched beliefs, attitudes, customs, and norms that have been deliberately designed to intimidate and control.

The central pillar of neocolonialism is dependency on Western countries, the most visible string of which is resources. But the more insidious and effective tool is the control of the psyche. The long-term strategy for perpetuating dependency is the propaganda that the West is the center of the universe, that Western culture is the progressive and inevitable culture of humanity, and that the African people need to emulate it or be doomed. This is coupled with the notion that African culture is primitive and retrogressive, and that Africans are dim. African ethnicity is portrayed as anathema to development, an evil to be rooted out. Instead, development and modernity are said to come from homogeneity not diversity. African politics are immature, and their states corrupted by a self-interested middle class. Africa is depicted as diseased and conflictual and therefore cannot survive without development aid.

These messages are delivered to African children from their birth. Many think, believe, accept, and become this myth. This then is Africa's collective consciousness. When African children see visions of who they could become, they unfortunately fall back on this negative consciousness. They find that thoughts, words, and actions are already cut out for them. Thoughts of survival on a doomed continent, words of protest, and empty workshops . . . talking and more talking, or else food relief and more food relief, or legal education and more legal education, or writing grant proposals with words that are in vogue, and developing logical frameworks and strategic plans that lead nowhere. Africans are left with no time to think, reflect, and remember who they are or what they want to be. When African intellectuals actually do these things, they have to clear their reports and innovations by their benefactors first. The intellectuals have no links with the activists on the ground, and so their ideas usually do not get translated into tangible programs. Instead, there is more research, additional workshop reports, and endless publications on the shelves of donors. Information is power, but all the information on transformative and revolutionary ideas goes out to the West first. There is little change, and visions fade and become unreal, and the militant advocates and development workers go back to their survivalist treadmills.

This is the story of dependency on donors and how it affects visions of social transformation and social justice. Dependency on external resources means that one is operating on survival mode with the sole purpose of staying alive. Under these circumstances, it is difficult to question, define one's own interests, refine one's thoughts, visualize, draw lessons, and map long-term strategy to develop an alternative consciousness.

Framing an African Human Rights Protest

Framing protests is a concept developed in social-movement studies and speaks of the process by which ordinary people and activists interpret a social situation as unjust, define victims and perpetrators, identify causes, translate local griev-ances into broader claims, and set out a course of action. It is a process that combines intellectual or ideological work with political initiative. The intellec-tual work involves a rationalization and justification, and the development of a basis for contention from which the definition or naming of the situation ema-nates, and the political initiative involves a design of effective strategy for con-tention. The way issues are framed into protests, especially within the human rights framework in Africa, is mostly defined by the dichotomization of class between "intellectual" (urban, educated, vanguard, middle-class) and the "masses," and by the contractual nature of the donor/grantee relationship.

Visible human rights organizing in Kenya has been a middle-class monop-oly. This has been a product of several events and processes. One was the pro-scription of the popular rights movements immediately after independence and the use of the provincial administration and repressive colonialist legislation to quash civic virtue. It has been very difficult for visible, formal, organized popular protest by peasants to take root at the community level in rural Kenya. This, however, does not mean that there has not been any human rights activism and protest within rural communities. Associational life in rural areas is depoliticized and manifested in sporadic protests. A culture of using the rights framework to frame protests and processes of contention has not developed. The women's movement, for instance, and the social and economic approach it has taken in the communities, is a protest of the inequality of the patriarchal social, eco-nomic, and political status quo. However, the language used by women is neu-tral, safe, and apolitical, such as defining themselves as *akina mama* (women or mothers), rather than feminists because feminism is too political, radical, and brings with it the threat of real transformation. Yet even as it is politically neu-tralized, the women's movement, in its quiet protest, is effectively transforming the institution of the patriarchy faster from the community level than at the elitist middle-class women's rights level.

Donors bring concepts and a language of human rights wrought from the experience of their country of origin, which are then expressed in their funding policies and priorities. Their interpretation of local situations and events is from this perspective. They bring these interpretations to their relationships with grantees. Being a contractual relationship, which is skewed by financial power against the grantee, the perspective of the donor usually prevails, leading to the development of inorganic intellectual framework with ineffective political strategies. Often, grantees get carried away in their fervor to meet the terms of the contract, and to secure the next contract, and do not take time to reflect on the impact of the adopted frames and interpretations on the realization of their visions. They get stuck in a rut of short-term goals, speaking a language, such as that of empowerment, that they do not necessarily understand.[19] This process has become the way business is done, with the result of suppressing local intellectual innovation and creating intellectual dependency. After many years, human rights organizations such as KHRC are realizing that their efforts have really not led to much progress towards their vision, and they are revisiting the processes and methods of contention.

The example of democracy donors and their grantees is a good illustration of these charges. Following the end of the Cold War, the change in the agendas, focus, and priorities of multilateral and bilateral donors, especially American, led to a change in the content and type of framing and organizing of protests by rights activists. The authoritarian state suddenly became illegitimate and undesirable and needed to be reformed. On this count, the view of democracy donors agreed with middle-class human rights activists. There was, however, a difference in the definition of victims and beneficiaries of the political initiative. For democracy donors under neoliberal democracy, the expected results of democratic reforms were not intended for the people but for the market, to facilitate economic reforms. The people were a secondary victim and beneficiary. To donors, the legacy of the authoritarian regime had led to the excesses of the state and the suppression of market forces. The donors targeted authoritarianism, the overextended state, corruption, and mismanagement. Their cure was political pluralism and freedom, state retreat, good governance, scaling down, opening up, privatization, order, property legislation, and a rights-based culture.

In the view of most human rights activists in the region, democracy meant claims for pluralism and political freedoms. Linkages to social and economic issues were not always expressly articulated as one of the expectations of political democracy. The middle class, the foot soldiers of democratic reforms, has been blind to the economic suffering of the masses. Its failure to focus on social and economic rights has been a real disservice to the poor, who are the majority of the population.

Following the inception in 1992 of pluralistic politics by the oppressive Moi regime, donors began dishing out "protest" money to civil society organizations to demand further political reforms from the state. The organizations needed the financial support that the donors gave it selectively and purposively. Donors dictated issues of priority, such as corruption, gender inequality, criminal justice, due process, property law, and judicial reform. The state was demonized as the only violator of human rights. Rights organizations became the perceived "saviors" of the masses. This made the rest of the population victims, and not actors. The culture of "human rights awards" exacerbated this perception with individual persons being seen as hero soldiers, martyrs, and experts.

Several leadings NGOs, such as the Kenya Human Rights Commission, FIDA(K), and the ICJ(K), focused almost exclusively on the excesses of the Moi regime and were blind to the economic privations of the population. They did not notice the unaccountable corporate sector and the proliferation of multi-national corporations. Throughout the 1990s, Unilever, a giant corporation, marketed essential household items to virtually every one in Kenya, affecting accessibility with its pricing mechanisms. Del Monte, the food conglomerate, was consolidating itself, and the export processing zones were being developed fast. Unregulated flower farms and other greenhouses were mushrooming with horrendous terms and conditions of labor and potential for environmental hazards. And the *Jua Kali* (informal) sector was threatened with forceful extinction. Inflation, commodity prices, unemployment, and poverty increased rapidly. Yet the priority issues of the activists and donors were police brutality, criminal injustice and judicial malfunction, violation of prisoners' rights, lack of legal aid, inequality and oppression of women, constitutional reform, and civic education for elections, among others. The language was that of "sensitization" and "empowerment."

One classic case of donor framing is that of the basket funding for civic education. The National Civic Education Program (NCEP) was replicated every two years after the 1997 elections. The donors designed the political initiative and framed its content and definition. Such donor interference, though it may have had certain practical advantages, stifled innovation and created the illusion of "movements" or networks that were inorganic, illusory, and temporary just like the funding that supported them. This was how bilateral democracy donors arguably hijacked the agency of human rights. For most of the 1990s, the interests of the donors dictated the agenda. However, it is important to remember that donors are not a homogeneous group. Each has its own individual interests, and the way it affects the framing of claims and the use of the agency of human rights depends on those interests. These interests change continually depending on preferences in the home countries. Their support is therefore not dictated by the reality as experienced in East Africa.

Several examples illustrate this point. For instance, the Scandinavians brought the campaign to end capital punishment as a result of the wave of demands for the abolition of the death penalty in their own countries. They influenced the concept and rationale for the campaign by using organizations such as KHRC. Another example is a donor like the Ford Foundation that will not fund an initiative that uses "lobbying" as a strategy or legislative change as a goal because it is against their policy. To obtain their funding, organizations have to use alternative strategies or language and not pursue legislative change, even where this would have been the most expedient strategy. This has also meant that development of indigenous human rights language and initiative wrought of local experiences and visioning is stunted.

The support of middle-class human rights activism has meant that other popular intellectuals who frame protests and design political initiatives within the peasant and working class populations are ignored. Their initiatives do not get the support they need to develop into popular transformative action. This has entrenched the dichotomy between urban rights activism and rights framing and organizing on the ground. It splits the vision of social justice and dilutes the possibility of creating a collective consciousness that would form the basis of a larger and more representative human rights movement. The cost of this dichotomy to both the democratic project and human rights work is only now becoming evident.

The KHRC, after a decade of human rights work, realized that it had made little progress towards its stated vision of a people-centered human rights culture. It found that donor policies and funding styles affected the way it organized and prioritized its work. In 1998, it called a donor roundtable and negotiated a way of doing business that left it in charge of its agenda and priorities even as it purported to respect the values and priorities of each donor. The KHRC did this by creating a funding basket to which donors willing to support its long-term plan would put their funds. The KHRC was able to bring both conservative and liberal donors together in one basket and remove the sensitivities of some key conservative donors. This gave it some limited protection from the dictates of strong donors, and freedom and flexibility to initiative, speak its own language, make links with community groups, extending to them the benefit it had just earned, that of self-expression and framing of own issues.

This was KHRC's big ideological break and the beginning of a more comprehensive approach to human rights. In this space, it began to champion economic, social, and cultural rights and changed from the "saviors" of the masses to partners in the struggle. The KHRC began to provide public visibility to the struggles of workers and farmers. It started with the rice farmers in Mwea and the plantation workers for Del Monte in Thika.[20] In the process, the KHRC realized the deep levels of human rights understanding and perception of the workers that was illustrated in the simple and clear articulation of their issues—labor rights, the environment, and corporate social responsibility. The activism of the workers in Thika that the KHRC organized shook the multinational corporation in Kenya. Del Monte brought its global representative to Kenya to participate in an unprecedented negotiation with workers, with KHRC and others as mere observers. This is a great example of the positive work of human rights agencies when workers are given the power to define their own priority issues and strategies.

Influence on Organizing and Advocacy

Human rights organizations are traditionally issue-focused with specific and pre-determined outcomes. These positions are couched in terms of strong opposition to the status quo. This practice has been exacerbated by short funding cycles by donors who require illustrated returns on their investment in order to keep support from the donor states. Donors therefore favor and encourage short-term focused initiatives with specific outcomes. This continues even though it is now clear that by itself the politics of protest is unlikely to yield many of the answers to complex social and economic problems. This short-term perspective does not leave room for research and learning, two prerequisites for the development of alternatives that are properly grounded.

The Basic Rights Campaign in Kenya is a case in point. The campaign was not based on profound research and did not submit itself to adequate testing and debate before it was put forth to the government. It sought to get the government to officially accept a duty by endorsing basic needs as rights as a prelude to their incorporation in the constitution. Because these rights are economic and require extensive investment, especially in the context of poverty rights, proposals for governments to accept them are rarely successful.

The strategy of the Basic Rights Campaign suffered from a lack of ideas about how the outlined rights might have been realized. The thrust of the campaign was for government alleviation of poverty and the deprivation for the majority. A little research would have revealed that alleviation of suffering and deprivation (provision of aid), though very important, are only small elements of basic rights. The other important elements involve ensuring that the subject acquires the ability to address their own needs and to stay out of deprivation in the future. This approach has been well extrapolated by Amartya Sen in his groundbreaking book *Development as Freedom*, and by other analysts of the concept, such as Henry Shue[21] and the UN High Commission for Human Rights.

Rather than seek quick outcomes in terms of government policies, which may yield unsustainable results, the campaigners might have taken the longer-term approach, which may have entailed trying to influence state economic policy on credit provision to the poor, land ownership, employment generation, labor rights, price control for basic food commodities, farm inputs, and infrastructure construction such as roads and marketing networks for small producers to enable the poor to live dignified lives. This would not have meant the abandonment of aid for the suffering, but it would provide a feasible process of progressively getting more people out of deprivation. The campaign was successful, however, in bringing the issue of basic rights to public debate and making it a legitimacy issue with the government. Even so, the campaign may legitimately claim some credit for the policy moves towards free primary education and the proposed public health scheme by the NARC government.

Slogans Without Constituencies for Change

> The revolutionary war is a war of the masses; it can be waged only by mobilizing the masses and relying on them. (Mao Zedong, 1965)[22]

Human rights organizations have traditionally used the conversion strategy, that is, getting the target to move from their position to the proposed position, without regard for engagement that aims to support a process of dialogue. Donors have played a role in the development of this strategy in two main ways. This has been done through technical support and capacity building programs. Donors have imported the advocacy strategies of northern organizations by bringing human rights "campaign experts" and practitioners from the West to teach local organizations how to design campaigns. This has led to the adoption of sloganeering campaign methods, complete with ill-afforded T-shirts, caps, mugs, and bumper stickers.

Secondly, donors view the state as the perpetrator that should therefore be the target for all activism. Their interests are on specific reform outcomes in the form of infrastructural and institutional changes through specific legal reforms, rules and regulations, policy documents, codes of conduct, and practices. They do not provide resources for the engagement of citizen constituencies around these issues because they believe the middle class is best suited to lobby lawmakers and policymakers. Support for citizen engagement has mostly come in the form of civic education in elections so that antireform regimes are voted out. Some donors, such as the British, may not support the mobilization of protest at the community level for fear of creating instability that may imperil their economic interests. For donors, democratization is about creating good institutions, and not building citizenship. Human rights organizations such as KHRC have realized that codes of conduct and human rights education for the police, for example, are of little use unless they are backed by large-scale citizen pressure to enforce them. They have found it more productive to influence the public context in which the police work instead of attempting to change each individual police official.

A good illustrative case is the evolution of the strategy for constitutional reform in Kenya from the 1980s to the 1990s. The evolution of the strategy began from the conception of the initial radical reform ideas expressed through the sloganeering approach of KHRC in the early 1990s. It then evolved through KHRC leadership into the Citizens Coalition for Constitutional Change (4Cs) which sought to build a broader coalition of mostly urban middle-class civil society organizations, but that lacked broad citizen constituency. The 4Cs, realizing its limitations, provided the leadership, vision, and mobilization that resulted in the formation of the National Convention Preparatory Committee (NCPC). This coalition brought together NGOs, churches, and all political parties except KANU. The representation in this body gave the process public legitimacy. When the body was transformed into the National Convention Executive Council (NCEC), it mobilized and presided over a series of large protest rallies and other forms of mass action and civil disobedience to pressure the government. That is why the state conceded and initiated the process of comprehensive constitutional reforms before the elections in December 1997.[23]

This evolution culminated in the National Convention Assembly (NCA) that sought to create a constituency from all over Kenya, with euphoric results before the Inter-Parliamentary Parties Group (IPPG) hijacked it. The increasing political clout that the organizations amassed by engaging grassroots support was illustrative of the power of constituency building for social transformation. The case of KHRC's engagement with workers at Del Monte was also illustrative of the transformative power of constituencies. Engaging more deeply in constituency building does not mean abandoning campaigns or surrendering the power of protest, but it calls for a better balance between traditional forms of advocacy and deliberate, longer-term work on the causes of social injustice.

Conversionism often leads to dead gains. Laws and rules have no life of their own. Alone they are just principles and value statements. It is people who give them life through invoking them and occasioning the development of jurisprudence and behavior around them. For instance, one can only legislate gender parity, only the principle. It is only by people's adherence to such principles that gender parity can be accomplished. Practice normalizes and makes custom. Only the engagement of people in the development of new laws, policies, and regulations can lead to the consolidation of the gains made in the enactment of such legislation because then they would own it and understand its relevance to their life situations, and therefore create the demand for their enforcement.

Straitjacket Organizing in NGOs

Human rights work starts from the heart, from a passion and belief that society can improve and that the love of mankind can achieve ambitious goals. Most problems that human rights work seeks to address are human ones, embedded in people, their political organizations and communities. Such human complications render whatever outcomes human rights interventions bring to bear appreciably less certain than science would dictate. This inability to assure intended results has led to the invasion of human rights work by a new orthodoxy of rationalism and managerialism. Donors have to account to the taxpayers in their home countries. They have to show that the funds are being put to some progressive cause. So they have required protocols to show that they have made a measurable difference. Tools of planning and organizing have been introduced from the private sector such as strategic plans and logical frameworks. These bring with them monitoring, evaluation, impact assessment, and other time-consuming processes. The more value-driven, mission-centered approach to human rights work is being replaced with a technically based, efficiency-driven, outcome-centered one—in short, the supplanting of art with science. A significant amount of time and funds are expended every year by human rights organizations to plan and design their strategies. Though developing indicators for human rights work is very difficult because of problems of attribution, organizations have found it necessary to comply. This is because the danger of becoming irrelevant in a market- driven society where bottom lines and the metrics of efficiency eclipse nonquantifiable values and social missions is very real. Unequipped as they are to offer little more than anecdotes about their successes and impact, human rights organizations, like other nonprofit organizations worldwide, have willingly embraced the metrics of the profit sector, and with the digital evolution, situated themselves in alignment with the new economy.

The challenge in this arrangement is the ability of human rights organizations to retain their values, instincts, passion, and volunteerism, factors that are the hallmarks of the movement. This trend is very worrying in East Africa with the growing crop of private for-profit management firms that have turned into development capacity building firms. There is a danger that the values of the for-profit sector will infiltrate the not-for-profit sector and contaminate the essence of its delivery system. Many of the scientific tools being implemented are rigid and restrictive, especially considering the often fluid and volatile environment of human rights work that requires quick changes of strategy. Most donors supporting a strategic plan require negotiation before strategies can be changed. Monitoring, evaluation, and impact assessment processes are also problematic as they tend to stop at the level of mission and do not seek to establish progress at the vision level. This leads to a practice of merely implementing programs without stopping to reflect on the gains to social transformation. It is this practice that sees some organizations engaging in the same activities for decades even when the context calls for change in strategy.

Deficit Financing Versus Asset Development

The funding rationale between donors and NGOs is based on the notion of deficit financing. It proceeds from a presumption of scarcity and asks the question: What do they need? This logic creates the vicious circle of dependency and indignity. An alternative paradigm, which is not given much consideration, is one that would proceed from the presumption of abundance, and instead ask the question: What do they have?

The deficit paradigm, which is implemented through the mechanism of proposal writing, socializes organizations to always think of what they do not have and what they should ask for. Rarely will the question be: What do we have? If they did, the sheer shift in thought and questioning would be dignifying and liberating. It would enable an organization to notice forms of resources that it already has but did not regard as resources. These would include resources such as time, membership, a board of directors, similar organizations, passion and resolve, local volunteers, and well-wishers. Notice would be taken of the perpetual tradition of African philanthropy and mutual support. They might even remember Africans in the Diaspora—learned, well-to-do people remitting large sums of money annually to Africa. NGOs might also engage the middle class that is yearning to make contributions to the country.

Organizations need to be open to more innovative ways of doing business. One new approach would be the vogue idea of corporate social responsibility that encourages businesses to support local causes. NGOs could also utilize the power of the Internet through e-philanthropy. The government could be a donor to NGOs through tax exemptions and donor deductibility incentives. In addition, civil society groups could build assets, including buying or building permanent rent-free premises. The difference in the shift in thinking would be stark. The donor-driven deficit paradigm is detrimental to the psyche of African NGOs and should be abandoned because it encourages parasitism and dependency.

Easy Money and Expensive Habits

Civil society organizations are continually dependent on donors because they have cultivated expensive business habits. The endless workshops, seminars, retreats, and conferences in expensive tourist resorts, high-end vehicles, costly and "networking" trips abroad, the expensive office rentals, and the high salaries all speak to a sector that is addicted to luxury. And the donors back it all up. Because the currencies of the northern donor countries are so strong compared to local currencies, the grant makers can afford to be very charitable. That is why they can fund these expensive tastes for years without end. The tastes of NGOs would doubtless change were they only able to raise money from local sources.

Networking and Donor Influence

Networks are essentially mechanisms of communication and influence. They mobilize energy and resources within civil society. New ideas, designs, and perspectives get elaborated through new ways of relating with each other. The cutting edge issues in development, advocacy, and society get communicated in a more informal and nonhierarchical manner since new ideas entail critique and departure from the established modes of functioning. The existing institutional frameworks of state, market, and academia tend to curtail such possibilities. Networks around socially difficult issues, such as violence against women, child labor, environmental protection and regeneration, peace, human rights, democracy, and freedom, are able to mobilize individuals and groups and promote linkages among them.

Donors generally do not fund networks except those that they initiate and control. This is attributable to the fact that responsibility within networks is spread out among many constituents and is not as easily enforced as a contractual relationship with one grantee. The donor and grantee relationship is by its terms and conditions developed by the donor with little input by the grantee. Within this relationship, it is easy for the donors to pursue their own interests. In contrast, it is difficult to direct the agenda and priorities of an independent network or to disable it by cutting off or withholding funds if it threatens a donor's interests. Therefore, independent networks are not as effective of a tool for pushing donor agendas as are individual grantee relationships. By reducing traceability to any particular organization, networks have a lot of flexibility that makes conservative donors nervous. Moreover, in Kenya the view of networks as partners for donors or as units of civil society organizing has not taken root with donors who prefer to work with the more formal units of NGOs. Funds for networks are therefore scarce and, as such, networks are weak, inconsistent, and cannot engage in long-term programs. It also does not help that networks in Kenya, such as the Human Rights Network, are sporadic and episodic. This inconsistency does not instill confidence for investment by donors.

Donors, Individualism, and Favoritism

In his research, Wachira Maina found that key donors in Kenya considered the reputation of the leaders of an NGO to be a critical factor in funding an organization. The same study also found evidence of obvious favoritism:[24]

> In one case it was clear that the donor was partial to one organization, describing the executive director of a favorite organization as almost his "son." In another case, one organization was clearly favored, receiving more than a quarter of a donor's total funding to civil society over a two-year period. In yet another, more than 50% of the donor's support for capacity building in civil society went to one organization alone.

These dynamics breed jealousies among civil society individual actors and organizations, making it difficult to work together. Another problem is the sectoral approach taken by human rights donors. Donors distribute funds according to sectors such as prisons, land rights, police brutality, legal reform, and gender rights, among others. This leads to unhealthy competition by organizations for limited funds within vogue issue categories. As a result, it becomes difficult for losers to work with winners.

Donor-Initiated Networks

Donors have forced the formation of alliances and coalitions to ease the implementation of a specific agenda or priority project. Individual donors, or groups of donors, whose interests coalesce around a priority issue, have done this. This is done through the basket-funding mechanism. Donors only permit organizations with the capacity to carry out the prescribed objectives to become members of the network. These networks are short-term, inorganic, and often acrimonious. Negative constituent experiences with these networks have led to skepticism about the possibility of effective networking. Examples have been the National Civic Education Project (NCEP), a basket-funding project by some democracy like-minded donors and the Kenya Land Alliance imposed by the UK Department for International Development.

But one example of a positive networking experience was that of the Ufungamano Initiative on the constitutional review process in Kenya. Ufungamano emerged as a result of the mutual needs of NCEC, NCA, and religious organizations to present a united front in the struggle to reform the Kenyan state through a democratic constitution. Because of its relative independence from donors, the network survived and was able to mobilize action quickly and to conduct business with efficiency.

Trade and Labor Mobility Regimes

For the sake of human rights work, the relationship between donors and the organizations they fund needs to improve. This chapter rejects the resigned view that Africa will always need development aid. Rather, it focuses on the search for opportunities to reduce the necessity for aid. Whereas the relationship serves an instrumental purpose for both parties, it ultimately stunts the development of human rights organizations and dissipates their potential for occasioning social transformation. Development aid is not an innate necessity; it is the result of structural international relationships that created its ostensible necessity. It is characterized by unequal and unfair international trade terms and oppressive and restrictive immigration regimes that inhibit the labor mobility from Africa to the global North. These regimes make Africa a marketplace and its population consumers of ill-afforded junk products from the North.

The development agenda of African governments and civil society will never be free of Western influence as long as the need for development aid continues to be so critical to the survival of both. The better utilization of resources is essential to the reduction of the necessity of aid. Civil society organizations are strategically attempting to reduce the need for development aid through the renegotiation of international trade and immigration regimes. These efforts are seen in campaigns promoting fair trade and increased international labor mobility and terms. Organizations such as Oxfam, Action Aid, and ECONEWS in Kenya, and the Debt Network in Uganda are doing this work.

Cultivating Local Resources

Rhetoric about local resource mobilization for development work has been around for a decade now following what was termed "donor fatigue" in the 1990s. Donors began asking for proof that organizations had verifiable plans for program/project sustainability. Organizations began talking of establishing endowments and even approached a few corporate donors for donations. They began to develop skills for local fund-raising. Fund-raising workshops were organized and models that had developed in the West were applied.

However, not much information was offered about where resources were situated in Kenya, how and why Kenyans give, and what Kenyans think of NGOs. The general belief among NGOs was that there were no resources in Africa that could be harvested. And so, dependency on foreign donors continued, with only a few organizations such as FIDA-Kenya, keeping up the efforts to utilize African resources. Although aid levels from foreign donors have decreased, for instance that of USAID, donors did not withdraw. They continued to support the same organizations and are not showing signs of leaving soon. So the urgency for developing financial independence has not been great. Fund-raising workshops continue, with international fundraising organizations such as Resource Alliance joining the bandwagon. The treadmill moves on, and dependency stays.

The Concept of Sustainable Development

The notion of sustainable development, cultivated in the 1990s, has not faded away for some progressive independent donors with shared visions and values with certain African civil society organizations. Private foundations such as the Aga Khan Foundation, the Rockefeller Foundation, and the Ford Foundation have kept the debate alive by supporting research and encouraging innovations. As a result, there is a growing movement to support the growth of local philanthropy. This movement is manifested in the growth of organizations focused on the search for local resource mobilization strategies with a focus for asset development by communities.

The Centre for Philanthropy and Social Responsibility (Ufadhili) is an organization that catalyzes giving from the sites where resources are situated such as corporations, individuals, and governments. Another example is that of agencies working to build the capacities of organizations that seek to build permanent resources and groups that are making grants from their own sources, or as intermediaries for big donors such as Allavida, a UK research program commissioned with the support of Ford Foundation. Allavida's preliminary reports indicate that there are resources available for social causes in the three East African countries and the resources are situated in various sites in African societies.[25]

Utilizing and Developing Local Resources

Within East Africa, there is a very strong traditional culture of giving to social causes that has evolved over time and is still alive and thriving. This is a culture based on the traditional African communal values of reciprocity and mutual aid, and on the principle of *ubuntuism* from which they emanate.[26] In Kenya, this was manifested in the institution of Harambee. Contrary to popular belief, Harambee is not dead; it has only retreated away from public space to the safer lines of trust and affinity from which it came. The foundation is still there.

Second, the corporate sector is a viable resource. In Africa, there is a strong, sizable, and growing corporate sector with an established history of giving to social causes, albeit in an episodic, sporadic way. Previous giving by the sector was mostly a public relations gimmick. This has changed with the wave idea of Corporate Social Responsibility (CSR) that calls for companies to establish and implement policies for supporting communities with whom they work as part of good business practice and as social investment. For example, the support for initiatives that advocate for the rule of law and order is something that many companies that work in the central business district in the city of Nairobi appreciate. After waves of crime and destruction that almost destroyed their businesses, some of them started listening to CSR advocates. Some, in particular, the Barclays Group and the Sand 'n' Sand Club, developed policies and mechanisms for supporting communities in their vicinities. This is a potential that has not been cultivated or exploited in any organized way by civil society.

Third, there are anywhere between 600,000 and 1.2 million Kenyans in the diaspora that bring in remittances making up 63 percent of all foreign exchange that flows into the country (including bilateral loans, grants, and other aid-in-kind). This inflow is in the form of cash aid to family members, and personal and other investments. Uganda was expected to earn over US$499 million in the 2000–2001 financial year from its nationals abroad. Private transfers from Ugandans abroad peaked in the 1998–1999 fiscal year, earning the country US$539 million. There is a solid base of wealth situated in the numbers of qualified African professionals in the Diaspora. Africa lost an estimated 60,000 middle- and high-level managers between 1985 and 1990, and about 23,000 qualified academic professionals emigrate each year in search of better working conditions.[27]

It is clear that there is a foundation for Diaspora philanthropy for East African civil society organizations. Diaspora philanthropy is the process through which immigrants in the Diaspora allocate a certain portion of their remittances to fund development projects in their societies of origin. There is already some philanthropy going on through organizations such as the Kenya Community

Abroad and the Uganda North America Association among others. It is, however, not consistent or organized. Examples of successful tapping and development of Diaspora philanthropy for the support of civil society groups exist in India, the Philippines, and Latin America where the infrastructure for mobilizing, stewarding, and linking to home projects has been developed. East African groups may want to borrow a leaf from these examples.

Fourth, there is a growing middle class in Africa. Charges have been made that the African middle class will not support certain civil society work because they benefit from the status quo and do not want to be seen to support subversive elements.[28] This same middle class has developed its own ways of supporting development through "home-town Diaspora giving," as demonstrated by the South Imenti Association and others in western Kenya in which professionals and business persons in Nairobi form associations that support development projects in rural areas. Though these may be discounted on account of the demonized ethnicity, it will serve critics better to remember that ethnic groups are geographically localized in one area, and ethnic and kinship affinities will therefore occur along those geographical patterns. Wachira Maina has made this point well:

African middle class straddles the twilight zone between individualism and communitarianism. They are not just members of a class, they are also sons and daughters of a tribe.[29]

My contention is that no serious investment has been made to tap the middle class to support civil society. Even though it operates at the crossroads of different and diverse loyalties, it is not a position unique to the African middle class. The most well-endowed international NGOs such as Oxfam and Action Aid are supported by gifts mostly from the middle class in their home countries. Gifts need not be big and can be publicly given as Africans are socialized in this type of giving. Individual gifts can be small. "Thinking small to make big" may be an approach that is unfamiliar to organizations that are socialized to receive millions of shillings at a time, but yet it is a gem of African wisdom: "Haba na haba hujaza kipapa" (Kiswahili for "little by little will eventually fill the basket").

Fifth, with their embrace of information technology, organizations can take advantage of the developing e-philanthropy trends. Electronic philanthropy refers to giving, or organizing for giving, on the Internet.[30] Civil society organizations, especially in the North, are setting up Web sites for fund-raising. The American Red Cross, for instance, raised US$2.5 million in 1999 alone through Web sites. Some CSOs with experience in e-philanthropy offer interactive services. For example, Vitualfoundation.org links donors to sustainable development projects. Duo.org enables groups or individuals to donate to charities assisting in disaster relief. Other fundraising Web sites include: www.donate.net; www.donaire.net; www.fund-online.com; www.givetocharity.com; www.redcross .org. For East African organizations, e-philanthropy may be used to tap Diaspora resources or resources from those in the world who may be sympathetic to their causes.

Last, but not least, is volunteerism. This is the most abundant, least costly, yet most undeveloped resource available to CSOs. There are volunteers everywhere: the youth, students and graduates, retired professionals such as teachers, accountants, doctors, civil servants, and active professionals. This needs to be organized and exploited as a strategic resource. Volunteers do not necessarily take the place of professional staff; they supplement them and enable more work to be done in a shorter period of time. They bring not only their skills, but also new enthusiasm and different perspectives and experiences.

CHAPTER EIGHT

Contradictions in Neoliberalism: Donors, Human Rights NGOs, and Governance in Kenya

Karuti Kanyinga

FOR OVER A century, the state has been the main variable of analysis of society in Africa. The state-centric view looks at events from the perspective of the center. It is predicated on the assumption that the state is responsible for social-political relations in society. Whatever takes place at the local level unfolds in a process of passive reflection of events at the national level. In the 1980s, the deepening of structural adjustment reforms led to a rapid "withering" of the state in studies of the practice of politics. With the increased contestation of state authority by different groups, commentators influenced by neoliberalism argued that the state was not the only actor influencing development. Nonstate actors were as important as the patrimonial state in development and politics.[1]

This view spurred thinking on the study of society and political events in Africa. Western scholars began to give primacy to dynamics at the base of the society. Literature on this approach specifically underlined the fact that the patrimonial nature of the African state stifled the potential for liberalization by civil society.[2] Others pointed to the potential of civil society as an institution that could countermand state power and liberate society. They pointed to the need to support civil society to make it a check on the "future career" of the state in Africa.[3] Positioned outside these two schools of thought was the popular politics approach, in which many Africanists in the Leninist tradition underlined the need to study the class content of politics to resuscitate popular struggles.[4] To

the adherents in this school, the postcolonial state in Africa privileged the bour-
geoisie and created a state framework for accumulation. Therefore, the state had
to be treated as the major object of popular struggles for social transformation
of society to occur.[5] It was imperative to reorganize the state and its institutions
through struggles and civil society social movements.

Neoliberalism overshadowed other approaches with the growing influence
of donors in public throughout Africa. The rise of governance and its influence
on donor policies after the failure of Structural Adjustment Programs
(SAPs) led African governments and the middle class to adopt neoliberalism.
Both gave primacy to free markets and socioeconomic and political pluralism.
There was consensus that organizations outside the state would offer better
solutions to democracy and development problems. Civil society was increasingly viewed as the "midwife" for the transition to multiparty democracy. Civil
society was seen as the antidote to statism and authoritarian regimes. The
career of civil society thus grew in tandem with the need to build institutions
to buttress the transition to multiparty democracy. The struggle to disengage
the postcolonial one-party state deepened and spread, especially in urban areas
in Africa.[6]

In the late twentieth century, struggles for liberation from postcolonial authoritarianism occupied the entire social-political and economic space in a manner similar to the case in the 1950s and 1960s when the peasantry waged a
concerted struggle against the colonial state. Although the peasantry was at the
forefront of the decolonization struggle, it appeared to be in the periphery of
the struggles against the postcolonial state. The African middle class, comprising
youthful professionals and a broad array of human rights and good governance
NGOs, took up the struggle for neoliberal values. The struggle sought a free
market economy, respect for human rights, independent media, social pluralism,
and open elections. Collective and communitarian values faded in the quest for
"democracy" as the emphasis shifted to individual liberties and political pluralism. The centrality of collective rights and the need to promote socioeconomic
opportunities for the vast majority of Africa's poor diminished in importance.
The domination of neoliberal values eroded the basis of social citizenship.[7] Second, with the support of Western donors, human rights and good governance
NGOs multiplied in number. They, and opposition political parties, became
the main champions of neoliberal political and economic liberalization.

This chapter examines the relations between civil society and donors in
Kenya in the context of governance programs. Secondly, it discusses how the
relations between donors and NGOs affects the organization of civil society. It
critically assesses the implications for donor-donee relationships.

Human Rights NGOs and Donors: A Conceptual Approach

The definition of civil society has remained elusive given its different labels. Its meaning has changed over time and with tradition. Peter Gibbon extensively discussed the history of the concept and noted its varied meanings.[8] Suffice to note that neoliberalism attaches importance to civil society only in relation to rights, citizenship, rule of law, free markets, freedom of information, and democratic representation. It concerns civic institutions whose activities are geared toward enriching liberal democracy. But, contemporary sociological theory borrows from the Hegelian tradition that associates civil society with autonomous groups of free individuals organized separately from the state and the family. In discussions of civil society, this includes social movements and organizations that articulate social concerns outside of the state. It sees civil society as the realm in which social relations are reproduced and articulated to foster the social good. Examples of civil society organizations include the Kenya Human Rights Commission in Kenya or Amnesty International, the London-based human rights group.

The associations of free and equal individuals are responsible for the internal contradictions and differentiation of civil society. It is the bedrock of heterogeneity. Civil society is neither homogenous nor free. It is "an ensemble of contradictory social relations."[9] Moreover, there is an organic relationship between the state and the civil society: both are products of similar social realities constructed in the public realm. The state and civil society should be seen as two opposites that stand in opposition to each other, but in a mutually reinforcing way. The role of civil society in the promotion of democracy and the transformation of the state is one example how the two mutually reinforce one another.

Donors have been critical to the development of civil society. The emergence of neoliberalism and social-political pluralization gave associational life an added impetus in rural and urban Africa. There was an increase in the number of voluntary associations such as self–help groups and professional associations. The erosion of social citizenship that accompanied the SAPs and the withdrawal of the state from the delivery of social services gave rise to civil society organizations. Thus NGOs and community-based organizations (CBOs) filled the lacuna left by the state. The quest for social pluralization required forces to countermand the intransigence of the authoritarian regimes that dotted the African political landscape. With the emphasis on good governance by donors, many groups organized to articulate long-held grievances against undemocratic regimes. This had one important consequence—the proliferation of human rights and good governance NGOs.

Starting in the early 1990s, Western governments and international aid agencies began to direct increased assistance through civil society. Donors began to link aid to the promotion of democracy, human rights, and good governance. The assistance was directed to human rights and good governance NGOs on the assumption that building that sector would have a positive impact on political liberalization. Because of the antidemocratic tendencies of the state, donors felt they had no choice but to channel political aid through the civil society. Most of the aid went into the areas of civic education, human rights, democracy, and governance.

Political aid has been the only thread joining civil society to the donors. More than anything, it is this aid that has shaped relations between donors and NGOs in Kenya. Willy Mutunga provides an elaborate conceptual framework for analyzing donor-donee relations.[10] Mutunga's arguments provide an important entry point to understanding the evolving relations between human rights NGOs and aid agencies. Basing his arguments on classical and neoclassical contract theory, Mutunga points out that the relations between human rights NGOs and donors are best understood from a "democracy contract" perspective because the doctrine of good faith is the foundation of any good contract. There must be good faith between the parties—both parties should be honest and transparent when they enter into the relationship. They make free choices. No one interferes with the other until one of the parties fails to meet its obligations. In view of this, Mutunga observes that the contractual relationship between donors and NGOs is not based on market principles in which parties exchange commodities. Rather, their relations are premised on fundamental economic, social, cultural, and political interests.

Mutunga argues that the best relationship between donors and NGOs is one governed by a democracy contract, whose features include common interests, transparency of both interests and transactions by both parties, and transparency in the performance of contracts. He notes that the length of the contract, enforcement mechanisms, and the nature of its content determine the sustainability of an NGO project. This framework is suitable for an analysis of the relations between human rights NGOs in Kenya and aid agencies. It could be used to settle a fundamental question: to whom are human rights NGOs accountable? What interests do donors vindicate by supporting civil society initiatives?

The Development of Civil Society in Kenya

Civil society in Kenya has experienced two distinct historical phases—state-dominated and state-free. State domination obtained largely during the colonial period in which the state occupied the social-political and the economic arena to the detriment of most groups in society. This form of domination carried over into the postcolonial period until the early 1990s. The colonial state maintained domination of civil society in several ways. As argued by Mahmood Mamdani with regard to the rest of Africa, the colonial state exerted this domination by extra-economic means.[11] This shaped relations of production in the countryside. Coercion, extortion, and expropriation underlay this strategy. The second, and quite relevant with respect to Kenya, was the ethnicization of society. The creation of native reserves for different ethnic groups made ethnicity an important variable in associational life in both the countryside and urban areas. In the latter, the multiethnic population notwithstanding, ethnicity and other primordial values crept in through welfare organizations. In this approach, the state did not restrict ethnic-based welfare societies. The ethnic character of those associations was essential for the divide-and-rule strategy through the colonial regime spread and deepened its hegemony over society.

The ethnicization of civil society took place in tandem with destruction of indigenous relations of production. This brought about deep socioeconomic inequalities as groups allied to the state accumulated wealth by extra-economic coercion. That is how otherwise popular indigenous organizations became appendages of colonialism. Even so, a number of popular organizations emerged out of these social-economic and political inequalities to lead the struggle for decolonization. Some organizations formed to articulate the social, cultural, and religious concerns of the black and Asian African populations. Several were later transformed into political nationalist movements. Between 1945 and 1952, for instance, several quasi-nationalist religious-based organizations grew rapidly. Dini ya Msambwa in western Kenya, Nomia Church in Luo Nyanza, and Dini ya Kaggia and other independent churches in central Kenya are notable examples in this regard. All had a base in ethnic settings: they were not open to broader national constituencies because of the limitations imposed by the colonial state.

These social movements had one basic objective: democracy and decolonization. They arose to articulate collective grievances by different social groups. The Mau Mau peasant movement, which articulated decolonization and economic concerns of the black African peasantry, either evolved from or was allied to some of the movements. The Mau Mau later became an important popular force in the colonial period. Its struggle against the colonial state over political space led to increased surveillance of popular organizations and a preclusion of social and political pluralization. Thereafter, the state accelerated the process towards ethnic-based associations and prevented the consolidation of a national social movement. The result was undesirable: organizations such as the Kenya

African Union, the Luo Thrift and Trading Corporation, the North Kavirondo Central Association, Ukamba Members Association, and Taita Hills Association combined efforts to intensify the struggle against colonial oppression. In effect, they cultivated the ground upon which ethnic-based political parties were later formed.

Predictably, the colonial state restricted the growth and development of self-help organizations for fear they would collaborate with the politically oriented social movements to undermine colonial hegemony. The state only allowed state-friendly groups like Maendeleo ya Wanawake, an organization of the wives of colonial administrators, to organize without restriction. Unfortunately, the legacy of the colonial state was passed on intact to the post-colonial state. The postcolonial state maintained demobilization of civil society to keep it feeble as a strategy to undermine any challenge to state authority. That is why the first postcolonial government saw no contradiction in banning political parties. Like the colonial state, it also personalized political institutions but maintained a laissez-faire attitude towards ethnic welfare associations so long as they did not practice politics contrary state patronage.

Post-Colonial State-Civil Society Relations

The highly centralized bureaucracy inherited at independence played a key role in the social-economic and political process of independent Kenya. Virtually no major changes were made in the police, military, and provincial administration, whose powers were quickly concentrated in the hands of President Mzee Jomo Kenyatta, Kenya's founding head of state. The provincial administration, which was run by the Kikuyu, Kenyatta's ethnic community, was a tool of civil control and regulation.[12] The state also recognized the significance of Harambee (Kiswahili for "pulling together") and accorded civil society initiatives special policy attention. Basic services at the grassroots level were provided by voluntary community initiatives such as churches and NGOs.[13] The apparent liberal attitude to civil society operations, however, was narrow in scope. Although it led to the consolidation of ethnic welfare associations, it restricted them to the social-economic arena and denied them access to political space. Civil society thus became increasingly depoliticized.

In spite of depoliticization, however, the civil society provided an important bridge between ordinary citizens and the state. Ethnic associations became the main platform around which political careers were constructed. Harambee organizations, which were important civil society initiatives, were institutionalized and integrated into mainstream politics of development. Generally, ethnic organizations provided a base for political activity, though limited in scale. Only the Gikuyu, Embu and Meru Association (GEMA), which was founded in the 1970s, assumed significant political character because its leading members were Kenyatta courtiers. Activities of other organizations such as the Luo Union were confined to welfare. This gave rise to the view that GEMA was the state and the state was GEMA.[14]

More credence was given to the political significance of GEMA when the organization's factionalists, alarmed by Kenyatta's advanced age and probable demise, sought to change the constitution to deny the vice president the right of automatic succession. The constitution provided that the vice president would assume office in an acting capacity following the disability, resignation, or death of the president. But GEMA was uncertain of its continued political domination if the office was occupied by any person other than one of its members or a person from Kenyatta's Kiambu inner court. The move to change the constitution began in 1976 but was shelved by Kenyatta once it became clear that it would divide not only his cabal but also the Kikuyu in general. But the domination of GEMA in national politics did not end. In fact, political activism by other actors in civil society depended on the ability of the leaders of various ethnic communities to establish clientelist relationships with Kenyatta and his Kiambu GEMA cabal.

The absence of effective popular movements in civil society and the subsequent demobilization of those already in existence created a lacuna in the social-political space. The result was that very few organizations were critical in the area of governance. The churches, as argued by Mutahi Ngunyi and Kamau Gathiaka, remained silent owing to their relationship with the ruling state elite.[15] The University Academic Staff Union and the Nairobi University Students Union (SONU), two left-leaning university organizations, were the only outspoken nonstate actors. The only other voice of dissent was a tiny maverick parliamentary backbench.

As noted above, self-help voluntary organizations and the formal NGOs were vibrant players in the country's development during the Kenyatta period. Self-help groups became an important force in the development process. Additionally, although Harambee efforts were heavily patronized by political elites, they managed to retain some degree of autonomy from the state. NGOs were also autonomous from the state and actively supplemented state development endeavors. However, NGOs were only active in relief and development efforts. Their relationship with the state remained cordial because they did not compete with it in the development process: they merely supplemented the state's efforts.

After Kenyatta, the government of President Daniel arap Moi actively carried out the demobilization and destruction of civil society organizations. Moi proscribed national welfare organizations that articulated ethnic interests. The government introduced measures to stifle agrarian social formations such as the cooperatives. Self-help groups were incorporated into administrative and political structures so that they could not undertake any development projects without the knowledge of local state agents. The government required these groups to register with the Ministry of Culture and Social Services, and those that did not were excluded from government and donor grants. The government also introduced District Focus for Rural Development (DFRD), in essence a decentralization development strategy. This framework benefited areas that provided political support to the state. The regime also gave opportunities for state-friendly political elites to create their basis of support through entrenchment and control of civil society organizations such as the Harambee development projects.

The state and the political elites at the center of state power transformed development projects into "centers of clientelism." Harambee projects became a platform for politics and conduits for the state through which patronage funds were disbursed to loyal groups. Moreover, contributions to Harambees were extracted through coercion and intimidation by the provincial administration. As a consequence, the Harambee spirit gradually slackened. A local dependency culture was created by perpetual reliance on the presidential Harambee entourage of senior government officials, politicians, and favor seekers. The result was a popular de-participation in both politics and development.

The deconstruction of the Kenyatta hegemony did not end at the political level. It penetrated deep into the civil society when Moi began to build a base to support his patron-client networks. A project to silence maverick politicians began in earnest. Through patronage and detentions, Moi silenced the opposition groups located in civil society. That is why several underground "social movements" by intellectuals and disengaged politicians came into being. The state deflated the organizations opposed to patronage politics. For example, the state became increasingly opposed to progressive religious organizations such as the National Council of Churches of Kenya and the Catholic Church. In an effort to create viable avenues to the grassroots, KANU, the state party, coopted Maendeleo Ya Wanawake, the umbrella women's organization and made approaches to labor unions, cooperatives, and self help hirable groups. By late 1980, most radical civic institutions had either been deregistered or co-opted.

More blatant attempts to demobilize civil society began in 1989 when the state made it clear that NGOs would be co-coordinated and supervised by the state. The reason for state anxiety was the opposition by NGOs to the change of electoral rules and introduction of queue voting, or *mlolongo*, in 1987. Amid threats to deregister the NCCK, the state began to design a legislative and administrative strategy to deal with antagonistic groups. In 1990, the government introduced legislation to facilitate coordination of NGOs. The law was meant to clip the wings of civil society organizations such as the NCCK and others critical of the government. But NGOs gathered in force to mitigate the attacks on their autonomy. They constituted themselves into a committee to negotiate with the government over the proposed law. But the government was reluctant to agree to any of these demands. However, pressure mounted when donors sided with NGOs. The government acquiesced somewhat and only pushed through less draconian measures. This in itself positioned the NGOs—and civil society in general—in politics. They now had acquired some skill and courage to confront the authoritarian state. The struggle for democratization had started in earnest.

Civil Society, Donors, and Democracy in Kenya

From 1991 to 2002, Kenya had three important interrelated political moments. Human rights groups shaped each and provided the direction of change. But international donors played a role too. Donors were a conspicuous feature of each of the moments. They either fanned the flames or directed the events. In the first moment, international donors put pressure on the government to open up the political and social space. This added to the pressure that domestic civil society and opposition politicians had put on the state. The withdrawal of donor funds forced the government to amend the constitution to allow for reintroduction of multiparty democracy. As a result, in December 1992, Kenya's first multiparty general elections were held since independence.

The second moment was a package of things: the defeat in 1992 and 1997 of the opposition political parties by KANU, the ruling party; the increased politicization of human rights organizations and civil society; and rise in donor funding to CSOs involved in public awareness programs. Combined, these events made civil society an indispensable feature of Kenya's political life. Moreover, they transformed civil society into alternative "opposition forces."

The third moment had several elements to it as well. These included the defeat by an opposition coalition in December 2002 of KANU, Kenya's ruling party since independence. The other was, inexplicably, a weakening of civil society organizations. More specifically, the third moment resulted in a weaker civil society and a tendency by donors to shift attention towards the government. This was a radical departure from the past.

The First Moment: Pressure for Change (1990–1992)

In this first period of transition, there was an organic relationship between the opposition pro-democracy groups, the civil society, and a group of progressive donors. Civil society organizations also evolved as an important training ground for opposition politics. Those who were involved in the reform movement used the civil society platform to promote the agenda of change and engagement in opposition politics. The distinction between civil society and opposition groups narrowed as the state procrastinated about reforms. Human rights organizations became important avenues for promoting change and shielding political activists from the excesses of the state. In fact, the Forum for Restoration of Democracy (FORD), the first opposition political party, drew membership from the civil society and political community. It provided the necessary foundation on which opposition groups and civil society would mobilize support for democracy. Donors were supportive as well. They withdrew aid to the government and openly supported pro-democracy reforms. The United States and Scandinavian countries were especially vocal and emphasized that aid would only be resumed after the government had committed itself to comprehensive democratic and governance reforms.

Moreover, donors provided support to the civil society organizations to monitor the progress in the opening of the political space after the reintroduction of open politics. Some donors gave discreet support to various groups to promote voter civic education while others funded logistics to mobilize support for reforms. Professional associations, churches, and human rights and democracy advocacy groups combined to oppose the state domination of the political space. They kept guard at the gate of political space until the December 1992 elections. During the elections, they carried out voter education emphasizing the value of the vote in a democracy. NGOs also monitored the conduct of the elections. In effect, civil society prevented a relapse into the old culture of authoritarianism.

In spite of the authoritarian tendency of the state, civil society groups—human rights NGOs in particular—advanced some changes in the political sphere. But their focus was on neoliberal reforms and the reintroduction of multiparty politics. Some of them saw political liberalization as an end in itself. The activities they engaged in focused on political pluralization. Most spent little effort on the advocacy for the democratization of the state and its institutions. Donors were partially responsible for this limited approach. Most of the donors were inclined to support neoliberal reforms anchored in the Western neoliberal tradition: a predictable electoral cycle or conduct of regular elections; unlimited political competition; an active parliament; and increased numbers of political parties and civil society organizations. The focus on the number of institutions and structures became an end in itself.

It is important to note that the rolling back of the state from the development, privatization, and the creation of room for social-economic pluralization were already policies in the North. These demands on Kenya were therefore an extension of the policies of donor states. The collapse of the Berlin Wall speeded up the spread of neoliberalism to ensure global conformity. Infatuation with the American version of neoliberalism did not pay attention to the need to democratize the state and its institutions. Civil society became the mouthpiece of neoliberal policies only because the West had an interest in removing some authoritarian governments from power. It is questionable whether they intended the reform of the state and its institutions. The state was thus the object of the struggle by donors and civil society, but for different reasons. The introduction of uniform political standards was important to donors. But civil society sought a little bit more: the removal of an authoritarian regime and the installation of a better government. This narrow focus on reforms left the state intact throughout the first moment of the transition.

The Second Cycle: Rekindling Civil Society (1993–1997)

The defeat of opposition political parties in the 1992 elections occasioned deep fragmentation within the opposition. Opposition political parties were so weakened that they could not forge a united challenge to the government in spite of their large numbers in parliament. Divisions deepened after the government co-opted some members of parliament from the opposition. Some opposition MPs defected to the government side through by-elections supported by the KANU state.

Without a strong opposition, civil society organizations assumed the role of the effective opposition in the state. NGOs began to articulate issues on comprehensive constitutional reforms and the review of repressive laws. Increasingly, donors worked in cahoots with civil society organizations. Because of renewed donor interest in human rights and democracy, the number of human rights and good governance NGOs rapidly increased. The number went from fewer than ten in 1990 to about one hundred later in the 1990s.[16] The activities of NGOs also became diverse. From simple voter civic education, many groups started to engage in general civic education and paralegal work. Donors funded civic empowerment projects—civic education—that sought to equip citizens with skills and knowledge to participate more effectively in public affairs. With support from donors, human rights NGOs spread human rights education to the countryside through community-based organizations, their grassroots partners.

NGOs also provided education on good governance, democracy, and constitutionalism. This covered issues of equality and social justice. These programs had a profound impact in local communities. Groups of ordinary citizens organized protests against the existing modes of governance. Public protests were staged in rural and urban areas of Kenya. People protested against repression by the provincial administration. Others organized protests against economic exploitation by state marketing agents. They demanded the total liberalization of the economy and the rolling back of the state from their lives. One important consequence of these movements was the proliferation of grassroots human rights and democracy organizations at the neighborhood level. Many evolved to become monitors of human rights while others fought for good governance.

Civic education, rights awareness campaigns, and paralegal education prepared citizens to reinterpret their relations with the state in the areas of political and economic governance. The result was a more informed citizen. Regrettably, the gains of civic education were somewhat eroded by the ethnicization of politics. The political elites that lost after the collapse of opposition politics deployed ethnicity to slowly reconstitute themselves. The political elites reverted to mobilizing their ethnic constituencies in preparation for the 1997 elections. Any focus on broad governance and democracy reforms was lost in the stampede to the elections. Although the citizen was now relatively better informed about governance and democracy, there was a tendency among civil society organizations and international donors to reduce the struggle for reform to a simplistic tunnel vision: a Moi-must-go agenda. Rather than focusing on governance, the "Moi-must-go" slogan became the rallying call for the unity of civil society and opposition groups.

The civil society became highly politicized during the second moment. It became increasingly involved in the struggle for constitutional reforms and sought to foster unity among opposition political parties ahead of the 1997 elections. Donors provided the bulk of funds for the civil society constitutional reform initiative. Out of these efforts came the conviction that opposition unity was critical to the removal of KANU so that a new government could effect comprehensive constitutional reforms. Civil society organizations mobilized support for the constitutional review process when it became clear that the state would not start the process. From 1994 to 1995, the Kenya Human Rights Commission (KHRC) led other NGOs to form the Citizens Coalition for Constitutional Change (4Cs), the focal organization to lead the struggle for constitutional reforms. In 1995, they came up with a model constitution that depresidentialized the state. The model devolved more powers to popularly elected bodies.[17]

The reaction of the government was immediate. The KANU state argued that the model constitution was a project by the opposition Kikuyu elites and did not reflect the interests of the society. But in April 1997 the NGOs held a convention and developed a program of action underlining civic defiance to force changes in the constitution. Thereafter, civic defiance spread to rural and urban areas under the leadership of civil society and radical opposition political parties. The moderates and the government saw these developments as an ominous loss of control of the political processes. They became concerned that the civil society was now leading the process for constitutional reforms that, in their view, was the proper province of parliament.

The fear of losing civil society—human rights organizations in particular—led the opposition political parties to seek a dialogue with the government over constitutional reforms. Civil society correctly argued that this was an attempt to hijack the reform process. Consequently, it mobilized against the elections if they were conducted without comprehensive constitutional reforms. It also resolved to constitute a sovereign citizen's constituent assembly to write a new constitution. The government took this as a threat to form a parallel government. From then on, the government violently repressed any meetings organized by civil society.

However, the government agreed to a dialogue with the opposition parties with civil society locked out. The parties agreed to discuss the future of the country within parliament. They formed the Inter-Parties Parliamentary Group (IPPG) to design a strategy for instituting the reforms. This split the NCEC from the opposition parties that had been key to the mobilization of civic defiance for the NCEC. The reform loci eventually moved away from the ambits of civil society to the corridors of government. The NCEC's clout faded as did that of the radical opposition MPs, who were ambivalent on whether to participate in the elections. The IPPG provided minimum reforms and underlined the need for a constitutional commission after the elections.

The second moment of political transition in Kenya had several contradictions. Although the opposition parties had been weakened by the deep ethnicization of politics, they reconstituted themselves to fence off civil society from the political space. The fear of losing the reform agenda to what they considered radical human rights groups prompted both the government and the opposition political parties to form an alliance to defeat the civil society. That is why the types of reforms introduced by the government were not comprehensive, but administrative and procedural in character. The same opposition political parties that would have benefited from an expanded political space ironically defeated the reform agenda. The second contradictory tendency was over the politicization of civil society and its inability to take control of the political space. Although civil society organizations were able to direct political processes, they were unable to consolidate their hold on political space. Because of this failure by civil society, the moderates hijacked the process and stopped any feasibility of comprehensive constitutional reforms. Interestingly, some donors also feared that civil society organizations were becoming too political. They were afraid that the government would associate the struggles by NGOs with donor funding. Many refused to fund NGOs because of these risks. The second moment of transition produced truncated reforms.

The Third Cycle: Donor Support for NGOs and Opposition Victory

Immediately after the 1997 elections, civil society groups focused their attention on three important areas: public education on democracy and governance; constitutional reforms; and the unity of opposition political parties. Many had argued that only civic education would equip citizens with the skills and knowledge necessary to participate in public affairs. Concerned that the government was using state-controlled media for propaganda, NGOs developed an elaborate program on civic education. Donors were concerned that the state was using the state-owned media to transmit state-censored information and political values to the society. These concerns eventually culminated into an approach for a national civic education.

There was a general consensus among donors and NGOs that previous attempts at civic education did not equip citizens with skills to participate effectively in public affairs. Citizens were inadequately prepared to consolidate a mature political culture. This thinking pointed at the ethnicization of politics and voting patterns that mirrored Kenya's ethnic demography and geography. It was clear that the gains for civic education had been limited. Furthermore, civic education was usually an initiative of urban based groups provided without any coordination. These critiques to the formation of a national program for civic education—the National Civic Education Program (NCEP)—would be delivered by a select group of NGOs with the support of several donors. The focus of the program was on democracy, governance, and constitutionalism. The program focused on constitutional reforms because it was launched in 2000, a time when that was the key plank of the struggle for change. The NCEP promoted individual awareness and knowledge about the constitutional reform agenda. Evaluation reports of the program showed that it promoted an individual sense of civic competence, skills, and knowledge to engage with the political system.

It was the argument of civil society that a flawed constitutional framework had enabled KANU to win elections and fragment the social basis of support for opposition political groups. What was required was a review of the constitution to reconstruct the institutions of the state and enhance the space for democratic change. NGOs contended that divisions among opposition parties—especially ethnic divisions—had become a crevice through which KANU won. They worried that the failure of opposition unity would pave the way for another defeat by KANU—and another five years of waste, corruption, and bad governance.

The merger of KANU and the opposition National Development Party (NDP) of Raila Odinga, whose ethnic base was among the Luo ethnic group, gave urgency to the need for opposition unity and alliance building. The unity of KANU and LDP pushed the other opposition parties to come together. NGOs played a guiding role in opposition unity. Civil society identified the constitution review process as the basis for unity and merger. But the opposition groups and NGOs took the demand a step further and established a reform process of their own, independent of the government. This led to the formation of the People's Commission of Kenya out of the Ufungamano Initiative.

The Ufungamano Initiative led to several attempts at unity among opposition parties. Many MPs joined to mobilize support for the Ufungamano Initiative. They formed Muungano wa Mageuzi (Kiswahili for "Movement for Change") to drum up support for reform. Because of the support they received—even in KANU's heartland—the government banned their activities. In March 2001, at the urging of NGOs, opposition parties made another attempt to work together. The result was Umoja wa Wakenya (Kiswahili for "Unity among Kenyans"). UKenya was meant to counter the KANU/NDP merger as the basis for opposition unity. But the group failed to agree on which other parties to bring on board, and remained inactive.

But NGOs continued to demand opposition unity. In response, leaders of the mainstream opposition political parties joined human rights groups to form the National Alliance for Change (NAC). NAC constituted a forum to discuss opposition unity. Once again, civil society provided the leadership in the formulation of NAC's vision and its programs. Under the leadership of civil society, NAC developed a Memorandum of Understanding that was signed by participating parties. As a show of commitment to political change and to demonstrate that it would not centralize power in the presidency, the alliance developed a new structure with the position of Prime Minister. It created a secretariat and formally joined the National Party of Kenya (NPK) after which it became the

National Alliance (Party) of Kenya (NAK). NAK, the new party, became an umbrella group of thirteen political parties and two civil society groups—NCEC and Progressive People's Forum.

NCEC's grassroots network in the countryside was a key entry point for the mobilization of citizens. Religious organizations were also channels for communicating the agenda of the new political force. Civil society groups provided intellectual and other input to bolster opposition unity. NGOs became the intelligentsia of the opposition. This had one consequence: to cement relations between the opposition political parties and human rights civil society organizations. Ironically, this relationship weakened civil society and prevented it from taking an active antigovernment role once NARC came to power after the 2002 elections.

On October 14, 2002, divisions within KANU splintered the party into two factions. One faction, the Rainbow Alliance, walked out of KANU to join NAK. Together, they became the National Rainbow Coalition under a Memorandum of Understanding crafted with the help of civil society groups. In December 2002, NARC won the elections and formed the new government.

It is not in doubt that civil society founded the coalition of political forces and contributed to the defeat of KANU. Civil society achieved this by providing "knowledge" to opposition parties. It was within civil society that thinking about opposition unity took shape and was transmitted to the political arena through meetings convened by parties and/or civil society groups. Secondly, civil society groups achieved opposition unity through concerted efforts. It provided "shuttle diplomacy" by carrying "messages of dialogue" from party to party and by providing a programmatic vision to all the parties that eventually formed NARC.

Civil Society and the NARC Government

A close relationship formed between the new government and civil society once NARC assumed office in 2003. In certain instances, the government was seen as a civil society government while in other civil society elites were seen as government errand officers or government officials in waiting. This perception owed much to a number of factors. First, the NARC government included leaders from civil society, particularly those with whom it had collaborated while in the opposition. Second, some individuals from civil society were elected to parliament. This was in line with the preelection vision. Civil society had mobilized many individuals to engage the political space by fighting for parliamentary seats. This was meant to ensure that there was a substantial number of "reformers" in parliament to champion reforms.

Ironically, the organic relationship between civil society and the new government became the basis for weakening civil society and for tensions between the government and civil society. To begin with, the new government started to speak "civil society" language, the idiom of rights and democracy. The government also designed programs similar to those of human rights and good governance NGOs. Over time, these developments created a crisis of legitimacy and relevance among NGOs. Civil society became "irrelevant" once the government started to address corruption, human rights abuses, transitional justice, and correction of historical wrongs.

NGOs were reluctant to criticize the new government that was composed of their friends. Many adopted a "wait and see" attitude. Personal relationships between leaders of NGOs and officials in government created a muddled environment. This led to reduced vigilance of the government by civil society. While few were critical of the state, others were waiting for appointment to government positions. The result was silence from many NGOs, although there were many that battled to identify and understand their roles and responsibilities in the new political dispensation.

While the organic relations between civil society and government weakened the former, it produced similarly negative tendencies in latter. Many in government became oblivious to the role of civil society and intolerant of its critical eye. Initial attempts by NGOs to point out wrongs were met with cynicism and contempt from government with origins in civil society. They claimed that civil society did not appreciate how the government works or that it was too soon for civil society to judge the new government. Intolerance gradually grew to open outbursts against civil society. Unfortunately, civil society was itself too disorganized to develop a common front or collective strategies to deal with the government.

Civil society has evolved into two main factions: those opposed to working with the government and those willing to collaborate with it. The former had other divisions particular to themselves—some were driven by ethnic factors while others had ideological objections. Although the ethnic divisions are obscured from public view, they are fused to the disagreements over the constitution review process and the vexed question of how to deal with the poor performance of the government in the area of corruption.

The faction of civil society opposed to the government claimed that NARC betrayed the reform platform on which it was elected. It argued that the government hijacked the constitution reform process to make a constitution suited to those in power. In this view, the government was no longer interested in providing a new constitution save one that matched the interest of those in power. The implication was that the state had not changed in its form; its institutions remained the same: opposed to Kenya's reform agenda. To this faction of the civil society, the struggle for democratic reforms had to continue to be embedded in the country's social-political life in spite of the transition. It contended that civil society could not be on the same side with the government; instead, it had to lead the struggle for change against NARC.

The faction of civil society that was opposed to the government ideologically was very small and remained incoherent in its approach to critical questions. A running theme in its discourse was the need to keep the government on its toes to ensure the delivery of services. Some were concerned about basic services while others were critical of the government for the sake of being on the opposing side. But others were interested in monitoring the government to protect society from the excesses of state power.

Those NGOs willing to work with the government were relatively few and did so based on the argument that correcting government depends on knowledge of its operations. They argued that change could come from working within the state. Within this group, there were also significant differences. On the one hand, there were groups with long-term relations with individuals in power. Because of these personal relations, they found it difficult to be critical of the government. Still, there were others who opted to work for or support the government for ethnic reasons because they were aligned with the ethnic elites in power. The group willing to work with the government was also relatively small and uncoordinated in its approach to national issues. It had not taken openly strong progovernment positions, in part because civil society in Kenya has always been known to be antigovernment.

On the whole, civil society was deeply divided along several lines. It had been severely weakened by these fractures and could not speak with one voice on national issues. One manifestation of this weakness was the inability to address the question of internal governance within the National Council of NGOs, the umbrella body for registered NGOs. The Council had experienced internal governance for years but NGOs were unable to address this because of steep divisions within the sector. These divisions continued to erode the legitimacy of civil society.

Conclusion

Suspicion and mistrust have characterized the relationship between the state and civil society since the colonial period. The reason for this lies in the raison d'etre of both the state and the civil society. The state was forged by the use of force and for the purpose of exploitation. It has been antidemocratic and antipeople. Civil society on the other hand, has existed as the space through which citizens exert themselves in the social-political arena. Human rights NGOs have played an important role in this regard. They have created a platform for articulating societal interests. They also became a training ground for political activism and eventually for opposition political parties.

The analysis in this chapter shows that the focus of reforms in the country has been narrow and particular. Reasons for this include infatuation with the neoliberal agenda that is in line with the demands and interests of donors to see political reforms in terms of numbers and activities. In the political sphere, the focus has been limited to multipartyism and the number of political parties rather than the democratization of political space. Little attention is paid on the quality of popular struggles for democratic reforms. Donor support for the activities of civil society has limited their focus. In many ways, civil society has become the courier of the donors' neoliberal agenda. Civil society organizations have generally been co-opted into the neoliberal ideology in spite of its weak potential to foster popular democracy. The ethnicization of politics has also eroded gains made by civil society. The dominance of ethnicity in the political space has diminished issue-based politics and increased the prominence of ethnic-based politics. This explains the continued truncation of reforms at the cusp of success. It also explains, for instance, why ethnic elites in the opposition political parties and the government prefer to work together rather than accept civil society leadership of the reform agenda. Both are afraid of genuine civil society reforms that would alter the existing structures of power.

The coming to power of a new government resulted in a weak civil society because civil society took a long "wait and see" approach. Some were careful not to criticize "friends in government" while others lacked a programmatic approach to the new space. On the whole, the new government's rise to power exposed the institutional weaknesses of civil society. Glaringly, civil society was yet to craft strategy to address grand corruption in the government.

But there were other challenges facing civil society. One less visible challenge was the quandary over how to engage the opposition. One view was that civil society should continue to work with opposition parties to monitor the government. Unfortunately, KANU dominated the opposition. Some civil society groups felt that working with KANU would not produce any democratic returns given the party's history of gross abuse of power in the past. The second and quite audible view was that civil society must remain vigilant because governments never change their disposition. This view warned that the NARC government had gone off the tracks, much like KANU before it. These types of challenges could only be resolved if civil society developed a proper vision and strategic approach as a sector. It had to take deliberate steps to institutionalize networks and partnerships at the local and national levels. Local community groups would have needed to be integrated in human rights and good governance programs to facilitate the consolidation of democracy at the local level. The creation of a strong and coherent civil society will be a long and laborious process, but it is necessary for the success of democracy in Kenya.

PART IV

State/Civil Society Relations

CHAPTER NINE

State and Civil Society Relations: Constructing Human Rights Groups for Social Change

Livingstone Sewanyana

THE HUMAN RIGHTS movement in Africa has come under intense scrutiny in recent years, due largely to the slow pace of democratic reforms. Even countries that were viewed as having made some progress, such as Uganda, Ethiopia, Eritrea, Ivory Coast, and Kenya, have registered significant setbacks in recent years. Human rights NGOs, which are part of civil society, have been viewed as an important actor in the democratic reform process. However, critics argue that not enough has been done by this specialized sector to advance reforms in the region. One key challenge to the functioning and success of human rights groups is the lack of response by the state to the demands of the sector. Only a clear understanding of the relationship between human rights groups and states in East Africa can put these expectations in perspective and provoke positive action.

This chapter analyzes the role of civil society organizations in promoting political democracy and argues that human rights groups in East Africa will have to undertake profound institutional and tactical changes to have any influence on states and the pace of political reforms. These strategies include, but are not limited to, broadening their constituencies, becoming more politically assertive, improving accountability, especially strategic accountability, creating stronger coalitions, using nonviolent civil disobedience, widening local resource base for greater sustainability, enhancing professional competence, and forging stronger partnerships with the so-called international civil society movement.

Civil Society and State Relations in East Africa

The traditional view of civil society/state relations is that civil society, in its plurality, is a rival to government power. The question is how powerful should civil society be relative to government? How is civil society defined, and what is its democratic function? Larry Diamond describes civil society as the realm of organized social life that is voluntary, self-generating, self-supporting, autonomous from the state, and bound by a legal order or set of shared rules.[1] It involves citizens acting collectively in a public sphere to express interests, passions, and ideas, exchange information, achieve mutual goals, make demands on the state, and hold state officials accountable. Diamond gives four distinctive attributes of civil society that differentiate it from "society" in general: civil society is concerned with *public* rather than *private* ends; civil society *relates to the state* in some way but does not aim to win formal power or office in the state (seeks policy changes, relief, redress, or accountability); civil society encompasses *pluralism* and *diversity* (does not tolerate extremism, fundamentalist, revolutionary, or chauvinist ideology; and civil society allows *partialnes*s (no group monopolizes community interest).

The four distinguishing features presuppose that civil society has a strong interest in democratic governance and that it assigns itself as the chief counterweight to the state. The idea of counterweight cultivates a new relationship with the state, that of being a sphere of action that is independent of the state and is capable of energizing resistance to a tyrannical regime. Civil society therefore would be viewed as a burden to any state, whether democratic or authoritarian.

Robert Putnam, however, categorizes civil society into Civil Society I Organizations and Civil Society II Organizations.[2] He argues that Civil Society I Organizations are associations that provide "networks of civic engagement" within which reciprocity is learned and enforced, trust is generated, and communication and patterns of collective action are facilitated. These include social clubs, cooperatives, and cultural associations. These exist for the common good and pose no serious threat to the state. Civil Society II organizations focus on enhancing democracy or curbing authoritarianism and are an enigma to the state. This includes groups that enable citizens to mobilize against tyranny and counter state power and in so doing bring out the conflictual potential of civil society.[3]

Alexis de Tocqueville subscribed to the latter view of civil society and contended that these groups thrive better with a vibrant system of political associations in place. Indeed, Tocqueville argued "that where political associations are forbidden, civil associations will always be few, feebly conceived, unskillfully managed and either never form any vast designs or will fail in the execution of them."[4] Put in the context of East Africa, all post-independence regimes have often circumscribed civil society groups. They have been emasculated or live in fear of repressive regimes in the region. This has been true whether in Uganda under President Museveni, Kenya under President Moi, or Tanzania under President Nyerere.

The descriptions of civil society here emphasize the nonpolitical nature of these associations. Political parties are excluded, although they are considered useful and strategic allies. Civil society must confront the state while upholding its authority. Consequently, the state and civil society are intimately linked. According to Nelson Kasfir,[5] "where the state's capacities contract or collapse, civil society will weaken. Associational life may grow when the state becomes less effective and more arbitrary, but civil society is likely to shrink." This description may reflect the status of human rights groups in East Africa. They are mainly civic and nonpartisan. Generally, they seek to improve the political system to make it more democratic through human rights monitoring, voter education and mobilization, poll watching, campaigning against corruption, and promoting human rights education.

Civil society can therefore be seen as a support for the state, but also as a bulwark against state power. What roles, then, should civil society and government play to increase human freedoms? This requires an examination of the traditional relationship between the two in terms of the mutual benefit that accrues to each. First, the state has the primary responsibility to protect and promote human freedoms and has been mandated to do so under international treaties and national law.[6] But civil society needs the civic space within which to operate. The state is necessary to guarantee that political space to civil society. The existence of a sympathetic government is central to the existence and effectiveness of civil society. Without such space civil society is unlikely to exist. It has been said that civil society needs a "touchstone" or a "canvas" for its activities. Although civil society is viewed as separate from the state and is often in opposition to it, it relies on the state for its existence as a focus for activities.

This requirement of civic space is both positive and negative. Human rights groups require some form of regulation to avoid a situation where individuals pursue selfish interests at the expense of society. This regulation can also be a major constraint to the freedom necessary for groups to function effectively. Within East Africa, states have enacted laws that seek to ensure that groups can only operate if they are registered. This may not be bad per se, but NGOs are required to operate without violating the "public interest," a term that may be used to coerce them into toeing the government line or risk deregistration.

In Uganda, the 1989 NGO registration statute requires regular renewal of a license and makes it an offense to operate without it. The 2006 NGO Amendment Registration Act imposes a criminal liability—a prohibitive fine or imprisonment or both—on any individual who operates without a permit. The effectiveness of human rights groups and their ability to take radical approaches is constrained by legal bottlenecks that generate persistent fear. The behavior of human rights groups has consequently been more conformist and ineffective in mobilizing public disobedience against state excesses, corruption, torture, arbitrary arrests, and state failure to deliver social services.

Second, the state is an important precondition for civil society. The delivery of social services and development in general are facilitated by the state. The economic, social, and political infrastructure that civil society needs in order to function is provided by the state, although support from other sectors is important. If the state denied human rights groups the infrastructure for their activities, there is no doubt that they would be disabled. Just imagine what would happen if the state denied NGOs access to banking, water, and communication services. They would be pushed to extinction.

But the state needs civil society for a variety of reasons. First, civil society acts as a bridge between the state and citizens. Normally, monolithic states are brought closer to the people through institutions of civil society. This improves government decision making as more people are stimulated to participate. This is true of human rights groups in East Africa. East African States have been undergoing political transitions that require the adoption of new constitutions. In this process of constitutional reform, human rights groups have been central to the mobilization of people to present views and to debate them. Civil society groups generate alternative views and debates are fostered.

Civil society is also an instrumental teacher, often providing leaders and inculcating democratic values. This educational role manifests itself in the very act of organizing institutionally to peacefully influence state decision making through negotiation and provides valuable learning about the conduct of democracy, otherwise known as the "school of compromise." This role includes being a source of future leaders for government as one of its instrumental values. Politicians in East Africa are not well known for compromise and skill, elements necessary for democratic governance. Civil society can be a good breeding ground for new leadership for the state. Kenya, for example, demonstrated this in the aftermath of the 2002 regime change with the new leadership that took over from the government of President Moi.

Civil society is an institution builder. This is best shown in the creation of formalized institutions of representation of varying interests. These institutions allow a plurality of views to be represented to government. There are hundreds of groups speaking for different constituencies, such as women, children, the disabled, minorities, and pastoralists.

Civil society is best known for providing a democratic information infrastructure. Civil society often takes the lead in disseminating information and fermenting ideas within society. This ensures organized and informed debate with the government on relevant issues. Perhaps this is one area in which human rights groups in East Africa have excelled. They have been at the forefront of generating information through publications, seminars, and radio for transmission to state agencies. The extent to which this information is utilized in policy formulation and debates would be an important subject of study.

Finally, according to Michael Foley and Bob Edwards, civil society can be a builder of social capital, facilitating governability through cohesion by decreasing social cleavages and enhancing social capital.[7] This mutual relationship between the state and civil society and their interdependence helps to define the context in which civil society, especially human rights groups, can expand human freedoms.

Addressing the Democratic Deficit

Michael Mann contends that "infrastructural power," in contrast to despotic power, should be the ultimate aim of every state.[8] He argues that infrastructural power is gained through state interactions with society-power through society, not over society, by intertwining the state with society. Despotic power over a people is maintained with a powerful and active military, as is the case in many developing countries such as Uganda. Liberal democracy, he argues, arose out of infrastructural power at the expense of despotic power. In its interaction with the state, civil society therefore aims to expand the scope of people's participation to increase their choices and limit state power. This is only possible through a set of well-focused and strategically articulated set of democratic functions.

Larry Diamond articulates several basic democratic functions of civil society that are relevant for human rights groups in East Africa. The first and most critical democratic function is to provide "the basis for the limitation of state power, ensuring control of the state by society, promoting democratic political institutions as the most effective means of exercising that control."[9] This function entails two aspects: monitoring and restraining the exercise of power by democratic states and the democratization of authoritarian states. It entails mobilizing civil society to expose abuses and undermine the legitimacy of undemocratic regimes. This function has often created the notion that civil society is in opposition to the state.

States in postconflict societies and those in transition to democracy are very prone to corruption, lack strong democratic institutions, and often exhibit the "strongman" syndrome in their leadership. This is true for Uganda, Kenya, Tanzania, Ethiopia, and Eritrea. Groups seeking to limit state power must have the capacity to expose abuses in a most coherent, objective, and timely manner, ensuring public scrutiny and spearheading legal reforms. They must be able to act in concert with each other in order to mobilize public involvement.

Few groups in the region are able to effectively chastise the state, and those that do have a limited capacity to challenge the status quo. Because of the repressive nature of the African state, few dare to confront the state directly. Instead, groups have resorted to soft options such as disseminating human rights information, workshops and symposia, debates and lectures. Although these activities are equally important in human rights promotion, they do not question the unlimited power of the state. The unresponsive state finds it convenient to receive the recommendations and then do nothing.

Policing the state entails a process of constructive dialogue. But NGOs must be armed with credible research data. Unfortunately, the space is still constrained for action in this regard. States have not passed enabling legislation to ensure effective access to information that would facilitate the collection of information. The "public interest doctrine" favors "classification" of information such that it would be impossible for anyone to demand access to military information or intelligence data that implicates a state official in wrongdoing. The collection of information and the unwillingness of state officials to respond pose a significant challenge in this regard. The establishment of information nets to facilitate information gathering is key to a timely collection of data. A robust and inquisitive press working closely with civic groups and a vast array of grassroots activists would greatly boost this function.

Ensuring the autonomy of civil society groups is essential if they are to check state power. However, it is important to recognize that engagement with government, the private sector, and other organs of society is essential even as groups guard their autonomy. This is the case because constructive relationships between sectors proliferate, moderate, and mainstream the actions of others. It is important to create a healthy tension and avoid a situation of perpetual hostility. Constructive engagement based on agreed objectives, outcomes, and roles aids this function greatly.

A second function of civil society groups is the development of democratic norms and attributes such as tolerance, moderation, compromise, and respect for divergent views. NGOs can enhance these values through interactive programs that teach the dynamics of consensus, respectful debate, and cooperation. This is a function that can nurture leadership. African leaders are very intolerant and strongly believe in the use of force. The region has become a haven for conflict and large refugee flows. Developing a democratic culture through extension of programs to schools and among adult citizens would go a long way in creating a new culture of rules that values consensus and shuns violence.

A third function of civil society groups is the promotion of democracy through the mobilization of traditionally disadvantaged groups such as women and racial and ethnic minorities to articulate, aggregate, and represent their interests and access positions of power. Such empowerment helps vulnerable populations join the ranks of pressure groups from below to advance social equality, responsiveness, and legitimacy. This function can enhance popular participation and influence at all levels of governance, particularly within local government. The acquisition of the requisite skills is essential for effective public policy participation

There have been positive developments in the mobilization of groups at the grassroots level, although a lot of work remains to be done. The region boasts hundreds of women's organizations and networks, and scores of associations that champion minority interests. However, these groups tend to view their existence as a privilege given by the state and are rarely prepared to rock the boat. These groups also present a very limited and soft agenda focused on self-empowerment and do not address larger issues of democracy. The challenge lies in integrating larger democracy issues in their agenda and promoting strategic linkages with mainstream democracy groups. In turn, democracy organizations must be challenged to mainstream gender and minority issues in their work plans.

The fourth function of civil society is to promote values of diversity. Ethnic tension and cleavages have contributed to the rampant conflicts across the Great Lakes region. Ethnicity is not entirely bad as it offers a sense of identity. It is the manner in which it is exploited to serve selfish interests that harms the peaceful coexistence of diverse peoples. It is important to recognize that individuals can have either narrow or multiple interests that could be religious, ethnic, partisan, and regional. These diverse interests can be utilized positively if they can marry their narrow individual interests with similar or larger concerns of others. The new attitudes that emerge could neutralize militant approaches and encourage tolerance for diversity and a spirit of compromise.

Unfortunately, many human rights groups in East Africa do not promote values of diversity. Many groups still only employ members of one tribe in their ranks. Such employees are often related to the initiators or managers of the project. This limits the value of plurality and creates inward tendencies of "them" against "us." A strategy that promotes ethnic diversity and inclusiveness along the lines of gender, tribe, religion, and other identities within these groups would contribute to new thinking.

The fifth function of civil society is the training of political leaders and candidates for political office. Leadership is a virtue and a skill. The state in Africa does not put sufficient emphasis on merit as the basis of leadership. Political leadership needs to learn the art of participatory management and acquire the administrative and technical skills and normative standards of public accountability and transparency. Even many civic organizations do not have a pool of people with these requisite skills. Civic organizations could deliberately take on this task. The curriculum could address issues such as how to motivate people, debate issues, raise funds, publicize programs, administer staff, negotiate agreements, formulate budgets, and build coalitions. The tasks are important for leadership building. Candidates for political office need these skills to function effectively.

Sadly, the political elites in Africa are rarely skilled in the basic requirements of leadership. They shoot or bribe themselves into power or elective office without sufficient public scrutiny. Accountability is an alien concept to them. Even political parties that are traditionally known to practice these values exhibit a sense of emptiness as witnessed in Uganda and Kenya. A strategy of civic engagement of the political leadership both in government and the opposition would stimulate democracy in the region. A new cadre of leadership would revitalize democracy and renew its legitimacy.

The sixth function of civil society is to assist in democracy building. Democracy building in Africa and East Africa requires a multipronged strategy. There are many interventions that can check state authority. But most require civic involvement. These include poll watching, reforming the electoral system, democratizing political parties, strengthening the legislature, and enhancing governmental accountability. Judicial, legal, and prison reform are all strategies that promote institutional building. East Africa is replete with groups that have initiated programs on many of these issues with good results.

However, democracy building requires the active participation of the state. Accreditation by the state is required for a group to observe the electoral process. The announcement of election results is a monopoly of the state, even when frauds are evident. The legislature is dominated by ruling party loyalists, and political parties operate as family enclaves that are in urgent need of reform. Judicial independence is threatened by executive interference and corruption, and prison inspections need prior clearance. Elections that are the basis of state authority have been marred with fraud, and governments come to power without legitimacy. Strategies are therefore needed to promote institutionalization of norms and procedures to challenge these antidemocratic practices.

Information is power. States hide a lot of information from the people. A free press is an important vehicle for providing information and exposing abuses. However, the media is self-interested and is often driven by commercial motivation. Civil society is an important instrument in disseminating information to citizens to defend their rights. The right to know is vital for democracy. It is only those who are well informed who can contest government policies or defend their interests. Knowledge of military or defense policy is often lacking among the ordinary people, and it is in this sector that governments commit serious abuses. When human rights groups contradict official lies, they make it more difficult for the state to cover up repression and abuses of power.

But human rights groups in East Africa have not been able to overcome the culture of official secrets that denies people key information necessary to keep states in check. Lobbying for access to information legislation should be a key strategy deal with this dilemma.

The seventh function of civil society is the mobilization of interest groups, political coalitions, and consumers to resist unfair state economic policies. This helps the society understand the new international economic order. Economic reforms sweeping the world have not spared East Africa. States have embraced new economic reform policies that center on the privatization of state enterprises. Privatization per se may not be a bad public policy objective, but the speed and manner in which it is executed leaves a lot to be desired. In East Africa, the process is not well understood, even though its consequences are far reaching. State functionaries who stand to gain from these processes hardly explain to the people how the policy benefits them. Farmers, small-scale entrepreneurs, and the consumers deserve a minimum degree of involvement that is often denied. Democracy cannot thrive in such opaque economic arrangements, and it is here that human rights groups become even more relevant. The creation of strategic alliances with other actors such as the media, the legislature, and think tanks is necessary to address this menace.

These civil society functions serve to strengthen the state so that it can govern more accountably and effectively. States need citizenries that act independently of them to advance their own welfare. States can only enjoy respect and obedience when they are accountable, responsive, inclusive, and effective. States should realize the benefits of a free citizenry that is able to effectively participate in development. Unfortunately, states in East Africa are uncomfortable with the demands for freedom by the people. In fact, state responses have often been brutal when people protested to express dissatisfaction with the regime. Civil society has to devise appropriate strategies to deal with governments in the region so that they can allow free expression.

Human Rights Advocacy for Social Change

The human rights movement in East Africa needs new tactics for effective advocacy. A process of reflection, strategic thinking, and internal reform will be needed to bring about the desired social changes. A new agenda could comprise the following strategies.

Broadening Constituencies

Human rights groups in East Africa are new, lack social roots, and are heavily dependent on external funding. Although they have been credited with playing a crucial role in building pressure for democratic transitions and constitutional reforms, they are still very weak and lack the capacity to strike deep social roots. If civil society is to be strong, it must defend the interests of citizens. It should be seen as an autonomous sphere of social power within which citizens can pressure authoritarians for change, protect themselves from tyranny, and democratize from below. Such strength will require a reasonable degree of local ownership and a grassroots base to succeed. Nelson Kasfir questions the sort of democracy that can be created by organizations that do not represent the interests of the majority of citizens.[10]

The success of democratization ultimately depends on the broad acceptance or acquiescence by citizens in the distribution of social power. That is why organizations that promote democracy must themselves be connected to the social roots of society. Only when NGOs are strong shall they be able to activate and engage the populace. Civil society organizations should therefore rise above individual interests and mobilize for social pressure to bear on states.

NGOs in East Africa will need to address the notion of nonpartisanship. When human rights activists distance themselves from politics, the ability to advance citizen interests is severely limited. Advocacy without political representation may have limited practical meaning, particularly in an unresponsive state. Institutions are either undemocratic or democracy is ill- suited to respond to citizen demands where the state is unresponsive. Then frustrated citizens may aggressively respond through militant action. This can be avoided if human rights groups offer alternative processes, such as nonviolent civil disobedience, for demanding change.

Broadening the social base will necessitate building strategic alliances and partnerships with other actors who have an influence on the state. These include the private sector, faith groups, the informal sector, the media, and transnational civil society groups.

Improving Strategic Accountability

Jeffrey Garten notes that with the growth, influence, and effectiveness of nongovernmental organizations, the demands for accountability and governance have increased from all spheres including the government, the private sector, academia, and the general public. He notes that "NGOs have had too much of a free ride in identifying themselves with the public interest. They have acquired the high ground of public opinion without being subjected to the same public scrutiny given to corporations and governments. . . . It is time that companies and governments demand more public examination of NGOs."[11]

Effective advocacy for reform requires credible actors. Human rights groups are not exempt from this demand. They must strengthen their accountability mechanisms as well. Accountability takes two forms. The first, short-term or functional accountability, requires information about resources and the group's immediate impact that donors and trustees require. The second, strategic or long-term accountability, requires information about the impact of the group that should be given to the intended beneficiaries in the wider environment.

Managing short-term accountability in cases of multiple funding sources is now normal practice in many NGOs. But achieving long-term accountability among NGOs is still a difficult task. If human rights groups are to be effective catalysts for social change at the grassroots level, they need to promote empowerment and qualitative changes through strategic accountability.

Enhancing Professional Competence

Effective advocacy involves understanding international treaties, local legislation, and comparative experiences. This is key to engaging the state proactively. Developing the professional competence of staff to devise the appropriate strategies is a precondition to successful civic engagement with the state. This involves maintaining high democratic credentials, ensuring sufficient education for staff, respecting divergent views internally, undertaking careful research and reflection, guarding against cooptation by outside forces, and devising alternative agendas.

Strengthening Partnerships with Transnational Groups

International nongovernmental organizations (INGOs) are increasingly regarded as important because of their capacity to influence global policy on general development, poverty alleviation, sustainable development, and human rights. They have marshaled experience to engage global institutions and governments. The experience gained in international advocacy helps them to link microlevel experiences with macrolevel policies. This comparative advantage over grassroots organizations needs to be exploited by local groups to engage unresponsive states. But INGOs need to learn about the situation on the ground to understand the context within which engagement can be initiated and to promote accountability with their intended beneficiaries. Through joint research, lobbying of key individuals within governments, bilateral and multilateral agencies, and through deliberate networking, the capacity of local NGOs can be strengthened.

An NGO human rights summit convened in Kampala in September 2003 with representatives from national NGOs and international NGOs examined these working relationships and adopted a declaration on strengthening the human rights movement in Africa (see Appendix).

Widening Local Revenue Base

The human rights movement in East Africa, and much of Africa, is heavily dependent on external financing. This raises the issues of sustainability and ability to promote democratic reform. Too often, human rights groups have been accused of acting under foreign influence and of not being "nationalistic" enough. Although it is a simplistic attack, which is peddled by perpetrators of human rights abuses, it is made possible by the external dependence of local NGOs. Human rights work will always need a certain amount of external support, but efforts aimed at exploiting local revenue should be stepped up. These may include consultancies, expert missions, publishing houses, and local philanthropy.

Conclusion

East Africa still faces the challenge of appalling levels of poverty, inequality, and social injustice. Robust political institutions are needed to implement political and economic reforms for sustainable growth and development. Civil society has a role to play in promoting political reforms and democracy. But civil society needs a responsive state to accomplish these goals. Civil society groups will need to balance the tensions between autonomy and cooperation, vigilance and loyalty, skepticism and trust, and assertiveness and civility. New tactics will be needed to achieve this, but more important is the deepening of social roots to overcome patronage and promote genuine reforms is obligatory.

Appendix. The Kampala Declaration on Strengthening the Human Rights Movement in Africa

We the delegates to the Africa Human Rights NGO Summit on "Strengthening the Human Rights Movement in Africa; Prospects and challenges," representing human rights organizations from Africa and International human rights organizations; having met at the Grand Imperial Hotel in Kampala, Uganda from September 22nd to 26th 2003:

HAVING examined the human rights movement in Africa including:

- Civil society priority needs and agendas in democratizing Africa;
- The critical question of NGO leadership development and management for the human rights movement in Africa;
- The global campaign against terrorism and its implications on the respect for human rights in Africa;
- The relationship between international NGOs and their African NGO counterparts in the promotion of human rights and democracy;

NOTING that a strong human rights movement is a precondition for the promotion of democracy, human rights, the rule of law, peace and stability in Africa;

ENCOURAGED by the continuing growth and strength of African Human Rights NGOs in:

- Networking with local and international NGOs in the promotion of human rights, democracy and the rule of law;
- Mobilizing and managing human and material resources in creating awareness about human rights on the continent;
- Building expertise and professionalism in the struggle for human rights;
- The evolving international human rights institutions, norms and standards;

CONCERNED that in spite of these strengths there are still perceivable weaknesses in:

- Over reliance on the global north for financial and material support;
- Developing closer linkages between human rights NGOs and their target constituencies, particularly the rural poor;
- Accountability systems both to the target population and the donor community;

AWARE of the challenges that lie ahead for the human rights movement in Africa in terms of:

- Sustainability of the Advocacy campaign;
- Enforcement and observance of human rights and Constitutional reforms;
- Ensuring full implementation of treaties signed by our respective governments and making these work in our domestic environment;
- Threats to human rights posed by recent attempts of nations to counter terrorism;
- Protecting human rights defenders on the continent;
- (Re)-defining our platform of engagement with the state;
- The ineffectiveness of regional human rights institutions and the absence of an African Court on Human Rights;

FURTHER AWARE of the challenges faced by human rights organizations in terms of:

- Improving transparency and accountability in the work of human rights NGOs
- Capacity building of human rights organizations including improvement in the management and leadership skills of human rights activists;
- Restrictive legislation regarding the registration and operations of human rights NGOs in some countries;
- Enhancing effective partnerships between African NGO's and their Northern counterparts.

DO HEREBY recommend as follows:

1. African human rights NGOs and their international counterparts should strengthen their relations based on the principles of:

- Cooperation in the exchange of information and expertise.
- Joint ownership of projects and recognition of the same.
- Avoidance of duplication, including substitution of local capacity, in projects of local NGOs by International NGOs.

2. Human rights NGOs should define a platform of constructive engagement with the state based on:

- Principled cooperation and non-patronage.
- Strong networking among the key stakeholders in the promotion of democracy—the judiciary, legislature, the executive and wider civil society.

3. Human rights NGOs should create and seek opportunities for organizational capacity building and leadership training for activists.
4. Human rights NGOs should take stock of best practices with the view to replicating them across the continent.
5. Human rights NGOs should cooperate more towards developing strategies for the protection of human rights defenders especially those working in conflict situations.
6. Human Rights NGOs should advocate for Democratic Reforms to strengthen pluralism and the respect for the separation of power and the rule of law.

Both African NGOs and their international counterparts should explore ways of reducing donor dependence.

1. An Africa Human Rights Day should be declared to highlight the state of human rights and the work of human rights NGOs on the continent.
2. Human Rights NGOs should urge African states to speedily ratify both the Optional Protocol establishing an African Court on Human Rights and the Optional Protocol of Women's Rights in Africa.

Done at Kampala this 26th day of September 2003.

CHAPTER TEN

Governance and Democracy in Kenya: Challenges for Human Rights NGOs

J. Wanjiku Miano

SINCE THE LATE 1980s, democracy, governance, and human rights organizations[1] have greatly influenced the democratization process in Kenya after the failure of the postcolonial state to bring about development.[2] At a time of scarce resources, the KANU state adopted a development culture that rewarded ethnic groups that supported it, but punished those that opposed it.[3] These exclusionary and vengeful practices led to the emergence of an organized civil society to challenge the legitimacy of the state. The emergent groups rejected the notion that mass despondency and apathy were chronic conditions. They mobilized large sections of Kenyan society to oppose the draconian state and sought its transformation to a political democracy.

The Kenyan state had steadily decayed since independence in 1964. The colonial legacy of patronage, gross human rights abuses, and the predatory tendencies of the political elite had led to the collapse of a once promising economy. The KANU state entrenched autocracy and used its hegemony to usurp control over national resources. It zealously enforced repressive laws, fanned traditional rivalries among different ethnic communities, and undermined constitutional guarantees of the citizenry with impunity.

In 1991, the political landscape changed dramatically after the lifting of the ban on open political competition. Human rights, democracy, and governance organizations sprung up in several urban areas. These new organizations eclipsed development organizations that had found favor with the state largely because of their pacific apolitical approach and their accommodating character. Even apolitical sections of society realized that good governance could not simply be wished for. It became increasingly clear that meaningful human development would only occur if good governance replaced autocracy. As a result, even some development organizations adopted a governance approach to address development concerns.

Although Kenya witnessed a proliferation of civil society organizations, it is important to note that not all were sincere in the pursuit of genuine political, social, and economic transformation in Kenya. The development of civil society was affected by crippling donor support, state interference, and ethnic polarization that combined to reinforce the prevailing culture of patronage. This led to the growth of a fragmented civil society. Nevertheless, a vigorous civil society became a fact of Kenyan life, even if at different times it pursued contradictory goals. Even though all manner of civil society organizations burgeoned, it was the human rights and governance groups, including faith-based organizations that played the most prominent role in expanding the democratic space.

The Road to Constitutional Review

Jubilation over the repeal in 1991 of Section 2A, the clause in the Constitution of Kenya that prohibited multipartyism, was short lived when people realized that the framework and machinery of the repressive state remained intact. Although further revisions to the law were made in July 1992 to facilitate multiparty general elections, it was clear that President Daniel arap Moi would tinker with the system and not accept its transformation. Indeed, he bought more time by promising more comprehensive reforms after the elections.

However, despite the historic multiparty elections in 1992, the gross human rights abuses continued unabated. Arbitrary executions and harassment of innocent Kenyans by the police, the violation of the personal liberty of government critics through surveillance, the gagging of the press by confiscating or destroying printing equipment and publications, the violation of freedoms of assembly and association, denial of permits to opposition politicians to hold meetings, violent disruption of public gatherings by opposition politicians, and corruption were widespread. In spite of political liberalization, genuine democracy remained a mirage. Most Kenyans were convinced that democratization could only be accomplished through a critical review of the constitution.

The first significant attempt by civil society to debate the democratic process in Kenya was a forum organized by the Law Society of Kenya (LSK), Kenya Human Rights Commission (KHRC), and International Commission of Jurists

(ICJ-Kenya) in September 1993. Participants at the forum confirmed that there was a constitutional crisis because of bad governance and the lack of accountability. They resolved that a national convention be held to determine the democratic future of Kenya.

A number of leading institutions were part of the KHRC-led forum. They included the Faculty of Law of University of Nairobi, Centre for Law and Research International (CLARION), International Federation of Women Lawyers (FIDA), Release Political Prisoners (RPP), Legal Education and Aid Project (LEAP), Mazingira Institute, Kenya Ex-Political Prisoners and Exiles Association, African Academy of Political Science, National Council on the Status of Women, and Council for the Development of Social Sciences Research in Africa (CODESRIA). The forum ignited a national debate on the review of the Constitution. Further meetings by civil society on this initiative led to the production in 1994 of a Proposal for a Model Constitution.[4] The publication, which was widely disseminated, excited constitutional debate nationwide and served as a catalyst for the protracted constitutional review process.

From 1993 to 1997, civil society began a variety of constitution-making initiatives. The most significant were the Citizens Coalition for Constitutional Change (4Cs) Model Constitution, the National Convention Planning Committee (NCPC), which brought under its wing faith-based organizations, political parties, civil society organizations, and the National Convention Assembly (NCA). The NCA and its radical wing, the National Convention Executive Committee (NCEC), ultimately assumed the face of a credible nonpartisan mass movement of proconstitutional reform. The NCA call for a mass election boycott on July 7, 1997, unless the government agreed to comprehensive reforms catapulted it to the forefront of the struggle for democracy. The boycott, which turned violent when security forces wantonly attacked protestors, propelled the constitutional debate beyond the parochial confines of a limited audience. Henceforth, the struggle for a democratic constitution became a national project.

Even though the NCA effort did not result in comprehensive reforms, the matter would haunt the country for the next decade. In the meantime, KANU and the opposition hijacked the reform agenda from civil society through an extraparliamentary forum known as the Inter-Parties Parliamentary Group (IPPG) in which political parties agreed on piecemeal reforms to facilitate the 1997 general elections. Out of the IPPG emerged the Constitution of Kenya Review Bill, a law to revise the constitution. This betrayal demonstrated the proclivity of politicians to act out of expediency and not principles. But the opposition had once again been duped by KANU because the IPPG left it with huge political advantages.

The 1997 general elections once again demonstrated KANU's mastery over the state. The fractured opposition was defeated and the Moi-KANU state returned to power. With the second defeat in as many multiparty elections, opposition politicians were dispirited, weak, and vulnerable. As a result, many sought alliances with civil society organizations in order to reconstruct their reputations and reengineer the reform agenda. But the NCEC had also lost much of its enthusiasm and lacked a clear strategy on its next course of action. That is how religious institutions assumed the leadership of the constitutional debate. Religious groups brought together the Ufungamano Initiative, a collection of diverse civil society organizations that constituted a parallel constitution review process to counter the one created by KANU and the National Development Party.

The Constitution of Kenya Review Act of 1997 provided for a broad representation of the people in the review process and subjected Parliament to the will of the people. However, a rift emerged in 1999 when some politicians sought a parliamentary process that would exclude civil society organizations affiliated to the Ufungamano Initiative. Most civil society organizations wanted a more inclusive process. The KHRC, NCEC, Greenbelt Movement, Law Society of Kenya (LSK), and the Presbyterian Church rejected the KANU-engineered parliamentary driven process in strong language.

We totally reject Parliament as the only forum for constitution making. We don't recognize it as a representative of all the voices in Kenya. We do this appreciating that there is already a stated national consensus that the constitution properly belongs to all people of Kenya. We unequivocally state that the constitutional review process is irreversible and must be people driven.[5]

In 2001, a controversial merger between the civil society Ufungamano Initiative and the Constitution of Kenya Review Commission (CKRC) were legislated into law even as some human rights organizations expressed vehement opposition to it. These tensions notwithstanding, a number of democracy, governance, and human rights organizations conducted civic education to prepare Kenyans in rural and urban areas to submit their views before the CKRC. The Constitution and Reform Education Consortium (CRECO) became a leading provider of civic education under the National Civic Education Program (NCEP). It reinforced efforts by the government through the CKRC to reach millions of Kenyans throughout the country. Kenyans enthusiastically turned out in large numbers at designated venues to give their views to the CKRC. Later, the National Constitutional Conference (NCC) produced a Draft Constitution. Of the 629 delegates at the NCC, 126 delegates were drawn from civil society.

Another impressive civil society initiative was the Campaign to Safeguard the Gains of Women in the Draft Constitution. It was created by human rights and governance organizations to advocate for social justice, gender equality, and respect for diversity and equity. In February 2003, the Institute for Education in Democracy (IED), the KHRC, the Federation of Women Lawyers (FIDA), and the League of Kenya Women Voters (LKWV) formed the Campaign to Safeguard Gains of Women in the Draft Constitution. The coalition successfully engaged with conference delegates, women's organizations, politicians, and political parties with a view to safeguarding and strengthening gains for women.[6] Even though a constitution has yet to be enacted, there is no doubt that civil society organizations played a leading role in ensuring a broadly representative process.

While a number of gains were made on broad national interests, there are major challenges for civil society groups. The clamor for a comprehensive and inclusive constitution review process has been viewed as a threat to the present status quo that favors the political elite. Similar to KANU, the government of the National Rainbow Coalition (NARC) developed inertia over the constitution review process. In an attempt to restore its legitimacy, KANU as the official opposition party, courted civil society into pushing a democratic constitution. But the natural inclination by the state is to wrestle power from influential groups and to subjugate the people to state interests ostensibly in the name of national interest.[7] The roles of KANU and NARC were dramatically reversed.

Though Kenyans participated in the constitutional review process, it is too early to say whether a deep sense of ownership has been instilled in them. Can it overcome the culture of patronage that governs relations between the political elite and the ordinary citizen?[8] Mutahi Ngunyi, a political analyst, has argued that a traditional form of governance based on patronage and social exchange inhibits a culture of constitutionalism. If a culture of constitutionalism is to take root in society, it is the role of civil society organizations to begin a deconstruction process of the existing power relations to enable citizens to articulate claims based on the constitution once it is enacted.

It is lamentable that though solidarity through unity of purpose was demonstrated through most of the difficult phases of the constitution review process, civil society organizations were not insulated from the political intrigues and factional interests. This resulted in diminished capacity for civil society organizations to influence the process. Civil society owes it to the people of Kenya to redefine its relationship with the state and other political actors to ensure that its reputation as an effective agent of positive transformation is restored.

The Campaign Against Impunity

While the constitution review process involved most sectors of civil society, the Campaign Against Impunity largely drew its advocates from human rights and governance organizations. Inspired by the concept of universal jurisdiction,[9] and the belief that shielding human rights violators retards justice, the Kenya Human Rights Commission embarked on a high-voltage campaign against impunity. The campaign was launched in September 2001 at a multistakeholders forum to address the lack of accountability for past wrongs. At the forum, civil society organizations constituted networks on advocacy and activism, early warning systems and rapid response, legal remedies, peace and conflict resolution, and relief assistance. The Kenya Human Rights Network (K-Hurinet)[10] agreed to take up distinct areas that each member organization had the capacity to address.

The key areas identified by the campaign were corruption, torture, politically instigated violence, sexual violence against women and children, political assassinations, land grabbing, and environmental degradation. Every effort was made to complement ongoing initiatives around the question of impunity by each organization participating in the campaign. The campaign set out to create public awareness on the culture of impunity, introduce mechanisms for truth telling and remedies for victims, provide reparations for survivors, administer justice to the perpetrators, establish constitutional safeguards to hold perpetrators accountable, and ensure a peaceful electoral and political transition. Some of these objectives have already been realized.

Survivors and families of victims of past atrocities were hopeful that the 2002 regime change would lead to justice. In February 2003, K-Hurinet arranged for the representatives of survivors of various human rights abuses to meet with Kiraitu Murungi, then minister of justice and constitutional affairs. The survivors presented a memorandum to Minister Murungi. In it, they highlighted their critical needs and called for the establishment of a truth and justice commission. The survivors told the minister that an official apology for past wrongs would be inadequate. They emphasized that the truth had to be known so that perpetrators would be identified and the reasons for the atrocities exposed. This was viewed as a first step in a long healing process. For its part, K-Hurinet recommended to Minister Murungi that known perpetrators had to be prosecuted, and the suspected investigated to establish the truth; that survivors and families of victims be compensated and rehabilitated; and that a commission facilitate truth and reconciliation. Minister Murungi assured the meeting that the government would explore viable machinery for addressing past wrongs after taking into account the peculiarities of the Kenyan experience.

In March 2003, in response to the popular demand by victims of past wrongs, the KHRC in conjunction with Transparency International (TI-Kenya) organized a forum to provoke a public debate on the establishment of a truth, justice, and reconciliation commission. Consensus on a truth commission for Kenya was reached although participants felt that such an institution would only be legitimate if victims mandated it. Secondly, the process would have to be informed and inspired by Kenya's needs and created at an opportune moment for the nation.

These events provided the impetus for the establishment of a task force by the government in April 2003 to explore the viability of establishing a truth, justice and reconciliation commission. The task force consisted of eighteen members, the bulk of whom were drawn from civil society and faith-based organizations. Makau Mutua, a professor of law and leading scholar on human rights, was appointed chair of the task force. The task force drew its recommendations from a comprehensive and open process of fact finding, research, public hearings, data collection, interviews, and wide consultations. Ninety percent of those who submitted their views to the task force confirmed the need for establishing a truth commission.

Although the task force submitted its report to the government in August 2003, no action was taken. The government refused to establish a truth commission. Efforts by civil society organizations to pressure the National Rainbow Alliance for Change (NARC) government to establish a truth telling and justice delivery mechanism were futile. It was an erroneous assumption that a government that civil society had helped elect would immediately warm up to implementing radical and necessary reforms. The agenda for the establishment of a truth commission was largely civil society led but like the constitution, the government chose to shelve the report without acting on the recommendations.

Lessons and Recommendations

Redefining the role of civil society in a postauthoritarian state is a huge challenge. Once regime change takes place, and democracy is ostensibly instituted, civil society must reformulate its purposes. The cohabitation between politicians and civil society organizations, particularly those in the human rights and democracy sector, becomes a delicate matter. In Kenya, it did not take long after regime change for civil society to be disillusioned by its former allies who were now in government. Once in power, there is a tendency to abandon ideals that may be in conflict with immediate political interests. In reality, politicians will inevitably remain civil society's strange bedfellows by reason of their influence on the polity. That is why civil society should not risk sacrificing its noble ideals by identifying too closely with politicians. From the failed experience of constitution making in Kenya, civil society should seek, where possible, a popular base that is independent of politicians.

Civil society in Kenya has been seriously depleted with the absorption of its luminaries into government as politicians, senior civil servants, or heads of newly established reform state organs. Since deliberate tutelage for leadership was not provided, the youthful crop of new civil society leaders is ill prepared for leadership in challenging circumstances. As a result, a previously vibrant civil society sector that achieved landmark successes has been robbed of effective leadership. In the meantime, new cadres are preoccupied with learning the ropes, redefining relationships with the state, their grant providers, and an array of other key stakeholders.

During the constitution review process, most civil society organizations and their networks addressed similar issues. This diluted the overall output as a result of the proliferation of networks and subnetworks because it overstretched the effectiveness of most members who were part of the same networks. It also undermined the cohesion of networks particularly because of competition and rivalry for scarce resources.

Another major challenge for civil society is ethnicity. Unlike religious institutions, most civil society organizations lack a lead institution around which they can gravitate. For instance, during the KANU era, the church was the only civic institution that was less polarized along ethnic lines. It also suffered little under political control and offered sanctuary to organizations that the government would otherwise criminalize. In fact, most human rights organizations used churches as cover when they offered civic education.

That is, human rights NGOs need to expand their base of support. It is critical that human rights organizations mobilize popular support within civil society and at the community level if they are to become more vibrant. In addition, overreliance on donor funding has hampered the ability of civil society organizations and their networks to address issues in a sustainable manner. It is time that local human rights organizations become more aggressive in local fundraising and begin to create projects that translate into income-generating organs of their organizations.

Approaches to deal with the government have to change while retaining independence and autonomy. Strategies, such as radical activism, might have to be rethought. This is necessary in view of the repressive environment that was characterized by the KANU government's intolerance of dissent and hostility towards civil society. More political space under the NARC government, often seen as a form of disarmament by skeptics, indicated that government was more open to dialogue and consultations as a means of enhancing citizen participation in matters affecting them. It is this space that civil society organizations must not cede to government.

Advocacy and research that constitute the bulk of civil society work should be more proactive in the future, and research done ought to reflect the necessary expertise. This would enhance the leverage of civil society when bargaining or negotiating with government over concerns that require policy changes or other administrative or legislative action.

Human rights organizations must pursue causes that attract popular support. An organization's mission to challenge human rights violations, for instance, is a strong moral case for legitimacy. This is due to the value attached to human life. Organizations can enhance their legitimacy by seeking wide support among the people it seeks to help. Such a human rights organization is more legitimate than one that does not have this support. Similarly, an organization with the wide support of allies can claim more legitimacy of the issues it addresses.

Legitimacy can also be derived from knowledge and expertise that an organization possesses. Knowledge of the issues that a human rights organization seeks to address is a great source of its legitimacy. In addition, performance for a human rights organization should be seen not only in the documentation of cases of human rights violations but also in practical interventions to avert violations.

According to Slim Hugo, accountability by human rights organizations should be viewed broadly. He defines accountability as the "process by which an organization holds itself openly responsible for what it believes, what it does and what it does not do in a way which shows it involves all concerned parties and actively responds to what it learns."[11] This means that a human rights organization must identify all the stakeholders to whom it is accountable. But accountability should not only be construed from a financial perspective. As a practice, accountability must be construed liberally to include feedback on relationships, intent, objectives, processes, methods, and impacts. Accountability processes must involve key stakeholders through representative meetings, research, representative assemblies, or voting systems. What a human rights organization says about itself, or what it reports others as saying about it, must be true, easily available, and accessible to all. There is no gainsaying that integrity and reputation are critical to the success or failure of a human rights organization.

Once human rights organizations have built legitimacy and accountability, they are in a better position to seek domestic support. The corporate sector provides fertile ground for financial and moral support. Corporate bodies by nature provide charities to attest to their social responsibility as citizens. They seek publicity through the work of human rights organizations. Giving them awards and publicizing their good deeds in communities is one way of enhancing their public image. But caution must be exercised to avoid being compromised or misunderstood by the public.

Finally, urban-based human rights organizations must work towards broadening the mass base of their constituents to reach more Kenyans. Identifying community-based organizations that human rights organizations can partner with to strengthen community networks would be a good place to start.

Conclusion

It is increasingly apparent that human rights organizations must be able to justify their existence by proving the unique value they can offer. Inevitably, only those that endeavor to adapt to the changing times will survive. Reinvention and reinvigoration will require thorough introspection and subsequent redefinition to provide clear institutional frameworks through which individual and collective goals of the human rights movement can be attained.

PART FIVE

NGO Institutional Case Studies

CHAPTER ELEVEN

The African Women's Development and Communication Network: Pan-African Organizing in Human Rights

L. Muthoni Wanyeki

THE AFRICAN WOMEN'S Development and Communication Network (FEM-NET) is a Pan-African network that was set up by African national women's networks in 1988 to coordinate African women's participation in the Fourth World Conference on Women held in 1995 in Beijing, China. FEMNET, based in Nairobi, Kenya, has substantially evolved since its formation. Its advocacy mandate—to provide strategic information on regional and international policy processes relevant to African women—was meant to ensure that African women effectively participate in the negotiating processes on women's rights. In addition, FEMNET has worked with the United Nations Commission on the Status of Women (UNCSW) in its annual sessions to review progress on the implementation of the Beijing Declaration and Platform for Action (PFA). It has also done intermittent work with other UN processes such as the World Conference Against Racism (WCAR) and, more recently, has moved into global governance work as a whole. The programs and projects of FEMNET are detailed in the Appendix to the chapter.

At the regional continental level, FEMNET works with the African Union (AU) and its specialized mechanisms. This work has focused on the evolution, adoption, and ratification of the Protocol to the African Charter on Human and Peoples' Rights on the Rights of Women in Africa, the evolution of the AU's

Economic, Social and Cultural Council (ECOSOCC), the New Partnership for African Development (NEPAD), and the African Peer Review Mechanism (APRM). FEMNET has advocacy projects that seek to understand why there has been little movement in areas where regional and international policy commitments exist. The first project addresses the relationship between culture, religion, and women's human rights. The second deals with gender and macroeconomic modeling, and the third looks at men's roles in promoting gender equality.

FEMNET enjoys legitimacy among members, partners, and peers as a coordinating mechanism for the African women's movement with respect to regional and international policy. It also works as a coordinating mechanism to ensure that key concerns of the African women's movement find reflection in international policy. To support its advocacy, FEMNET has a training and communication mandate. It pioneered training on how to apply frameworks and models for gender analysis mainstreaming in Africa, and developed its own framework and model for gender mainstreaming. Its training work has been done with both the membership and national governments—initially the gender machineries only, but now also with relevant government ministries. FEMNET includes as a measure of its success the demand for its training, training materials, and tools.

In the critical area of communication, FEMNET provides several channels to facilitate the exchange of information from the international and regional levels to the national levels, as well as the exchange of information across Africa in women's human rights issues. These channels include a monthly electronic bulletin, a triannual membership newsletter called *FEMNET News*, and a biannual thematic newsletter called "Our Rights." In addition, FEMNET runs several list serves—some for its board of directors, national focal points and general membership, and others for its members and partners working on specific international and regional policy institutions and processes such as the CSW and the AU. The mandate of FEMNET has evolved over time because of changes in its membership. Its initial membership has expanded from national women's networks to include national women's organizations as well as individual women.

FEMNET's Core Challenges

FEMNET has faced many challenges by virtue of its identity as a network. But these challenges have been compounded by the fact that it is a Pan-African network. A key challenge is the demand—and necessity—to work across linguistic and subregional divides that are historically determined but are often presented as being conceptual or ideological. This chasm has been complicated by the failure to determine the best and most effective institutional and structural arrangements to make FEMNET a genuinely Pan-Africanist network. As an example, the question of whether an Anglophone, even bilingual, executive director based in Anglophone Africa can effectively serve Francophone Africa, let alone Arab-speaking and Lusophone Africa, highlights these challenges.

These challenges of perception make it difficult to recruit bilingual staff at a regional level and fundraise on a pan-African basis. Although FEMNET has attempted to fashion structural and logistical solutions to these challenges—through various formulations in the organization's history—an optimal solution has yet to be found. This has raised the question as to whether the challenges can even be solved structurally, or whether the solutions should be located at the conceptual and ideological levels. To put it more directly, what are the prospects for a Pan-African feminist project in the context of such deeply felt linguistic and subregional cleavages that are reinforced by the operational context in the country where FEMNET is based and the funding questions with which it has to contend?

Internal Challenges

Internally, FEMNET is faced with other conceptual and ideological challenges. These internal challenges are structural, constituency-based, social, and logistical. As is the case with many African women's organizations, both national and Pan-African, FEMNET tends to assume that working on gender and women's human rights presupposes a shared vision of African women's development, equality, and other human rights. But this assumption is obviously false—as evidenced by the persistent perception that African women's organizations and their leaders are elite and urban. Even so, FEMNET has yet to develop a vision on the basis of mutually shared principles to which members and staff must adhere and openly uphold. On the one hand, however, this lack of vision gives FEMNET's Board of Trustees, Executive Board, and Regional Secretariat room to maneuver, depending on the ideological outlook of its leadership and staff at any given time. But this absence of vision means that FEMNET's board of trustees, executive board, regional secretariat, and general members sometimes find themselves at odds with one another.

Although more African women's organizations now term themselves feminist as compared to the time when FEMNET was formed, feminism is not a homogenous belief system or political ideology. Many variations, which are subject to multiple interpretations depending on belief systems and political ideologies, exist. These variations depend on class, race, dependency, and hegemony analyses, among others. Among African women's organizations, however, the struggle has tended to be implicit rather than explicit and such subtleties are often lost. During the past decade, the dividing line between those who termed themselves feminist and those who did not was among who openly aligned themselves with the movements for political pluralism across the continent and those who did not—regardless of the ideological difficulties posed by such an alignment. Today, the divide is between pro-choice advocates and those who are pro-life, and those who view sexual orientation as a matter of equality and those who do not. It is on African women's bodily integrity, autonomy, and choice with respect to reproductive and sexual rights that the conflict invariably emerges.

FEMNET is a Pan-African network with a mandate of advocacy on regional and international policy. This means that it should not advocate or provide services—beyond strategic information—at the national level. The assumption is that anything else should be the work of its national members. However, the acceptance of this positioning varies greatly across the continent, depending on the state and strength of various national women's movements. In practice, this necessitates constant management of the membership's expectations of FEMNET to ensure that it remains relevant to the expressed needs of its diverse membership without doing different things in various countries.

FEMNET includes in its statement of purpose the intention to play a catalytic role with respect to issues that African states are unable or unwilling to address. In practice, however, FEMNET is constrained, as most African civil society structured as nongovernmental organizations is, by insufficient financial and human resources. In short, the ability to stretch the financial and human resources provided by available program and project funding is limited. The question is whether an African women's movement—or any other African social movement—can be effective and viable when forced to frame both proactive and reactive initiatives into programs and projects with scarce monetary and personnel resources.

External Challenges

FEMNET's has not had a contentious relationship with African states, including Kenya, where it is based. Gender and women's human rights, although deeply threatening at the individual and community level, have not been viewed with alarm at the state level. Most African governments have been perfectly willing to compromise women's human rights when pushed by community, customary, and religious lobbies.

It should be remembered that national women's networks formed FEM-NET at the end of the 1980s when such networks were explicitly or indirectly linked to the ruling political parties at the time. It is only in the past decade that more autonomous African women's organizations have arisen to align themselves overtly with the democratic and human rights cause. That is why in the past decade, FEMNET has actively sought to join the cause of democratization. Even so, FEMNET has been able, at the regional and international levels, to more successfully work with states than its national members and partners. The reason is that states see FEMNET, which does not directly address specific country issues, as less threatening than its national members.

Similarly, FEMNET's relationships with grant-making organizations have tended to be mutually beneficial. For example, FEMNET's core funding arrangement is based on the provision of one month's advisory services to its key grant-making organization. There are some grant-making organizations from which FEMNET will not accept funds, but that has more to do with FEM-NET's staff's ideological positions than on any written policy. FEMNET's board of trustees and its executive board have supported these positions because they share them in some instances and because FEMNET's funding is secure in other cases. The core funding and relative financial security have led FEMNET to be more flexible and autonomous in its choice of priorities. Grantors approach FEMNET on the basis of its on-going work rather than on what the donors would like to fund. However, FEMNET has yet to find a way out of its dependency on grant-making organizations. The organization could not survive on membership contributions alone.

Perhaps the question is whether civil society organizations anywhere in the world can be financially sustainable. Many in the global North depend on corporate and public grants. Although Africa may not be in a place—conceptually, financially, or politically—to do the same yet, perhaps the obsession for sustainability in the classic sense may be unrealistic.

Emerging Human Rights Issues

FEMNET's experience demonstrates the importance of addressing certain questions in the relationship between the human rights and women's movements in East Africa, and at the continental level at large. The first is about regional and international law as compared to regional and international policy as a tool to advance women's human rights. Generally speaking, human rights organizations in the subregion have chosen to utilize law over policy, while women's organizations have chosen to utilize policy over law. There are some exceptions with the more legally oriented women's organizations. This means that human rights organizations have engaged legally binding treaty bodies at regional and international levels whereas most women's organizations work with the policy-making bodies. These divergent strategies have implications for implementation at the national level.

It is true that constitutional and legal reform to bring the states of the subregion in line with their international and regional legal commitments is a concern of both the human rights and women's organizations. However, the follow-up to establish supportive policy frameworks and institutional and financing arrangements to implement state programs—outside the justice, law and order sector—is the primary concern of women's organizations. But this is changing as traditional human rights organizations move beyond monitoring and documentation. This has also changed with the emergence of differentiated human rights organizations that address concerns relative to so-called second-generation human rights—economic, social, and cultural rights.

The second issue deals with human rights issues typically considered to be the domain of either human rights organizations or women's organizations respectively. More human rights organizations have taken up reproductive and sexual rights issues. But they are apparently unable to consistently apply reproductive and sexual rights standards to communal conflict where violations of those rights are the norm. They appear uncomfortable with other key reproductive and sexual rights issues, particularly those relating to abortion and sexual orientation. Similarly, an increasing number of women's organizations now address civil and political rights, but only as they relate to women's political participation. But they seem not to address the context within which women's economic, social, and cultural rights can be realized. They will work on gender budgeting, for example, but not the macroeconomic framework and the monetary and fiscal policy on which such budgeting is based. This is baffling because issues such as structural adjustment, debt, aid, and trade deeply affect the questions on which they advocate.

The third issue is the difficult relationship between equality rights, customary law, and religious law. While most human rights organizations now take a firm stand on the violation of women's rights by certain customary laws, they seem unable to address the violations of women's rights by religious Islamic law. In the post–September 11 world, many human rights organizations find it difficult address this issue for fear of alienating Muslim women. Even so, much work has been done by women's organizations in Africa with respect to the interpretation of Islam from both theological and secular standpoints in line with human rights standards. That work should be drawn upon by both human rights and women's organizations in this subregion to move forward on this issue.

The fourth and final issue is about citizenship rights at the subregional and regional level. The past decade saw the emergence of subregional intergovernmental organizations (IGOs) such as the East African Community (EAC) and the AU. These organizations promise more freedom of movement. Despite these advances, the ability of organizations such as FEMNET to genuinely operate at a regional level continues to be curtailed by bureaucratic immigration procedures that threaten Pan-Africanist projects. This is an issue that ought to be taken up by both human rights and women's organizations in the subregion.

Conclusion

Many criticisms have been leveled at FEMNET. These include what the organization is or ought to be doing, how it carries out its mandate, and the impact of its work. Without doubt, much of the criticism is justified. Both the mandate and the vehicle of FEMNET suggest grand accomplishments. Yet, it is clear that the organization has not lived up to its potential as a feminist Pan-Africanist network.

The question is why. Is it a question of the organization's mandate? I believe that this is red herring. FEMNET's mandate is so broad that the leadership and staff can interpret it liberally to accomplish virtually any goal it deems appropriate. Is the leadership—the board of trustees, executive board, and staff—the problem? Maybe. The various levels of leadership have rarely worked in unison or pulled together in the same direction. Is the answer related to FEMNET's membership? Possibly. The membership is more institutional than individual. Hence, allegiance to FEMNET as an organization is often dependent on its own institutional needs at any given time. FEMNET is not necessarily seen as a vehicle through which to engage with the pan-African feminist project: to debate the similarities and differences among African women. Perhaps the answer to FEMNET's future lies in the commitment and passion that African women feel for each other.

Appendix: Programs and Projects

The African Women's Development and Communication Network (FEMNET) was set up in 1988 to share information, experiences, ideas, and strategies among

African women's nongovernmental organizations (NGOs) through communications, networking, training, and advocacy so as to advance women's development, equality and other women's human rights in Africa.

A constitution and the following governance and administrative structures govern FEMNET.

- National focal points in African countries whose representatives attend a triannual programming conference and General Assembly;
- An elected eleven-member executive board that includes two board members per subregion and a chairperson. In addition, there are two ex-officio board members (immediate past chairperson and the executive director);
- An elected seven-member board of trustees to oversee FEMNET's assets; and
- A Secretariat that implements FEMNET's programs and is headed by an executive director. Since its inception in 1988, FEMNET has played a leadership role for African women's NGOs at regional and international decision making and policy forums. FEMNET works in three main program areas.

The Advocacy Program

The advocacy program includes projects designed to evolve approaches and methodologies for dealing with barriers to the implementation of the outcomes of the Beijing process.

(a) Monitoring Implementation of the Dakar and Beijing Platforms for Action
Engaging with international IGOs—notably the United Nations Commission on the Status of Women (UNCSW)—is of increasing importance to African women. But advocacy at the UNCSW by African women has been hindered by a number of factors.

The aim of this project is therefore to improve the quality of African preparations for, engagement with, and follow up to the UNCSW sessions. The project seeks to initiate and enable a cohesive regional response by African women in civil society to the Beijing process. The project thus hopes to develop the capacity for advocacy and improve the quality of advocacy around African women's human rights at the international level.

(b) Regional Protection for African Women's Human Rights: The African Commission on Human and Peoples' Rights and the African Union
Engaging with emerging regional institutions—notably the AU and its African Commission on Human and Peoples' Rights—is of increasing importance

to African women. Two opportunities in this respect are worthy of noting. First, the intensified efforts for regional integration as evidenced by the transition process of the AU and its New Partnership for African Development process. Second, the elaboration of the Protocol on the Rights of Women in Africa and the appointment of the Special Rapporteur for Women's Human Rights at the African Commission on Human and Peoples' Rights.

The project's activities seek to initiate a cohesive regional response by African women to regional integration as evidenced by the AU's transition process and to the regional legal protection mechanisms around the Protocol. The project will concretely address existing advocacy gaps by providing a framework for regional intervention as well as informed national intervention. Finally, the project aims to identify entry points for long-term work on gender mainstreaming within the AU so as to ensure the AU is able to proactively advance African women's human rights. By so doing, the project hopes to develop the capacity for advocacy around African women's human rights at the regional level.

(c) Culture, Religion, and Human Rights: African Women's Access to and Control over Land

This project is implemented in partnership with the Law and Religion Program of Emory University and focuses on women's access to, and control over, land. It seeks exemplify and address the project's core theme—achieving cultural and religious transformation from a human rights perspective. The project also aims to link research and analysis with advocacy and contribute toward equalizing gender relations in Africa and promoting the ability of African women to achieve economic independence and realize other human rights.

The project's activities seek to build a case for African women's land rights that take into account their cultural and religious contexts in seven African countries. The activities also seek to make policy-making and policy-enforcement mechanisms, including cultural and religious mechanisms, gender-responsive in terms of improving women's representation and engendering both their content and their processes.

(d) Economic, Social, and Cultural Human Rights: Gender Mainstreaming Implementation of Poverty Reduction Strategy Papers

Many expected and unexpected problems attended the process of Poverty Reduction Strategy Papers (PRSP) formulation in Africa. The understanding that emerged was that the consultations helped target expenditures more efficiently but did not provide new insights to macroeconomic policy. The macroeconomic framework of the draft PRSPs therefore fails to acknowledge women's triple work burden (productive, community, and reproductive) in national production. Subsequently, it does not recognize approaches to reduce this burden, identify economic rights commensurate with this burden, or measures to secure access to and control over economic resources for women.

Related to these problems and a challenge to PRSP implementation is the fact that the consultations did not affect economic reform agreements between respective governments and the International Monetary Fund. These reforms and associated conditionalities were not subject to review by citizens. This was a major PRSP contradiction. Existing macroeconomic arrangements need to be evaluated in the light of poverty's prevalence, particularly among women, and governments be allowed to review these arrangements with lending institutions such as the World Bank and the IMF on the basis of this evaluation.

This project therefore seeks to document the experiences of gender lobbies in the PRSP process and provide an analysis of women's poverty in direct relationship to the national macroeconomic policy. The project encourages the creation of national gender networks that influence the national budget through economic literacy among civil society organizations. The project also aims to develop gender awareness among economists and economic planners.

(e) The Regional Men-to-Men Project

The gender approach to dealing with the issue of violence requires analysis to understand its root causes. Analysis has revealed that men are the key perpetrators of violence and women are the key survivors and victims. In the past, interventions have tended to focus on the survivors and victims of violence who are women. However, as awareness and consciousness of dynamics of the problem have become clearer, the need to address men has been identified.

FEMNET has worked with men in the gender-training program throughout the last decade and has identified partnerships with men as key to achieving gender equality and eliminating gender-based discriminatory attitudes, behavior, and practices. FEMNET mobilizes men to support the campaign for the elimination of gender-based violence. Such efforts have already begun in several countries, including Botswana, Kenya, Malawi, Namibia, South Africa, and Zimbabwe. It is on the basis of these experiences that FEMNET hopes to organize a regional initiative to involve men as advocates for the elimination of gender-based violence. The project therefore aims to create teams of male advocates of gender equality and societies free of violence against women in several African countries.

The Training Program

FEMNET has developed a model for the training of trainers in gender mainstreaming which is applicable to the twelve priority areas outlined in the African and Beijing Platforms for Action. The model has been tested at the national level in a number of African states and is currently being developed so as to more explicitly address sectoral concerns. To better address implementation of the outcomes of the Beijing process, the current training program targets civil society, governments, and intergovernmental representatives involved in gender mainstreaming and/or in communicating this work to wider audiences.

The Communications Program

FEMNET produces a monthly electronic bulletin as well as two newsletters in both English and French for its membership. "FEMNET News" focuses on sharing membership experiences of and strategies for African women's development and equality. "Our Rights" includes analyses of gender and women's human rights issues in Africa.

FEMNET has established a Web site at http://www.femnet.or.ke, which is updated quarterly. Work on accessing and using new information and communications technologies (ICTs) for better membership networking and more effective advocacy is one of FEMNET's priorities for FEMNET as evidenced by the growing number of the list serves it runs.

FEMNET also runs a documentation center specializing in materials related to gender in Africa. Academics, researchers, students, as well as African NGOs and Community based organizations re regular visitors to and users of the documentation center.

The current communications program also focuses on communications for advocacy. Within organized civil society, African women still lack the means to consistently share strategic information on initiatives to address the advocacy problems outlined above. The sharing of lessons learned from these initiatives—from the community to the diplomatic levels—is still rare and has proven difficult. It has not been participatory when conducted for the constituencies served by African women's grassroots organizations and NGOs. This project focuses on building content and capacity with respect to information and communications on gender in Africa. The project seeks to enable the collection, analysis, and dissemination of strategic information through content production and to provide capacity building for such content production. The production and dissemination of strategic information on the outcomes of and follow-up to the Beijing process as they pertain to African women is part of the project. The project also aims to extract and popularize concerns and proposals for action in the five critical areas of concern through the print and electronic media. In so doing, the project's activities exemplify the use of participatory communications for advocacy to advance the concerns and solutions of African women.

CHAPTER TWELVE

Social Transformation in Uganda: A Study of Grassroots NGOs

Dani W. Nabudere

THIS CHAPTER LOOKS at how several grassroots organizations in northeastern Uganda worked with pastoral and agricultural communities to enhance human rights, encourage peace building, and foster adult learning. The organizations broadened their collaborative activities to include the rights of women and the youth to enhance self-empowerment. The goal was to improve their lives and survival while at the same time raising awareness about their communal roles. In so doing, they established new grassroots organizations to empower the communities to solve local problems and secure basic human rights.

It is through these activities that the networks acquired skills to deal with donor organizations while retaining their visions and obtaining new ideas and strengthen themselves. In addition, they acquired skills of negotiation and dialogue that made it possible for them to become better conciliators. By engaging other organizations in a dialogue, they learned from each other's experiences and knowledge. In the end, this proved mutually satisfactory and sometimes led to a deeper friendship between the organizations and the individuals involved. This in turn led to new types of collaborative activities and relationships through exchange visits, cross-cultural interaction and understandings.

Through processes of self-understanding, the pastoral communities engaged in action research to disentangle the causes of conflicts between themselves and their agriculturalist neighbors. This resulted in new kinds of activities for their communities, including contacts with scholars. The collaboration between scholars, practitioners, and indigenous knowledge custodians made it possible for the organizations to engage in "field building" activities with the communities. These activities brought together and compared knowledge acquired through research on similar issues to make it accessible to all the users, instead of restricting it to closed registers that could not be accessed by its intended beneficiaries.

Eventually, the dialogue came to include intellectuals who were empathetic to the efforts of the organizations. However, these contacts raised philosophical and ethical questions that found expression in the development of an epistemology of knowledge-creation that could advance self-confidence in the communities. It was felt that the combined knowledge so achieved could bring about a better human and social science to recognize African indigenous knowledge as valid in its own context in new forms of institutions. The view of the six collaborating organizations under this study was that such an approach would best highlight the plight of the marginalized pastoral and agricultural communities.

The study attempts to show that what eventually came to constitute the central understanding of "human rights" in these communities was the need to raise the whole epistemological and cosmological question of how to conceive "human rights" and "development." This was tied with the need to create both community-based learning institutions as well as new educational institutions that can create conditions for rural communities to participate in higher education through processes of accreditation in life-long learning institutions. This inevitably meant creating educational institutions to prioritize the production and transmission of African indigenous knowledge so that the communities could understand problems in ways internal to them.

The six organizations in this chapter were founded as grassroots awareness institutions with the mandate to promote grassroots emancipation through self-empowerment. But others emerged later, embarking on new activities that were linked to the old structures but which opened up new avenues for engagement. The organizations were not created at one time, but took shape as the needs arose. Their formation at different stages became a function of the needs, skills acquisition, and the creativity of the people involved. The six organizations can therefore be described as "peoples institutions" to the extent that their creation was part of a series of learning experiences and activities. As such, the institutions cannot be said to be the end product but a continuing search for self-empowerment on the part of the communities involved. The organizations were: Yiga Ng'okola (Learn as You Work) Folk Institute, Association for World Education, Afrika Study Center, The Mandela Afrikan Peoples College, The Pan-Afrikan Endogenous Knowledge Systems Network (PAEKSNET), and the Marcus-Garvey Pan-Afrikan Institute.

Yiga Ng'okola Folk Institute: Women, Gender, and Dialogue

Origins and Philosophy

Formed in 1993, Yiga Ng'okola was registered as a local NGO in Mbale, northeast Uganda in 1994. As its name implies, its mandate was to bring about learning through community activities and the sharing of those experiences. The organization's conceptual and operating values were based on the African cultures of community work and life-long learning through human activity and interaction. By way of cross-cultural exchange, the philosophy also drew inspiration from the Danish humanistic educational philosophy advanced by Bishop Fredericks Grundtvig, which promoted education for "enlightenment" through dialogue and "education for life."

The activities of the member groups were initiated by *cultural animation*. The member groups were encouraged to begin their activities by first carrying out a collective cultural activity such as singing a song, engaging in a dance, telling a story, or retelling a proverb that had a bearing on what the groups was trying to achieve. This set a cultural framework and context to inspire members and create an environment that was conducive for the activity. This approach placed culture at the forefront of the endeavor, a process that would enhance the legitimacy of the exercise and its outcome. Often, all activities ended with a similar cultural animation of a congratulatory or critical kind so that the members who had done best were recognized and those who had not done as well were critically encouraged to do better in the cultural context. This was done within the African philosophical underpinnings which hold that knowledge does not belong to a single person but to all, as expressed in the Luganda proverb: "Amagezi ssi gommu." This cultural approach was intended as a bottom-up transformation instead of the top-down model characteristic of many state-sponsored "development" programs.

Democratizing the Organization

The most important objective of Yiga was for member groups to define the objectives of their organization in the process of their becoming members. Dani W. Nabudere started the organization as a resource center without a democratic structure and only three workers: a director, program officer, and secretary. The director was the chief executive and held all power. This was an inevitable model given the lack of membership or internal structures of democratic governance. However, the first ten community-based organizations (CBOs) to use the Center challenged the way it was run and operated. In particular, they questioned the mandate of the Center and voiced concern about the divergence of its objectives from their needs. They sought skills such as accounting and record keeping to support and improve upon family income-generating activities.

Yiga's transformation was due to the new members who joined it. As the membership expanded, it forced the organization to create new structures to accommodate varying interests and modes of decision making. For example, a general assembly was created to address the rights and duties of members. This allowed participants to define membership, the application process and conditions for membership, and the manner of participation and decision making. That is how members created a constitutional framework for Yiga, including structures such as the governing council that was elected by the general assembly to run the organization in concert with the director. The director was renamed "coordinator" and his term of service limited to five years. The members also formalized the rules and conditions of employment for the coordinator and staff.

Members took other measures to internalize democracy within the organization. As they became more aware of what the Center could do for them, including fund-raising, the members started to closely monitor whether their chosen representatives were faithful to them. In one telling development, the members decided to suspend relations with their donors so that the Center could establish a modus operandi for dealing with them. In particular, the members were concerned that the relationship between donors and the Center be streamlined in accordance with the philosophy and objectives of the individual member organizations. This process took an entire year after which relations with donors were resumed.

Gender Relations and Culture

The member groups that belonged to the Yiga Ng'okola Resource Center were women's community-based organizations. They were drawn from a wide variety of groups promoting women's rights and encouraging income generation for families. Several were religious groups pursuing similar objectives but through the umbrella of a mother's union. Others were credit unions in which their members were engaged in various economic activities. Some were "burial societies" that combined community solidarity and the creation of credit. But they discovered, through their own experiences, that too much attention was given to women's groups but none to men, a phenomenon that did not promote family cohesion. In their view, this partially resulted in the disempowerment of men and resulted in excessive drinking.

All thirty six-member groups conducted, with the facilitation of the Yiga Center, individual dialogue programs on the alienation of men and husbands with a view towards integrating them in household chores and family activities. This exercise took six months and produced intriguing results on gender relations. The dialogues facilitated open and critical exchanges between husbands and wives. The women complained that their husbands did not help them in the home. The husbands retorted that the women made it difficult for them to help. For example, the men argued that if they went to the kitchen the women would feel possessive of the space, or that if a man carried water on his head from the village well women would ridicule him. Many of the men admitted that they felt peer and social pressure to drink with the other men. They charged that women were spending too much time in women's groups where foreign donors lavished too much money on them.

However, the two genders agreed that both had to change their attitudes. In one member group in Bugiri district, all twenty-four female members brought an equal number of men—either husbands or brothers-in-law—to the dialogues. In this particular group, both the men and the women agreed to establish a division of labor according to the current needs of the family—such as who was to care for children at certain times and which party would do shopping for the kitchen, bedrooms, or living rooms. In another group where no man turned up, the women nevertheless discussed similar issues and strategized on how best to include men and motivate them to participate in the life of the family.

The groups evaluated themselves in a general assembly meeting one year after these dialogic exercises were completed. Virtually all the groups reported that, in their view, the men had substantially changed their views and attitudes toward women's rights and the role of women in the home. Interestingly, these shifts in attitude were reported even for the men and husbands who had refused to attend the sessions. When asked how this had been possible, the group's chairperson reported boys who had been watching and listening to the dialogues through the windows had reported back to the absentee fathers, who in turn engaged their drinking partners in debates about the exercise. One group that had intense debates about men fetching water reported that the men had engaged in "self-criticism" about their attitudes after the women had left the room. The result was that many men and husbands were using their *boda boda* bicycles to fetch water for the family.

This experience demonstrated that changes of behavior and attitude are possible through an appropriate strategy of dialogue in the community. It is important to note that these changes were achieved without any external pressure or lectures on human rights and gender equality. It is true that such seminars and workshops had been conducted by the government and nationally based NGOs. They may have empowered women. But the critical phase occurred when women themselves became direct agents of change. One of their concerns was the marginalization of men and their exclusion from donor funding. They believed that their welfare would be incomplete unless men became engaged and equal partners in the life of the family. The communities were able to transform an aspect of gender relations through a self-affirming cultural experience and module.

This experience illustrated that human rights as advanced by donors and governments is a complex question. It demonstrated that rural communities tend to take into account their own norms and values. The questions of human rights and gender, which the donor community had pushed as a boilerplate concern, in the discourses of "Women and Development" (WAD) and "Women in Development" (WID) had produced a counterreaction in women, the beneficiaries of the donor funding. The women concluded that such an approach could create disharmony in families by alienating the men and making them resentful of donor intervention. The norms the women perceived as most important were keeping the family together and developing complementary and mutually supportive gender roles. The women embraced some of the values of the human rights corpus in their own cultural context.

Relations with One "Donor Partner"

Yiga Center's programs were funded by the Danish volunteer organization MS Uganda. The Danish charity provided limited funding to promote capacity at the center and its affiliate CBOs. Relations between Yiga and MS Uganda were based on consultation and dialogue. Yiga insisted that MS Uganda limit its involvement to "survival activities," or efforts to enable communities to survive the failures of national development policies. However, in the second year of the relationship, the Yiga management felt that some of the member groups looked upon it as a conduit for donor funds. Yiga felt that member groups were using it to siphon money for them from MS Uganda for their own purposes. In addition, there was talk about sending a Danish development worker to assist Yiga. Yiga management disagreed with this approach given the differences on how to address development. The management also developed reservations about those who looked at Yiga as a fund-raiser for them. This showed a lack of a mutual understanding about the objectives and philosophy of the organization. Moreover, the management noticed that some of the CBOs were not democratically organized, as only one or two people consistently attended Yiga meetings and training.

It was because of these tensions that member groups met to discuss Yiga's relationship with MS and to review Yiga's internal structures. As a result, Yiga decided that it needed to visit each of the member groups in their villages and hold general meetings with their members to evaluate governance structures and decide which would remain affiliates. It was agreed that Yiga would assist member groups in writing democratic constitutions, including in cases where none existed. It was at this meeting that Yiga decided to suspend its relationship with the MS until further notice. The idea was to allow the organization to undergo a democratic overhaul from the grassroots in order to ensure that the members understood both their role and that of Yiga. It was felt that once this was done, the membership would be strengthened and the relationship with the donor-partner redefined. The exercise took a year.

In the end, the number of members was reduced when those that lacked democratic constitutions were rejected. Those that were readmitted had to redefine the role of Yiga in their own organizations in line with Yiga's philosophy and objectives. A new constitution for Yiga was written, taking into account the years of experience and self-understanding. Then the organization was renamed the Yiga Ng'okola Folk Institute. Relations with MS were then restored after MS and Yiga entered into a new Memorandum of Understanding. Relations between the two improved substantially with the negotiation of long-term (five-year) partnership agreement. It is in this context that Yiga allowed a Danish development worker to become involved, although her role was limited to restricted matters.

In addition, the CBOs improved their internal management and financing through locally generated credit schemes. They avoided microfinancing projects. The decision to set up and operate internal credit creating structures among CBOs was the result of an internal struggle about how to finance the groups. Once they discovered that the donor was not providing funding, they engaged in a series of discussions, workshops, and training in fund-raising techniques. While some of the groups decided to join microfinance organizations, they found out that the credit schemes were onerous in terms of interest charges and administrative costs. As a result, many the women's groups found other ways of creating credit among themselves, a fact that led to self-reliance in their activities.

The Future of Yiga

Yiga Ng'okola's success will be dependent on its ability to grow and expand. The name itself seems to attract attention and interest from a cross section of society. The first impression when people are told about the name of the organization is to smile. When asked why they smile, they just repeat the word "Yiga" and its link to "work." The organization started as a "Resource Center," which it never became. Instead, it was changed in its operational objectives while the vision remained the same. It started with ten women's groups joining and immediately beginning to define its objectives according to their needs. The Institute has expanded to seven districts in Uganda and created a system of "subcenters" because of the new members. Member organizations, which feel they have many local organizations that want to join, can recruit them through the subcenters and organize local joint activities, including local training and dialogues. Five such subcenters have been created in four districts and this has expanded the number of community groups linked to Yiga to over 150.

The Association for World Education: Traditional Conflict Resolution

Origins and Philosophy

The first attempt to address agricultural-pastoral conflict was undertaken by the Yiga Ng'okola Folk Institute. The organization utilized conflict management by tapping into the cultural experiences of agropastoral peoples in conflict management. But Yiga was not well equipped for the task and it outsourced the initiative to other organizations with which it had a working relationship. Since the coordinator for Yiga was also the vice-president of the Association for World Education (AWE), he linked the two in a partnership for this venture. In 1970, Danish and American college educators established the AWE to promote the concept of world education. Established first in the United States, the organization sought to create conditions in which students elsewhere would not only be educated about their own countries but the wider world as well. AWE was premised on the notion that a nation can fully appreciate itself only when it learns about other countries and cultures.

International Organizations and Local Communities

This case study demonstrates another positive experience gained by linking local communities to international organizations. The experience also shows how African intellectuals can be conduits for the transmission of cross-cultural influences in their communities. Key to this experience was the participation of AWE at the United Nations Educational Scientific and Cultural Organization's International Conference in Adult Education in Hamburg, Germany, in 1997 known as CONFINTEA V. Nabudere, who was associated with AWE, attended the conference and participated in the theme on adult learning for the twenty-first century. In this assignment, AWE demonstrated one technique of adult learning by simulating a conflict resolution game and role-play in which forty participants from different regions of the world took part. This role-play was replicated in the work of AWE when it established chapters in Uganda, Kenya, Tanzania, and Sudan.

The results from the experience and subsequent participatory research on the role-play revealed that the communities preferred to use traditional techniques of resolving conflicts with their neighbors, even though political and economic conditions had exacerbated and complicated the conflicts. For example, in the past, whenever cattle raids took place and conflicts arose between pastoralists and the agriculturalists, the postcolonial state would violently intervene to repress the community it deemed culpable. Such intervention made it difficult to establish the facts and to deal with them in a satisfactory in a fair, legitimate, and proportionate manner.

This research on the possibilities of alternatives to traditional techniques of conflict management in pastoral and agricultural communities was extended across the border into Kenya. The results from these limited experiences tended to show that the use of traditional techniques to resolve and manage new conflicts in changed situations was complex and required further research and sharing of experiences across borders and countries. That is why three organizations hosted an international conference on "Adult Education and Conflict Resolution" at which different experiences in traditional techniques were exchanged. The conference seemed to affirm the importance of traditional systems of knowledge and wisdom to conflict resolution processes. New ideas that emerged included the use of modified traditional techniques, the practice of networking between different actors across communities and organizations to share experiences, using nonformal techniques to compliment and enhance traditional techniques, the revival of cultural institutions, and the establishment of adult learning centers and their linkage with traditional leaders.

AWE Program in the Communities

Immediately after the international conference, Yiga Ng'okola Folk Institute agreed with the AWE Uganda Chapter that the work in the pastoral communities on conflict management and adult learning should be shared but primarily handled by the AWE, while Yiga would concentrate on agricultural communities with some links to the pastoralists. The recommendations of the conference set the stage for a new program on pastoral communities based on expanded participatory action and research. In 2001, the AWE confirmed most of the earlier research findings carried out by Yiga. The researchers found that new social forces had transformed the pastoral economy. The introduction of guns and a free market, capitalist commodity economy had transformed the social and spiritual basis of the economy. Increasingly, traders and merchants assumed a greater role with assistance by the state. New treatment methods for cattle raised survival rates and increased flocks. The population also rose in both the pastoral and agricultural communities, creating pressure on the cattle economy.

These factors were analyzed by the CBOs with the communities. As a result, a program of action was created to address the conflict in northeastern Uganda. The program was adopted by the AWE general assembly and then referred it back to the communities for group discussions, self-reflection, and the determination of which approaches would be most effective in their local areas. This program became the basis for dialogue and negotiations with MS Uganda, the partner organization, out of which emerged workable program that was implemented by communities.

Afrika Study Center: Collaboration Through Research

Following the international conference, the Afrika Study Center, an NGO registered in 1994, developed a structured grassroots academic research program to reinforce the action participatory work of the AWE. The Harry Frank Guggenheim Foundation of New York funded this four-year research program. The research theme was to end violence arising out of cattle raids between the pastoral communities and their agricultural neighbors, and to deepen the theoretical understanding of these problems in East Africa. The ASC's objective was to reinforce the research undertaken by the AWE in order to create synergies in the work of the two organizations. There also appeared to be complex cultural and social problems that had been further complicated by new globalization pressures. There was some research on these matters in monographs and other forms of literature to contribute to the global understanding of the pastoralist communities that have been under pressure of further marginalization. However, much of this research was not accessible to the affected communities. The research carried out by ASC was geared at producing locally usable literature and knowledge that would be more readily accessible to the communities.

"Field Building" and the Pooling of Knowledge Resources

"Field building" research was conducted by the Program Committee on Global Security and Cooperation of the Social Science Research Council of New York

(GSC-SSRC) with the participation of Dani Nabudere, one of its members. The Committee had awarded four-year postgraduate, doctoral, and postdoctoral grants on themes covering human security in all regions of the world. A few select candidates from "conflict zones" were awarded small grants to undertake research for two years involving scholars and practitioners. In this research effort, members of the GSC-SSRC were expected to carry out "field-building" research in their own institutions and countries. The idea was to encourage the pooling of knowledge from different countries and make it easily accessible to all users. Scholars and the practitioners in the community were supposed to create synergy with each other.

In May 2002, Nabudere argued for the expansion of actors and participants in these research efforts. He insisted that scholars and practitioners were not the only ones involved in research and knowledge production. In his view, people living in the rural communities produced large amounts of knowledge based on their individual life experiences in the communities. It was therefore necessary to add a third category to the list—indigenous knowledge custodians and experts. A study project on this question was approved by the Committee and placed under the supervision of Nabudere.

This new effort became a fertile ground for collaboration between scholars, practitioners, and traditional scholars. A workshop on "field-building" research activity highlighted various concepts of research phenomena in different cosmologies. Catherine Odora, the keynote speaker and an academic, pointed to the need for African traditional knowledge and wisdom to be researched on a different cosmological basis because it called for a new epistemology. Historically, research by scholars and practitioners has had a Eurocentric bias that evacuates African realities and therefore fails to expose the true conditions under which the Africans live. This initiative led to soul-searching about how to undertake field-building research in pastoral, agricultural, and agropastoral communities.

Provisionally, the research methodology adopted in field building was multidisciplinary. It drew reference from the region and the globe, and enabled researchers to analyze situations holistically in a cross-disciplinary and cross-cultural way. This meant that the referential framework was at once local, regional, and global. While the national level was obviously to be part of this matrix, it was submerged under the regional level. In short, analysis of events in Uganda and Kenya was looked at in a wider regional context.

There was a growing awareness to go beyond multidisciplinary approaches and to adopt an open-ended hermeneutic approach that could establish viable fields of knowledge and research able to bring about collaboration between practitioners and traditional researchers in the communities. This would create valid new sites of knowledge in the communities. Research on the knowledge located in communities required a form of methodology that acknowledged and recognized the epistemological and cosmological foundations of such knowledge as found in the communities.

The new understanding that emerged in the field-building exercises made clear the need for a broader conception of security as the basis for understanding the causes of violence in pastoral communities. This broader concept included an understanding that localized small-scale conflicts, weapons proliferation, ethnic conflicts, environmental degradation, international crime, and human rights abuses were central to security for these communities and needed to be viewed at the local, regional, and global levels. It was obvious from the research that scholarly studies should reflect this holistic, comprehensive approach to issues that cut across many boundaries.

The scholars, practitioners, and traditional scholars of human security in pastoral communities produced papers that opened up new avenues in collaborative research with the target communities. One major paper, which was produced by Nabudere, synthesized the experience. Titled "Epistemological and Methodological Foundations for an All-Inclusive Research Paradigm for Global Knowledge," the paper was published by the African Association of Political Science in Pretoria and has become the basis for opening new forms of institutions to promote knowledge production that is all-inclusive. It advocates that a new epistemology based on the people's self-understanding be adopted for future research.

This exercise became the ideological basis on which new forms of research have been developed. On this basis, the Marcus-Garvey Pan-Afrikan Institute at Mbale, Uganda, was established. Additionally, the Pan-Afrikan University was built, with one pillar at the official campus and the other pillars at traditional "sites" of knowledge in the communities. The experience is still evolving as people become more conscious of their role and their rights. The SSRC, the Harry Frank Guggenheim Foundation, and the Harry Frank Foundation have supported this research effort.

The Mandela African Peoples' College: The Mobile Community College

In July 2001, the Afrika Study Center, in collaboration with the AWE chapters of Kenya, Uganda, Sudan, and Tanzania, organized a two-week "school" called the Peter Manniche International Folk High School. Women and youths from pastoral communities of these countries took part so as to draw on each of their cultural experiences. The idea was to commemorate the work of a Danish adult educator, Peter Manniche, who had created the International Peoples College in Ellsinore, Denmark, for cross-cultural learning and collaboration after the experiences of World War I.

During the exercise, a one-day school was organized in a *Manyatta,* or a kraal, in Namalu, Karamoja, in Uganda. At the one-day school, the idea of an adult learner's college was introduced and tested through a dialogue between men, women, and youths about conditions in pastoral communities. Women and youth from Kenya, Sudan, and Tanzania observed the dialogue. Participants were asked whether they thought it was a good idea for them to develop a similar institution in their own areas. The reaction was extremely positive and participants decided to form their own adult education college, which they named the Mandela African Peoples' College. They also decided that forty facilitators would be trained for the Mandela College community. The colleges were to conduct research, teach human rights, and engage in other forms of learning, including youth sporting activities. The training would include leadership skills, peace building and peace making, sports, culture, development, adult learning, and participatory research. This initiative coordinated regional adult learning and peace-making activities that involved young women and the male youths from pastoral communities in sports and other productive activities. This was considered a viable way to steer them from recruitment into cattle-rustling activities or forced early marriages.

In order to create more opportunities for young women and men, peace building, sports, work camps, and weekend schools with a cross-cultural focus were to be established in the communities. Young women and men would form groups in their local areas to produce bricks and blocks by utilizing vocational skills such as masonry and carpentry. These activities would promote nonviolence while teaching them alternative means of earning a livelihood. In the long run, it is hoped that these activities will transform the economic life of the region and improve security. It is regrettable, however, that many of these activities have stagnated for lack of funding.

The participants of the school wrote a personal letter to Nelson Mandela asking for the use of his name for the college. Within a month, he said yes and wished them success. He also acceded to their request to send an autographed picture of himself, which they displayed as inspiration for their activities. It is expected that limited funding will support a small building at the site where the community had a dialogue in the agropastoral area to symbolize the headquarters of the college and an address for mail purposes. The principal lives near this site that may one day become a "Site of Knowledge" for the Marcus-Garvey Pan-African Institute.

The Pan-Afrikan Endogenous Knowledge Systems Network (PAEKSNET)

PAEKSNET arose out of a field-building experience addressing the production of African indigenous knowledge on new epistemological foundations. The traditional knowledge custodians and scholars sympathetic to this new effort decided to form a network that would specifically promote African indigenous knowledge systems and wisdom with a view to institutionalizing it and turning indigenous ideas into products for commercial purposes.

The network was composed of a group of lawyers and a judge interested in developing protocols for the protection of African intellectual property rights and the collective rights of the communities to those rights. Other areas of interest included African taxonomy and the development of plants and plant medicine, as well as herbal and spiritual healing. The effort also involved individual organizations promoting particular fields of African knowledge, traditional agriculture, and African methods of addressing crop pests. The members formed a network to promote the production of knowledge and to help professionalize the different branches of the knowledge. This would lead to the recognition of the practitioners of the particular area of knowledge. The group felt that it had an adequate knowledge base from which to classify, categorize, and name particular areas of knowledge and the practice of it. But they knew that there was need for an academic institution that could support their work, train new cadres, and develop a professional teaching curriculum.

The network decided that it would help to identify and locate sites of "Afrikan knowledge and wisdom." It sought to assist in the teaching of the knowledge to students who could then be certified for particular branches of classified knowledge. The sites would work closely with the new institutions of higher learning to impart such knowledge while at the same time developing as centers of learning for rural communities. This created the need for an institution to complement the work of the Mandela Peoples' College and the Pan-Afrikan Endogenous Knowledge Systems.

The Marcus Garvey Pan-Afrikan Institute

In the course of these initiatives, it was felt that there was a need to set up a new institution to support the work of the communities. Consequently, the board of trustees of the Africa Study Center created a new institution that would link high-level research in African indigenous knowledge and wisdom to learning in rural communities. This decision was made in 2003 and was the first phase in a five-year process of establishing the Marcus Garvey Pan-Afrikan University in Uganda. The creation of the Pan-Afrikan University is a long-standing project that was envisioned by many pan-Africanists over many years. However, the project has stalled because of the chokehold of the Western worldview and its control of the African continent and the African Diaspora.

African independence did not resolve the problem of neocolonialism. The first attempts to transform the university colleges that had been established by the colonial powers into instruments of African independence and nation building failed because of the of colonial powers' determination to maintain Western cultural domination over Africa. This domination was ensured through the special relationships created between the new university colleges in Africa and the University of London, French universities, and other European metropolitan universities.

The Marcus Garvey Pan-Afrikan Institute would identify researchers to locate sites of knowledge and wisdom, and help them develop into centers of learning in the communities. This would create a horizontal relationship between the Institute and the sites. The new institution would stand on two pillars—one at the Institute and the other at the sites of knowledge in the communities. The objectives of the Institute would include carrying out joint research programs on Africans and the African Diaspora with a view to creating an African epistemology and methodologies to highlight and mainstream African indigenous knowledge and wisdom. It would engage in curricular development on African indigenous knowledge and wisdom.

The creation of Life Long Learning Centers would facilitate the establishment of information and communication technologies in the communities and create networks with other institutions, including health centers, secondary schools, primary schools, and other rural communities for e-learning and e-health programs. Such new forms of information technologies would assist the communities in developing their own knowledge bases and eventually utilize this knowledge development in the era of globalization. African people must increase their production of scientific knowledge based on their epistemologies and use such knowledge to join the Knowledge Society and, in the process, make such knowledge available to others in the human family on the basis of mutual reward and acknowledgment.

In order for the Marcus Garvey Pan-Afrikan Institute to eventually become a university, it will be necessary during the five-year phase to create affiliations with existing universities and other tertiary institutions. Such collaboration will allow the existing universities to access the new curricula developed by the Institute, while at the same time strengthening the Institute to further develop its capacities in new directions. Such collaborative efforts could create space for innovations by the new institutions while spurring less creative institutions to new vitality.

Conclusion and Prognosis

The experiences presented in the six case studies sought to demonstrate that a genuine human rights movement in East Africa could only develop if it is rooted in the experiences of the vast majority of the people in the region. This means that the bulk of the movement must be based in the rural areas, where most people live. It must view people as citizens of the movement and not objects of pity and development. A people-based human rights movement must be guided by the following conclusions.

- The *human rights discourse and the practice of human rights should arise out of people's life experiences* and must not be imposed from the outside. The case studies show that it is possible for rural communities to interrogate their own cultures and conceptions of human rights through dialogues. It is through this process that this discourse can become a universal reference point.
- The concept of *human rights should be holistic* and encompass all aspects of the people's lives. A rights-based understanding of development should be nuanced to accommodate the people's conceptions of rights rather that the rights-based perspective itself being a metaphysical idea that they cannot follow and implement.
- Pastoral communities understand *security* to mean many things. This understanding has turned out to be the conceptual framework that is being advocated in certain high level scholarly institutions on global security as *human security*. The field-building research experience showed that working with communities can help them confront their problems and fashion policies to resolve them.
- East African scholars need to work closely with rural communities in order to further develop and strengthen their capacities to learn human rights. This relationship must include people in academia and policy. But research must be carried out with an open-ended hermeneutic approach that recognizes indigenous people as producers of knowledge in their cultural contexts. The results of such collaboration can lead to the self-empowerment of the communities while scholars gain the experience of working in communities as active participants. This can strengthen the

ability of scholars to produce relevant and workable knowledge in those communities.

- For grassroots community-based organizations to grow and become visible as part of the global human rights community, they must find ways of linking up with regional and global organizations. The working slogan of the AWE chapters in East Africa is: THINK LOCALLY; ACT GLOBALLY; THINK GLOBALLY—ACT LOCALLY. This is the way forward. The experiences from the six case studies indicate that for this to happen, East African intellectuals should act as the link between their communities and the global people-centered solidarity movements. Intellectuals must be integrated first in their communities.

- The center of all human rights discourse must be the recognition that people of different cultures have a right to their culture, identity, language, and the right to produce knowledge on the basis of their cosmologies and epistemologies. They also have the right to their resources on which basis they can sustain their cultures. One implication is that no human rights discourse should be imposed on other human rights discourses, which may have different meanings attached to certain rights. Another implication is that in order to create a truly universal human rights code outside existing liberal conceptions—which are themselves culturally and ideologically loaded—human rights activists must develop a new ethic of tolerance that recognizes dialogue among cultures.

- The right to life should be recognized by all cultures. The East African experience seems to confirm that for this basic human right to be realized, people must be assured of the control of their natural resources and that no state imposition is legitimate unless it can be shown and demonstrated that the exploitation of such resources by the state, private individuals, and multinational corporations is for the greater good of the people to whom the resources belong. Any other justification that marginalizes the vast majority of the people on their ancestral lands and resources is a continuation of colonialism.

- The experience of pastoral communities reveals that where the state lack the capacity to protect the life and property, either because its institutions are weak or it has collapsed, the state can no longer claim the right to the monopoly of the instruments of violence. In such a situation, the people have the fundamental human right to reclaim their sovereignty and constitute new states and political entities that can advance their interests. This is a basic human right that no state can take away.

PART VI

South/South and North/South NGO Relations

CHAPTER THIRTEEN

The Death Penalty in East Africa: Law and Transnational Advocacy

Margaret A. Burnham

ONCE WIDESPREAD IN Africa, the death penalty is rapidly disappearing from the continent as more states either abolish it or abstain from its use. East Africa is on the cusp of this continent-wide trend. Although the penalty remains lawful in all three countries, the presidents of Kenya, Tanzania, and Uganda have refrained from signing death warrants since 2002, and hundreds of prisoners have had their death sentences commuted in Kenya and Tanzania. However, although the international campaign to abolish the death penalty has won major victories in the last decade, entrenched and important holdouts remain. China, where 80 percent of the world's executions take place, is firmly committed to the death penalty, as are the United States and the nations of the Commonwealth Caribbean. As long as such important states retain the death penalty, it is hardly a foregone conclusion that East Africa will join the abolitionist camp.

Disengagement from the death penalty has proceeded along three tracks: outright abolition, abstention from carrying out the sentence, and reformation of the capital punishment system to render it more reliable. In East Africa, where enormous challenges plague the criminal justice system, measures to abolish the death penalty have been largely ineffectual. Put simply, these three states cannot afford the death penalty, a notoriously expensive legal tool. Experienced—and therefore usually high-priced—legal counsel, forensic expertise, and thorough, transparent, and meticulous adjudication are all required to ensure due process in these high stakes cases. The problem-ridden legal systems of the three states under study, where inefficiencies and corruption abound and courts are understaffed and underfinanced, are simply not adequate to handle capital cases.

Two cases starkly illuminate the corrosive character of the death penalty for the human rights project as a whole in East Africa. In Kenya, Amnesty International took up the case of a young man sentenced to death in 1999 for robbing a Swiss tourist of US$600. The sentence was imposed less than twenty-four hours after the crime on a guilty plea accepted by the Mombasa Magistrate's Court, even though the defendant was unrepresented. In Uganda, a man was released from prison in 2000 after eighteen years under sentence of death when it was determined that the man he was convicted of killing was alive and well.

Despite these grotesque cases, many regard the death penalty as a low priority next to other human rights issues confronting Africa. Some retentionist states in the global South protest that the focus on the death penalty is excessive and fetishist, and that it detracts from the more severe, catastrophic, and costly human rights crises linked to neocolonialism and globalization. There is a sense that the European-led campaign reprises Europe's "civilizing" mission, imposing "human rights" on the "other" while engaging in economic practices that continue to hold hostage a continent bedeviled by unsustainable foreign debt, recovering from despotism, ravaged by HIV/AIDS, and mired in poverty. Claiming the death penalty, rather than, say, wealth redistribution, as the acid test of human rights compliance reinforces the classic dichotomy between first and second generation rights, allowing the North to stake out the moral high ground while escaping any real accountability for policies that perpetuate scarcity, need, and oppression in the global South.

As the region explores how it will institutionalize and acculturate human rights, it will consider what importance to attach to the death penalty issue. Indisputably, the death penalty can be an informative marker on the scale of human rights progress. But it is also not entirely clear what the correlation is between the use of the death penalty by a state and its overall human rights record. Some failed states with catastrophic human rights records, like Haiti, have abolished the penalty, while others, like Barbados, are enthusiastic supporters of the death penalty but rank high in overall human rights performance.

These empirical and ideological ambiguities notwithstanding, there are solid reasons for NGOs in the region to continue to devote human rights resources to the abolition of the death penalty. First, the timing seems particularly propitious. Total abolition in Africa, where several key governments recently have announced their opposition to the penalty, and where South Africa has dramatically broken new ground on the constitutionality of the penalty, is not an unattainable aspiration.

Second, owing to the straightforward nature of the state role in the administration of capital punishment, the issue holds symbolic value that may be said to outweigh its actual cost in human lives. Many of the human rights issues confronting the region, like extrajudicial killings, involve violence perpetrated by non-state actors proceeding, perhaps, with the tacit approval of the state. State nonfeasance regarding these "private" political crimes in, for example, the failure to police, prosecute, or punish is often difficult to establish. However, the death penalty presents a tidy case of the state violating rights, the solution for which—abolition—is equally clear-cut.

Third, although no single paradigm covers all the states still applying the death penalty, it is often deployed by states with weak criminal justice infrastructures and unstable political regimes in the misguided belief that repressive measures will restore order and stem violence. Certainly this is the case in East Africa, a region that continues to be vulnerable to political violence, escalating economic crime, and the ready availability of small arms. In these circumstances the death penalty may seem an apt remedy. But as the South African Constitutional Court made clear in the *Makwanyane*[1] case, there is no reliable evidence correlating the incidence of violent crime and the death penalty. Moreover, the penalty is inconsistent with the state's exemplary role in constructing a culture of human rights.

Fourth, where the death penalty remains on the books, as in East Africa, but is deployed in a random manner, its use is often associated with political crimes. Such selective use undermines the rule of law. Events in Kenya illustrate the point here, for although the death penalty is a prominent feature of the criminal justice system, the last executions there were of the death row prisoners accused in the 1982 coup attempt.

Finally, and as this chapter attempts to demonstrate, the death penalty debilitates and corrodes the criminal justice system of which it is a part. The common problems of underresourced and poorly administered criminal justice systems are a fertile breeding ground for human rights abuses such as custodial deaths, police killings, prison torture, official corruption, and judicial misconduct. Because they sanction physical violence, death penalty systems inure the public to other human rights violations, such as extrajudicial killings. Moreover, they absorb enormous resources that could be more evenly and productively distributed across a range of criminal justice objectives, including expanding access to courts and free legal defense services.

This chapter explores several factors likely to influence the direction of the death penalty campaign in East Africa. It summarizes the current legal and political trends in East Africa. Using a comparative method, it considers the history that led to a human rights backlash in the Commonwealth Caribbean, where strong support for the death penalty pushed against United Kingdom initiatives to abolish the penalty or compel better controls over its operation. It discusses the tension that has emerged between the abolitionist states of Europe and the retentionist states of the Americas, as Europe has adopted abolition as a preeminent foreign policy objective. It hypothesizes that executive initiatives, such as moratoria and acts of clemency, may be the engines of change in East Africa, where the courts have not yet created a dynamic human rights jurisprudence, and where constitutional reform efforts have so far failed to abolish the penalty totally.

Developments in Africa

While its deepest roots are in Europe and in Latin America, the movement to abolish the death penalty has accelerated dramatically in Africa.[2] In 1965, no sub-Saharan country had abolished the penalty, but as of 2003, almost half the countries on the African continent were de facto or de jure[3] abolitionist. The highest number of states in the world with either an official or unofficial moratorium—eight of thirty-two—is in Africa.[4] The most striking shifts have been in southern Africa and West Africa. Between 1965 and 1990, the penalty was abolished in Angola, Mauritius, Mozambique, Namibia, and South Africa, and the presidents of Malawi and Zambia vowed not to sign any death warrants while in office.[5] Among the West African states, Senegal, Cape Verde, Guinea Bissau, and the Ivory Coast have abolished the penalty, and the Sierra Leone Truth and Reconciliation Commission has termed abolition an "imperative."[6] In Rwanda, legislation in 1996 reduced the scope of the penalty, and it was excluded as a sanction available to the International Criminal Tribunal for Rwanda.[7]

However, although many states are abstaining from executing prisoners, the death penalty remains an enormous barrier to fair and equal justice in Africa. Where the penalty is still lawful, judges are imposing it. Indeed, in the many instances where the penalty is mandatory, the courts have no choice in the matter. The crimes it covers extend beyond murder, and in murder cases typically the sentence is mandatory without regard to critically important mitigating factors such as the degree of individual culpability and the nature of the offense. When the mandatory sentence operates in tandem with exceedingly unreliable proceedings to determine guilt, awful miscarriages of justice are unavoidable. Delay plagues the system and compromises justice from beginning to end. Figurative death comes slowly first in the long wait, often ten years or more, from conviction to execution, and the actual act is finally accomplished by means of the ancient and torturous noose.

It is plain that moratoria on executions, while effective symbols of a state's movement toward abolition, are not sufficient to reduce the enormously corrupting effect the death penalty has on the rule of law, especially where, as in Kenya, Tanzania, and Uganda, the state's judicial and penal machinery are underresourced and its legal code outmoded.

Developments in East Africa

Colonial legal history casts a long shadow over the use of the death penalty in East Africa.[8] Death by hanging was the mandatory sanction for homicide in the United Kingdom and its colonies until the postwar era when the death penalty became the subject of controversy in the UK. Even after it was abolished in the UK, it remained in use in virtually all of its territories, including in East Africa. The death sentence was deployed to police race and class boundaries in those colonies, such as Kenya, with large settler populations. Although rape was not a capital offense in the UK, crimes of sexual assault, called "black peril" offenses were until 1955 punishable by death in Kenya if the victim was white and the perpetrator African. Although in the UK executions took place in prison, until the 1930s in the African colonies they were public events carried out in the open, often at the scene of the crime. After World War II, British activists garnered support for abolition with the publication of the British Royal Commission on Capital Punishment in 1948, leading to the halt of executions in Britain in 1965.[9] However, as a bulwark against the liberation movements, Britain retained the penalty in the colonies and after their independence in the 1960s, the new states increased the number of offenses for which the penalty could be imposed.

While Kenya, Tanzania, and Uganda all retain the death penalty and hold significant numbers of inmates, either convicted or pending sentencing, on capital crimes, some of the elected political leadership in these states stand opposed to capital punishment, and executions have been infrequent since the 1990s. These states, like Africa as a whole, have reached a critical juncture on the death penalty. They could abolish the penalty, following the path of South Africa, Namibia, Mozambique, and Angola, or they could reject this international trend, as has the Commonwealth Caribbean, and retain the penalty.

As of this writing, Kenya had not carried out an execution since the 1980s.[10] There have been no executions in Tanzania since 1995.[11] In Uganda the last civilian executions were in 1999, when twenty-eight men were hanged, and in March 2002, after summary trials utterly lacking in due process, military firing squads killed a number of soldiers for murder, provoking enormous controversy.[12] But even while executions have been dramatically curtailed in these three states, there remain pressing human rights concerns about the continuing prosecutorial and judicial use of the sanction, the failure of recent constitutional reform efforts to limit the use of the penalty, and the status of death row prisoners. In short, the central architecture of the colonial death penalty system remains in place: the execution is by hanging, the penalty is mandatory for a range of crimes that are broadly defined, and the true sentencing authority lies in the unfettered discretion of the president, who has the power to grant a reprieve from a mandatory sentence.

The Role of Executive Policymakers in East Africa

Senior officials in East Africa have expressed their opposition to capital punishment. In Kenya, policymakers have been particularly outspoken. In 2003, the newly elected President of Kenya, Mwai Kibaki, released twenty-eight prisoners who had been on death row for fifteen to twenty years, and commuted to life the sentences of 195 others. Shortly before this presidential clemency, Kiraitu Murungi, then justice minister of Kenya declared that he was personally opposed to the death penalty and that his government intended to abolish it within six months.[13] In 2004, Kenya underwent a constitutional review process, and Murungi, the leading figure in the call for abolition, urged the National Constitutional Conference to reject the death penalty. However, despite Murungi's appeal, in March 2004, the Kenyan Constitutional Review Conference produced a draft constitution that leaves room for the death penalty to be imposed for the most severe crimes.[14] As of 2008, the government had not acted on its promise to abolish the death penalty.[15]

In Uganda, the government of President Yoweri Museveni favors the death penalty, and has endorsed a constitutional change that would retain the mandatory penalty for murder as well as several nonhomicidal crimes.[16] However, other public officials, including the commissioner of prisons, the Uganda Prisons Service, and the assistant commissioner of police have condemned the penalty.[17] The last executions in Uganda were in 1999, when twenty-eight prisoners, some alleged to be political adversaries of President Museveni, were executed over two days.

In Tanzania, there have been no executions since former President Mkapa assumed office in 1995,[18] and there has been no indication that President Jakaya Kikwete, who assumed power in December 2006, will deviate from Mkapa's practice. Some officials in Mkapa's government registered support for the penalty,[19] while others opposed it. Mkapa himself commuted the sentences of 100 death row prisoners in 2003 out of regard for the right to life.[20] In a related development, in 2004 Mkapa pardoned and released about 4,000 prisoners held on less serious crimes to reduce overcrowding in Tanzanian prisons.[21]

The prison heads of Kenya, Tanzania, and Uganda have all called for abolition of the death penalty because of harsh death row conditions, the harms associated with prolonged incarceration, the ill effects on executioners, and because in their experience innocent prisoners have been executed.[22]

Legal Challenges to the Death Penalty

All three states are party to the African Charter on Human and Peoples' Rights and to the ICCPR. The African Charter permits the use of the death penalty, and the African Commission on Human Rights has held the penalty does not violate the right to life, which, along with protection against inhuman treatment, is secured by the Charter.[23] However, in 1999 the Commission adopted a resolution encouraging states to consider a moratorium and to limit the imposition of the penalty to the "most serious crimes."[24] The Commission's guidelines governing the right to a fair trial apply in capital cases.[25] Moreover, the African Charter on the Rights and Welfare of the Child, which came into force in 1999, prohibits imposition of the death penalty on children and protects their right not to be subjected to inhuman or degrading treatment.[26] The constitutions of each of the three states protect a qualified right to life and to be free from inhuman or degrading punishment or treatment.[27]

Efforts to eliminate or limit the scope of the penalty in the domestic courts are likely to bear fruit, as has been the case in other jurisdictions such as in the Caribbean region. Two major challenges mounted in Uganda are under judicial consideration. In the principal case *Kigula v. Attorney General*, the Foundation for Human Rights Initiative, a Ugandan NGO, is pursuing, on behalf of 417 death row prisoners, a claim that the penalty contravenes the constitutional prohibition against torture, cruel, inhuman, or degrading punishment.[28] In June 2005, the Constitutional Court ruled on the petition in *Kigula*. While it stopped short of rejecting the penalty altogether, the Court struck down mandatory sentences for some capital crimes and ruled three years to be the limit for holding condemned prisoners. The Court observed that protracted detention in "depressing and intolerable conditions . . . often results in the death of very many prisoners before their actual execution." Both the government and the prisoners appealed the judgment of the Constitutional Court to the Ugandan Supreme Court

The second case, brought on behalf of the Uganda Law Society, challenges the firing squad death of two soldiers in 2002.[29] In this matter, the men who were charged with the murder of a priest and his two workers were killed at a public execution after a Field Court Martial proceeding. Tried without benefit of counsel, the men claimed they were not guilty and attempted unsuccessfully to withdraw their confessions at the trial, which took place within a week of the crime. There was a public execution within three hours of the conviction.[30] The constitutional case challenges the lack of fundamental fairness in court martial proceedings.[31]

One case decided by the Tanzanian courts reflects much of the debate over the status of the death penalty in international and constitutional law. In *Mbushuu v. Republic*,[32] the Court of Appeals reversed the lower court, ruling that while the penalty is inhuman, cruel, and degrading, the right to be protected from it is derogable. The Tanzanian Constitution protects the right to life "subject to law"[33] and to be free from inhuman or degrading punishment. In *Mbushuu*, Judge Mwalusanya of the High Court called the penalty an unconstitutional deprivation of the right to life and to human dignity and an inhuman or degrading punishment.[34] Relying heavily on foreign and international materials, Judge Mwalusanya observed that there was an

emerging consensus of values in the civilized international community as evidenced by the UN human rights instruments, the decisions of other courts and the writings of leading academics . . . that the death penalty is a cruel, inhuman and degrading punishment.[35]

In response to this appeal to international developments, the Tanzanian government suggested to Judge Mwalusanya that abolitionism "presupposes that only one set of values [liberal Western values] is "civilized." They exclude the values of the Third World."[36] To the contrary, the government proclaimed, "civilization . . . is going down particularly in the decadent West."

The Court of Appeal rejected Judge Mwalusanya's conclusion that the death penalty was inconsistent with the right to life. It did conclude, however, based in part on foreign and international trends, that the death penalty "has elements of torture" and that death by hanging is "inherently inhuman, cruel and degrading."[37] But, reversing Judge Mwalusanya's decision, the Court found the penalty saved by a clause in the Constitution permitting derogations from human rights in the public interest that are not arbitrary and are proportional.[38] The Court concluded that the death penalty, while "inhuman" and "degrading," was nevertheless necessary in Tanzania. It reasoned:

Court decisions of other countries provide valuable information and guidance in interpreting the basic human rights in our

Constitution. . . . But when it comes to what is reasonably necessary to protect our society we have to be extra careful with judicial decisions of other jurisdictions. . . . In societies where owning a firearm is almost as simple as owning a penknife, the death penalty might not be necessary to protect the public. But in societies like ours, where people go to the extent of sacrificing dear sleep to join vigilante groups, popularly known as Sungusungu, in order to protect life and property, the death penalty may still be reasonably necessary.[39]

The Mandatory Sentence

In each of these jurisdictions, the death penalty is mandatory for murder. Many tribunals have condemned the mandatory death sentence as cruel and inhuman for the reason that it denies an opportunity for individual mitigation before its imposition.[40] A case from Kenya illustrates starkly the mercilessness of the mandatory sentence. In Kenya, death is mandatory not only for murder and treason but also for the crimes of robbery with violence (armed robbery), and attempted robbery with violence.[41] Capital murder and treason cases go to the High Court where defendants who qualify receive free legal aid. However, a capital robbery case can be heard either in the Magistrate's Court, where legal aid is not available, or in the High Court.

In December 1999, Boniface Lukoye, a twenty-three-year-old orphan, was sentenced to death in a Mombasa Magistrate's Court within twenty-four hours of his arrest for the armed robbery of $600 from a tourist. His case proceeded on a plea without benefit of counsel. After the judge imposed the mandatory penalty, Lukoye sought to interpose mitigating factors, including his status as an orphan, but the court had no power to grant relief from the mandatory sentence. Both the Law Society of Kenya and the Kenya Human Rights Commission condemned the proceedings, which violated international legal standards, as a gross miscarriage of justice.[42]

In Uganda, the Constitutional Court ruled in *Kigula* in 2005 that the penalty was not mandatory for murder as well as for the offenses of treason, armed robbery, smuggling, kidnapping, rape, and defilement.[43] Of the 417 death row prisoners who challenged the death sentence in *Kigula*, 415 were imprisoned for murder or aggravated robbery, both of which carry the mandatory sentence.[44] Justice Okello, the leading judge in *Kigula*, observed that mandatory sentencing violates due process because "courts are compelled to pass the death sentence because the law orders them to do so but not all the offences can be the same."

The Death Row Phenomenon

Prison conditions in all three states are harsh and unforgiving. Long appellate delays at the judicial and at the mercy phase exacerbate the anguish of awaiting death. Men and women incarcerated on death row for prolonged periods with no control over their fate and little reason to expect mercy experience a living hell that courts have termed the death row phenomenon.[45]

In Kenya, although the numbers are difficult to fix with certainty, there are well over 1,000 capital prisoners held in the country's overcrowded and danger-ous prisons.[46] Many death row prisoners were convicted on questionable evi-dence, received grossly inadequate trials, or were tried and sentenced without benefit of counsel. Few have had the benefit of timely appellate review and most have spent years awaiting the final disposition of their cases. Hence, although no death row prisoner has been executed in Kenya since 1985, there are neverthe-less over 1,000 people, including many, such as Boniface Lukoye, convicted for crimes less serious than murder, held in the shadow of the gallows, where, save for executive commutation or judicial intervention, they shall remain either for life or until they are hanged. Although the clemency extended in 2003 by Presi-dent Kibaki, who in February that year ordered the release of twenty-eight death row inmates and the commutation of 195 others, was commendable, it fell short of correcting the human rights violations inherent in death row captivity.

Prison conditions in Tanzania, where, as of this writing, over 300 prisoners are on death row for the crime of murder,[47] are similarly harsh. A parade of horrors assaults the death row convict who is typically held in virtual solitary confinement for preexecution periods that can extend in the range of ten years.[48] In concluding in *Mbushuu* that the penalty is cruel and inhuman, Tanzania's High Court Justice Mwalusanya observed that "It is not just the final act of stringing up the prisoner which is an ugly matter; but the protracted torment to which we subject the prisoner before finally dispatching him, makes the whole process even nastier."[49]

The conditions on death row in Uganda, where about 500 inmates are under detention, are grim and the delays agonizing. The former superintendent of the Uganda Prisons urged the *Kigula* court to declare the death penalty un-constitutional because of inhuman conditions in the prison and the traumatizing effects of hanging on prison staff.[50] One man, Edmary Mpagi, released in 2000, served eighteen years on death row before his innocence was established when it became known that the man of whose murder he was accused was still alive.[51] As is the case in Kenya and Tanzania, it is not unusual for Ugandan prisoners to spend ten years on death row.[52]

The Scope of Capital Punishment

As elsewhere in the Commonwealth states, the definition of murder is overly broad, including killings without intent and joint enterprise. Moreover, the penalty is applied to a range of crimes that do not result in death. By making the penalty applicable in such broad circumstances, all three states are in violation of the international standard of proportionality, as reflected in a resolution adopted by the African Human Rights Commission calling upon states to limit use of the penalty to "the most serious crimes."[53] This issue is particularly acute in Kenya, where the penal code was changed in 1973 in response to rising crime rates to render capital the crimes of robbery and attempted robbery with violence. Similarly, in Uganda, in response to public concerns about the spread of HIV/AIDS, a 1999 change in the penal code made capital the crimes of rape and defilement.

The International Initiative for Abolition

In the English-speaking world, from the tiny states of the Caribbean to the American South to the United Kingdom, acting together with the European Union and its various organs, there is a broad-ranging campaign to abolish the death penalty. In some venues, notably the Commonwealth Caribbean, this initiative has met with stiff resistance as retentionist states have distanced themselves from the international human rights legal regime. Some countries, such as the United States, protest that the death penalty is not a matter of human rights at all. Fortunately, considerably less rigid attitudes are shaping the debate in East Africa. The pro-death penalty majority is not as strong there as it is in the United States and the Caribbean,[54] and government opinion leans toward abolition. Admirably, important policymakers in East Africa have attempted to lead, rather than be held hostage by public opinion on this issue. But as the debate over the death penalty moves ahead in East Africa, NGOs addressing the issue there can draw useful lessons from the abolition campaigns of other regions, particularly those where, as here, UK-based INGOs have been very active.

Harmonizing Municipal and International Law

On the legal front, the United Kingdom and abolitionist international human rights organizations (INGOs) have pursued a mixture of strategies to establish the abolition of the death penalty as an international norm.[55] Seeking to integrate the abolitionist principle into domestic legal regimes, the legal campaign has expanded the normative reach of international instruments and held parties to their treaty obligations. Multiple, and oftentimes parallel, approaches to the death penalty in domestic and international law have emerged as tribunals have construed similarly the rights-granting clauses of international and municipal instruments. Domestic courts have deployed international and foreign law as an interpretive guide in constitutional jurisprudence. Thus, normative support for international abolition can be found in judgments from the European Commission on Human Rights and the United Nations Human Rights Committee, as well as the domestic courts of South Africa and Zimbabwe, and the Judicial Committee of the Privy Council and the Supreme Court of Canada.[56] These leading cases and many others have created both a dynamic interstate constitutionalism and a rich body of international law on the subject of the death penalty.

However, the strategies to render domestic constitutional law compatible with international law have generated backlash as some states with otherwise adequate human rights records have rejected international standards in an effort to escape scrutiny on the death penalty.[57] Two retentionist states in the Commonwealth Caribbean, Trinidad and Jamaica, have denounced their treaty obligations, while a third, Barbados, has amended its constitution. A state's disengagement from a treaty regime harms not only potential death penalty petitioners seeking to vindicate their human rights, but other human rights claimants as well. The effect of the acts of these states in their quest to avoid the abolitionist principle is significant.

But, where constitutional courts have taken the lead in limiting or abolishing the penalty despite majority public support for it, the democracy costs can redound to affect the stability of the constitutional regime. Death row defendants require judicial protection precisely because they are a despised minority. However, courts have not always made clear why, in the case of the death penalty, they are better suited than the political branches to determine the precise scope of the constitutional right to life or to be protected from torture and other cruel, inhuman, or degrading treatment.

Abolition and the European Foreign Policy Agenda

In Europe, the long-standing debate over capital punishment concluded with the adoption of Protocol 6 and Protocol 13[58] to the European Convention on Human Rights on the abolition of the death penalty. In 1998, Protocol 6 was incorporated into British domestic law. As of this writing, Protocol 13, opened for ratification in 2002, has been ratified by thirty-six of the member states of the Council of Europe and signed by eight others.[59] The Parliamentary Assembly of the Council of Europe adopted a resolution in 2002 calling on member states to refuse extradition of terrorist suspects who might be sentenced to death, and the Charter of Fundamental Rights of Europe prohibits such extradition.[60] Some European states have conditioned other forms of prosecutorial cooperation on representations regarding the death penalty.[61]

The European Union has placed human rights at the center of its relations with third countries. In 1991, the Council of Europe affirmed that "human rights are an essential part of the European Community's international relations." This policy was reinforced in the 1993 Treaty on the European Union (TEU), which set as an objective of the EU's Common Foreign and Security Policy the "respect for Human Rights and fundamental freedoms."[62] When the TEU was amended in 1999 and again in 2003, the promotion of human rights within and outside the EU was again included as a fundamental objective. New applicants must demonstrate their commitment to human rights principles,[63] and member states whose practices persistently contravene human rights principles can be suspended. Progress on human rights is an "essential element" of all EU regional and bilateral instruments for trade, development, and diplomatic relations with third countries. The Cotonou Agreement, which applies to agreements with African, Caribbean, and Pacific states, specifically requires respect for human rights as an "essential element" of the partnerships of ACP states with the EU.

Aggressively proselytizing in retentionist regions, the EU and European NGOs have pursued both a popular campaign and a legal assault targeting the constitutional regimes and the treaty obligations of retentionist states. In 1998, the EU adopted guidelines regarding its relationships with death penalty states. Accordingly, the guidelines proclaim the goal to be universal abolition, and call for the progressive restriction in the use of the penalty and adherence to trial and appellate safeguards. The EU and other European-wide organs have filed amicus curiae briefs in death penalty cases outside their borders; issued numerous demarches on the subject in international human rights forums; and marshaled legal resources to assist death penalty defendants and their counsel in retentionist states the world over, including the United States, Africa,[64] and the Caribbean.

The Abolitionist Campaign in the Caribbean

The twelve states of the Commonwealth of the Caribbean have a shared history with the states of Kenya, Tanzania, and Uganda in that their legal systems comprise an amalgam of laws and legal practices from the colonial and postcolonial eras.[65] Achieving their independence from the United Kingdom in the 1960s, the English-Speaking Caribbean (ESC) states adopted new constitutions that included expansive bills of rights. The bills of rights were derived from two sources: the Nigerian Constitution, which was the model for the Caribbean charters that followed it, and the European Convention on Human Rights of 1950 (ECHR), which the United Kingdom ratified in 1951 and applied to its colonies in Africa and in the Caribbean.[66] As is true of the East African constitutions, the bills protect the right to life and the right to be free from inhuman and degrading treatment.

In the 1980s, many of the ESC states experienced a dramatic increase in violent crime. The increased crime was attributable to heightened political violence, to the violent drug activity that ensued as the region became a crossroad between the producers to the south of them and the consumers to their north, and to the social disasters of globalization. In response, these states adopted harsh policies to battle the growth in crime, including reinvigorating the death penalty apparatuses that had lain fallow in the decades since independence. Executions resumed and the death row populations swelled.[67] In Jamaica there are four times as many death row inmates per capita than there are in the United States.

However, given the inadequacy of police and judicial systems, a criminal justice crisis was virtually inevitable. When they returned to the death penalty in the 1980s, the ESC states were without the infrastructure to protect against miscarriages of justice. As in East Africa, lawyers were ill-trained and underpaid, judicial resources were inadequate, procedural protections against unfair police and prosecutorial practices were weak, and death row conditions, where convicted men were held for prolonged periods of time, sometimes decades, were atrocious.

This was the context in which Caribbean human rights NGOs sought support from their British counterparts. Conferences organized by the INGOs such as Interights, Penal Reform International, Amnesty International, and Human Rights Watch brought to bear resources from outside of the region to address the resurgence in the use of the death penalty as well as other serious human rights problems, particularly extrajudicial police killings, and deaths in custody. The INGOs provided technical and resource assistance to domestic groups, and they began to focus their human rights reporting and documentation on the region and to stimulate international concern over the escalating death row numbers.

Lawyers in the UK partnered with those in the Caribbean to bring cases to the human rights tribunals. The legal campaign had the features of traditional law reform litigation efforts. Lawyers strategically selected their issues, forums, and clients in order to maximize the impact of their work. That the Caribbean states utilized the Judicial Committee of the Privy Council as their court of last resort was a critically important asset to the campaign, for it meant that the British lawyers could wage their legal battle on territory that was proximate and familiar.

While the local NGOs sought to build popular support among the religious community and elsewhere for abolition, the lawyers proceeded on two fronts. First, they sought review in the tribunals of the two international human rights treaty systems to which the ESC states belonged.[68] Armed with clear authority from the human rights tribunals, the lawyers then addressed the relevant constitutional provisions on the domestic side. The lawyers provided their services on a pro bono basis to the death penalty defendants. Without this assistance the vast majority of these cases would not have reached the appellate tribunals because most of the legal aid systems in the ESC states granted no services for appeals.

What ultimately transpired surprised all participants. The Privy Council, a London-based, virtually all-white colonial relic, became, in effect, a strong proponent of international human rights while the Caribbean states decried the intervention of the former mother country as an assault on Caribbean national sovereignty. Some of the ESC states reneged on their international obligations to escape the sanctions of the international tribunals, while some governments sought to amend their constitutions to avoid having to give effect to the decisions of the Privy Council. Ultimately the ESC states would move to establish their own regional supreme court and sever ties with the Privy Council.

In 1989, the Caribbean campaign was propelled forward when the European Court of Human Rights decided the *Soering* case establishing that extradition to a death penalty jurisdiction where the defendant was likely to experience the "death row phenomenon" contravened Article 3 of the European Convention on Human Rights.[69] *Soering* provided the lawyers with a chisel with which to gain entry into the death row dungeons in the Caribbean islands of Trinidad and Jamaica.

In 1993, the Privy Council decided the landmark case of *Pratt and Morgan*.[70] Following *Soering*, the *Pratt* case raised the question whether long-term detention on death row, triggering the "death row phenomenon," violated the Jamaican constitution and international human rights treaty guarantees. When the Privy Council decided the case in 1993, the *Pratt* defendants had been on death row for fourteen years. In its 1993 decision, the Privy Council determined that the prolonged delay violated the Jamaican constitution and international human rights standards. It ordered the death sentences remitted to life and it set a limit of five years on all appellate processes in capital cases. The decision required a massive overhaul of the capital punishment systems in the ESC states. Of the 450 prisoners on death row before *Pratt*, at least half had their sentences commuted to life terms as a result of that case.[71] Following *Pratt*, the campaign turned its attention to other aspects of the death penalty, specifically the automatic penalty, the failure to allow closure of international appeals before issuing the death warrant, and the inadequate protections inherent at the mercy phase of the proceedings.

As in East Africa, in most ESC states the penalty was mandatory for all categories of murder, including felony murder, and in some systems the law did not recognize certain common defenses, such as drunkenness or duress. Again, as in East Africa, this failure properly to classify homicide offenses violated the international norm that the sentence should be reserved for only the gravest crimes.[72] In 2002, the Privy Council declared that the mandatory penalty contravenes protections against inhuman treatment.[73] Similarly, in the same year, the Inter-American Court of Human Rights struck down the mandatory penalty as an arbitrary deprivation of life.[74]

In 2000, the Privy Council had turned its attention to the mercy phase and, in another landmark case from Jamaica, *Lewis*, it ruled that these post-trial executive proceedings are subject to judicial review. The Court accorded to the accused the right to notice of the proceedings, to submit materials in mitigation, and to review materials submitted by the trial judge and others to the commutation decision maker.[75] *Lewis* also established that it is unlawful to proceed on a death warrant before a prisoner's appeals to international human rights bodies have concluded.

The human rights rulings of the Privy Council and the international tribunals provoked a "human rights backlash."[76] As crime continued to climb, so did support for the death penalty, leaving little room for political actors to initiate the broad human rights reform the judicial bodies were urging, if not ordering. Instead of refocusing the question as one of penal policy rather than popular opinion, political leaders in the region muddied the waters by condemning the international courts for failing to grasp the social conditions of their societies, and invoked sovereignty to shield their states from outside criticism. The governments took steps to undermine the authority of the human rights bodies and sever the historic ties to the Privy Council.

After the Privy Council decision in *Pratt*, Trinidad and Tobago, and Jamaica claimed they could not comply with its mandate because of the risk that the appellate process in domestic and international forums could not be concluded in five years. In 1997, Jamaica became the first state ever to withdraw the right of individuals to file petitions with the United Nations Human Rights Committee under the Optional Protocol. In 1998, Trinidad and Tobago denounced the American Convention on Human Rights and withdrew from the Optional Protocol. It then re-acceded to the Protocol subject to a reservation barring its citizens from appealing death penalty matters to the Human Right Committee. Guyana took the same action, although Guyana was not subject to the *Pratt* judgment. In December 1999, the UN Human Rights Committee ruled that Trinidad and Tobago's attempt to bar appeals under the Protocol was invalid. In March 2000, Trinidad and Tobago responded by withdrawing from the Optional Protocol.

Following the Privy Council's 2002 decision limiting the mandatory penalty, Barbados amended its constitution to avoid the result in that case and to shield from constitutional scrutiny the automatic penalty. In 2000, Trinidad and Tobago's attorney general introduced a bill to amend the constitution to escape *Pratt* and other cases. Among other changes, the bill provided that the execution of a condemned prisoner could be carried out without violating due process even if there were a pending petition before a human rights body.

Among the several responses the governments made to the legal assault on the death penalty, the most consequential was the decision to separate the region's judicial system from the Privy Council that had been the court of last resort since the early nineteenth century. In February 2001, thirteen states in the region signed an agreement to establish a regional court. The Caribbean Court of Justice, launched in 2005, replaces the Privy Council for the states of Barbados and Guyana, with other states considering affiliation to the new court. It is still an open question whether the new court will follow the decisions of the Privy Council and of the international tribunals on the death penalty, or take the opportunity to rechart this territory.[77] What is a virtual certainty is that the appellate legal services that had been heretofore available to death row inmates will be severely reduced if not altogether eliminated.

Taken together, the actions of these ESC states limit the scope of judicial review of these cases, narrow appellate forum options, and reduce the opportunity for defendants to take advantage of a source of highly experienced and free legal assistance.

The Abolition Campaign in East Africa

As NGOs in East Africa press the campaign to abolish the death penalty, fruitful lessons can be drawn from the successes and disappointments the international movement has encountered in the Commonwealth Caribbean and the United States. The collaboration between human rights advocates in Britain and the

Caribbean established new standards for the administration of the death penalty in that region, resulting in reprieves for scores of death row prisoners whose confinement violated the new rules, and in important law reform. Indeed, human rights lawyers from the UK who helped to design the attack on the death penalty in the Caribbean have assisted litigators in East Africa and in Nigeria, adapting many of the same legal arguments that were first deployed in the Caribbean. The Ugandan judgment in *Kigula* condemning mandatory sentencing follows the logic of judgments that preceded it by a few years in the Judicial Committee of the Privy Council and in the Eastern Caribbean Court of Appeal.[78]

However, one objective to be taken from the Caribbean experience would be to avoid a human rights backlash that could set back efforts on other fronts. In part, the backlash reflected a sense among Caribbean people that abolition was a standard imposed by foreign elites indifferent to local mores and values. A second goal would be to counter the ideological claim, frequently advanced by both the United States and the Caribbean, that the death penalty is not an issue of international human rights but rather one of national sovereignty.

On the first matter, East African countries stand on more solid ground than the Caribbean countries because their leaders have not yielded to or hidden behind public opinion. Rather, with the notable exception of Uganda's President Museveni, they have made clear that it is their responsibility as public officials to exercise their own independent, informed judgment on matters of penal policy. In contrast to the Caribbean countries, they have accepted the validity of abolition as a norm and recognize that their current practice deviates from that norm.

On the second point, the idea that the death penalty is not properly within the human rights legal system should hold no purchase in states such as Kenya and Uganda, where human rights is not only a legal regime but a moral wellspring for newly emerging democratic movements seeking cultural and institutional barricades against the horrible excesses of the past. Seen through this lens, an expansive vision of human rights manifestly includes abolition, even if international law has not yet embraced it as an enforceable norm. Abolishing the death penalty is a salient indicator of the transition to democracy for states with histories of repression, as evidenced by the experiences of Namibia and Hungary, where the penalty was abolished in 1990, and of South Africa.

Because recent constitutional reform efforts in Kenya and in Uganda have failed to abolish the death penalty, it may well fall on the courts to do so. This was the pattern that occurred in South Africa where, famously, the constitutional framers left the text silent on the matter, deferring to the Constitutional Court. In the case of the Caribbean, the savings clause in domestic constitutional law prevented the Privy Council from striking down the death penalty.[79] The Privy Council has been limited to constricting the use of the penalty. The legal campaign in the Caribbean enjoyed success in the Privy Council, narrow though it was, because it first created favorable law in the international tribunals and thereby triggered momentum for domestic judicial oversight of the penalty. The Privy Council could then incorporate international and foreign law in its death penalty judgments.

The jurisprudence of the African Commission on Human and Peoples' Rights, while promising, lags somewhat behind that of the two tribunals of the American Human Rights Convention.[80] However, arguably the most progressive domestic law on the death penalty, at least in the English-speaking world, has come from South Africa and Zimbabwe, and the constitutional courts of the East African states should find ample models for interpreting the right to life, and to be protected from cruel and inhuman punishment, in those landmark cases.

Ultimately, in East Africa as elsewhere, executive branch initiatives and progressive jurisprudence will likely both play a role in abolishing the death penalty because it has rarely been abandoned as a result of public referendum. In the United States, although the Supreme Court has adamantly refused to strike down the penalty and remains self-consciously indifferent to international human rights norms, state governors and state courts, troubled by wrongful convictions and arbitrary enforcement, have demonstrated more flexibility.[81] Government executives hold significant power to influence the abolition movement. They can, as have the presidents of Kenya and Tanzania, exercise the power of clemency in capital cases, establish moratoria on executions, recommend legislation to abolish or constrict application of the penalty, appoint abolitionists to criminal justice positions, or create commissions to study the issue.

Working closely with international legal organizations, NGOs in East Africa are developing litigation strategies to break the logjam on the death penalty. In 2003, the British Institute of International and Comparative Law launched a project funded by the European Commission to assist lawyers and NGOs in Africa in death penalty cases. The intent of the project, which addresses capital punishment in thirteen countries, including Kenya, Tanzania, and Uganda, is to produce a cadre of lawyers skilled in challenging the death penalty in the region. International and foreign law will support the central claims of such a campaign, and can figure prominently in domestic cases, as it did in *Makwanyane, Catholic Commission for Justice and Peace*, and the High Court decision in *Mbushuu*.

In sum, where, as in East Africa, the death penalty has popular support, it is critical to retain the government as an essential partner in the campaign to educate the public regarding necessary reforms in the administration of the penalty and the arguments in favor of total abolition. The more effective death penalty campaign will be placed in the context of overall reforms in the criminal justice delivery system and improved human rights enforcement. Finally, the Caribbean experience reinforces the obvious caution that the overall direction and pace of the campaign must be in the hands of those from the countries with the most at stake.

CHAPTER FOURTEEN

Democracy Organizations in Political Transitions: IDASA and the New South Africa

Shaila Gupta and Alycia Kellman

IN 1986, AGAINST the backdrop of apartheid South Africa, Fredrick Van Zyl Slabbert and Alex Boraine resigned their positions as members of the South African Parliament. Their departure was a protest to the bankruptcy of government and the politics of exclusion, repression, and resistance fostered by the apartheid state. For Slabbert, the last straw was the betrayal he felt in 1985 when Foreign Minister Pik Botha assured him that South African military forces were no longer involved in the "destabilization effort" against the antiapartheid government of neighboring Mozambique. The frustration of Slabbert and his colleague Boraine, then chair of the Federal Council of the anti-apartheid Progressive Federal Party, was the irrelevance of Parliament. The government's so-called reform policy of a tricameral parliament rhetorically exchanged the apartheid system for a unitary state system.

In the 1980s, South Africa was a highly polarized and violent society. It was characterized by vast ignorance on the part of the white population about the situation of the black majority and its political organizations including the African National Congress (ANC), the Pan-Africanist Congress (PAC), Inkatha, and the Azanian People's Organization (AZAPO). Most whites unquestionably accepted the government's description of the ANC as a violent terrorist group without a domestic constituency. More generally, the oppressive conditions of blacks were almost entirely invisible to white South Africans.

After traveling the country speaking with a wide cross section of political leaders, both black and white over a period of eight months, Boraine and Slab-bert determined that in order to most effectively participate in the struggle to end apartheid and usher a new society, there was a need to establish an independent institute with democracy as its major focus. That is how the Institute for a Democratic Alternative for South Africa was born. IDASA opened its first office in Port Elizabeth on November 1, 1986. IDASA was not founded as a political party, an advocacy group, or popular movement. Its aim was to generate discussion and engagement—the politics of negotiation—across a highly polarized society, and to work with forces for change toward the ultimate goal of a nonracial democratic South Africa.

IDASA was born out of a mission to educate, especially the white population, to counter a systematically imposed ignorance. It was an initiative of white people for white people with support from the largely black anti-apartheid movement. The theory was that change could occur if white resistance to change was overcome. IDASA stressed the strategic importance of involving the white community in the struggle for nonracial democracy out of their self-interest in change, not mainly by moral exhortation. IDASA sought to bring whites out of their insulation to create a commitment to the nonracial democratic goal.

Immediately upon conception, it was subject to intense public criticism, both from the white elite and distrusting black communities. The critics' frequent charge of elitism suggested obliviousness to the grassroots commitments of the organization. Yet, over the years, IDASA has been able to prove itself as a worthy organization and make clear its commitment to democracy.

IDASA has been able to adapt through extremely contentious and volatile times. While most nongovernmental organizations that existed before the transition had to completely overhaul their staffs in order to shift from working against an oppressive regime to facilitating the establishment of a new government, IDASA kept virtually its full leadership team with very little discontinuity. As a result, though IDASA currently focuses on vastly different subjects than it did when it was first initiated, the spirit in which it operates has not changed.

The uniqueness of IDASA and its ability to develop and adapt along with the circumstances in which it operates can provide valuable lessons for other organizations across the globe that wish to help bring about democratic reform in their own countries. IDASA has shaped and reshaped its objectives and strategies many times throughout its history. While each organization will obviously have its own individual political, economic, and social circumstances, IDASA's development suggests that its institutional policy shifts can be molded into a general methodology for organizations that hope to facilitate transition and consolidate democracy, both on the African continent and elsewhere.

Building a Climate for Democracy (1986–1990)

Between 1986 and 1990, in its initial years of existence, IDASA worked mainly toward establishing a climate for democracy. In order to accomplish this goal, IDASA first consolidated itself as an organization and established guidelines for its operations. In this respect, IDASA's leadership created an institutional approach that was based on four major premises.

First, the organization needed a realistic understanding of South Africa and the fundamental issues facing the country then. IDASA thus committed itself from the outset to constantly analyze the socioeconomic and political situation of South Africa. During the early months of 1990, IDASA in partnership with the Friederich Naumann Foundation of West Germany hosted a three-day conference on the South African economy, its growth, and justice. The conference was an attempt to bring together political organizations, labor, and business to analyze and understand South Africa's economic climate and forge an economic policy that delivered both justice and growth. A group of twenty-five top businesspeople, academics, and ANC delegates concluded early on that, "a nonracial, democratic political system would be meaningless without economic restructuring."[1]

Second, the organization realized it had to devise strategies firmly based on the prevailing socioeconomic and political landscape. They argued that IDASA should seek to establish clear priorities and stick to them. However, the third premise mandated that strategy should never be elevated to principle. The organization recognized that it must always be ready to abandon unsuccessful strategies to seek new ones. Last, IDASA aimed to be democratic not only in its goals, but also in the process of realizing those goals. This meant being clearly committed and ready to consult widely with other movements, communities, and organizations as well as seeking consensus within IDASA itself.[2] These four premises still guide the organization today.

During these years, IDASA's main objectives were to encourage South Africans of all races to reject apartheid and discover a nonracial and democratic alternative, to provide forums, to encourage citizens to find democratic solutions to South Africa's problems, and finally to conduct research relating to a democratic alternative and to produce and publish this information.[3]

Toward these ends, IDASA's first years were marked by milestone meetings to create conversations and spaces for engagement and dialogue, sometimes in full public view, often behind the scenes, that would break down stereotypes and educate South Africans about each other across racial, economic, and ideological lines. There was so much hatred, suspicion, misunderstanding, and fear in South Africa at the time that it was seen as vital to have all sides become acquainted and to hear and discuss each other's views on ways to induce change. The first of these meetings was a major conference on democracy in May 1987. More than 400 delegates from all over South Africa met in Port Elizabeth for a program of lectures, workshops, and general discussions. One of the most striking features of the conference was the large component of delegates from the black community, giving the conference a concrete sense of reality in a society plagued by the illusions of "wit Baasskap."[4] At the conference, the implications of democracy were examined on seven major areas of society: government, labor, business, education, law, media, and the church. The conference gave focus to the work of the organization and helped to establish IDASA as a national movement.

However, it was the dramatic meeting in Dakar, Senegal, which gave IDASA the high profile it enjoyed after only a few months of existence. It was IDASA's view that if discussions of democracy were to have any meaning, they had to take place between the major protagonists. In July 1987, for the first time in history, a group of 61 white South Africans including leading scholars, business people, political, and church officials met with the outlawed ANC. In an intense three days of meetings, the two sides exchanged views and debated questions such as the role of violence in the antiapartheid struggle. The conference was an attempt by IDASA to demystify the South African government's depiction of the ANC. The IDASA conference helped to expose the myth of a terrorist ANC that the apartheid regime used to justify emergency rule.

In the October 1987 issue of *Democracy in Action*, Boraine gave two reasons for IDASA's mission to Dakar. First, he states, "Our initiative arose out of deep concern for our country which is so hopelessly divided and the victim of escalating violence."[5] He concluded that the state could not perpetually operate in a state of emergency and that the ANC could by no means overthrow the state by force alone. Second, "the reason why we went to Dakar arises from our experience in talking with leaders of the Black community and with organizations in those communities." The conference was a tremendous success and ended with the Dakar Communiqué in which all participants unanimously expressed their preference for a negotiated resolution to the South African question and declared their commitment to the goal of a nonracial democracy.

The realization of IDASA's inaugural goals was by no means reached without overcoming significant obstacles. Boraine documented in September 1987 that the "State President delivered a very scathing attack on IDASA and on the Dakar meeting when he spoke in Parliament recently."[6] As a result of the Dakar meeting, the state issued a warning stating, "the state will have to reconsider granting passports to those who wish to participate" in any further meetings with the then exiled ANC.[7] And finally, in late 1987, the state warned that the state president would consider cutting off all overseas funding for IDASA.

Though much of the media attention focused on the dramatic meetings taking place outside South Africa, IDASA was also extremely busy inside the country at a grassroots level. There remained considerable suspicion within the black community as to IDASA's agenda. As a result, the organization was compelled to spend an enormous amount of time and energy in meetings with various groups, attempting to establish a climate of trust. Beginning in 1987, IDASA started to encourage and facilitate local forums. The forums focused on a variety of issues, but each of them had the effect of bringing people together and building confidence in the intentions of IDASA.

An important initiative during this time was a national conference on the Freedom Charter. The conference, The Freedom Charter and the Future: A Critical Appraisal, was held in Cape Town, July 15–16, 1988, and was attended by over 400 delegates.[8] The conference was intended to give whites an opportunity to gain a deeper understanding of the aspirations and anger of the South African majority, thereby allowing them to deal with their own fears and hopes for the future, while acquainting them with the ideas of the ANC Freedom Charter.

Another significant process held by IDASA was the Constitutional Options debate. In March of 1989, IDASA launched the "Options for the Future" debate series on constitutional proposals for South Africa at various forums and workshops across the country. The question then facing South Africans was not whether negotiations over power sharing were to take place, but when they would take place, before or after war. Preventing violence and war by bringing all concerned parties to the negotiation table and jointly evaluating constitutional proposals for South Africa was the ethos of the conference. As Boraine stated, IDASA stood squarely in the arena of negotiation politics where it could urge people to negotiate away from apartheid toward a democratic society with real power sharing.[9]

During this period of oppressive government, IDASA was guided by its intention to sow the seeds of democracy. It based its operational policy on the belief that to accomplish its objectives of constructing strategies for change, it had to build national unity, establish areas of commonality, expose people to the reality of the "other," address their fears and prejudices, and develop a common destiny through holding debates on the future.

A Critical Ally in the Transition (1990–1993)

On February 2, 1990, the political circumstances in South Africa changed dramatically. In a speech to the Parliament, State President De Klerk unbanned the liberation movements and allowed their leaders to return from exile. This historic development had profound effects on the work of IDASA. IDASA had grown into a fair-sized organization employing about fifty staff nationally. It operated six regional offices in Pretoria, Durban, Bloemfontein, Port Elizabeth, East London, and Cape Town. In light of these new developments, the challenge for IDASA was to reevaluate its strategies and structures while at the same time avoiding operational paralysis.

The changing political face of South Africa and IDASA's role in the transition process were scrutinized during a two-and-a-half-day staff workshop held at Gordon's Bay in June of 1990. Directors and coordinators from all six regions of South Africa and members from the IDASA head office met and discussed political developments in the country and the goals and challenges facing the organization in the 1990s. In light of the institution's goals and objectives, a broad working document merged. From then on, IDASA would engage in the following activities: promoting progressive and democratic ideals and practices; addressing the fears, prejudice, and anger in South African society as obstacles to the transition; strengthening "pacting" between the major actors of South Africa; providing information to all groups on all levels on critical issues confronting South Africa; and facilitating discussion of constitutional and development issues for a post-apartheid South Africa.[10]

Consequently, IDASA's staff met in August 1990 and discussed the organization's continuing role in the pursuit of a democratic alternative. They identified six possible ways in which IDASA could continue to play a significant role. First, in a time of competing loyalties and alliance building, it was extremely important that IDASA maintain its independence. As a critical ally of the transition process, IDASA, they argued, would be well positioned to encourage action and decisions that could assist the transition process toward genuine negotiation. This did not mean sitting on the sidelines and criticizing, but rather seeking to be a critical ally of the transition to democracy by working with any and every party, by any constructive means possible, to achieve this goal.

Secondly, against a background of widespread confusion, fear, and uncertainty about the political situation, IDASA would take the role of interpreter seriously. Emphasis was placed on analyzing the political and historical events, putting them in perspective and distributing this information. The importance of the interpreter's role for IDASA was highlighted by the government's inability to educate its own people.

Thirdly, IDASA committed itself to continuing its innovative work. Organizational flexibility at all times would be necessary in order to adapt quickly and competently to changing situations. Pioneering work still needed to be done in order to assist the transition process. Fourth, IDASA would continue with its role in the facilitation process. As Boraine stated, "IDASA is well placed to continue its work as a facilitator in this regard. Indeed, where breakdowns occur, as they will occur, IDASA may well be asked to assume the mediating role between groups and individuals."[11] Widespread skepticism, suspicion, distrust, and violence throughout the country made facilitation an urgent necessity.

Fifth, IDASA committed itself to work in the field of education. In particular, IDASA saw itself as having a responsibility and an opportunity to give people at every level a greater understanding of what democracy meant; not only in constitutional terms, but especially in how it affects their daily lives and the institutions of which they are a part of. Last, IDASA made a commitment to become an active change agent. In the past, IDASA had stage-managed events and sought to act very much as a facilitator. IDASA's leadership and personnel had not been prime movers. IDASA explicitly acknowledged that it would have to face the question as to whether or not it would go beyond the role of facilitator and begin actively participating. These conclusions translated into IDASA's guiding principles during this period.[12]

It became apparent during 1990–1991 that if South Africa were to have a democratic future, it would not be enough to focus on high level talks. Every element of society needed to take part in, support, and understand the process. Additionally, violence during the early 1990s highlighted the need for civil society to take an active role. In response, IDASA established in 1992 the Training Center for Democracy in Johannesburg. The center enabled IDASA to take its workshops, seminars, and conferences a step further and offer in-depth training on the philosophy of democracy, its history and the skills necessary to develop a democratic society. In other words, IDASA was developing a sustained and continuing focus on grassroots citizen education. "Central to IDASA's work method has been the belief that people learn best about democracy through practicing it," explains the Training Center's brochure. As Alison Curry, tutor with the Training Center stated, "We have lived so long in a culture of blame, it has become difficult to envisage any other way of being."[13]

Between 1990 and 1993, IDASA was involved in facilitating a large number of regional forums on issues concerning economic justice, education, human rights, the media, and grassroots involvement. It encouraged both black and white South Africans to take part in the political development of the country. In June 1990, IDASA hosted a conference, "South Africa in Transition" at the East Cape Training Center in Port Elizabeth. The conference was an undertaking by IDASA to educate South Africans about specific issues relating to the process of transition and create a climate of openness. International speakers discussed lessons learned from transitions in Eastern and Central Europe, and Latin America.[14]

In addition to local forums to build a culture of democracy, IDASA also recognized that there was a need to ensure stability by beginning to transform the security forces. In May 1990, IDASA held a conference in Lusaka, Zambia, that brought together a large group of white South Africans involved in the South African Defense Force (SADF) and members of the military wing of the ANC, Umkhonto we Sizwe (MK). The focus of the meeting was on the future security and defense force in a new South Africa and was one of the first initiatives to address the question of SADF/MK relations.

In 1992, IDASA held a conference entitled Policing in South Africa in the 1990s that brought together members of the South African Police Force (SAPF), political leaders, and intellectuals to examine policing in the context of the transition. IDASA recognized that while the SAPF had been an essential instrument for maintaining white domination, it was the only police force in South Africa, and to not engage it would be to invite anarchy. The conference aimed to decrease the credibility gap between the police and communities in order to further the democratic transition. "It is in facing up to the truth that we will be freed to work toward a police force which will enjoy the confidence and respect of all South Africans."[15]

Continuing its role as an innovative change agent, IDASA became active in organizing programs for international visitors. Academic establishments such as North Park College in Chicago working with IDASA arranged for students and professors to visit South Africa on a cultural exchange. These programs included visits to townships and church services with community members. The ultimate goal for IDASA was to break down misconceptions on the international front.[16]

In the period before the first-ever free and fair elections in South Africa, IDASA saw itself as an organization within civil society that sought to be impartial and yet not neutral. It sought to be independent and thus able to be forthright in its criticism of any or all political parties and leaders who delayed or attempted to thwart the birth of a democratic society. IDASA's efforts to interpret the transitional process, to encourage and build support for transitional mechanisms, and to articulate citizen needs and aspirations to the negotiating partners, made it an invaluable ally of the transition process during this period. As Boraine noted, "If ordinary South Africans, who are fearful of their future and the future of their children, and are fed up with the on/off negotiations, can be galvanized into putting pressure on all political parties, this would indeed be democracy in action."[17]

Support for the Founding Elections (1993–1995)

In July 1993, Jannie Hofmeyr, an independent researcher, reported on the findings from a survey he conducted. The findings suggested a despondent attitude within the country with most South Africans wanting to "escape." There appeared to be a reemergence of racial stereotypes between blacks and whites, and a feeling of alienation among 41 percent of the African population who had no commitment to racial harmony. It was within the context of these findings that Hofmeyr stated that the only way to save the country was through the strengthening of the "middle group" that was still committed to forging a peaceful future.[18] It was in this climate of uncertainty with the prospect of civil war that IDASA moved into the third phase of its history.

Though IDASA was continuously working to ensure stability and encourage a peaceful transition through dialogue and educational initiatives, it was during the period leading up to the first election that the organization gained a new focus. From 1993 to 1995, IDASA worked to educate voters, including those within the military, and to create nonpartisan spaces that would build legitimacy for the electoral process. Free and fair elections were considered to be crucial to the development of a democratic South Africa. As an institute based specifically on democracy, IDASA felt a particular responsibility to participate in this endeavor. IDASA was involved in preparing for the 1994 elections in a number of ways, from policy processes and the monitoring of electoral legislation to voter education and observer training.[19] It continues these activities today through its Political Information and Monitoring Services (PIMS) to, among other things, build civic capacity to participate in democratic institutions.

Immediately after the 1994 elections, the organization changed its name to the Institute for Democracy in South Africa, as it was no longer necessary to seek a democratic "alternative," although it kept the well-known acronym IDASA. By this stage, the organization had again doubled in size, employing a staff of over 100 and making it one of the larger NGOs in South Africa.[20] While the work of regional offices in the preelection period had been characterized by a high degree of responsiveness to regional needs and realities, in the postelection period IDASA projects began to converge toward a number of key themes including government monitoring and training and civil society capacity building.

IDASA recognized that mere elections would not create a democratic society without sustained education and monitoring. It initiated a number of projects to build democratic ideals. In 1993, to address the challenges facing South Africans during the transition period and to simultaneously emphasize the role of civil society, IDASA cohosted a seminar, "The Role of Civil Society in an Emerging Democracy." The meeting of journalists, local academics, and NGOs led to a distillation of factors that could threaten South Africa's transition to democracy. These included the maldistribution of socioeconomic wealth and ethnic tensions and conflicts. Larry Diamond, senior research fellow at the Hoover Institution in California stated, "The transition to democracy in South Africa is easily the most complex transition in the world."[21]

In light of the many barriers to a smooth transition, IDASA felt that the most crucial need for South Africa was political will and leadership. As a result, it organized public hearings with various groups of stakeholders to discuss the constitutional process, including specifically youth, women, religion, and labor. Drawing from examples such as Cambodia, the Training Center for Democracy continued working on voter education programs. The Center operated under the belief that effective voter education needed to be deepened beyond the erection of voting mechanisms. Through project development and implementation, the Center began to tackle fundamental issues such as fear that could cloud the voting process.[22]

Even though a large portion of IDASA's transition work concentrated on national initiatives, the organization was working to build capacity at the local level as well. In 1993 in a meeting entitled "Conference on Peace, Development and Democracy," IDASA aimed to explore what peace, democracy, and development meant to those working at local levels. By promoting active information exchanges, the organization encouraged participants to interact with each other and explore conference themes.[23]

In this short period, IDASA worked diligently to establish a nonpartisan space for civil society to discuss its views, to strengthen election bodies, to empower voters, and to contribute to free and fair elections. It saw its role as a facilitator of democracy that would help to consolidate and direct the newfound optimism in the country.

Building Democratic Institutions (1995–1998)

In 1993, Alex Boraine wrote, "We are convinced that long after the first free and fair election in South Africa has been held, there will be a need for an organization like IDASA to continue to focus on democratic values and thus to challenge any possible abuse of power from whatever source."[24] In the post-election period, this was precisely the direction in which IDASA turned. Rather than working toward removing a repressive government, the organization now focused its energies toward building those democratic institutions that would help to strengthen a newly elected, but inexperienced, government. IDASA respected the mandate of the new government, the legislative moral role of political leaders, and the responsibilities of public institutions. Yet, its focus now shifted to an understanding of democracy as involving the rhythms, patterns, and cultures of the broad array of institutions and communities in society—democracy as a way of life, not simply periodic elections. In order to do this, IDASA was radically restructured. There had to be a shift from being inimical to government to a willingness to work with it.

One of the main ways in which IDASA facilitated cooperation with government was through its Public Information Center (PIC), established in March 1995. The PIC's mission was to collect, collate, analyze, and provide information on public policy with a view to enhancing government transparency, accountability, and effectiveness. Mamphela Ramphele, who later went on to become managing director for the World Bank, headed the PIC. It attempted to break the tendency to adopt oppositional approaches to public policy questions and instead worked to foster a new civic ethos to constructively influence government and participate in public policy debates.

The PIC was conceived as a project that would serve as an ally of change, providing the government of national unity with information, support and, where appropriate, criticism and feedback. Then executive director of IDASA, Wilmot James noted that access to information was key to good government. The voting public, he said, "elected as well as appointed public officials at all levels of government, and actors in the wider South African society will be better served by an open flow of reliable, in-depth information. The PIC is therefore geared to bridge the information gap which exists in our society."[25]

In another attempt to work with the government in democracy building, IDASA began working on constitutional development issues. In a little known effort of great importance, IDASA organized five high-level constitutional "safaris" for drafters of the new South African Constitution. The group examined the constitutions of England, Switzerland, Portugal, the United States, Canada, India, and Australia. The purpose was to expose South African writers to fascinating lessons from other countries and emphasize the fact that constitutions were products of history. Basic elements such as bicameral versus unicameral parliaments, bills of rights, and voting processes were addressed. In Australia, for example, the place of the Aboriginal people's had been a very sensitive one. They had been subject to policy and legislation determined by each state. But in 1967, a nationwide referendum approved the inclusion of Aboriginal people in the census figures on which electoral allocations are based. It also established the principle that the commonwealth could legislate for all races. The lesson in Australia was that systems can manage to meet internal and external challenges and that South Africans were fortunate in being able to learn from others and in having the will and creativity to design a system best-suited to their conditions.[26]

Another initiative was Community Policing Forums. These were an extension of IDASA's already existing work in the security field. Community policing is a philosophy or approach that guided the methodology of policing. It is based on the assumption that the objective of policing—the provision and maintenance of safety and security for all individuals and communities—can only be achieved through the collaborative effort of the Police and the communities where they operate. Therefore, a major objective of the Community Policing Forums was to establish an active partnership between the police and public through which crime problems could be determined and appropriate solutions designed and implemented. IDASA was successful in establishing a community-policing forum in most South African policing districts.

During this period, IDASA focused its work on assisting in the reconstruction of the state, developing civic virtues, encouraging democratic practice, and procedures, and consolidating the new constitution. The regional offices, whose programs had begun to resemble each other and whose locations no longer reflected the new provincial divisions in South Africa, were closed and two amalgamated Democracy Centers were established, one in Cape Town and the other in Pretoria.

Empowering Citizens (1998–2000)

By 1998, South Africa had undergone one democratic election and was quickly approaching another. Though the first free and fair election in a country has obvious significance, it is the second election that determines how firmly entrenched democracy truly is. IDASA recognized the importance of the second election and sought to play as large of a role, if not a greater, than in the 1999 elections. IDASA coordinated 165 workshops and trained close to 450 voter educators in seven different provinces. It produced and published a voter educator's package, "Your Vote Counts," and distributed over 4,500 copies across the country.

The Curriculum Development and Citizenship Education Unit (CDCE) concluded its Training for Democracy Educators project in 1998. By the end of 1998, 380 community-based democracy educators had participated in an intense five-day training program. The CDCE also designed a groundbreaking course for traditional leaders as part of the KwaZulu-Natal Democracy project, which aimed at enhancing democratic interaction at the local level.[27] The Budget Information Service (BIS) unit was also worked on new and innovative research that would ultimately lead to a more informed and empowered citizen. The Provincial Fiscal Analysis Project within BIS established a provincial network of legislature monitors that assisted in initiating an exciting research program providing immediate responses to critical provincial finance issues.[28]

In accordance with the theme of empowering citizens, IDASA consolidated many of its ongoing projects into two new national programs including the

Local Government Center and the Citizen Leadership Programme. The Local Government Center sought to empower municipalities and local communities for effective and accountable governance and service delivery. The Citizen Leadership Programme, which later became the Citizen and Community Empowerment Programme (CCEP), strengthened the capacity of civil society leadership to participate in policy development and implementation.

Strengthening Capacity for Democracy (2000–2004)

Though IDASA has worked diligently and determinedly toward its goals, the initial excitement and jubilation that marked the beginning of the transformation process in South Africa is all but forgotten. When asked to express their views on the state of affairs in South Africa, most citizens will refer to the high levels of crime and violence, increasing unemployment, poverty, and the perceived inability of the government to make things right.[29]

IDASA believes that many of these challenges are connected and can be addressed by dealing with certain weaknesses in society and deepening democracy by building the capacity of citizens and the state. The organization's primary objective has become to build this capacity. IDASA's current mission statement asserts that it is "an independent public interest organization committed to promoting a sustainable democracy in South Africa and elsewhere by building democratic institutions, educating citizens, and advocating social justice."[30] To do this, the organization has decided to concentrate on building government and civic capacity for democracy particularly through training and related activities. IDASA's goal is to provide empowering and critical education, not merely the transmission of narrowly defined skills competence.

In order to achieve this objective, IDASA has identified three critical interrelated competencies that must be strengthened. The first is "Enforcement and Consent," by which is meant the competency of the state to enforce all laws and the willingness and ability of people to comply with these laws. The second is "Representation and Participation," the ability of the state and government to represent through all statutory institutions the needs and interests of people, and the willingness and ability of people to directly participate in processes to meet their own interests and needs. The last critical competency is "Delivery and Demand," the ability of the state to deliver social services and the rights expressed in Chapter 2 of the Constitution and the willingness and ability of people to make demands based on the Constitution. These three critical competencies form the theoretical framework that IDASA's programs. IDASA recognizes that there is a connection between the competencies, and knows that while action is required in all three, action in one will affect the whole system.

IDASA runs a number of programs serving both national and international capacity building needs including the Budget Information Service, the Citizen and Community Empowerment Programme, the Community Safety Programme, the Governance and Aids Programme, the Local Government Center, the Political Information and Monitoring Service, the Right to Know Programme, the Public Opinion Service, and the Southern African Migration. Though these programs are aimed at strengthening vastly different capacities of disparate target groups, they all serve to reinforce IDASA's long-term commitment to promoting sustainable democracy.

IDASA: A Movement Beyond South Africa

IDASA's emergence as a professional institution has roots in the struggle for democracy in South Africa. However, in the last several years, IDASA has become increasingly involved in assisting democratic processes in other African countries as well as other projects that cross borders. IDASA's international programs are guided by the belief that democracy is a common struggle that must be met by ordinary citizens and leaders from all over the world. As such, the struggle requires solidarity. For example, the Southern African Migration Project (SAMP) addresses the highly controversial flow of migrants and refugees between many Southern African countries. SAMP is a network of institutions in eight countries in the Southern African Development Community (SADC) region. It includes a research program on migration and has helped organize international forums in which migration officials from all the Southern African countries meet with each other and with immigration advocacy and research groups.

Created in 2001, IDASA's Governance and Aids Program (GAP) is based on the belief that the impact of HIV and AIDS poses a serious threat to democratic consolidation. It seeks to mobilize political leaders across Southern Africa to act collectively as legislators. Conducting breakthrough research on the implications of HIV/AIDS on elections, particularly citizen participation and electoral models, and introducing original training programs targeted at government communicators and speechwriters, GAP raises governance issues on HIV/AIDS at the various national levels. High-level leadership within the executive in South Africa and the ministers of health from Mozambique and Namibia has put GAP on the map as a leader in this field.

Afrobarometer, an IDASA flagship project working in the Public Opinion

Service (POS), is one of the most effective governance and democracy research tools on the continent. It recently received the 2004 Data Set Award of the American Political Science Association's Comparative Politics Section. Afrobarometer is driven by the belief that capacity for democracy entails citizens that are knowledgeable about government and can demand their rights. It follows the notion that democracy requires elected government officials, political parties, and civil society organizations that can effectively represent citizens. POS monitors, researches, and disseminates information about popular opinion by conducting periodic attitude surveys, looking at the development of African values, their assessments of democratic institutions, their perceptions of social justice in terms of how they are treated by those institutions, and their quality of life. The work of POS is to match its strategic sense of what is important and relevant with the perceptions of African citizens from fifteen countries. Over time, it will also enable IDASA to measure the impact of democracy promotion work in Africa.[31]

As IDASA has expanded its work in the rest of Africa, it has also taken on an increasingly self-conscious "African" identity and perspective on what democracy means. Recent work in Nigeria is illustrative. In 2002 IDASA, with two other partners, won a two-year USAID tender for a project in Nigeria titled "The Partnership for Advocacy and Civic Empowerment" (PACE). The project aim was to strengthen and build capacity within Nigerian civil society in areas of electoral support, constitutional reform, transparency, and peace building. One of the first efforts was monitoring and responding to the potential violence that could have threatened the 2003 elections. Because IDASA was one of the few democracy organizations working on the continent, it worked in partnership with churches and trade unions to establish an Alternative Information Network. As a result of IDASA's election observation work, the organization released a statement after the polls closed saying that the election, while not perfect, was definitely an advance. This judgment had a large impact on international opinion about the election's credibility and could have been a key factor in the government's decision to hold the next round of elections.

The 2002 elections in Kenya provided IDASA with another opportunity to contribute to the building of democracy in Africa. Prior to the elections, Kenya embarked on the process of producing a new democratic constitution to guide the election. The lack of political leadership to drive the constitutional debates left the country without a democratic constitution. Forecasting uncertainty in the 2002 elections and realizing the potential for change, IDASA took an assertive approach and initiated discussions with a wide range of NGOs in Kenya. The dialogue focused on the potential for institutional capacity building and "Post-Democracy Political Skills." The success of similar projects in Zambia and Zimbabwe reinforced IDASA's belief that capacity building in times of contentious elections was not only possible but also necessary. It is the understanding that Kenya that forms a building block to construct a democratic force in Africa that drives IDASA's motivation and commitment to create this project.

By making use of the South African experience and expertise working with colleagues and partners IDASA hopes to build, deepen, and strengthen democracy within Africa.[32] The question facing IDASA today is what strategic direction it should take to continue being a leading Africa-wide democracy building organization. IDASA has always maintained that it does not represent civil society but rather operates as a professional institution. The road ahead can lead in one of two ways—either IDASA becomes a Pan-African NGO with offices in South Africa or it remains a South African NGO that operates select programs in other African countries.

Relationships with External Parties

Nearly all NGOs operating within the context of a donor-recipient relationship must answer the question of how those relationships contribute to strengthening constituency bases, whether it is by enhancing horizontal linkages between autonomous actors, or vertical relations of dependence.[33] The context of a relationship is critical in defining autonomy: are these relationships based on individuals or organizations as agents of change, and are they based on personal relationships or results?

By employing a laissez-faire approach where horizontal relationships are built on the organization as an entity and individuals within as agents of change, IDASA has maintained unique relationships with international and domestic donor institutions. Throughout its history, the institution has been firm on setting its agenda while other organizations in similar situations within and around South Africa have become victims of donor dictated projects and programs.[34] While most organizations struggle with the question of autonomy or dependence, IDASA has clearly maintained its freedom to determine its own strategic direction and development without undue pressure from external actors.

The core component in preserving this level of independence is the process of creating an overall mission without reference to donors. The strategic direction of IDASA has been to collectively decide its mission, search for ways to achieve the mission objectives, and seek funding opportunities. In contrast, many NGOs seek funding and then tailor their objectives accordingly. IDASA's ability to maintain its objectives despite donor intervention has allowed the organization to become more competitive in the fight for scarce resources.

IDASA occasionally sets the donor agenda as well. Through interaction at high policy levels and consultative processes, donor agencies have bestowed upon IDASA the standing of one that is well immersed in priorities within the South African community. The combination of concrete objectives coupled with the diversity of funding by domestic and international donors has helped foster the lack of conformity to traditional donor-recipient relations (see Appendix A for IDASA's current funding landscape). This independence does not preclude IDASA from participating in formal systems of accountability to donors. Recipient organizations are understandably concerned about institutional development. The beauty of IDASA is that it has managed to work beyond accountability systems put in place by donors. Some of these systems have on occasion have served to undermine internal methods of control.

The defining distinction of IDASA that lends itself to this autonomous relationship with donors is its reputation as a productive organization of high quality work with results-oriented projects and commitment to change. What makes IDASA exceptional is the boldness, size, and multidimensionality of its political approach for the twenty-first century. This reputation can be attributed to two key organizational characteristics: strong and inspiring leadership and groundbreaking initiatives.

From its conception, IDASA has been under the direction of strong and capable leadership. Boraine and Slabbert created an institution of change based on their credibility as policy makers, and with a clear vision for success. Boraine, a former president of the Methodist Church of Southern Africa, served twelve years in Parliament before creating IDASA. Slabbert, a social scientist and former leader of the Opposition in Parliament, brought with him expertise as the chairperson of the Witwatersrand Metropolitan chamber and the University of Witwatersrand Graduate School of Business. The original board of trustees, kept intentionally largely white to adhere to and execute IDASA's mission, included members such as André du Toit, the founding editor of Die Suid-Afrikann magazine, James Leatt, the former vice chancellor and principal of the University of Natal, Stuart Sanders, the principal and vice chancellor of the University of Cape Town, and Archbishop Hurley, a former Catholic Archbishop of Durban (see Appendix B for a full list of original board members).

For almost two decades, these qualities have continued to sustain IDASA's direction. Both past and future leadership have uniformly managed the institution under an air of openness and equality, creating a supportive organizational culture. The leadership recognizes that producing an environment where everyone can express themselves and is treated equally is the key to sustainability. The low attrition rates within IDASA indicate the level of dedication and commitment the organization generates. The flexible nature of IDASA's leadership to change with the times in regards to community and internal needs has been a significant contributor to its reputation. After the 1994 elections, for instance, the need to develop leadership within the black community became apparent. Consequently, IDASA shifted its concentration from the distinct but small white power base to developing leadership programs within the black community.

IDASA's ability to create and sustain truly groundbreaking initiatives has also been vital to its success. The many successful projects and conferences IDASA has held over its lifetime directly contribute to the positive reputation it enjoys. The Dakar conference held in Senegal during its infancy launched IDASA as a national organization. In conjunction with that conference, IDASA was also critical in organizing a group of South African artists' visit to exiled South African artists in Lusaka, Zambia, and a group of South African women's visit to exiled women in Harare, Zimbabwe. Beyond the scope of its original mission and the Dakar conference, IDASA's role in the first free democratic elections was also critical. The creation and full implementation of the Independent Electoral Commission (IEC) came only three months prior to the elections. The IEC therefore lacked the ability to appropriately conduct all required election duties. During these elections, IDASA acted as the election administrators in absence of a fully capacitated IEC.

IDASA's role in facilitating a peaceful dialogue between Zulus and Indians in KwaZulu-Natal in 2002 was another successful groundbreaking initiative. Many Indians, and some among the black community, continued to experience economic advancement in the early 1990s while the majority of the Zulu community experienced stagnant or even worsening economic conditions. To address the bitter divides between the two communities, IDASA decided to create a dialogue. In June 26–27, 2002, diverse civil society leaders in Durban participated in a dialogue that included a series of exposure tours with Indians and Zulus going into each other's communities. The tours were successful eye-openers dispelling distorted ideas both groups had about each other. With over 400 participants in the conference, IDASA considered the dialogue a success.

The achievements of these conferences and its capacity building work throughout Africa have brokered trust and peace between conflicted parties and helped built sustainable civil society organizations. It is this trust and confidence which organizations and individuals have granted IDASA that makes these relationships so hopeful and fruitful.

The IDASA Approach

Throughout its history, IDASA has believed in and practiced political tolerance and the engagement of government with citizens. It considers the establishment of constitutional democracy, the building of democratic institutions, the habits and virtues of democratic citizenship, and increasing economic and social equality to be the best guarantors of peace in a world where conflict is inevitable. The changing role of civil society is located in the context of an ongoing process of transformation in South Africa. IDASA's history and development have been closely tied to the evolution of democracy in South Africa. While it has changed focus and strategy numerous times over the years, its commitment toward a democratic ideal has never wavered. IDASA has been able to participate in projects and activities covering the widest spectrum of democratic transition and consolidation. It has operated under the apartheid regime, a state of emergency, a transitional government, and two democratically elected parliaments.

IDASA's strategic phrase is that it builds capacity for democracy. This means capacity of government and the capacity of citizens and civic institutions such as NGOs, community organizations, schools, and the press. It also includes the ideas of democratic governance, which is about the quality and culture of citizen-government interaction. Democratic governance involves a culture of accountability, transparency, responsiveness, and permeability of government and civil society boundaries. Developing people's skills involves expanding their ability to engage with others across lines of racial, cultural, economic or ideological differences to accomplish public tasks such as conflict resolution and problem solving. Through public work and deliberation, IDASA has developed these capacities. This emphasis represents an older understanding of politics as negotiation among a plurality of interests to accomplish public tasks.

Politics, with its bad reputation around the world, is nonetheless the master language of decision making, goal setting, engagement of interests, and power in complex, diverse societies. When politics become increasingly professionalized most people are shut out of the serious work of making critical decisions about their world. Citizenship either thins out or is reduced to righteous demands and complaints. Perhaps most novel in a world where professionals increasingly dictate the terms and frameworks of politics, IDASA has sought to retrieve the nonprofessional understanding of politics. In IDASA's view, politics has always belonged to the people.

IDASA's approach to philosophically democratic and constructive politics has been formed by a quest to find its roots in African traditions and experiences, not models imported from Europe or the United States. Explicit attention to nonpartisan politics that empowers citizens is apparent in the faith-based organizing networks developing among low-income church communities in Johannesburg, Cape Town, Port Elizabeth, Durban, and elsewhere. This approach has deep roots in older South African traditions that emphasized the everyday work of organizing, developing local leadership, and creating public goods such as clinics and cooperatives like the Black Consciousness Movement of the 1970s.

The constructive politics that IDASA pioneers challenges "politics as usual" across the world. The world today is confronted by large problems that cannot be solved without government, but which governments alone can never address. IDASA has understood from the beginning a crucial truth of democracy building in our age: to create flourishing democracies and a global environment hospitable to such democracies will require deep respect for the interests, talents, and intelligence of all stakeholders. Without a doubt, each country has its own unique barriers to the elimination of injustices. But the institutional framework developed by IDASA offers good lessons. It is a model that works to build national unity and seeks democratic alternatives through dialogue and workshops and lays the groundwork for free and fair elections, empowers citizens, and deepens the capacity of government and civil society. It provides a powerful example that organizations the world over can use to inform their own efforts to establish democratic reform. IDASA's distinctive flexibility, its interest in innovative and creative projects, and its willingness to work with any actor committed to the goal of democracy makes its operational philosophy a valuable and useful example for any organization working toward social justice.

Appendix A: IDASA's Funding Landscape

As evident from Figure 1, much of the funding for IDASA came from sources external to South Africa. This was illustrative of a poor local philanthropic base and the difficulty of attracting domestic funding for human rights and democracy NGOs during apartheid.

Appendix B: IDASA's Original Board of Trustees

Dr. Nthato Motlana was a leading community figure in Soweto and a medical doctor. He was founder president and then honorary president of the Soweto Civic Association. Over the years he has played an important role in primary health care, small business development, education and community-based projects.

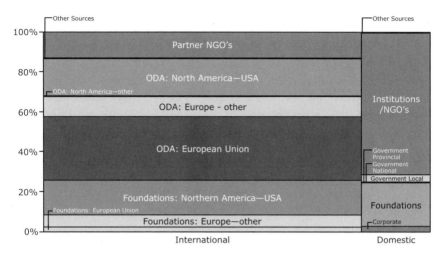

Figure 1. IDASA funding.

Professor Andre du Toit was professor of political studies at the University of Cape Town and deputy dean of the social sciences and humanities faculty. He was the founding editor of Die Suid-Afrikann magazine and has written numerous scholarly articles and authored several books.

Professor James Gerwel performed duties as rector and vice chancellor at the University of the Western Cape. His primary interest was the transformation of the education system in South Africa and he held office with several education bodies.

Dr. Alex Boraine, former executive director of Idasa, was president of the Methodist Church of Southern Africa. He was a Member of Parliament for twelve years before founding Idasa.

Dr. Fredrick Van Zyl Slabbert, a social scientist and former leader of the opposition in Parliament, was the director of policy and planning of Idasa. He also served as chairperson of the Witwatersrand Metropolitan Chamber, and a visiting professor at the Wits Graduate School of Business.

Professor James Leatt was vice-chancellor and principal of the University of Natal. He has published widely in the fields of religious studies and applied ethics and works as a consultant to various companies on industrial relations, dispute resolution and corporate social responsibility.

Mr. Enos Mabuza was Chief Minister of kaNgwane between 1977 and 1991. Respected across the political spectrum in South Africa in 1978 he founded the

Inyandza National Movement. He was also part-time executive director of the Independent Development Trust and served on the boards of several major companies.

Ms. Elizabeth Mokotong was executive director of the Vocational Guidance and Education Center and Hluvukani (a development agency) on the Reef. Her interests have been in development of women, children and conflict management.

Dr. Beyers Naude, a prominent religious leader in South Africa, lived under a banning order between 1977 and 1984. He was honorary vice-president of the South African Council of Churches and was active in several organizations. As the first chairperson of Idasa's Board of Trustees, he retired at the end of 1991.

Professor Wiseman Nkuhlu, principal and vice chancellor of the University of Transkei, was very active in the field of economic development and served on the boards of the Development Bank of Southern Africa, the African Bank and the Independent Development Trust.

Dr. Stuart Saunders was principal and vice chancellor of the University of Cape Town (UCT). He previously served as professor and head of the medical school at UCT. He is a past president of the South African Institute of Race Relations and has had links with a range of educational and health organizations.

Archbishop Denis Hurley retired in 1991 after holding a position of the Catholic Archbishop of Durban for forty years. The social application of the Christian gospel was his field of interest. He served on the council of Diakonia and was chairperson of the Natal Church Leaders Group.

Reverend Mteteleli De Villiers Soga was a minister of the Reformed Presbyterian Church in Port Elizabeth. He also served as chairperson of the Eastern Cape Council o Churches and was president of the Port Elizabeth branch of IDA-MASA (Inter-denominational African Ministers Association of South Africa).

Professor Peter Vale was codirector of the Center for Southern African Studies at the University of the Western Cape. The author of over 100 academic publications, he has taught and done research in the field of international relations.

Reverend Canon Zundu was archdeacon of Diaz in Port Elizabeth and chairperson of the Eastern Cape Council of Churches. He was a member of the management committee of the Port Elizabeth Child Welfare and Family Life and a board member of the Equal Opportunities Foundation.

Conclusion: Coming of Age: NGOs and State Accountability in East Africa

Chris Maina Peter

> *It must be accepted that ultimately, Africa is responsible for its own develop-
> ment; the role of outsiders—NGOs, private companies, governments, inter-
> national agencies—is merely to assist. Even in terms of democratization,
> foreigners should not be solely relied on to pressure recalcitrant regimes to
> democratise. Internal forces especially within the civil society are responsible,
> in the first instance, for inducing Africa's turn around.*
> —Kivutha Kibwana

Placing NGOs in Society

NGOS AND CIVIL society now occupy a central place in the governance of East
Africa. This is fact in spite of attempts by certain sectors of society to discredit,
belittle, or dismiss NGOs. NGOs are here to stay because they have a fundamental role to play. Their place is entrenched and secure because it is not
granted on a silver platter. It was fought for and earned. What's more, the
people of the region—the constituency that matters the most—supports civil
society organizations

This concluding chapter broadly examines the rise of civil society as a key
political player during the era of one-party dictatorships and looks at the hide-
and-seek games NGOs have played with the regimes in power in order to survive. It explores the relations between NGOs and the donors that sustain them.
It also looks at attempts by governments to coopt NGOs into governance. It
addresses legislative attempts by the state to control civil society and their resistance to such maneuvers. It concludes by examining some of the weaknesses
within the NGOs that have been exploited by their detractors in order to belittle
their contribution to governance, rule of law, and democracy in the region.

Civil Society and the Independence Struggle

There was a close relationship between nationalist leaders and various civil society organizations during the struggle for independence in East Africa. In some respects, it was almost impossible to separate the two groups.[1] Peasants in cooperative movements and the working people in various trade unions provided the nationalist leaders with a way to address the public legally without going through the rigors of procuring the required permits for meetings from the authorities. In Tanzania for instance, even social organizations such as football clubs like the Young Africans Sports Club and Taarab clubs like the Egyptian Musical Club in Dar es Salaam were among the civil society groups that assisted the nationalist movement in its struggle for the country's independence.[2] These were the recruitment centers for the new political organizations, particularly the Tanganyika African National Union (TANU). Tatu Mzee, a leading TANU activist who later became a member of the party's National Executive Committee, said:

> We tried to keep in mind what type of people to look for. We looked
> for *lele mama* dance groups and beer brewers because these were groups
> that had many people. And through these groups we could spread pro-
> paganda about our organization. . . . We used to pick those who were
> courageous.[3]

There were many civic groups in up-country Tanganyika organized by Muslims to oppose colonial rule. Many of the political actors of the period such as Mwalimu Julius Kambarage Nyerere, Bibi Titi Mohamed, Oscar Kambona, and Zuberi Mtemvu have died without leaving behind a written record of the rich history of this close relationship between political actors and members of the civil society.

Kenya was no different. Citizen organizations led the way to political emancipation. Civil organizations such as Young Kavirondo Association, Young Kikuyu Association, Taita Hills Association, and Ukamba Members Association—though narrow in their "native" demands for better working and living conditions and the right to organize themselves—were the training grounds for politicians who came to take over the country later.[4] According to Ngunyi, as long as these distinct groupings—organized mainly along "tribal" lines—did not network and remained parochial, the colonial administration was happy to permit their existence because their effectiveness was minimal and thus posed no threat to the status quo.[5]

Trade unions made significant contributions to the independence struggle in Kenya. Their leaders were so active that the colonial state targeted some of them for detention. The colonial regime detained Makhan Singh, who is regarded as the father of modern trade unionism in Kenya.[6] An important fact is that trade unions and civil society actors did not feel limited by the colonial boundaries. They operated regionally wherever workers were oppressed. Trade union leaders like Tom Mboya, Fred Kubai, and Dennis Akumu were as East African as they were Kenyan.[7]

In Uganda, those civil societies that were active in the colonial period were transformed into formidable political parties. A good example is I. K. Musazi's Uganda African Farmers Union that championed the interests of farmers. It later worked closely with the Uganda National Congress.[8] Earlier, the Bataka Movement had managed to establish itself as a formidable anticolonial peasants' organization.[9] Another interesting civil society organization to emerge during this period was the Buganda African Motor Drivers Union, the first union to be formed in Uganda, in 1939. Together with domestic servants, motor drivers formed the most articulate section of workers in the country.[10] These organizations soon joined other middle-class groups such as Uganda African Civil Servants Association, Uganda African Welfare Association, Uganda African Farmers Union, and later the Transport and General Workers Union. Workers in institutions linked to the East African High Commission that operated East African-wide activities like the railways, harbors, and posts and telecommunications tended to organize as East Africans, not merely as Ugandans.

The role of civil organizations during the colonial period cannot be underestimated. They were crucial in bringing together large numbers of people to demand freedom. The cooperative movement and the trade unions are worth noting. But this amicable and supportive relationship changed after independence.

Marginalization of NGOs Under One-Party Dictatorship

The 1960s and 1970s witnessed a movement from the multiparty democratic political system hurriedly introduced by the departing colonial power towards one-party dictatorships. The single ruling party was declared supreme and all political activity subjected to it.[11] Unfortunately for Uganda, this development was followed by a military dictatorship under the late Idi Amin Dada.[12] An important casualty of this change was the people and their civic organizations. The only avenue open for any form of organization was the single party. Civic organizations that had effectively struggled against colonialism such as cooperatives and trade unions were declared "mass organizations" and placed under the supreme ruling party. In the Tanzanian context, Juma Mwapachu articulately captures the impact of this development:

> Because of close to three decades of one party rule, civil society in Tanzania suffered serious damage. The abolition of co-operatives . . . removed from the political mainstream a voice that represented the people at grassroots level. Trade unions had also been absorbed into the political party structure, and so were women and youth organizations.[13]

Henceforth building new organizations of civil society would not be an easy task:

> To rebuild civil society after destruction of the environment upon which civil society breeds, nourishes and thrives has been an awesome and arduous challenge. Thus, even with the re-entry of multi-party political system. . . . Tanzania is yet to build organs of civil society that are strong and bold.[14]

Faced with autocratic rule elsewhere in the region, people took refuge in organizations that were beyond the reach of the state. These organizations enjoyed wide support, making it difficult for government to attack them. Primarily, these were faith-based organizations. In Kenya in particular, the faith-based organizations played a central role in championing the wishes and interests of the people without fear.[15] Their leadership was clear and articulate against autocratic rule.[16] Some actors in this sector sacrificed their lives in the hands of the ruthless ruling clique who felt threatened by their vocal leadership.[17] Some died in such suspicious circumstances that their fate couldn't be separated from the struggle for a better Kenya.

Civil Society: The Flagship for Change

NGOs and civil society have played a central role in ushering change in East Africa. They have been active in the struggle against economic and social poverty. They have been in the forefront of educating populations about political participation and governance during electoral periods. NGOs have enabled common people to make political choices for their leaders from an informed standpoint.

Some civil society organizations have been active in economic matters by enabling members of the public to access loans and grants. Others have addressed the environment, energy, and conservation measures; health, food and nutrition; water and sanitation; population matters; shelter; relief services; the disabled, children, youth, and women, destitution, and religion; communication; the informal sector and empowerment; and education. These are the most vulnerable sections of the population but are given low priority by the government. In most cases, intervention by civil society actors has had a long-term impact on the population. The major advantage of having non-state actors is to empower the people and demystify the government and its power. It allows the people to realize how much power they collectively wield against the few bureaucrats who manipulate and misinform them.

NGOs and the State: Cat and Mouse?

The relationship between the government and NGOs in East Africa can be compared to that of cat and mouse. Central and controversial in this relationship is access to resources and people. Governments believe that NGOs are taking donor money, which in their view should be allocated to them for "development." States think that donor monies in the hands of NGOs is a serious waste of resources. On the other hand, donors have learned their lessons. Although they have been funding governments for years, they claim to see no tangible results. They equate funding governments to throwing money down a bottomless pit. Nothing comes out of it. This partially explains the search for alternative ways and going directly to the people through their own organizations instead of using the government as an intermediary. In some cases, this has paid high dividends. But it has often angered governments in power.

The second "headache" for the government as far as NGOs are concerned is access to people in the rural areas. By and large, the government survives through the ignorance of people about their rights. Therefore, whoever accesses the people and educates them on their rights is seen as a threat that must be dealt with. The civic programs conceived and prepared by NGOs in human rights and other fundamental rights and freedoms are seen as thorn in the flesh of the regime in power. It is undesirable for them to open the eyes of the people.

NGOs are therefore restricted in outreach. The government is only comfortable if NGOs can restrict their activities to urban areas. Urban areas dwellers are educated and already know most of their rights. However, they are in the minority. The rural majority hardly knows its rights.[18] According to the state, NGOs should, in every way, be prevented from reaching rural folk.

The state can be ruthless with NGOs that attempt to penetrate rural areas. A good example is the attempt by Baraza la Wanawake wa Tanzania (BAWATA) or the Women's Council of Tanzania that was established in 1995 by Anna Tibaijuka, a UN under-secretary-general. BAWATA irritated the ruling party Chama Cha Mapinduzi (CCM) for guiding women to vote for candidates with pro-women agendas in general elections. To add insult to injury, BAWATA concentrated its activities in rural areas starting at the village level. This was a new approach for women in the politics in the country. One commentator differentiates BAWATA from the hitherto existing women organizations in the following terms:

> The main difference between BAWATA and UWT [Umoja wa Wana-
> wake wa Tanzania—Organisation of Women of Tanzania established
> under the auspices of the ruling CCM] is that the former is much more
> concerned about the problems of women at grassroots level than UWT
> has ever been. While UWT expressed concern about the welfare of
> women in urban centres, BAWATA has concentrated on the bread and
> butter issues of womenfolk in the village.[19]

This government could not allow such "mischief" to continue. Therefore, without assigning any good reason, the Ministry of Home Affairs threatened to deregister BAWATA.[20] To date, a much-weakened BAWATA still operates under the protection of a court injunction.[21] There are similar stories in the other East African countries, and this trend of the restricting the access of civil society organizations to rural areas and special sections of the population—particularly women—is likely to continue.

NGO Relations with Donor "Partners"

The relationship between NGOs and the donors is tricky because the majority of civil society actors in the East African region are totally dependent on donors for their survival. This is a serious limitation to their freedom. It is well presented by Shivji:

> we are funded by, and rely almost exclusively on, foreign funding. This
> is the greatest single limitation. "Whoever pays the piper calls the tune"
> still holds true, however much we may want to think otherwise. In
> many direct and subtle ways, those who fund us determine or place
> limits on our agendas or reorient them. Very few of us can really resist
> the pressures that external funding imposes on us.[22]

NGOs without strong, well-thought-out agendas and programs can be easily confused and pushed around by donors.

There are two types of NGO donor-donee relationships. Take the case of NGOs that are well established with a track record of good performance. In most cases, these NGOs have worked hard for their reputation and thus have something to prove to donors. Donors seek them out and it is a privilege for them to be associated with this class of NGOs. There is a limited number of this type of donors in the region. Such NGOs even call a conference of donors to agree on which one of them would fund particular projects. This is the case with the Kenya Human Rights Commission. NGOs in this class can hold discussions with funders on an almost equal basis. This is because of the cultivated mutual respect. The only caution here is for the NGO to maintain its good performance and not let its success get in the way.

The problem of donor-donee relations is with small and emerging players in civil society. Some may be good and well-meaning organizations. Yet opportunists may establish others. Donors can usually distinguish the fake from the genuine. It is dangerous when NGOs readily accept everything suggested by the donor as it invites questions as to the genuineness of the organization, its leadership and its programs. Another group of suspect NGOs is those that move to and from program depending on what is fashionable with donors. Today it could be gender and tomorrow HIV/AIDS. The danger here is the fact that the NGO cannot build on its past work because of the short-term changes.

Unprincipled donors will attempt not only to control weak NGOs but also try to turn them into their own departments. With time, the donor many insist on the following: sitting in the meetings of the NGO; a veto in all decisions made by the NGO; making it mandatory for the NGO to adopt its employment criteria; insist on providing the NGO with technical assistance of its choice—in most cases a person hired from the home country of the donor.[23] These danger signs should be read early and the donor, however generous, be kept at arm's length.

The solution to the ever-changing relationship between donors and members of the civil society is for the NGOs to have a well-thought-out strategic program that is sustainable. Donors will not be there forever. Therefore, NGOs need to carefully and seriously consider having a viable way out of donor dependence. That is to say that donor funding should be seen and taken by the NGOs as a bridge towards self-sufficiency and not as an end in itself.

NGOs and Co-option into Government

A large number of members of the civil society in East Africa have been co-opted into government. This has happened in two situations. The first is where a radical activist decides to join competitive politics—stands for elections, joins parliament, and is later appointed into government. Whatever bright ideas such an activist may have, he or she is soon overwhelmed by "colleagues" in government and begins to tow the official line. They are then written off as useless to the causes of civil society. The second occurs when civil society joins with the opposition in the struggle against autocratic rule. This joint effort is successful, members of civil society join the opposition into forming the government and then the problems begin.

In Kenya, members of the civil society joined forces with the opposition to fight the government of former President Daniel arap Moi. This undertaking succeeded in December 2002 when a new government came into office. There was a lot of hope in Kenya and in the region in general. Members of the civil society who had been very critical to the Moi government were soon appointed into various offices of power.[24] However, a considerable number of them have proved to be a disappointment to those who supported them. With time, they joined the hard-liners in government who regarded the government as a master, and not a servant, of the people. From the experience in the region, it seems clear that NGOs, CBOs, and other people-based organizations should steer clear of direct politics and work as a check on state power.

Clipping the Wings of Civil Society

Governments in East Africa seem to have one common desire: to exercise a tight control over the civil society. This attitude has remained intact notwithstanding the adoption of policies ostensibly to open up political space. Of late, governments in the region have adopted policies to implement tighter legislation to govern the registration and operations of NGOs. Prior to the legislation, civil society in the region rejected such measures when it was given an opportunity to comment on them.

In Tanzania, it was easy at first for NGOs to circumvent the registration process tightly controlled by government. Originally, all civil society organizations were supposed to be registered under the 1954 Societies Ordinance. This is a colonial piece of legislation purposely enacted by the British to curb the activities of TANU, which was formed the same year. Under the law, the Ministry of Home Affairs took time to vet each applicant organization. No NGO with the words "democracy," "rule of law," or "human rights" in any of its documents was registered for years. To evade the this restriction, civil society organizations applied for registration either as companies with limited guarantees under the 1932 Companies Ordinance or as trusts under the Trustees Incorporation Ordinance.

However, the government soon discovered this "mischief." Today, registered NGOs are required to conform to the provisions of the 2002 NGOs Act.[25] Under this law, each civil society organization is required to register as an NGO and be provided with a certificate of compliance. It is an offence to operate as an NGO in the country without fulfilling the requirements of this law. The law provides for the establishment of an umbrella organization, the National Council for Non-Governmental Organizations, for all NGOs in Tanzania.[26] Though formed by members of civil society, it is state-sanctioned body.

This situation has been worsened by the enactment of terrorism legislation in Tanzania.[27] The terrorism law requires NGOs to indicate their sources of funding and account for every cent received from abroad. It has suggested that NGOs had been a conduit for funding of terrorist activities and groups. This new law allows for the control and easy deregistration of NGOs.

The situation in Kenya is not different. Prior to 1990, there was no specific institutional and legislative framework governing NGOs. Like Tanzania, NGOs were registered under various laws such as the Companies Act, the Societies Act,[28] the Ministry of Culture and Social Services, and the Trustees Act. Kameri-Mbote has captured this situation:

> There was no clear national framework for appreciating NGOs' role in development; institutional capacity weaknesses; poor co-operation and networking; tensions between NGOs and Government; and geographical maldistribution.[29]

By 1990 about 75 percent of all registered NGOs were located in the capital city of Nairobi, with the majority of the rest in other urban areas. There were very few NGOs based in the rural areas.[30]

The government of Kenya has always sought to control civil society in general and NGOs in particular. It was just a question of finding the opportune moment.[31] A number of factors conspired to bring about that moment. First, a number of problems in the 1980s escalated that made the presence of NGOs in the country clearly visible. These included poverty, civil strife, conflicts, internal displacements arising out of "tribal" clashes, and the degeneration of the socio-economic and political systems. NGOs seized the moment to fill the gap because the government was too slow to react to the plight of the population. This led people to question the government's leadership. The legitimacy of the state was eroded. This is a threat that the government could not be taken lightly. Second, some reports suggested that a number of NGOs were being involved in illegal activities. These included abuse of tax-free facilities to import luxury vehicles for sale and importation of arms, ammunition, communication facilities, and other equipment. The government perceived this as a statement about its own irrelevance. Third, donors indicated their dissatisfaction with the government because of its failure to provide basic services and protect fundamental rights. Donors then shifted their funding to NGOs. They cited corruption and embezzlement as among the reasons for change. As a result, the government increasingly viewed NGOs with alarm.

This background explains the enactment of the 1990 NGO Coordination Act.[32] This legislation came into force in January 1991 and defines NGOs and establishes the NGO Co-ordination Board, a government agency to regulate NGOs in the country.[33] In addition, the Act provides for a self-regulatory agency of NGOs—the Kenya National Council of NGOs.[34] This body handles matters such as funding, foreign affiliation, national security, training, and institutional building within the NGOs. This is done through a Code of Conduct adopted by the NGOs themselves.

However, power lies with the Board. It is the one that registers NGOs on the recommendation of the Council, although according to section 14 it may refuse registration for many reasons including the "national interest." It may also deny registration if the Council does not support the application. Appeals against such a decision goes to the Minister and if necessary to the High Court. It is an offence to operate an NGO in Kenya without registration under this act. The Board is empowered to deregister NGOs.

The government is wary of high profile NGOs. It does not hesitate to harass such NGOs or if possible remove them from the register. This is the case where NGOs are perceived as "political." One victim of these powers was the Centre for Law and Research International (CLARION). This organization was registered on in January 1994 and deregistered in February 1995 by the Board, allegedly for violating the terms of registration: publishing materials damaging to the credibility of the government and disseminating materials harmful to the country. The process did not follow the basic rules of natural justice. The Board did not give CLARION a hearing before reaching their decision. It took internal and external pressure and a decision of the High Court in June 1996 to restore CLARION's registration. It was only out of shame that the Board decided to rescind its own decision to deregister the organization. This indicates vulnerability of NGOs in Kenya under the current legal framework.[35] Other organizations that have also been the subject of harassment by the regime in Kenya include the Green Belt Movement led by Nobel Prize Laureate Wangari Maathai and the National Council of Churches of Kenya (NCCK).[36] The clergy have not been spared from threats and intimidation as demonstrated by the experiences of the Church of the Province of Kenya (CPK) and the Presbyterian Church of East Africa (PCEA):[37]

The situation in Uganda is not different from that in the rest of the region.[38] Most NGOs are urban-based. A small elite based in Kampala and other urban centers such as Entebbe and Jinja lead the majority of NGOs. The government is in total control of civil society following new legislation in 2001.[39] Three East Africas are birds of feather it terms of the way they view NGOs. The government in Uganda, notwithstanding its rhetoric on democratization and good governance, has not given breathing space to civil society. As donors endear themselves to civil society more, the relations between NGOs and the regime in Kampala can only become even more strained.

The government in Uganda pays a special attention to faith-based NGOs because of recent events that led to the loss of the lives of many believers. This was the case after the Kanungu mass murder of believers by the cult leaders.[40] Hundreds of innocent citizens died in an alleged faith-induced suicide. The event drove the state to give special attention to the charismatic churches and their born-again flock, which is easily led astray. To civil society and NGOs in the region, all these developments mean that the struggle for a free civil society is just beginning. There is need to remain alert in order to guard the gains so far achieved in the struggle and prevent losses in the democratization process.

Conclusion: Don't Preach Water and Drink Wine

There is no doubt that NGOs have played a very important part in the socioeconomic development of the region. They have not only concentrated in the areas of politics, democracy, the rule of law, and human rights, but some have guided peasants and workers in the economic and trade sectors. NGOs have not only fought social poverty but economic poverty as well. It is a contribution whose impact on the lives of citizens is incalculable.

However, it is important to deliver a warning to NGOs. They should not take things for granted and let their recent victories against autocrats in the region make them arrogant. If civil society in the region is to be taken seriously and be effective as a check against the excesses of the regimes in power, then NGOs and Community Based Organizations (CBOs) must stand out as shining example of good governance, transparency, and openness. It makes little sense for NGOs to point fingers at governments and criticize them while their own houses are not in order. There are a number of problems that NGOs must address to avoid paralysis.

The first is the *founder's syndrome*. In a number of NGOs, the people who originally established the organizations still serve as executive leaders more than a decade later. They jealously hold on to the organizations. They run them by remote control even when they are out of the country. Any major decision relating to the organization cannot be made without consulting the "boss," who may be abroad. Often, directives are given via e-mails. It is therefore not surprising that modern technology has nurtured a form of dictatorship where person can run an NGO in East Africa while on sabbatical for a whole year in Europe. This is not good governance. If terms of office for heads of state can be set, then NGOs cannot be exempt. Leadership in NGOs should be limited in order to allow for growth and fresh ideas.

The second is the *lack of internal democracy*. In many NGOs, there are no structures for democratic decision making. Instead, there is a small cabal of "rulers" who lord over everybody. They make all major decisions pertaining to the organization without any proper consultation and later formalize these decisions in boards of directors without meaningful discussion. Yet the structure of the governance of the organization given to the public and the donors indicates just the opposite of the practice. Meetings are called and in most cases a single individual makes decisions. Yet this type of civil society leader will shout their voices hoarse condemning the government of the day for being undemocratic and unaccountable.

The third is *transparency in financial matters*. A considerable number of NGOs are uncomfortable when it comes to the discussion of their sources of finance. The finance officer and the chief executive carefully guard this information. Often, the members of the board of directors are not privy to this important information. At the end of the year, board members get dry figures that most of them do not understand. They approve figures they cannot comprehend for fear of seeming stupid. A board member who understands finances is soon replaced for "other" reasons. NGOs need to be open on their sources and their income and how that income is spent. This should be made public for the organization to enjoy the confidence of those it sets out to serve: the people.

The fourth is *having and taking the people as a base*. NGOs should not be organizations of like-minded elites in the urban areas "exporting" democracy and good governance to the people in the rural areas through seminars and training sessions. Shivji puts this point well:

> most of our NGOs are top-down organizations led by elites. What is
> more, most of them are urban based. . . . NGOs did not start as a
> response to the felt need of the majority of working people. It is true
> that many of us within the NGO community are well intentioned and
> would want to contribute to some cause, however we may define it. It
> is also true that many NGOs do address some of the real concerns of
> the working people. Yet we must recognize that we did not develop as,

nor have we as yet managed to become, organic to the mass of the people. The relationship between NGOs and the masses therefore remains, at best, that of benefactors and beneficiaries. This is not the best of relationships when it comes to genuine activism **with**, rather than **for**, the people.[41]

NGOs will be irrelevant and of no use to society if they fail to identify with the people they are supposed to serve as their base and main reason for existence. In short, it is important that NGOs in the East African region exercise good governance. In terms of internal democracy and financial matters, they should be like Caesar's wife—beyond suspicion. It is only this openness that can give them the legitimacy of holding governments in the region to account. In other words, they should be prepared to practice what they preach—not preaching water and drinking wine. This is important because NGOs and civil society lead where governments have failed to show the way. Governments fail because they depend on dividing the people. Civil society must confront this challenge by addressing this "divide and rule" strategy squarely. In the words of Juma Mwapachu, "A key challenge confronting [the] civil society is how to build bridges across the national diverse cultures, beliefs, values, religion, race and even tribes."[42]

If this succeeds, then NGOs would have done their part in making East Africa a better place in live in.

NOTES

INTRODUCTION

1. See Mahmood Mamdani, *Citizen and Subject: Contemporary Africa and the Legacy of Late Colonialism* (Princeton, N.J.: Princeton University Press, 1996), 19.

2. Crawford Young, *The African Colonial State in Comparative Perspective* 22 (New Haven, Conn.: Yale University Press, 1994).

3. John Keane, "Despotism and Democracy: The Origins and Development of the Distinction Between Civil Society and the State 1750–1850," in *Civil Society and the State*, ed. John Keane (London: Verso, 1988), 35–36.

4. Ibid., 36.

5. Ibid.

6. Mamdani, *Citizen and Subject*, 19.

7. Ibid.

8. Robert Fatton, *Predatory Rule: State and Civil Society in Africa* (Boulder, Colo.: Lynne Rienner, 1992); John W. Harbeson, Donald Rothchild, and Naomi Chazan, eds., *Civil Society and the State in Africa* (Boulder, Colo.: Lynne Rienner, 1994); Richard Joseph, ed., *State, Conflict, and Democracy in Africa* (Boulder, Colo.: Lynne Rienner, 1999).

9. Paul Tiyambe Zeleza, "The Struggle for Human Rights in Africa," in *Human Rights, the Rule of Law, and Development in Africa*, ed. Paul Tiyambe Zeleza and Philip J. McConnaughy (Philadelphia: University of Pennsylvania Press, 2004), 1.

10. Ibid., 1–2.

11. Ibid., 2.

12. Joel D. Barkan, "Kenya After Moi," *Foreign Affairs* 83, 1 (2004): 87.

13. Joseph, "State, Conflict, and Democracy in Africa," in Joseph, ed., *State, Conflict, and Democracy in Africa*, 3.

14. Young, *The African State in Comparative Perspective*; John W. Harbeson and Donald Rothchild, eds., *Africa in World Politics* (Boulder, Colo.: Westview Press, 1991); I. William Zartman, ed., *Collapsed States: The Disintegration and Restoration of Legitimate Authority* (Boulder, Colo.: Lynne Rienner, 1995); Ali A. Mazrui, *The Africans: A Triple Heritage*, BBC with Nigerian Television Authority, 1986.

15. Marina Ottaway, ed., *Democracy in Africa: The Hard Road Ahead* (Boulder, Colo.: Lynne Rienner, 1997); Richard Joseph, *The Democratic Challenge in Africa* (Atlanta: Carter Center of Emory University, 1994); Michael Bratton and Nicholas van der Walle, *Democratic*

Experiments in Africa: Regime Transitions in Comparative Perspective (New York: Cambridge University Press, 1997).

16. Frank Holmquist, "Kenya's Antipolitics," *Current History: A Journal of Contemporary World Affairs* 104, 682 (May 2005): 209.

17. Alexis de Tocqueville, *Democracy in America* (New York: Library of America, 2004).

18. John W. Harbeson, "Civil Society and Political Renaissance in Africa," in Harbeson et al., eds., *Civil Society and the State in Africa*, 1–2.

19. Michael Bratton, "Civil Societies and Political Transitions in Africa," in Harbeson et al., eds., *Civil Society and the State in Africa*, 51–52.

20. Mamdani, *Citizen and Subject*, 13–14.

21. Ibid., 14.

22. See generally, Jotham C. Momba, "Civil Society and the Struggle for Human Rights and Democracy in Zambia," 216–34; Claude E. Welch, Jr., "Human Rights and Development in Africa: NGOs," 199–208; and Makau wa Mutua, "African Human Rights Organizations: Questions of Context and Legitimacy," all in Zeleza and McConnaughy, eds., *Human Rights, the Rule of Law, and the Development of Africa*, 191–97; Ann Fowler, "The Role of NGOs in Changing State Society Relations: Perspectives from Eastern and Southern Africa," *Development Policy Review* 9, 1 (1991): 80; David Gillies and Makau wa Mutua, *A Long Road to Uhuru: Human Rights and Political Participation in Kenya* (Montreal: Center for Human Rights and International Development, March 1993), 22–37.

23. William D. Carmichael, "The Role of the Ford Foundation," in *NGOs and Human Rights: Promise and Performance*, ed. Claude E. Welch, Jr. (Philadelphia: University of Pennsylvania Press, 2001), 248–60.

24. Mamadou Diof and Mahmood Mamdani, *Academic Freedom in Africa* (Oxford: African Books Collective, 1993); Africa Watch Report, *Academic Freedom and Human Rights Abuses in Africa* (New York: Human Rights Watch, 1991).

25. Joe Oloka-Onyango, *Civil Society, Democratisation, and Foreign Donors in Uganda: A Conceptual Literature Review* (Kampala: Center for Basic Research, 2000); Apolo Nsibambi, *Decentralisation and Civil Society in Uganda* (Oxford: African Books Collective, 1998); Julie Hearn, *Foreign Aid, Democratisation, and Civil Society in Uganda in the 1990s* (Kampala: Center for Basic Research, 1999). See, for example, Africa Watch, *Kenya: Taking Liberties* (New York: Human Rights Watch, 1991); Willy Mutunga, *Constitution-Making from the Middle: Civil Society and Transition Politics in Kenya, 1992–1997* (Nairobi: Sareat and Mwengo, 1999); Ole Therkildsen and Joseph Semboja, *Service Provision Under Stress in East Africa: The State, NGOs & People's Organizations in Kenya, Tanzania & Uganda* (Portsmouth: Heinemann, 1996); Chris M. Peter, *Human Rights in Tanzania: Selected Cases and Materials* (Cologne: Rudiger Koppe Verlag, 1997).

26. Claude E. Welch, Jr., *Protecting Human Rights in Africa: Strategies and Roles of Nongovernmental Organizations* (Philadelphia: University of Pennsylvania Press, 1995), 42–43.

27. Chidi Anselm Odinkalu, "Why More Africans Don't Use the Human Rights Language," *Human Rights Dialogue* (Winter 2000): 4.

28. Welch, ed., *NGOs and Human Rights*.

29. Peter Baehr, "Amnesty International and Its Self-Imposed Limited Mandate," *Netherlands Quarterly of Human Rights* 12, 1 (1994): 5; Henry J. Steiner, *Diverse Partners: Non-Governmental Organizations in the Human Rights Movement* (Cambridge, Mass.: Harvard Law

School Human Rights Program and Human Rights Internet, 1991); Steve Charnovitz, "Non-Governmental Organizations and International Law," *American Journal of International Law* 100, 2 (2006): 348.

30. See, for example, Athena D. Mutua, ed., *Progressive Black Masculinities* (London: Routledge, 2006).

31. bell hooks, *Feminism Is for Everybody* (Cambridge, Mass.: South End Press, 2000).

32. Athena Mutua, "Gender Equality and Women's Solidarity Across Religious, Ethnic, and Class Difference in the Kenya Constitutional Review Process," *William & Mary Journal of Women and Law* 13 (2006): 1. See, for example, National Constitutional Conference, *The Draft Constitution of Kenya 2004* (2004); FIDA-K, KHRC, IED, League of Kenya Women Voters, "Safeguarding the Gains for Women in the Draft Constitution: Model Proposals," January 2005.

33. David Beetham, "What Future for Economic and Social Rights?" *Political Studies* 43 (1995): 41; Henry J. Steiner, "Social Rights and Economic Development: Converging Discourses?" *Buffalo Human Rights Law Review* 4 (1998): 25; Shadrack B. O. Gutto, "Beyond Justiciability: Challenges of Implementing/Enforcing Socio-Economic Rights in South Africa," *Buffalo Human Rights Law Review* 4 (1998): 79.

34. See generally Julius E. Nyang'oro, ed., *Civil Society and Democratic Development in Africa: Perspectives from Eastern and Southern Africa* (Harare: Mambo Press/Mwengo, 1999).

35. Odinkalu, "Why More Africans Don't Use the Human Rights Language," 4.

36. Azzedine Layachi, "Algeria: Reinstating the State or Instating a Civil Society," in Zartman, ed., *Collapsed States*, 172.

37. Odinkalu, "Why More Africans Don't Use Human Rights Language," 4.

38. Kenneth Anderson, "The Ottawa Convention Banning Landmines: The Role of International Non-Governmental Organizations and the Idea of the International Civil Society," *European Journal of International Law* 11 (2000): 92; Mutua, "African Human Rights Organizations," 191.

CHAPTER I. HUMAN RIGHTS NGOS IN EAST AFRICA: DEFINING THE CHALLENGES

1. See, for example, Jean L. Cohen and Andrew Arato, *Civil Society and Political Theory* (Cambridge, Mass.: MIT Press, 1992); Claude E. Welch, Jr., *Protecting Human Rights in Africa: Strategies and Roles of Nongovernmental Organizations* (Philadelphia: University of Pennsylvania Press, 1995), 42–43; John Keane, "Introduction," in *Civil Society and the State*, ed. John Keane (London: Verso, 1988), 1–29.

2. As Welch, *Protecting Human Rights in Africa*, 43, correctly argues, African civil societies largely arose in the 1980s after it had become clear that the postcolonial state was itself the major, if not the leading, cause of social and economic crises, such as famine, civil wars, despotism, exclusionary practices, and economic collapse.

3. John Keane, "Despotism and Democracy: The Origins and Development of the Distinction Between Civil Society and the State Since 1750–1850," in Keane, ed., *Civil Society and the State*, 35.

4. Ibid.

5. Ibid., 50.

6. See G. W. F. Hegel, *Grundlinien der Philosophie des Rechts* (1821); Alexis de Tocqueville, *De la démocratie en Amérique* (1835); *Democracy in America* (New York: Library of America, 2004).

7. Azzedine Layachi, "Algeria: Reinstating the State or Instating a Civil Society," in *Collapsed States: The Disintegration and Restoration of Legitimate Authority*, ed. I. William Zartman, (Boulder, Colo.: Lynne Rienner, 1995), 171–72.

8. Ibid., 172.

9. Michael Bratton, "Civil Society and Political Transitions in Africa," in *Civil Society and the State in Africa*, ed. John W. Harbeson, Donald Rothchild, and Naomi Chazan (Boulder, Colo.: Lynne Rienner, 1994), 51, 56.

10. Welch, *Protecting Human Rights in Africa*, 44.

11. For a critique of African NGOs, see Chidi Anselm Odinkalu, "Why More Africans Don't Use the Human Rights Language," *Human Rights Dialogue* (Winter 2000): 4.

12. Paul Tiyambe Zeleza, "Introduction: The Struggle for Human Rights in Africa," in *Human Rights, the Rule of Law, and Development in Africa*, ed. Paul Tiyambe Zeleza and Philip J. McConnaughy (Philadelphia: University of Pennsylvania Press, 2004), 1.

13. Issa G. Shivji, "Minimum Legal Conditions to Begin the Process of Democratization in Tanzania," *Eastern Africa Law Review* 17 (1990): 134.

14. See Chris M. Peter, *Human Rights in Tanzania: Selected Cases and Materials* (Cologne: Rudiger Koppe Verlag, 1997).

15. Joe Oloka-Onyango and Justus Mugaju, eds., *No-Party Democracy in Uganda: Myths and Realities* (Kampala: Fountain, 2000).

16. Willy Mutunga, *Constitution-Making from the Middle: Civil Society and Transition Politics in Kenya, 1992–1997* (Nairobi: SAREAT; Hararee: MWENGO, 1999).

17. Henry J. Steiner and Philip Alston, *International Human Rights in Context: Law, Politics, Morals* (Oxford: Oxford University Press, 2000), 938–40.

18. Makau wa Mutua, "African Human Rights Organizations: Questions of Legitimacy and Context," in Zeleza and McConnaughy, eds., *Human Rights, the Rule of Law, and Development in Africa*, 194.

19. Makau Mutua, "Domestic Human Rights Organizations in Africa: Problems and Perspectives," *Issue: A Journal of Opinion* 22, 2 (1994): 31.

20. Samuel Huntington, *The Third Wave: Democratization in the Late Twentieth Century* (Norman: University of Oklahoma Press, 1991), 6–8.

21. Steiner and Alston, *International Human Rights in Context*, 988–89.

22. Henry J. Steiner, *Diverse Partners: Non-Governmental Organizations in the Human Rights Movement* (Cambridge, Mass.: Harvard Law School Human Rights Program and Human Rights Internet, 1991), 19.

23. See Makau Mutua, *Human Rights: A Political and Cultural Critique* (Philadelphia: University of Pennsylvania Press, 2002).

24. Philip Alston, "The Committee on Economic, Social and Cultural Rights," in *The United Nations and Human Rights: A Critical Appraisal*, ed. Philip Alston (Oxford: Clarendon Press, 1992), 473, 490.

25. Antonio Cassese, "The General Assembly: Historical Perspectives," in *The United Nations and Human Rights: A Critical Perspective*, ed. Philip Alston (Oxford: Clarendon Press, 1992), 26, 31.

26. Universal Declaration of Human Rights, G.A. Res. 217 (III), UN GAOR, 3rd Sess., 183rd mtg. at 71, UN Doc. A/810 (1948); International Covenant on Civil and Political Rights, Dec. 19, 1966, S. TREATY DOC. No. 2, 95th Cong., 1st Sess. (1977), 999 U.N.T.S. 171, 6 I.L.M. 368. See Makau wa Mutua, "The Ideology of Human Rights," *Virginia Journal of International Law* 36 (1996): 589.

27. In 2002, however, the Kenya Human Rights Commission argued for a more nuanced and political understanding of the principle of nonpartisanship as it endorsed Mr. Mwai Kibaki and the National Alliance Party of Kenya (NAK) for the presidential and general elections. See Willy Mutunga, "So, What Really Is Non-Partisanship?" in *Eyes on the Prize*, ed. Athena Mutua, (Nairobi: Kenya Human Rights Commission, 2003), 31. See also Issa Shivji, *The Concept of Human Rights in Africa* (London: Codesria, 1989).

28. Ian Martin, "The New World Order: Opportunity or Threat for Human Rights?" Edward Smith Lecture at the Human Rights Program, Harvard Law School, 1993, 6.

29. Law Society of Kenya, "Impunity: Report of the Law Society of Kenya on the Judicial Commission of Inquiry into Ethnic Clashes in Kenya," 2000.

30. Human Rights Watch, *Human Rights Watch World Report 2000: Events of 1999* (New York: Uman Rights Watch, 2000), vii.

31. Peter Baehr, "Amnesty International and Its Self-Imposed Limited Mandate," *Netherlands Quarterly of Human Rights* 12, 1 (1994).

32. Mutua, "The Ideology of Human Rights," 617–20.

33. United Nations World Conference on Human Rights, Vienna Declaration and Programme of Action (para 5), adopted June 25, 1993, reprinted in 32 I.LM. 1661 (1993), *Human Rights Law Journal* 14, 352 (1993).

34. Jack Donnelly, "Human Rights and Western Liberalism," in *Human Rights in Africa: Cross-Cultural Perspectives*, ed. Abdullahi A. An-Na'im and Francis M. Deng (Philadelphia: University of Pennsylvania Press, 1990), 31, 33.

35. Willy Mutunga and Alamin Mazrui, "Rights Integration in an Institutional Context: the Experience of the Kenya Human Rights Commission," *Buffalo Human Rights Law Review* 8, 123 (2002): 138–39. East Africa is not, sadly, unique in this respect. Almost universally, most human rights NGOs are not engaged in the advocacy and protection of economic, social, and cultural rights. However, there are some encouraging developments in some parts of the world. In Nigeria, for example, Felix Morka, an accomplished human rights advocate, has developed the Social and Economic Rights Action Center (SERAC) into what is arguably Africa's first serious human rights NGO focusing on economic, social, and cultural rights.

36. Some notable names include Joe Oloka-Onyango, Fred Jjuuko, and Sylvia Tamale at Makerere University, Issa Shivji and Chris M. Peter at the University of Dar es Salaam, and Karuti Kanyinga at the University of Nairobi.

37. Academics and human rights programs at Yale, Harvard, SUNY-Buffalo, Columbia, American, Minnesota, and other universities have been invaluable to human rights groups in the United States. Academics play important roles in mapping out the human rights discourse and providing intellectual guidance to human rights organizations.

38. These include Louis Henkin of Columbia Law School, Philip Alston of New York University Law School, Drew Days and Harold Koh of Yale Law School, Henry Steiner of Harvard Law School, Diane Orenthlicher of American University College of Law, Henry Richardson of Temple Law School, Adrien Wing of Iowa College of Law, Claude Welch of

State University of New York at Buffalo, David Weissbrodt of University of Minnesota School of Law, and Abdullahi A. An-Na'im of Emory Law School, to name just a few.

39. The East African Center for Constitutional Development.

40. Again, the Kenya Human Rights Commission is one local NGO that constantly reviews its mandate to stay relevant to the basic challenges facing Kenyans, even if it means innovating or adding new dimensions to its mandate.

41. Kenya Human Rights Commission, *Manufacture of Poverty: The Untold Story of EPZs in Kenya* (Nairobi: The Commission, 2004); Kenya Human Rights Commission, *Behind the Curtain: A Study on Squatters, Slums, and Slum Dwellers* (Nairobi: The Commission, 1996. See Mutunga and Mazrui, "Rights Integration in an Institutional Context," 138–44.

42. Steiner, *Diverse Partners*, 19.

43. Mutua, "Domestic Human Rights Organizations in Africa," 31.

44. See Preamble, Art. 55 (c), Charter of the United Nations, adopted June 26, 1945; International Covenant on Economic, Social and Cultural Rights, adopted December 16, 1966, entered into force January 3, 1976, G.A. Res. 2200A (XXI), UN Doc. A/6316 (1966), 993 UNTS 3, reprinted in 6 I.L.M (1967); International Convention on the Elimination of All Forms of Racial Discrimination, adopted June 21, 1965, entered into force January 4, 1969, 660 UNTS 195, reprinted in 5 I.L.M. 352 (1966); Convention on the Elimination of All Forms of Discrimination Against Women, adopted December 18, 1979, entered into force September 3, 1981, G.A. Res. 34/180, 34 UN GAOR, Supp. (No. 46), UN Doc. A/34/46, at 193 (1979), reprinted in 19 I.L.M. 33 (1980); Convention on the Rights of the Child, adopted November 20, 1989, entered into force September 2, 1990, G.A. Res. 44/25, 44 UN GAOR, Supp. (no. 49), UN Doc. A/44/49. at 166 (1989), reprinted in 28 I.L.M. 1448 (1989); Convention Against Torture and Other Cruel, Inhuman or Degrading Treatment or Punishment, adopted December 10, 1984, entered into force June 26, 1987, G.A. Res. 39/46, 39 UN GAOR, Supp. (No. 51), UN Doc. A/39/51, at 197 (1984), reprinted in 23 I.L.M. 1027 (1984).

45. Mutua, "Domestic Human Rights Organizations in Africa," 31.

46. It is encouraging that the KHRC has initiated within Vision 2012 projects that seeks to root human rights and democratic values in communities.

47. Odinkalu, "Why More Africans Don't Use the Human Rights Language," 4.

48. The KHRC, for instance, forged such relationships with a number of community human rights organizations, including the Nairobi-based Release Political Prisoners Lobby Group (RPP), Muslims for Human Rights (MUHURI), and ILIMU-SHERIA (ILISHE) in Mombasa, among several others around Kenya. See Mutunga and Alamin, "Rights Integration in an Institutional Context," 136–37.

49. Mutua, "African Human Rights Organizations," 196.

50. Odinkalu, "Why More Africans Don't Use the Human Rights Language," 4.

51. Larry Cox, "Reflections on Human Rights at the Century's End," *Human Rights Dialogue* 5 (Winter 2000).

52. Kenneth Anderson, "The Ottawa Convention Banning Landmines: The Role of International Non-Governmental Organizations and the Idea of the International Civil Society," *European Journal of International Law* 11 (2000): 92.

53. Cox, "Reflections on Human Rights," 5.

54. Odinkalu, "Why More Africans Don't Use Human Rights Language," 4.

55. This event, a first for FIDA-Kenya, which was attended by senior political figures,

government ministers, civil society luminaries, and elites from the professions, demonstrated the possibilities of tapping local support for human rights NGOs.

56. Mutua, "African Human Rights Organizations," 197.

57. Claude E. Welch, Jr., "Introduction," in *NGOs and Human Rights: Promise and Performance*, ed. Claude E. Welch, Jr. (Philadelphia: University of Pennsylvania, 2001), 3.

58. Makau Mutua, "Savages, Victims, and Saviors: the Metaphor of Human Rights," *Harvard International Law Journal* 42 (2001): 201, 202.

59. Andersen, "The Ottawa Convention Banning Landmines," *European Journal of International Law* 11 (2000): 91, 92.

60. Prominent former civil leaders who joined the NARC state included Maina Kiai, former executive director and board member of the KHRC, who later became Chair of the official Kenya National Commission on Human Rights, and John Githongo, former executive director of Transparency International (Kenya), who later became Permanent Secretary in charge of Ethics and Governance in the Office of the President.

61. See Makau Mutua, "The End of Reforms in Kenya," *Boston Globe*, August 14, 2004; Makau Mutua, "NARC Has Rejected the Path of Reforms," *East African Standard*, September 4, 2004.

CHAPTER 2. TO WHOM, FOR WHAT, AND ABOUT WHAT? THE LEGITIMACY OF HUMAN RIGHTS NGOS IN KENYA

Epigraph: Kumi Naidoo, "Civil Society Accountability: Who Guards the Guardians?" address before the United Nations, New York, April 3, 2003, http://www.civicus .org/new/media/NGO%20Accountability.doc, at 2 (accessed June 26, 2006).

1. "Who Guards the Guardians?" *Economist*, September 2000, 129.

2. See NGOWATCH, A Project of the American Enterprise Institute and the Federalist Society, http://www.ngowatch.org/ (accessed June 27, 2006). The American Enterprise Institute—a conservative NGO, has created an NGO watch Web site that attacks liberal and progressive NGOs and has links to information relating to their programs and finances. Some observers have likened this Web site to a "McCarthyite blacklist."

3. Chidi Anselm Odinkalu, "Why More Africans Don't Use the Human Rights Language," *Human Rights Dialogue* (Winter 2000): 3.

4. Ibid.

5. Michaela Serban-Rosen, ed., *Constitutionalism in Transition: Africa and Eastern Europe* (Warsaw: Helsinki Foundation for Human Rights, 2003), 354. This is certainly true of Kenya—the same individuals drove the human rights movement in the 1980s and 1990s. Willy Mutunga led the LSK, KHRC, 4Cs, and was coconvener of NCEC. Davinder Lamba led Mazingira and was coconvener of the NCEC. Kivutha Kibwana led CLARION and was coconvener of NCEC.

6. Hugo Slim, "By What Authority? Accountability of Non Governmental Organizations," International Council on Human Rights Policy International Meeting on Global Trends and Human Rights—Before and After September 11, *Journal of Humanitarian Assistance* (January 10–12, 2002), http://www.jha.ac/articles/a082.htm (accessed June 27, 2006).

7. "FIDA Kenya: Putting Women First," http://www.fidakenya.org/ (accessed July 3, 2006).

8. Law Society of Kenya, http://www.lsk.or.ke/ (accessed July 3, 2006).

9. The LSK came into its own during the tenure of Paul Muite and Willy Mutunga respectively. During Paul Muite's tenure as chair of the council, the Society officials were taken to court by KANU sponsored lawyers who wanted the LSK restrained from issuing what they conceived as political statements and from using the LSK as a platform to attack government.

10. Kenya Human Rights Commission, via http://www.khrc.or.ke/ (accessed July 3, 2006).

11. Amos Wako had served as UN Special Rapporteur on Extra Judicial Executions; as attorney general he presided over the politically motivated prosecutions of pro-democracy activists on trumped up charges. His tenure was characterized by extrajudicial punishment and torture. Given his international stature and professed human rights credentials, it was surprising that such events would occur on his watch.

12. Makau wa Mutua, Maina Kiai, Kiraitu Murungi, Peter Kareithi, and Willy Mutunga were among founder members of KHRC. All but Mutunga and Kiai were then in exile; Kiai became the first executive director of the Commission. Four of the original directors were Harvard-educated lawyers—Mutua, Murungi, and Kiai had Harvard law degrees, as did Mumbi Mathangani, another board member. Others such as Mutunga and Mazrui were renowned professors in their fields. KHRC was in many respects a very blue chip organization in knowledge and learning. Their revolutionary credentials were not in question either. Two of the directors had spent time in political detention under Moi's repressive regime and others were intractable critics of the Moi regime.

13. Willy Mutunga, *Constitution Making from the Middle: Civil Society and Transition Politics in Kenya, 1992–1997* (Nairobi: SAREAT; Harare: MWENGO, 1999).

14. See generally ibid. for a full discussion of the history of the constitution-making process in Kenya and the specific roles played by these organizations in this process.

15. Led by Professor Wangari Maathai, the Green Belt Movement core business is to plant trees; however, its large membership enabled civic education on a variety of citizens' rights and its members are among the most enlightened on human rights issues.

16. Mothers of political prisoners stripped naked in a protest at Uhuru Park's Freedom Corner in 1989 to campaign for the release of political prisoners. The Green Belt Movement thereafter planted trees at this protest spot to commemorate the mothers' action. The trees did not survive police brutality during the Moi era, either.In 1999, Maathai, a world renowned environmentalist, currently an assistant minister in the NARC government of Mwai Kibaki, was arrested and indicted on a charge of "public incitement to violence" along with John Makanga and James Orengo (Green Belt member and Opposition leader respectively) for leading protests against the grabbing of Karura Forest. The charges were subsequently withdrawn against Maathai but are still pending against Makanga and Orengo.

17. Literally "blowing the whistle" on corruption and land grabbers.

18. In October 2002, the Kenya Human Rights Commission, the premier human rights organization in the country, publicly endorsed the National Alliance Party of Kenya (NAK). Others like FIDA, its members, employees and elected officials, volunteered their time and resources to run the National Rainbow Coalition (NARC) campaigns and training sessions

under the guise of lobbying and advocacy. Citizens groups like the NCEC became members of the political coalition and eventual ruling party NARC.

19. Michael Edwards, *NGO Rights and Responsibilities: A New Deal for Global Governance* (London: Foreign Policy Centre, 2000). Edwards works for the Ford Foundation and has written extensively on NGOs.

20. L. David Brown, "Civil Society Legitimacy: A Discussion Guide," in *Practice Research Engagement for Civil Society in a Globalizing World*, ed. L. David Brown, Hauser Center for Nonprofit Organizations and CIVICUS: World Alliance for Citizen Participation (Cambridge, Mass.: Hauser Center, 2001), 63–80.

21. In Uganda, Rwanda and lately Kenya, first ladies have taken to heading NGOs that are engaged in HIV AIDS advocacy. In Ghana, Nana Rawlings headed the largest women's rights organization, the December 31st Movement.

22. See Mutunga, *Constitution Making*, for an interesting discussion of who the "people" are.

23. Brown, "Civil Society Legitimacy: A Discussion Guide," 63.

24. Mutunga, *Constitution Making*, 8

25. Ibid.

26. The Belmarsh Detention Center in the United Kingdom and the U.S. Guantanamo Bay facility in Cuba are institutions in which persons held under antiterrorism legislation languish in detention without trial. A majority of detainees at the two facilities are of the Islamic faith.

27. "Constitutionalism in Transition: Africa and Eastern Europe," in *Conference Report on Comparative Constitutionalism*, ed. Michaela Serban-Rosen (Warsaw: Helsinki Foundation For Human Rights, 2001), 354.

28. Issa Shivji, "Constitutionalism in Transition: Africa and Eastern Europe," in Serban-Rosen, ed., *Conference Report on Comparative Constitutionalism*, 354.

29. Ford Foundation, "Close to Home: Case Studies of Human Rights Work in the United States," Ford Foundation, New York, June 2004, 17–18, http://www.fordfound.org/publications/recent_articles/close_to_home.cfm (accessed June 28, 2006).

30. Ford Foundation, *A Revolution of the Mind: Funding Human Rights in the United States* (New York: Ford Foundation, 2002).

31. Mutunga, *Constitution Making*.

32. Miklos Marschall, "Legitimacy and Effectiveness: Civil Society Organizations' Role in Good Governance," *Global Policy Forum* (November 2002), http://www.globalpolicy.org/ngos/credib/2003/0529legit.htm#author.

CHAPTER 3. LAW, SEXUALITY, AND POLITICS IN UGANDA: CHALLENGES FOR WOMEN'S HUMAN RIGHTS NGOS

1. See Anne Marie Goetz and Shireen Hassim, eds., *No Shortcuts to Power: African Women in Politics and Policy Making* (London: Zed Books, 2003); Aili Tripp, "The Politics of Autonomy and Cooptation in Africa: The Case of the Ugandan Women's Movement," *Journal of Modern African Studies* 39, 1 (2001): 101–28.

2. Human sexuality, as used in this chapter, encompasses a wide array of complex ele-

ments, including sexual knowledge, beliefs, values, attitudes, and behaviors, as well as procreation, sexual orientation, and personal/interpersonal sexual relations. It touches a wide range of other issues including pleasure, the human body, dress, self-esteem, gender identity, power and violence. It is an all-encompassing phenomenon that involves the human psyche, emotions, physical sensations, communication, creativity and ethics.

3. It must be noted that while silence can work to reinforce oppression, it can also be a tool of resistance and struggle, especially for the marginalized. There is a legitimate silence surrounding African women's sexuality, a silence that is safe and ambiguous. Here, "silence" is different from the Western feminist approach that normally condemns it and describes it as a totally blank "voice." In many African cultures, while speech is necessary and empowering in sexuality, silence can be an equally powerful tool of agency.

4. See Patricia McFadden, "Sex, Sexuality and the Problem of AIDS in Africa," in *Gender in Southern Africa: Conceptual and Theoretical Issues*, ed. Ruth Meena (Harare: SAPES Books, 1992); Kofi Awusabo-Asare, John Anarfi, and Dominic Agyeman, "Women's Control over Their Sexuality and the Spread of STDs and HIV/AIDS in Ghana," *Health Transition Review* 3, Supplement Issue (1993): 69–83; Ayesha Imam, "The Muslim Religious Right ('Fundamentalists') and Sexuality," in *Women and Sexuality in Muslim Countries*, ed. Pinar Ilkkaracan (Istanbul: Women for Women's Human Rights, 2000); Mumbi Machera, "Opening a Can of Worms: A Debate on African Female Sexuality in the Lecture Theatre," in *Rethinking Sexualities in Africa*, ed. Signe Arnfred (Uppsala: Nordic Africa Institute, 2004); Sylvia Tamale, "Out of the Closet: Unveiling Sexuality Discourses in Uganda," *Feminist Africa* 2 (2003): 42–49; Assitan Diallo, "Paradoxes of Female Sexuality in Mali: On the Practices of *Magnonmake* & *Bolokoli-kêlal*," in Arnfred, ed., *Rethinking Sexualities in Africa*.

5. This is so despite the enormous leaps the sexual rights discourse has achieved internationally at UN conferences, notably, the 1993 Vienna Conference on Human Rights, the 1994 Cairo conference on Population and Development and the 1995 Fourth Conference Women's Rights held in Beijing.

6. The 7th African Regional Conference on Women was held in Addis Ababa, October 6–7, 2004. Over 200 NGOs from the five subregions of the continent were represented at this forum. The issue of lesbianism was extremely controversial at the NGO Forum, so much so, that even the watered down statement regarding "women's bodily integrity and autonomy . . . of choice" that appeared in the draft version of their recommendations was later dropped altogether. See 7th African Regional Conference on Women, "Synthesis from the NGO Forum," http://www.uneca.org/beijingplus10/synthesis_NGOs.pdf.

7. Ms. Fanny Ann Eddy, aged thirty and leader of the Sierra Leone Lesbian and Gay Association (SLLAGA), was attacked during the night of September 29, 2004, as she worked alone at the SLLAGA offices. She was repeatedly raped, stabbed, and her neck broken in one of the most gruesome acts of violence against women. See Human Rights Watch, "Sierra Leone: Lesbian Rights Activist Brutally Murdered," http://www.hrw.org/english/docs/2004/10/04/sierra9440.htm.

8. See Women of Uganda Network (WOUGNET), "Women Organisations in Uganda," http://www.wougnet.org/wo_dir.html.

9. Referring to Western perceptions of female genital mutilation in Africa, Oyeronke Oyewumi argues that today, the trend has changed from a *hyper-sexual* African woman to a *hypo-sexualized* one, caused by her presumed missing parts. See Oyeronke Oyewumi, "Alice

in Motherland: Reading Alice Walker on Africa and Screening the Colour 'Black,'" *Jenda: A Journal of Culture and African Women Studies* 1 (2001), http://www.jendajournal.com/vol1.2/oyewumi.html.

10. See Anne McClintock, *Imperial Leather: Race, Gender and Sexuality in the Colonial Conquest* (New York: Routledge, 1995).

11. Frederick Engels made the important link between women's oppression to property relations, demonstrating how monogamous family arrangements facilitate patriarchal domination. See Frederick Engels, *The Origin of the Family, Private Property, and the State* (1884; New York: Penguin, 1972).

12. In Africa, the process of separating the public-private spheres preceded colonization but was precipitated, consolidated and reinforced by colonial policies and practices. Where there had been a blurred distinction between public and private life, colonial structures (e.g., law, religion) and policies (e.g., educational) focused on delineating a clear distinction guided by an ideology that perceived men as public actors and women as private performers. Where domestic work had coexisted with commercial work in precolonial satellite households, a new form of domesticity, existing outside production, took over. Where land had been communally owned in precolonial societies, a tenure system that allowed for absolute and individual ownership in land took over. At the same time politics and power were formalized and institutionalized with male public actors. The Western capitalist, political ideology (liberal democratic theory) that was imposed on the African people focused on the individual, submerging the African tradition that valued the collective.

13. Also by keeping women in a subordinate position, capitalism can justify and profit from paying women who work outside the home lower wages and employing them under worse conditions than men.

14. See Ugandan Penal Code, Chapter 120 of the Laws of Uganda.

15. The Feminist Dictionary defines the term "Phallocentricism" as "male-centredness, which places the male-identified subject at the centre of intellect, perception, experience, values and language." See Cheris Kramarae and Paula Treichler, *A Feminist Dictionary* (London: Pandora Press, 1985).

16. Lord Chief Justice Hale established this principle in 1736 when he decided that "the husband cannot be guilty of a rape committed by himself upon his lawful wife, for by their mutual matrimonial consent and contract the wife hath given up herself in this kind unto her husband, which she cannot retract."

17. For example, in the year 2000, the Tanzanian parliament amended the Constitution to prohibit sexual harassment against women in the workplace.

18. See *The Monitor*, October 14, 2003, 4, where it was reported that Mr. Nelson Kawalya announced that the Buganda government is in the process of publishing a book on "Virgin Brides."

19. Penal Code Act, Chapter 120 of the Laws of Uganda.

20. See Richard Ssewakiryanga, "Sex Work and the Identity Question: A Study on Sex Work in Kampala City," Working Paper. 75 (Kampala: Centre for Basic Research, 2002).

21. See Luise White, *The Comforts of Home: Prostitution in Colonial Nairobi* (Chicago: University of Chicago Press, 1990); Laurie Shrage, "Prostitution and the Case for Decriminalization," *Dissent* 43, 2 (1996): 41–45; Carol Hauge, "Prostitution of Women and International Human Rights Law: Transforming Exploitation into Equality," *New York International Law Review* 8, 2 (1995): 23–50.

22. Forces beyond women's control (e.g., male supremacy, capitalism, globalization) coerce them into all kinds of exploitative jobs. Hence women are forced to make decisions between only different bad alternatives. Most women "choose" to do one exploitative job and not another. The choice ranges from domestic labor (as housewives or house maids) to factory work (e.g., the "AGOA girls" in Kampala). Adult sex work is no different. It is a form of work, "chosen" primarily for economic reasons.

23. Such a restrictive legal regime governing abortion pertains in over 40 African countries. Only three countries on the continent, viz., Tunisia, Cape Verde and South Africa, allow for unrestricted abortions (at least in the first trimester of pregnancy).

24. A 2001 study in Addis Ababa, conducted by the Ethiopian Society of Obstetricians and Gynecologists revealed that it accounted for 54 percent of maternal deaths. See "Unsafe Abortion Identified as Second Major Killer of Pregnant Women," *Addis Tribune*, March 16, 2001, http://www.addistribune.com/.

25. See Judith Butler, *Gender Trouble: Feminism and the Subversion of Identity* (New York: Routledge, 1990).

26. It is only in South Africa that discrimination on grounds of sexual orientation is prohibited. The long liberation struggle against apartheid forged a political self-consciousness within the gay and lesbian community in South Africa that resulted in this constitutional victory for them. However, this does not mean that gays and lesbians in South Africa enjoy their full rights similar to heterosexuals. For example, same-sex weddings are not recognized in South Africa.

27. See Stephen Murray and Will Roscoe, eds., *Boy-Wives and Female Husbands: Studies on African Homosexualities* (New York: St. Martin's, 1998); Deborah Amory, "Homosexuality in Africa: Issues and Debates," *Issue: A Journal of Opinion* 25, 1 (1997): 5–10.

28. See Jack Driberg, *The Lango: A Nilotic Tribe of Uganda* (London: Thorner Coryndon, 1923). Similar practices were recorded between the Iteso and the Karamajong of northeastern Uganda.

29. Jeremy Lawrence, *The Iteso: Fifty Years of Change in a Nilo-Hamitic tribe of Uganda* (Oxford: Oxford University Press, 1957); Musa Mushanga, "The Nkole of Southwestern Uganda," in *Cultural Source Materials for Population Planning in East Africa*, ed. Angela Molnos (Nairobi: East African Publishing House, 1973); Rodney Needham, "Right and Left in Nyoro Symbolic Classification," in *Right & Left: Essays on Dual Symbolic Classification*, ed. Rodney Needham (Chicago: University of Chicago Press, 1973), 299–341; Martin Southwold, "The Baganda of Central Uganda," in Molnos, ed., *Cultural Source Materials*.

30. John Faupel, *African Holocaust: The Story of the Uganda Martyrs* (New York: P.J. Kennedy, 1962).

31. Tamale, "Out of the Closet," 47.

32. Sylvia Tamale, "How Old Is Old Enough?: Defilement Law and the Age of Consent in Uganda," *East African Journal of Peace and Human Rights* 7, 1 (2001): 82–100.

33. Tamale, "Out of the Closet," 49.

34. Patrilineality refers to tracing one's descent exclusively through male relatives. Patrilocality is the marriage institution where a married woman moves—geographically and across the kinship system—from her natal home to that of her husband.

35. Frederick Jjuuko, "Matriarchy in Tribal Buganda, Uganda," *Journal of African Religion*

and Philosophy 2, 2 (1993): 88–120. In fact, a handful of matrilineal societies still exist in some parts of Africa such as Ghana, Congo, Tanzania, Zambia, Mozambique, South Africa, Malawi, Zimbabwe, and Namibia.

36. Engels, *The Origin of the Family.*

37. The traditional practice in which the bridegroom's family "pays" dowry to the bride's family. Under customary law, full payment of bridewealth is an essential requirement to the legal recognition of customary marriages.

38. See Sandra Burman, "Fighting a Two-Pronged Attack: The Changing Legal Status of Women in Cape-Ruled Basutoland, 1872–1884," in *Women and Gender in Southern Africa,* ed. Cheryl Walker (Cape Town: David Philip Publishers, 1990), 48–75.

39. J. H. Driberg, "The Status of Women Among the Nilotics and Nilo-Hamitics" *Africa: Journal of the International African Institute* 5, 4 (1932): 404–21, 413.

40. See Chief Justice Hamilton's judgment in the case of *R v. Amkeyo* (1917), E.A.P.L.R. 14, 19.

41. Women and the Law in East Africa (WLEA), *Report on the Study of Inheritance Laws and Practices in Uganda* (Kampala: WLEA, 1996).

42. The practice is commonly and euphemistically referred to as "female circumcision."

43. See Nahid Toubia, *Female Genital Mutilation: A Call for Global Action* (New York: Women, Ink., 1995).

44. See Eve Ensler, *The Vagina Monologues* (New York: Villard, 2001).

45. The literal meaning of the term Ssenga is "paternal aunt." However, when one speaks of "Ssenga matters" among the Baganda, it is at once understood to signify an institution that has persisted and endured through the centuries as a sexual initiation tradition.

46. World Health Organization, "Female Genital Mutilation: Information Pack," http://www.who.int/docstore/frh-whd/FGM/infopack/English/fgm_infopack.ht m (accessed September 19, 2004).

47. Today, many urban-based Ssengas are not fulfilling these duties and in their place has emerged some "commercial Ssengas" who can be hired for a fee by young women (including many non-Baganda) or their parents to perform the function of the traditional Ssenga.

48. See Sylvia Tamale, "Eroticism, Sensuality and 'Women's Secrets' Among the Baganda: A Critical Analysis," *Feminist Africa* 5 (2005), www.feministafrica.org/05-2005/feature-sylvia.htm (last visited on June 29, 2006).

49. See *Arise Magazine* 36 (Kampala: ACFODE, July 2004).

50. The term "cohabitation" as used in the DRB means "the fact of an unmarried man and an unmarried woman living together as if they were husband and wife." See DRB, Clause 3, 2003.

51. Jacqueline Asiimwe-Mwesige, Coordinator, UWONET, interview with author, September 9, 2004.

52. 16 Days of Activism Against Gender Violence is part of a global campaign for human rights that falls between November 25 and December 10 each year. The aim is to raise awareness that gender-based violence is a human rights issue.

53. Freire defines praxis as the dialectical union between "action and reflection." See Paulo Freire, *Pedagogy of the Oppressed* (Harmondsworth: Penguin, 1972), 96.

54. Ibid.

55. Aili Tripp, for example, argues that the women's movement in Uganda has quite

successfully challenged pressures from the state and is relatively autonomous. See Tripp, "Politics of Autonomy."

56. The record of the NRM administration on supporting women's rights is no doubt better than the previous regimes but again, there is little evidence to suggest that men in the NRM leadership are fundamentally different from the pre-1986 "old boys" in showing real commitment to women's emancipation: Underfunding the Ministry responsible for women's affairs, tokenistic appointments of women to cabinet positions, soft-peddling on the important Domestic Relations Bill and failure to institute the Equal Opportunities Commission, to mention but a few examples. See Sylvia Tamale, *When Hens Begin to Crow: Gender and Parliamentary Politics in Uganda* (Boulder, Colo.: Westview Press, 1999), 19–20.

57. The president said this during his official address on International Women's day, March 8, 2000. See *The Other Voice* 3, 5 (March 2000).

58. See Tamale, *When Hens Begin to Crow*, 19–20.

59. See the Non-Governmental Organisations Registration (Amendment) Act, 2005. The Coalition on the NGO bill (CONOB) made up of the NGO community in Uganda has challenged the law, arguing that it violates fundamental human rights and freedoms.

60. See Human Rights Network Uganda (HURINET), "The Non-Governmental Organisations Registration (Amendment) Bill 2001: A Challenge to Constitutional Guarantees and the Democratisation Process in Uganda," http://www.hurinet.or.ug/billlight.php (accessed September 29, 2004).

61. Anne Marie Goetz, "The Politics of Integrating Gender to State Development Processes: Trends, Opportunities and Constraints in Bangladesh, Chile, Jamaica, Mali, Morocco and Uganda," UNRISD contribution to the Fourth World Conference on Women (UNRISD, May 1995), http://www.unrisd.org/ (Geneva: UNRISD, 1995).

62. SWAP integrates resources at the sector level (e.g., health, education, agriculture, water, etc.) to the national fiscal management system. Basket funding involves various donors entering into a financial arrangement whereby they pool their resources together to support a selected sector budget (as opposed to a project).

63. For Nigeria, see Nina Mba, *Nigerian Women Mobilized: Women's Political Activity in Southern Nigeria, 1900–1965* (Berkeley: Institute of International Studies, University of California, 1982). For Anlu, see Shirley Ardener, "Sexual Insult and Female Militancy," in *Perceiving Women*, ed. Shirley Ardener (London: Malaby Press, 1975), 29–53.

64. See J. Oloka-Onyango and Sylvia Tamale, "'The Personal Is Political,' or Why Women's Rights Are Indeed Human Rights: An African Perspective on International Feminism," *Human Rights Quarterly* 17, 4 (1995): 691–731.

CHAPTER 4. NGO STRUGGLES FOR ECONOMIC, SOCIAL, AND CULTURAL RIGHTS IN UTAKE: A UGANDAN PERSPECTIVE

1. A special report in the *Economist* several years ago analyzed why this was so. "Righting Wrongs," *Economist*, August 18, 2001.

2. E. F. Ssempebwa, "The Constitutional Review Process," in *Towards Political Liberalization in Uganda: A Report of the Uganda Fact-Finding Mission*, ed. Othman Haroub and Maria Nassali (Kampala: Fountain, 2002), 90–91.

3. Cord Jakobeit, "World Bank and 'Human Development': Washington's New Strategic Approach," *Development and Cooperation* 6 (1999): 4–5.

4. See Peter Mijumbi, "Uganda's External Debt and the HIPC Initiative," Occasional Paper 15 (Kampala: Economic Policy Research Centre, 2001).

5. It is thus interesting to note that the United States has recently advocated debt cancellation for both Uganda and Tanzania. Kevin Kelley, "Cancel Uganda, Tanzania Debt, US Tells IMF," *East African*, September 20–26, 2004, 1.

6. "Uganda: The Challenge of Growth and Poverty Reduction," World Bank Report 14313 IBRD, Washington, D.C., June 30, 1995.

7. See Remigius Munyonyo, "An Evaluation of Uganda's Poverty Reduction Strategy Paper (PRSP) Using a Human Rights-Based Approach," in *Developing a Culture of Peace and Human Rights in Africa*, ed. Deusdedit Nkurunziza and Lewis Mugumya (Kampala: Konrad Adenauer Stiftung, 2003).

8. "Constitutional Day Message from the Uganda Human Rights Commission," *Monito*, October 8, 2003, 30.

9. See "Poverty Levels Soar," *New Vision*, November 12, 2003, 3. Although the economy is growing, the article argues that Ugandans are in fact becoming poorer, with the poverty level of 34 percent in 1999 increasing to 38 percent in 2002–2003.

10. "Uganda Human Development Report," United Nations Development Program (Kampala: UNDP, 2002), 14–20 (hereafter UNDP Report).

11. Warren Nyamugasira and Rick Rowden, "Poverty Reduction Strategies and Coherency of Loan Conditions: Do the New World Bank and IMF Loans Support Countries' Poverty-Reduction Goals? The Case of Uganda," April 2002, http://www.africaaction .org/docs02/ugan0204.htm.

12. John Pender, "Empowering the Poorest? The World Bank and the 'Voices of the Poor,'" in *Rethinking Human Rights: Critical Approaches to International Politics*, ed. David Chandler, (London: Palgrave Macmillan, 2002), 112.

13. See Wairama G. Baker, *Uganda: The Marginalization of Minorities* (London: Minority Rights Group International, 2001); Issa Shivji and Wilbert B. Kapinga, *Maasai Rights in Ngorongoro, Tanzania* (Hakiardhi: IIED, 1998).

14. Rugemeleza Nshala, "Granting Hunting Blocks in Tanzania: The Need for Reform," Policy Brief 5, Lawyer's Environmental Action Team (LEAT), 1999.

15. ACFODE, "The Proposed Equal Opportunities Commission for Uganda: Recommendations from Civil Society Organizations," February 2003.

16. For an incisive comment on this, see Michael Okema, "Alas, the Tribe Is Dead, the Nation Stillborn . . ." *East African*, September 6–12, 2004, 13.

17. See Nadia Hijab, "Human Rights and Development: Learning from Those Who Act," background paper for UNDP Report 2000, November 4, 1999.

18. Kenya Human Rights Commission, "Beauty and Agony: An Advocacy Research on the Working Conditions in the Flower Plantations in Kenya" (Nairobi: The Commission, 2001); FHRI, "The Right to Education in Uganda: A Myth or Reality?" Special Reference to the Universal Primary Education Programme (UPE) (Kampala: FHRI, 2001).

19. For a general critique of African human rights NGOs, see Makau Mutua, "The Politics of Human Rights: Beyond the Abolitionist Paradigm in Africa," *Michigan Journal of International Law* 17, 3 (1996): 606–7.

20. See Christian Ochoa, "Advancing the Language of Human Rights in a Global Economic Order: An Analysis of a Discourse," *Boston College Third World Journal* 23, 1 (2003): 69.

21. Justice Resources, "Beyond Workshops: Challenges and Strategies in Human Rights Interventions in Uganda" (Kampala: Justice Resources, 2002).

22. K. T. Akoyi Makokha, "Working with Community Organizations and Civil Society: The Case of Uganda," paper presented to the European Forum on Rural Development Cooperation, Montpellier, 2002.

23. Susan Dicklitch, *The Elusive Promise of NGOs in Africa: Lessons from Uganda* (New York: Macmillan, 1998), 15.

24. HURINET, *A Directory of Human Rights & Development Organizations in Uganda* (Kampala: HURINET, 2002), 83–114.

25. Samuel Mushi, *Development and Democratisation in Tanzania: A Study of Rural Grassroots Politics* (Kampala: Fountain, 2001).

26. For a history of ESCRs on the international scene, see Asbjørn Eide, "Economic, Social and Cultural Rights as Human Rights," in *Economic, Social and Cultural Rights: A Textbook*, ed. Asbjørn Eide, Catarina Krause, and Allan Rosas (Dordrecht: Nijhoff, 2001), 12–17.

27. For a background to the development of social and economic rights, see Henry Steiner and Philip Alston, *International Human Rights in Context: Law, Politics, Morals* (Oxford: Oxford University Press, 2000), 237–38.

28. On the operations of the Committee, see Allan McChesney, *Economic, Social and Cultural Rights: A Handbook* (Washington, D.C.: AAAS/HURIDOCS, 2000), 86–88, and Matthew Craven, "The UN Committee on Economic, Social and Cultural Rights," in Eide et al., eds., *Economic, Social and Cultural Rights*.

29. See Asbjørn Eide, "Economic, Social and Cultural Rights as Human Rights," in Eide, Krause, and Rosas, eds., *Economic, Social and Cultural Rights*, 17–34 .

30. Chidi Anselm Odinkalu, "Analysis of Paralysis or Paralysis by Analysis? Implementing Economic, Social, and Cultural Rights Under the African Charter on Human and Peoples' Rights," *Human Rights Quarterly* 23, 2 (2001): 335.

31. See U. Oji Umozurike, *The African Charter on Human and Peoples' Rights* (Dordrecht: Nijhoff, 1997), 45–50.

32. Manisuli Ssenyonjo, "Justiciability of Economic and Social Rights in Africa: General Overview, Evaluation and Prospects," *East African Journal of Peace & Human Rights* 9, 1 (2003): 8–24.

33. See J. Oloka-Onyango, "Beyond the Rhetoric: Reinvigorating the Struggle for Economic and Social Rights in Africa," *California Western International Law Journal* 26, 1 (1995).

34. See *Malawi African Association and others v. Mauritania.* [2000] Communications 54/91, 61/91, 98/93, 164/97, 196/97, 210/98.

35. See *Social & Economic Rights Action Centre (SERAC) and the Centre for Economic & Social Rights v. Nigeria,* [2001] Communication 155/96, http://www1.umn.edu/humanrts/africa/comcases/155–96b.html.

36. For an extensive analysis of the implications of this case, see J. Oloka-Onyango, "Reinforcing Marginalized Rights in an Age of Globalization: International Mechanisms, Non-State Actors, and the Struggle for Peoples' Rights in Africa," *American University International Law Journal* 18, 4 (2003).

37. SERAC decision, note 11, para. 71.

38. See Morné der Linde and Lirette Louw, "Considering the Interpretation and Implementation of Article 24 of the African Charter on Human and Peoples' Rights in light of the SERAC Communication," *African Human Rights Law Journal* 3, 1 (2003).

39. Upendra Baxi, "Taking Suffering Seriously: Social Action Litigation in the Supreme Court of India," in *The Role of the Judiciary in Plural Societies*, ed. Neelan Thiruchelvam and Radhika Coomaraswamy (New York: St. Martin's, 1987).

40. S. Muralidhar, "Economic, Social and Cultural Rights: An Indian Response to the Justiciability Debate," in *Economic, Social and Cultural Rights in Practice: The Role of Judges in Implementing Economic, Social and Cultural Rights*, ed. Yash Ghai and Jill Cottrell (London: Interights, 2004).

41. Rassie Malherbe, "A New Beginning: Introducing the South African Constitution and Bill of Rights," *Netherlands Quarterly of Human Rights* 18, 1 (2000).

42. Makau Mutua, "Hope and Despair for a New South Africa: The Limits of Rights Disclosure," *Harvard Human Rights Journal* 10 (1997).

43. Sandra Liebenberg and Karrisha Pillay, *Socio-Economic Rights in South Africa*, Socio-Economic Rights Centre (Cape Town: University of Cape Town, 2000).

44. See Section 7(1) of the Constitution of South Africa (1996).

45. Ibid., Sections 27, 27, 29 respectively.

46. Ibid., Section 7(2).

47. Asbjørn Eide, *The Right to Adequate Food as a Human Right*, Study Series 1 (Geneva: Center for Human Rights, 1989).

48. See respectively *Soobramoney v. Minister of Health, Kwazulu-Natal*, [1997] 12 BCLR 1696 (CC), also Malherbe, "A New Beginning," 55; *Grootboom v. Oostenberg Municipality*, [2000] (3) BCLR 277 (C); Geoff Budlender, *Justiciability of Socio-Economic Rights: Some South African Experiences*, in Ghai and Cottrell, *Economic, Social and Cultural Rights in Practice*, 33–41.

49. The recent Nevirapine case (where the litigants sought to get the South African government to provide free Nevirapine to all pregnant women with HIV/AIDS to prevent parent-to-child transmission (PTCT) of the disease) also highlighted how the right to health (especially the government obligation to take reasonable legislative and other measures), could be realized. See *Treatment Action Campaign and Others v. Minister of Health and Others*, [2000] (2) SA 1 (CC). For extensive comment, see Evarist Baimu, "The Government's Obligation to Provide Anti-Retrovirals to HIV-Positive Pregnant Women in an African Human Rrights Context: The South African Nevirapine Case," *African Human Rights Law Journal* 2, 1 (2003).

50. Ramkrishna Mukherjee, *The Problem of Uganda: A Study in Acculturation* (Berlin: Akademie Verlag, 1956).

51. John-Jean Barya, "Trade Unions and the Struggle for Associational Space in Uganda: The 1993 Trade Union Law and Article 40 of the Constitution," CBR Working Paper 63, Kampala, 2001.

52. Mahmood Mamdani, "Pluralism and the Right of Association," in *Uganda: Studies in Living Conditions, Popular Movements and Constitutionalism*, eds. Mahmood Mamdani and J. Oloka-Onyango (Vienna: Jep Books, 1994).

53. See Constitution of Uganda, 1962, http://www.kituochakatiba.co.ug/laws.htm.

54. Nyangabyaki Bazaara, "Mixed Results in Uganda's Constitutional Development: An Assessment," in *Constitutionalism in East Africa: Progress, Challenges and Prospects in 1999*, ed. Kivutha Kibwana (Kampala: Fountain, 2001).

55. For the history of the bill of rights in Tanzania, see Chris Maina Peter, *Human Rights in Tanzania: Selected Cases and Materials* (Köln: Rüdiger Köppe Verlag, 1997), 2–4.

56. Bazaara, "Mixed Results," 41–45.

57. 1995 Constitution, Chapter 4.

58. See Sylvia R. Tamale, "Gender and Affirmative Action in Post-1995 Uganda: A New Dispensation or Business as Usual?" in *Constitutionalism in Africa: Creating Opportunities, Facing Challenges*, ed. J. Oloka-Onyango (Kampala: Fountain, 2001).

59. 1995 Constitution, respectively Articles 31, 34, 35, 3.

60. See draft articles 67 to 73 and 76 of the draft Constitution of Kenya, adopted by the National Conference, March 15, 2004, http://www.kenyaconstitution.org/docs/constitutionbychapters.htm

61. Ibid., chap. 5.

62. Ibid., Articles 51–66.

63. Uganda Constitutional Commission (1993), "The Report of the Uganda Constitutional Commission: Analysis and Recommendations," UPPC, Entebbe, para. 7.60, 147.

64. Ibid., para. 7.102, 159, para.7.194, 193.

65. Ibid.

66. Ibid., para.7.148, 177–78. Indeed, the marginal note that covers workers rights in the Constitution is entitled "Economic Rights."

67. Ibid., chaps. 23, 24.

68. Ibid., 99.

69. See Recommendation 31.2 at 833.

70. Ibid.

71. See, for example, the debate on draft Article 67; ROU, 2116 to 2132.

72. 1995 Constitution, Article 30n.

73. See Lewis Mugumya, "Human Rights: An Insight into Uganda's Education Sector," in Nkurunziza and Mugumya, eds., *Developing a Culture of Peace and Human Rights*.

74. Richard Ssewakiryanga, "Applying RBA to Poverty Assessment: The Experience of the Ministry of Finance," *Your Rights* 6, 3 (July 2003): 15–16.

75. Sisule F. Musungu, "The Right to Health in the Global Economy: Reading Human Rights Obligations into the Patent Regime of the WTO-TRIPS Agreement," LL.M. dissertation, University of Pretoria, 2001.

76. See Constitution of the World Health Organization (WHO), 14 U.N.T.S 186, *Basic Documents of the World Health Organization* (1981).

77. See General Comment of the Committee on Economic, Social and Cultural Rights 14 (July 2000), para. 12.

78. Paul Hutchinson, "Combating Illness," in *Uganda's Recovery: The Role of Farms, Firms, and Government*, ed. Ritva Reinikka and Paul Collier (Kampala: Fountain, 2001).

79. Ibid., 415–18.

80. George Muwanguzi, "HIV/AIDS, Human Rights and the Legal Sector in Uganda: An Assessment of Compliance with the International Guidelines," LL.M, dissertation, Makerere University, 2003.

81. In dealing with this issue, the UN High Commissioner for Human Rights has explicitly stated that the RTF should be considered not the right to be fed, but rather the right to feed oneself: "The right to be free from hunger is the minimum essential level of the right to adequate food. See UNHCR, "Guidelines on a Human Rights Approach to Poverty Reduction Strategies" (Geneva, 2002).

82. Aliro Omara, "The Right to Food: National Implementation, the Uganda Experience," paper presented at National Seminar on the Right to Adequate Food, Oslo, April 10–11, 2002, 30.

83. Apollo Makubuya, "The Right to Adequate Food: Examining Uganda's Legal and Institutional Framework," paper presented at National Seminar on the Implementation of the Right to Adequate Food, January 23, 2003, 3, Human Rights & Peace Centre, Makerere University, Kampala, Uganda.

84. See Jacqueline Omara, "The Right to Food: Globalization and Its Impact on Food Security in Uganda," LL.B. dissertation, Makerere University, 2002, 25–33.

85. Republic of Uganda, *The Uganda Food and Nutrition Policy* (Kampala: Government Printer, 2003), 11.

86. See, for example, Gerald Tenywa, "Ugandan Scientists in Spirited Fight for Genetic Engineering," *New Vision*, July 9, 2003, 27; Patrick Luganda, "GMO Foods Safe," *New Vision*, August 27, 2003, 35.

87. Opiyo Oloya, "GMOs: Monsanto Had Their Agenda," *New Vision*, September 17, 2003, 10.

88. See Katrina Tomasevski, *Education Denied: Costs and Remedies* (London: Zed Books, 2003).

89. See Ritva Reinikka, "Recovery in Service Delivery: Evidence from Schools and Health Centres," in Reinikka and Collier, eds., *Uganda's Recovery*, 347, Table 1.

90. Ibid.

91. See UNDP, 2002, 9.

92. Simon Appleton, "What Can We Expect from Universal Primary Education?" in Reinikka and Collier, eds., *Uganda's Recovery*.

93. The 2000 Uganda Human Development Report noted that the quality of primary education had declined, 38, Table 13.

94. Fundamental rights questions (such as corporal and other forms of inhuman treatment and punishment) still remain. See Mugumya, "Human Rights," 121.

95. See "The Laying Down of Tools," Makerere University Academic Staff Association (MUASA) *Special Issue Newsletter*, May 2–18, 1989.

96. Katarina Tomasevski, "Report of the Special Rapporteur on the Right to Education," UN Doc. E/CN.4/2000/6/Add.1, Addendum: Mission to Uganda, June 26 to July 2, 1999, 111.

97. Ibid., 111–12.

98. Zie Gariyo, "Uganda: Aid and Education Development," in *The Reality of Aid: An Independent Review of Poverty Reduction and Development Assistance*, ed. Judith Randel and Tony German (London: Earthscan, 1998).

99. Ibid., 206.

100. Tomasevski, "Report of the Special Rapporteur," para. 29.

101. Ibid.

102. Ibid., para. 28.

103. Ssenyonjo, "Justiciability of Economic and Social Rights in Africa," 25.

104. Ssempebwa, "The Constitutional Review Process," 90.

105. Toriola Oyewo, *Constitutional Law and Procedure in Nigeria* (Ibadan: John Archers, 2000), 87.

106. *Société United Docks v. Government of Mauritius*, [1985] LRC (Const.) 801.

107. Thus in the case of *Minerva Mills Ltd & Ors. v. Union of India & Ors*, [1981] (1) SCR 206, 257, Chief Justice Chandrachud stated that the rights in the body of the Constitution need to be read together with the principles which form the "edifice" on which the Indian Constitution is built. And further: "Those rights are not an end in themselves but are the means to an end. The end is specified in the Directive Principles."

108. *NTN Pty Ltd & NBN Ltd. v. The State*, [1988] LRC (Const) 333, 352, per Barnett, J.

109. See judgment of Egonda-Ntende in *Tinyefuza v. Attorney General* (Constitutional Petition No. 1 of 1997), 18.

110. See *Grootboom* decision, para. 23.

111. See for example, "UHRC Lends Special Ear to Disability Issues," *Your Rights* 3, 10 (November 2000): 3–14.

112. Apollo Makubuya, "Breaking the Silence: A Review of the Maiden Report of the Uganda Human Rights Commission," *East African Journal of Peace & Human Rights* 5, 2 (1999): 217.

113. UHRC Annual Report (1998), 41.

114. The key question in realization of ESCRs is not resources. It is demonstrating a broad, constant, progressive movement toward the full realization of rights. In the words of the WHO: "Any deliberately retrogressive measures require the most careful consideration and need to be fully justified by reference to the totality of rights provided for in the human rights treaty concerned and in the context of the full use of the maximum available resources. In this context, it is important to distinguish the *inability* from the *unwillingness* of a State Party to comply with its obligations." "25 Questions and Answers on Health and Human Rights," Health & Human Rights Publication Series1 (Geneva: World Health Organization, 2002), 14.

115. See UHRC Annual Report (2000–2001).

116. See Chapter 4.

117. Ibid., 62–68.

118. "Editorial," *Your Rights* 6, 3 (July 2003): 2.

119. See Republic of Uganda, "The Uganda Food and Nutrition Policy," http://pma .go.ug / pdfs / food % 20and % 20nutrition % 20policy.pdf#search = % 22 % 22The % 20 Uganda%20Food%20and%20Nutrition%20Policy%22%22 (2003).

120. *Emmanuel Mpondi v. The Chairman, Board of Governors Nganwa High School*, [1999–2002] UHRR 68; Complaint 210 (1998).

121. Ibid., para.11, 71.

122. Complaint 501 of 2000.

123. Ibid., 4, emphasis added.

124. Ibid., 5.

125. See for example, *Salvatori Abuki & Anor., v. AG*, [1997] Constitutional Petition 2, confirmed in *AG v. Salvatori Abuki*, [1998] Constitutional Appeal 1.

126. Among the several cases concerning the right to a healthy environment, see *BAT Ltd. v. TEAN*, [2003] Misc. Appl. 27; *Pastor Martin Sempa v. AG*, [2002] Misc. Appl. 71; *Greenwatch v. AG*, [2002] Misc. Appl. 140.

127. *The Environmental Action Network (TEAN) v. National Environmental Management Authority (NEMA)*, [2001] Misc. Appl. 39.

128. But see also *British American Tobacco Ltd. v. Environmental Action Network Ltd*, [2003] Civ. Appl. 27.

129. *Joyce Nakacwa v. AG*, [2001] Constitutional Petition 2.

130. Ibid., 3.

131. Counsel for the respondent sought to keep the action alive in the public interest following the death of the petitioner, but the Court ruled he was not entitled to do so. See *Phillip Karugaba v. AG*, [2002] Constitutional Petition 11. The ruling has been appealed to the Supreme Court.

132. *Dimanche Sharon et al. v. Makerere University*, [2003] Constitutional Cause 1.

133. Ibid., 17–18.

134. See the analysis by Ann Seidman and Robert Seidman, "Assessing a Bill in Terms of the Public Interest: The Legislator's Role in the Law-Making Process," *World Bank Legal Review: Law and Justice for Development* 1 (2002): 207–56.

135. See Shadrack C. Agbakwa, "Reclaiming Humanity: Economic, Social and Cultural Rights as the Cornerstone of African Human Rights," *Yale Human Rights & Development Law Journal* 5 (2002): 177–215, esp. 210–12.

CHAPTER 5. FEMINIST MASCULINITY: ADVOCACY FOR GENDER EQUALITY AND EQUITY

This chapter does not represent the policy or position of the Ford Foundation. Jael Silliman, Elizabeth Orchardson-Mazrui, Jacinta Muteshi, Anzetse Were, Sharon Makoriwa, Tazim Elkington, Athena Mutua, Ousseina Alidou, Rakiya Omaar, Cynthia Mugo, Silvia Tamale, Silvia Federici, George Caffentzis, Conradin Perner (Kwacakworo), Reverend Dr. Timothy Njoya, Kennedy Otina, and Joe Oloka-Onyango read previous drafts of this chapter. The various comments by these feminist theoreticians, scholars, or activists are reflected and incorporated in the chapter.

1. Masculinity denotes dominance and oppression of women by men, and the juxtaposition may be a contradiction in terms. However, the term reflects the tensions and contradictions involved and may best problematize the men for gender equality movement. It is perhaps a better term to express the vision of the men for gender equality movement than masculine feminism, borrowed from feminist Christine Delphy. See also the vision Bell Hooks gives of the term feminist masculinity in *Feminism Is for Everybody* (Cambridge, Mass.: South End Press, 2000), chap. 12.

2. Silvia Federici, *Caliban and the Witch: Women, the Body and Primitive Accumulation* (Brooklyn, N.Y.: Autonomedia, 2004), 7–10; Amina Mama, "Gender Studies for Africa's Transformation," in *African Intellectuals: Rethinking Politics, Language, Gender and Development*, ed. Thandika Mkandawire (Dakar: Codesria; New York: Zed Books, 2005), 94.

3. In terms of organizing, note should be taken of the oppression of women in social

and nationalist movements and other forms of organizing where women's voices were marginalized. Indeed, women had to opt out of these formations and create their autonomous formations for their issues to be taken seriously.

4. Federici, *Caliban and the Witch*, 14: "the debates that have taken place among postmodern feminists concerning the need to dispose of 'women' as a category of analysis, and define feminism purely in oppositional terms, have been misguided."

5. See Federici, *Caliban and the Witch*; Smith, *Women and Socialism*; Mkandawire, *African Intellectuals*.

6. For male dominance, see Federici, *Caliban and the Witch*, 2. For the role of the body, see 15: "From the beginning of the Women's Movement, feminist activists and theorists have seen the concept of "the body" as key to an understanding of the roots of male dominance and the construction of female and social identity"; see also Jael Silliman, Marlene Gerber Fried, Loretta Ross, and Elena Gutierrez, eds., *Undivided Rights: Women of Color Organize for Reproductive Justice* (Cambridge, Mass.: South End Press, 2004), 10, "The rights to bodily and reproductive autonomy are fundamental to human rights." Sharon Smith argues that "The reduction of women's sexuality in popular culture to a sum total of body parts, instead of belonging to a whole person, helps explain the prevailing acceptance in society today, among both men and women that women's bodies exist for the pleasure of men. This notion is reinforced not only through the flourishing pornography industry, which took $10 billion in the United States last year, but more pervasively through commercial advertising, which uses women's bodies and acts of seduction to sell everything from beer and automobiles to movie tickets. The objectification of women's bodies both demeans women and dehumanizes sexuality—reflected in the high incidence of rape and battery suffered by women the world over. Roughly one in every three women worldwide has been beaten, raped or otherwise abused in her lifetime—and up to 70 per cent have never told anyone else about the abuse they have suffered." This conclusion was based on a review of over 1,000 articles in scientific journals and national reports conducted by John Hopkins University researchers, published in the journal *Population Reports* (1999) (*Women and Socialism*, 15–16). In "*Stamped" African Women: A Century of Postal Art in Africa* (mimeo, 2006), 8, Agbenyega Adedze concludes that "the African woman's body has been abused on postage stamps for over a century. It was stripped of its identity or rendered anonymous, eroticized, and stereotyped to become representatives of a continent, a country, or a region. The African woman's images were controlled and circulated by a male dominated philatelic industry supported by governments from colonial period to the present. With very few exceptions (late Ms. Mugabe and recent issue on Women Achievers from Ghana), the full spectrum of the African woman's responsibilities, contributions, and aspirations has not been represented. The postcolonial governments are equally guilty of this blatant sexism as their colonial predecessors." For men as beneficiaries of patriarchy, see Christine Delphy, *Close to Home*, 140. For violence, see Federici, *Caliban and the Witch*, 11. For capitalism and wage slavery, see 8.

7. "Sexuality refers to a core dimension of being human which includes sex, gender, sexual and gender identity, sexual orientation, eroticism, emotional attachment/love, and reproduction. It is experienced and expressed in thoughts, fantasies, desires, beliefs, attitudes, values, activities, practices, roles, and relationships. Sexuality is a result of the interplay of biological, psychological, socio-economic, cultural, and ethical and religious/spiritual factors. While sexuality can include all these aspects, not all of these dimensions need to be experi-

enced or expressed. However, in sum our sexuality is experienced and expressed in all that we are, what we feel, think and do." Rebecca J. Cook, Bernard M. Dickens, and Mahmoud F. Fathala, *Reproductive Health and Human Rights: Integrating Medicine, Ethics, and Law* (Oxford: Oxford University Press, 2003), 174–75.

8. Amartya Sen, *The Argumentative Indian: Writings on Indian History, Culture, and Identity* (New York: Farrar, Straus and Giroux, 2005), 224.

9. Current technologies that enable parents to determine the sex of the child do result in abortions of female fetuses. Class analyses emanate from discussions of relations of production and they are an important category in discussing feminist movement. The category "women" does not do away with class; nor does the category "gender."

10. Elizabeth Orchardson-Mazrui, "The Impact of Cultural Perceptions on Gender Issues" a keynote speech at the International Conference titled "Understanding Gender Inequalities" held at Egerton University, Kenya, August 5–8, 2004 (mimeo), 3.

11. Ibid., 6. When Charity Ngilu, the Minister of Health, was given bows and arrows as symbols of leadership and eldership of the Kamba community some men protested while others were able to advance the common stereotype that women political leaders are not women but "masculine women" who have refused to stick to their "province." It is important to mention that in the past, many African societies had dual sex political systems that provided for substantial female representation in political matters. For example, the position of the Queen Mother seen across Africa in Ghana among the Akan, Egypt, Uganda, Ethiopia and Rwanda, to name a few countries, gave women prominent and visible political authority in running their respective nations. In some societies, the King's wife (wives) also wielded considerable authority. The impact of colonialism on this positive status quo was to impose reactionary Victorian values of respective "provinces" for men and women. See Sen, *Argumentative Indian*, 233.

12. In the Kamba community a man or boy with many girlfriends is called "Mwendwa or Mbendwa," meaning the one who is loved. A woman or girl who has many boyfriends is called "Kilalai," meaning a prostitute.

13. Orchardson-Mazrui, speech, 11.

14. Ibid., 13.

15. Ibid., 14.

16. Elizabeth Orchardson-Mazrui and Kimani Njogu, "Gender Inequality and Women's Rights in the Great Lakes: Can Culture Contribute to Women's Empowerment? (mimeo), 2004.

17. Jacinta Muteshi, "Constructing Consciousness: Diasporic remembrances and imagining Africa in late modernity," *Critical Arts: A Journal of South-North Cultural and Media Studies* 17, 1&2 (2003).

18. Jael Silliman and Anannya Bhattacharjee, eds., *Policing the National Body: Race, Gender, and Criminalization* (Cambridge, Mass.: South End Press, 2002), xix.

19. Ibid., xx.

20. Silvia Federici, "Reproduction and Feminist Struggle in the New International Division of Labor" in *Women, Development and Labor of Reproduction: Struggle and Movements*, ed. Mariarosa Dalla Costa and Giovanna F. Dalla Costa (Trenton, N.J.: Africa World Press, 1999), 47.

21. Radical scholars have always maintained that societies that oppress other societies

also oppress their own citizens. I have found Michel Warschawski, *Toward an Open Tomb: The Crisis of Israeli Society* (New York: Monthly Review Press, 2004) extremely useful in reflecting upon this point.

22. Federici, *Caliban and the Witch*, discusses this issue.

23. Andrea Cornwall and Sarah C. White, eds, *Men, Masculinities and Development: Politics, Policies and Practice*, *IDS Bulletin* 30, 2 (April 2000). See also bell hooks, *Feminist Theory: From Margin to Center* (Cambridge, Mass.: South End Press, 2000), chap. 5. She argues, "After hundreds of years of anti-racist struggle, more than ever before non-white people are currently calling attention to the primary role white people must play in anti-racist struggle. The same is true of the struggle to eradicate sexism—men have a primary role to play. This does not mean that they are better equipped to lead feminist movement; it does not mean that they should share equally in resistance struggle. In particular, men have tremendous contribution to make to feminist struggle in the area of exposing, confronting, opposing, and transforming the sexism of their male peers" (83). See also Jackson Katz, *The Macho Paradox: Why Some Men Hurt Women and How All Men Can Help* (Naperville, Ill.: Sourcebook, 2006). Katz makes the great point, "Make no mistake. Women blazed the trail that we are riding down. Men are in the position to do this [men for gender equality] work precisely because of the great leadership of women" (7).

24. On the basis of the analysis in this chapter, the curriculum must surely include the following issues: the causes of men's disempowerment; men's privilege and their oppression of women; male supremacist ideologies; synergies for gender equality; imperialism/globalization and gender roles; the root causes of culture that produces violent men; organizing men in a sustainable movement for gender equality; men to men education; the socialization of boys and youth; a global movement for gender equality; and consolidating the feminist movement's leadership in this area of work.

25. Akwasi Aidoo, a Ford Foundation colleague, sent a message for the New Year that reflected on the dead and greeted the living. One of the stories in his message is about the late Abdulrahman Babu, the Zanzibari revolutionary and Pan-Africanist. Babu was a great cook and advised Dr. Aidoo as follows: "Comrade, you better learn to cook if you don't already know how to, because very soon we can tell a genuine male comrade from a fake one by whether or not he can cook. A male comrade who talks about women's liberation but can't cook is just a talker."

26. Delphy, *Close to Home*, 106–10, asks many of these questions.

27. See Margrethe Silberschmidt, "Male Sexuality in Context of Socio-Economic Change in Rural and Urban East Africa," http://www.Pambazuka.org/index.ph? Id = 31952; Anzetse Were, *Are African Men Disempowered?* (forthcoming, manuscript made available to author); Margrethe Silberschmidt, "Poverty, Male Disempowerment, and Male Sexuality: Rethinking Men and Masculinities in Rural and Urban East Africa," in *African Masculinities: Men in Africa from the Late Nineteenth Century to the Present*, ed. Lahoucine Ouzgane and Robert Morrell (New York: Palgrave Macmillan, 2005), chap. 11.

28. The superficial answers are that equality is the right thing and everyone benefits when the right thing is done; from a religious perceptive grace is won by fighting for the rights of others. More needs to be said to explain what the benefits of men are of gender equality.

29. hooks, *Feminism*, 70.

30. LGBTI Organizing in East Africa: The True Test for Human Rights Defenders (Nairobi: Urgent Action Fund, 2005); Beti Ellerson, "Visualizing Homosexualities in Africa—Dakan: An Interview with Filmmaker Mohamed Camara," in Ouzgane and Morrell, eds., *African Masculinities*, 61; Ronald Louw, *"Mkhumbane and the New Traditions of (Un)African Same-Sex Weddings,"* in *Changing Men in Southern Africa*, ed. Robert Morell (London: Zed Press, 2001) 287.

31. *Femnet News*, January–April 2004, 2.

32. Discussion Paper 12, *Women Taking a Lead: Progress Towards Empowerment and Gender Equity in Rwanda* (mimeo), October 2004.

33. Cornwall and White, eds., *Men, Masculinities and Development*, 5–6.

34. Amina Mama observes that "Only a small minority of African male academics are aware of the now substantial body of gender research that documents, historicizes and locates women's activism and women's intellectual contribution to African societies and scholarship." Mama, "Gender Studies for Africa's Transformation,"105.

35. Delphy, *Close to Home*; Sen, *Argumentative Indian*, 250, "Gender inequality is a far-reaching societal impairment, not merely special deprivation of women. That social understanding is urgent as well as momentous."

36. Cornwall and White, *Men Masculinities, and Development*, 2.

37. There have been debates about the content of the two categories human rights and social justice. My interpretation of the whole gamut of human rights addressed social justice concerns in their entirety. I use the category of social justice after human rights as a matter of emphasis and repetition. I have always thought that if one wants to capture the totality of the two categories through an example, the best one I have seen is by Sardar and Davies: "If America is the world, then resources of the world belong to America. This assumption amounts to much more that is suggested by the bare statistics that we come across routinely in the UNDP's Human Development Reports: that Americans consume over half of all the good and services of the world; that its people spend over $10 billion annually on pet food alone—$4 billion more than the estimated total needed to provide basic health and nutrition for everyone in the world; that their expenditure on cosmetics—$8 billion—is $2 billion more than the annual total needed to provide basic education worldwide; or that the three richest Americans have assets that exceed the combined gross domestic product of 48 least developed countries. Having cornered most of the world's resources, America now has its eyes firmly set on the last remaining resource of developing countries: the flora, fauna, biodiversity and the very DNA for the indigenous people of the world." See Ziauddin Sardar and Merryl Wyn Davies, *Why Do People Hate America* (New York: Disinformation, 2002), at 82. While discussing what America consumes it is important to bear in mind that there is extreme poverty in America itself that has to be problematized. See Sidney Lens, *Poverty: America's Enduring Paradox, A History of the Richest Nation's Unwon War* (New York: T.Y. Crowell, 1969).

38. Mahmood Mamdani, *Social Movements and Constitutionalism in the African Context*, CBR Working Paper 2 (Kampala: Centre for Basic Research, May 1989), 1–2: "Whenever there was (and is) oppression—and Europe had no monopoly over oppression in history—there must come into being a conception of rights. This is to say that the notion of rights cannot possibly have any fixed and immutable content, whether given by the American and the French revolutions or that formulated in a number of subsequent charters." Mamdani

gets support from other scholars. See Cecilia Jimenez, "Human Rights in the Post-Cold War Era: The Cases of North Korea, China and Burma," *Human Rights Dialogue* Ser. 1, no. 1 (New York: Carnegie Council on Ethics and International Affairs, May 1994); Norani Othman, "Grounding Human Rights Arguments in Non-Western Culture: Shari'a and the Citizenship Rights of Women in a Modern Islamic State," in Bauer and Bell, eds. *The East Asian Challenge for Human Rights*, 169–92; Amartya Sen, "Democracy as a Universal Value," *Journal of Democracy* 10, 3 (1999): 3–7. Debates over the origins of human rights still rage on. The major writers on human rights in the West claim that human rights are descended from the history of the Western state. See Jack Donnelly, *Universal Human Rights in Theory and Practice* (Ithaca, N.Y.: Cornell University Press, 2002); Michael Freeman, *Human Rights: An Interdisciplinary Approach* (Cambridge, Mass.: Polity, 2002); Rhoda Howard, *Human Rights and the Search for Community* (Boulder, Colo.: Westview Press, 1995. Angela Davis traces the birth of women's rights movement in the U.S. to 1832 in *Women, Race and Class* (New York: Vintage Books, 1983), chapter 2.

39. Willy Mutunga and Alamin Mazrui, "Rights Integration in an Institutional Context: The Experience of Kenya Human Rights Commission" *Buffalo Human Rights Law Review* 8 (2002): 123. In Amman, Jordan, in 2004 a Palestinian human rights activist told me that the human rights discourse did not help him. And he had a point because a human rights crusader there may be profiled as a terrorist. I told him that the discourse was relevant to others because it allowed them to support the Palestinian struggle.

40. Sidney Lewis, *Unrepentant Radical: An American Activist's Account of Five Turbulent Decades* (Boston: Beacon Press, 1980), 37–38.

41. Ibid., 39

42. For East Africa Yash Tandon, ed., *University of Dar es Salaam Debate on Class, State and Imperialism* (Dar es Salaam: TPH, 1982) and L. Khamisi, *Imperialism Today* (Dar es Salaam: TPH, 1983) provide unique and in-depth reading in this regard.

43. Tandon, *University of Dar es Salaam*; Issa Shivji, *The Concept of Human Rights in Africa* (Dakar: Codesria, 1989). Shivji states that "human rights talk constitutes one of the main elements in the ideological armory of imperialism" (5). She also argues that human rights discourse can be an ideology of resistance. There lies the "double-edgeness" of human rights and social justice discourses. See also Amy Bartholomew and Jennifer Breakspear, "Human Rights as Swords of Empire," in *The New Imperial Challenge*, ed. Leo Panitch and Colin Leys (London: Merlin Press, 2003), 124–145. One of the arguments of the authors is that the new global order requires that we do not rubbish international law and international institutions. Both have a role to play notwithstanding their known weaknesses.

44. Mutunga and Mazrui, "Rights Integration."

45. Reagan is said to have opined that social democracy was more dangerous than communism to capitalism Two sources of discussions on *why and what* really collapsed are Eric Hobsbawm, *The Age of Extremes* (New York: Vintage, 1996), chap. 16; Dani Wadada Nabudere, *A Critique of the Political Economy of Social Imperialism* (mimeo) (Harare/Helsingor, 1986).

46. The never-dying debates between "reform" and "revolution" still persist. For intellectuals calling for reform and who support globalization but want an alternative form, a form that mitigates globalization and market fundamentalism see, Joseph Sitiglitz, *Globalization and Its* Discontents (London: Penguin, 2002); Amartya Sen, *Development as Freedom*

(New York, Anchor Books, 1999); Peter Singer, *One World: The Ethics of Globalization* (New Haven, Conn.: Yale University Press, 2002).

47. The Declaration affirmed that various basic human rights are universal, indivisible, interdependent and interrelated. The international community was tasked to "treat human rights globally in a fair and equal manner, on the same footing and with the same emphasis." It was the duty of states, "regardless of their political, economic and cultural systems, to promote all human rights and fundamental freedoms." The conference also endorsed the "right to development" as "a universal and inalienable right and an integral part of fundamental human rights."

48. Arudhati Roy says that "Many resistance movements in poor countries which are fighting huge injustice and questioning the underlying principles of what constitutes 'liberation' and 'development' view human rights non-governmental organizations as modern-day missionaries who have come to take the ugly edge off imperialism—to defuse political anger and to maintain the status quo." Arudhati Roy, *An Ordinary Person's Guide to Empire* (Boston: South End Press, 2004). It can be argued rightly that human rights discourse mitigates market fundamentalism and constitutes a lifeline for the current global status quo. However, there are other faces associated with other human rights nongovernmental organizations that expose, demystify and resist the global status quo and thus form a strong basis for qualitative social transformation. See also Bartholomew and Breakspear, "Human Rights as Swords of Empire."

49. Vijay Prashad, *Fat Cats and Running Dogs: The ENRON Stage of Capitalism* (London: Zed Books, 2002), 1–10.

50. Morrell, "Men, Movements, and Gender Transformation in South Africa," 271. See also Morrell, ed., *Changing Men in Southern Africa*.

51. Morrell, "Men, Movements, and Gender Transformation in South Africa," 284.

52. Njoki Wainaina, *Femnet Review Report: Male Involvement in Programmes to Combat Gender Based Violence, Malawi and South Africa* (Nairobi: Femnet, 2002), 37.

53. Ibid., 38.

54. Ibid.

55. Nkosi has worked with various programs to combat gender violence, including running workshops for young people. Is this transformation? I guess in his case transformation related to his commitment and passion to struggle against GBV and to talk to men as perpetrators. Is this enough transformation? I would argue it could be a first step in a long journey of liberation of men, women, and society at large.

56. Some of the clear opportunities are access to this huge constituency of men in a country that is fanatically religious, and access to feminist theologians who are crucial allies to men for gender equality movement.

CHAPTER 6. WOMEN'S ADVOCACY: ENGENDERING AND RECONSTITUTING THE KENYAN STATE

Epigraph: Jerald Zaslove, "Constituting Modernity: The Epic Horizons of Constitutional Narratives," *Public Reading Our Rights* 9 (1994): 63–65.

1. Bessie House-Midamba, "Gender, Democratization, and Associational Life in

Kenya," *Africa Today* 43, 3 (July–September 1996): 294. Women secured 7 of the 27 places at the table of constitutional commissioners to the constitution of Kenya review process.

2. Valentine Moghadam, "Globalization and Feminism: The Rise of Women's Organizations in the Middle East and North Africa," *Canadian Women's Studies* 17 (Spring 1997): 76.

3. Moghadam, "Globalization and Feminism," 64–65.

4. FIDA-Kenya; Institute for Education and Democracy; Kenya Human Rights Commission; League of Kenya Women Voters.

5. Adriana Hernandez, *Pedagogy, Democracy, and Feminism: Rethinking the Public Sphere* (Albany: State University of New York Press, 1997), 29, citing Samuel Bowles and Herbert Gintis.

6. As the Coalition began its campaign within the conference other groups marginalized on the basis of ability, ethnicity, and location as women and as men supported the gender equality campaign for the Coalition, thereby expanding the content of the constitutional provisions on gender and human rights that were under review. This conceptualization of the intersections of harm, discrimination, and marginalization for particular groups proved powerful and positive in terms of identifying content and spaces for strategic alliances.

7. Association for Women's Rights in Development (AWID), "An Advocacy Guide for Feminists," *Ways and Means* 1 (Toronto) (December 2003).

8. Kimberlé Crenshaw, "Mapping the Margins: Intersectionality, Identity Politics, and Violence Against Women of Color," in *The Public Nature of Private Violence: The Discovery of Domestic Violence Abuse*, ed. Martha Albertson Fineman and Roxanne Mykitiuk (New York: Routledge, 1994), 93–118. Crenshaw first developed a theoretical tool to help explain the lived experiences of African American women in the United States; AWID, "Advocacy Guide."

9. Jacinta Muteshi and Athena Mutua, "Diversity of Women and Intersectionality," in *Safeguarding the Gains for Women in the Draft Constitution: Training Manual* (Nairobi: Kenya Human Rights Commission, FIDA-Kenya, Institute for Education and Democracy and League for Kenya Women Voters, 2003): 40–41.

10. This group, who presented themselves as "friends of the Commission," came to know as the "Palacina group" after the venue at which they held most of their meetings.

11. There had been an earlier presentation to this forum by gender activists before I was invited to participate. The early submissions had primarily outlined the positive provisions for women but there had been no follow up discussions or planning of the way forward.

12. The author ceased to be a director on the KHRC board in 2004.

13. Zaslove, "Constituting Modernity," 66.

14. Athena Mutua, a law professor from SUNY Buffalo, was consulting for KHRC and participating in the Palacina meetings. Jane Kiragu became the first and new executive director of the Kenya Anti-Corruption Campaign Commission in September 2004.

15. Zaslove, "Constituting Modernity," 75.

16. House-Midamba, "Gender, Democratization, and Associational Life," 296.

17. Hernandez, *Pedagogy, Democracy, and Feminism*, 30–31.

18. Ibid., 61.

19. Sonia Correa and Richard Parker, "Sexuality, human rights, and demographic thinking: Connections and disjunctions in a changing world," *Sexuality Research and Social Policy* 1 (January 2004): 23.

20. An important lesson learned was that there was need to clarify the organizational role and responsibility at the institutional level. With the exception of FIDA, who had been assigned the role of administration and fund management, the Coalition had focused only on specifying the roles and responsibility of the four director individuals representing the four organizations and assuming good faith on the part of the Coalition organizations. The core group also failed to grasp the wider political forces that would have effects on the political alignments made by their respective organizations. It frequently became increasing important to engage with these challenges through dialogue with each other and at times it even became necessary to recreated the strategic alliances and bring in new partners as organizations withdrew given their own internal struggles or resources constraints. Nevertheless, the Coalition continues to work in an ad hoc manner.

21. There were several other women's organizations that had also seized the moment and set out to inform and educate the public about the gains for women in the draft bill. Many were however acting as individual organizations within their mandates while others produced and published information collaboratively but did not undertake to organize joint activities nor seek consensus during the negotiation phases of the constitutional review conference.

22. Very early on however, these committees ceased to operate as formally constituted committees for the work required proved demanding and substantial on the time and resources of individuals and their organizations. Instead the various tasks of the committee that were retained as planned were divided up among the four core organizations and a few interested individuals supportive of the campaign. The Coalition then successfully fund raised to support these activities. However, a national media strategy was not developed given the number of tasks to be undertaken; instead media work was done as need arose.

23. Brigitte Mabandla, "Promoting Gender Equality in South Africa," in *Putting Women on the Agenda*, ed. Susan Bazilli (Johannesburg: Raven Press, 1991), 91.

24. Susan Bazilli, Introduction, in Bazilli, ed., *Putting Women on the Agenda*, 13.

25. Seeking to come out in solidarity with Muslim women who had lobbied for this qualification, the Coalition supported the retention of the Kadhi Courts on principles of social justice since many provisions of Islamic law, especially with regards to inheritance, seemed to result in equality in fact. The Coalition had also made proposals supported by Muslim women that Kadhi courts must become professionalized and consistent in their application of Islamic law.

26. Naila Kabeer, *Reversed Realities: Gender Hierarchies in Development Thought* (London: Verso, 1994), 188. Kabeer has pointed out that "women as mothers or would-be mothers are rarely perceived as competent actors, capable of making responsible choices in their own and in their families' interests. Instead, they are subjected to agendas which have been determined elsewhere."

27. United Nations International Research and Training Institute for the Advancement of Women (INSTRAW), "Engendering the Political Agenda: The Role of the State, Women's Organizations and the International Community," *INSTRAW* (Santo Domingo; 2000), 225. INSTRAW is based in Santo Domingo. The Coalition was pessimistic about its ability to resolve the differences within this issue because of the moral divide between the "person" and "non-person" dichotomy that was unbridgeable. On the one side there was sanctity of life arguments and the other side supported a woman's autonomy and control over her body.

The Coalition's strategy was to limit the types of issues that got dragged into the right to life provisions, but that was unsuccessful. The lessons from South Africa on reproductive rights and the right to choice are instructive. Their achievements in this realm sprung from a synergy of progressive health and rights activists in civil society and powerful women and men's voices within ANC seizing the political moment of transition from apartheid to entrench progressive claims for women.

28. Constitution of Kenya Review Commission, *The Draft Constitution of Kenya 2004* (Nairobi: Constitution of Kenya Review Commission, March 2004). The articles on land and property rights were a loss for women in so far as the gender-neutral language of "people" was used to state in article 78(1) that "All land belongs to the people of Kenya," while the bill of rights only recognized women's right to "manage" land.

29. Maria Nzomo, "Introduction," *Perspectives on Gender Discourse* 3 (1993): 10.

30. In 1997, Hon Phoebe Asiyo unsuccessfully offered a private member's motion seeking to legislate affirmative action that would require that all registered political parties in Kenya nominate at least one-third women candidates. The motion failed but what emerged was a network of women forming the Women's Political Caucus, who recognized that women would only be more strongly positioned to act and influence politics if they did so jointly. By August 1997 the Caucus had it first significant initiative when it presented demands for the effective representation of women in the constitutional review process and the inclusion of international human rights instruments pertaining to women in the new constitution.

31. Koki Muli, "Mixed Member Proportional Representation," in *Safeguarding Women's Gains in the Draft Constitution*, 64–67.

32. The Coalition carried out a series of educational sessions and discussions on the MMPR system with a wide variety of women delegates and lobbied for its entrenchment in the draft. For the Coalition it was clear that MMPR would substantively altered the way male dominated political parties' interacted with women seeking party membership since MMPR would pull women into party politics.

33. Zaslove, "Constituting Modernity," 75.

34. Jacinta Muteshi, "The Gender Commission," in *Safeguarding Women's Gains in the Draft Constitution*, 50–51.

35. Hernandez, *Pedagogy, Democracy and Feminism*, 56.

36. Anannya Bhattachannjee, "The Public/Private Mirage," in *Feminist Genealogies, Colonial Legacies, Democratic Futures*, ed. M. Jacqui Alexander and Chandra T. Mohanty (New York: Routledge, 1997), 326.

37. Athena Mutua, "The Constitutional Review Process: A Gender Audit of Bomas," in *Step by Step: Backwards or Forwards?* Annual Report (Nairobi: Federation of Women Lawyers Kenya, 2003): 9.

38. The Coalition believed that language was a pivotal point of entry in the constitution through the legal and social order could be transformed.

39. Hernandez, *Pedagogy, Democracy and Feminism*, 61.

40. Although positively supporting equality, several of these positions have remained unsecured in the context of a stalled constitutional process in March 2004 after the completion of the conference.

41. Mabandla, "Promoting Gender Equality," 78.

42. Ibid., 79.

43. Ibid.

44. At the start of the conference, access by the Coalition to all women delegates who had formed a caucus and met twice a week at the conference site was made very difficult. Hostility to civil society organizations may have been a result of the suspicions circulating throughout the conference that experts would take over the review process. Entry for the Coalition occurred when we only targeted delegates representing women's organizations for the Coalition members were its constituency; after this it eventually became possible to lobby diverse women delegates although our core target remained the delegates who had been selected to the conference as representatives of women's organizations.

45. Safeguarding Women's Gains in the Draft Constitution.

46. *Yawezekana: Bomas Agender* (Nairobi: Kenya Human Rights Commission, FIDA-Kenya, Institute for Education and Democracy, League for Kenya Women Voters and Noel Creative Media, 2003–4).

47. Anne M. Goetz, *Getting Institutions Right for Women in Development* (London: Zed, 1997); Shirin Rai, ed., *National Women's Machineries in Perspective* (Manchester: University of Manchester Press, 2001).

48. Tatjana Sikoska and Nuket Kardam, "Introduction," in *Engendering the Political Agenda: The Role of the State, Women's Organizations and the International Community* (Santo Domingo: United Nations International Research and Training Institute for the Advancement of Women, INSTRAW, 2000): 4. INSTRAW carried out comparative studies on engendering the political agenda in countries that had recently undergone political transition: Dominican Republic, Romania, and South Africa.

49. Sikoska and Kardam, "Introduction," 4.

50. United Nations Development Programme, *Human Development Report 2004: Cultural Liberty in Today's Diverse World* (New York: Oxford Press, 2004).

51. Wambui Kimathi, "Making Women's Demands Real," in *Step by Step*, 9–22.

52. President Mwai Kibaki's inaugural speech, cited in ibid., 10.

53. *Engendering the Political Agenda*, 8.

54. The Heinrich Boell Foundation-Kenya created and supported several gender forums and publications to raise discussion on engendering Constitutional issues. The Coalition also received donor support from DANIDA (Danish International Development Assistance), SIDA (Swedish International Co-operation Agency) and UNDP (United Nations Development Programme) for all of its activities.

55. The Coalition assigned its members to each negotiating site and session of the review conference to observe, keep abreast of issues and report back to the core coalition for purposes of strategizing.

56. Natasha Walter, *The New Feminism* (London: Little, Brown, 1998).

57. Ayesha M. Imam, "The Dynamics of WINning: An Analysis of Women in Nigeria," in Alexander and Mohanty, eds., *Feminist Genealogies, Colonial Legacies, Democratic Futures*, 303; Sikoska and Kardam, "Introduction," 17. A site of conflict is the divisions not only between intellectuals and activists, but also between women and men; and rural and urban women with a key point of contention arising around speaking on behalf of others, and who is defining the issues of oppression. Underscoring that the oppressed have a right and necessity to say what it is they feel in defining their oppression and which issues need to be dealt with. Ayesha Imam has nevertheless, argued that "felt oppression is not the privileged

last word in the analysis of that oppression . . . a developed consciousness can reflect and analyze experience which is not immediately one's own, and produce knowledge about it admittedly, it is not *experiential* knowledge." Sikoska and Kardam have cautioned that "women's lack of gender equality consciousness is an important obstacle for engendering the political agenda . . . it may result from women's formulation of their own personal needs as within and part of concealed inequalities of power."

58. Imam, "The Dynamics of WINning," 297. The fact of one's oppression does not make them more understanding of the causes of that oppression, or what will change it. It does not give one a keener sense of justice. . . . It does not necessarily make them more effective. The way out of this dilemma, explains Imam, is to "move from who is speaking to what is being said."

59. Jane Kiragu, Koki Muli, Jacinta Muteshi, Athena Mutua, and Grace Okello, who had replaced Cecelia Kememia.

60. Moghadam, "Globalization and Feminism," 67.

61. Imam, "The Dynamics of WINning," 297.

62. Jacinta Muteshi, Koki Muli, Jane Kiragu, Mary N. Mutinda, Immaculate Njenge, Betty Murungi, Vicky Karimi, Wanyiri Kihoro, and Josephine Mutungu, *The Coalitions' Model Proposals for the Draft Constitution* (Nairobi: January 2004).

63. Three of the original Coalition organizations, FIDA-Kenya, IED, and LKWV remained members of the Coalition, which expanded to include Urgent Action Fund and National Council of NGOs until 2004. KHRC ceased being a member of the Coalition.

64. For example, FIDA-Kenya, IED, Urgent Action Fund, and I have recently worked together educating and lobbying MPs and ministers to help garner parliamentary support to table the Family Protection Bill.

65. *Engendering the Political Agenda*, 281.

66. Correa and Parker, "Sexuality, Human Rights, and Demographic Thinking," 23.

67. Moghadam, "Globalization and Feminism," 64.

68. Marilyn Porter and Saparinah Sadli, "Is Global Feminism Possible: Developing 'Partnership' in a University Linkage Project," *Canadian Women's Studies* 17 (Spring 1997): 76.

69. Cameron McCarthy, *The Uses of Culture: Education and the Limits of Ethnic Affiliation* (New York: Routledge, 1998), 112, 46. At this time of the transition the role of universities would be to develop new understandings and to forge new alliances that will, as Cameron McCarthy argued, "guide us through the events and challenges of the present era." McCarthy went on to declare that educators and intellectuals can "intervene in this discursive field at the critical and strategic points of production and reception."

70. Imam, "The Dynamics of WINning," 299.

CHAPTER 7. DONORS AND HUMAN RIGHTS NGOS IN EAST AFRICA: CHALLENGES AND OPPORTUNITIES

1. Alison Van Rooy, ed., *Civil Society and the Aid Industry* (London: Earthscan, 1998); Hulme and Edwards 1997); David Hulme and Michael Edwards, eds., *NGOs, States and Donors: Too Close for Comfort?* (Basingstoke: Macmillan, 1996).

2. Hulme and Edwards, eds., *NGOs, States and Donors*.

3. Adebayo Olukoshi and Mkandawire Thandika, eds., *Between Liberalisation and Oppression: the Politics of Structural Adjustment in Africa* (Dakar: Codesria, 1995).

4. World Bank, *Annual Report 1997* (Washington, D.C.: World Bank Group, 1997).

5. Wachira Maina, "Kenya: The State, Donors and the Politics of Democratization," in *Civil Society and the Aid Industry*, ed. Alison Van Rooy (London: Earthscan, 1998), 134.

6. Ibid.

7. Smith Hempstone, *Rogue Ambassador: An African Memoir* (Sewanee, Tenn.: University of the South Press, 1997).

8. Ibid.

9. Alison Van Rooy and Mark Robinson, "Out of the Ivory Tower: Civil Society Assistance and the Aid System," in Van Rooy, ed., *Civil Society and the Aid Industry*, 31.

10. Maina, "Kenya: The State, Donors and the Politics of Democratization."

11. Ibid.

12. Ivor Chipkin, "What Civil Society in South Africa? Political Conceptions of the Relationship Between Civil Society and Democracy," in *Leadership, Civil Society and Democratization in Africa: Case Studies from South Africa*, ed. Abdalla Bujra and Sipho Buthelezi (Addis Ababa: Development Policy Management Forum, 2002).

13. See B. Andreasson, Wachira Maina, and Mutahi Ngunyi, *Promoting Democracy Through Civil Society in Kenya* (Oslo: Norwegian Human Rights Institute, 1996); Mutahi Ngunyi, *Democracy and the Aid Industry in Kenya: An Assessment of Grant making to the DG Sector of Civil Society in Kenya* (Leeds: University of Leeds/SAREAT, 1999).

14. Archie Mafeje, "Democratic Governance and New Democracy in Africa: Agenda for the Future," paper prepared for African Forum for Envisioning Africa Focus, Nairobi, April 26–29, 2002.

15. Abdallah Bujra, "Introduction," *Proceedings of the Conference on Democracy, Sustainable Development and Poverty Reduction: Are They Compatible?* (Addis Ababa: Development Policy Management Forum, 2001).

16. Jacques Maritain, *The Range of Reason* (New York: Scribner, 1952; University of Notre Dame Jacques Maritain Center), http://www2.nd.edu/Departments//Maritain/etext/range13.htm#p179.

17. Mafeje, "Democratic Governance and New Democracy in Africa."

18. Rwekaza Mukandala, "Presidential Address to the 13th Biennial Congress: The State of African Democracy," *African Journal of Political Science* 6, 2 (2002): 1–10.

19. Maina, "Kenya: The State, Donors and the Politics of Democratization."

20. Willy Mutunga, Francesco Gesualdi, and Steve Ouma, *Exposing the Soft Belly of the Multinational Beast: The Struggle for Workers' Rights at Del Monte Kenya*, Kenya Human Rights Commission Report (Nairobi: Kenya Human Rights Commission, 2002).

21. Amartya Sen, *Development as Freedom* (New York: Anchor Books, 2000); Henry Shue, *Basic Rights: Subsistence, Affluence, and U.S. Foreign Policy* (Princeton, N.J.: Princeton University Press, 1980).

22. Mao Zedong, "Be Concerned with the Well-Being of the Masses, Pay Attention to Methods That Work," *Selected Works of Mao Tse-tung*, 5 vols. (Beijing: Foreign Language Press; New York: Pergamon, 1975), 1: 147.

23. Maria Nzomo, "Civil Society in the Kenyan Political Transition: 1992–2002," in

The Politics of Transition in Kenya: From KANU to NARC, ed. Walter O. Oyugi, Peter Wany-ande, and C. Odhiambo-Mbai (Nairobi: Heinrich Boll Foundation, 2003).

24. Maina, "Kenya: The State, Donors and the Politics of Democratization," 158.

25. Connie Ngondi-Houghton, *Philanthropy in East Africa: The Nature, Challenges and Potential* (Allavida, 2004).

26. Ibid.

27. Ibid.

28. Maina, "Kenya: The State, Donors and the Politics of Democratization."

29. Ibid., 138.

30. Ngondi-Houghton, *Philanthropy in East Africa*.

CHAPTER 8. CONTRADICTIONS IN NEOLIBERALISM: DONORS, HUMAN RIGHTS NGOS, AND GOVERNANCE IN KENYA

1. Naomi Chazan, Peter Lewis, Robert Mortimer, Donald Rothchild, and Steven Sted-man, *Politics and Society in Contemporary Africa*, 2nd ed. (Boulder, Colo.: Lynne Rienner, 1992). Also, see generally Robert H. Jackson and Earl G. Rosberg, *Personal Rule in Black Africa: Prince, Autocrat, Prophet, Tyrant* (Berkeley: University of California Press, 1982).

2. Donald Rothchild and Naomi Chazan, *The Precarious Balance: State and Civil Society in Africa* (Boulder, Colo.: Westview Press, 1988).

3. Göran Hydén and Michael Bratton, eds., *Governance and Politics in Africa* (Boulder, Colo.: Lynne Rienner, 1992).

4. Peter Anyang-Nyong'o, *Popular Struggles for Democracy in Africa* (London: Zed Books, 1987)

5. Mahmood Mamdani, "State and Civil Society in Contemporary Africa: Reconceptu-alizing the Birth of State Nationalism and Defeat of Popular Movements in Africa," *Africa Development* 15, 3/4 (1990).

6. Hydén and Bratton, eds., *Governance and Politics in Africa*.

7. Stephen N. Ndegwa, "Citizenship and Ethnicity: An Examination of Two Transition Moments in Kenyan Politics," *American Political Science Review* 91, 3 (1997)

8. Peter Gibbon, "Some Reflections on Civil Society and Political Change," in *Democ-ratization in the Third World: Concrete Cases in Comparative Theoretical Perspective*, ed. Lars Rudebeck, Olle Törnquist, and Virgilio Rojas (New York: St. Martin's, 1998)

9. Issa Shivji, *Not Yet Democracy: Reforming Land Tenure in Tanzania* (London: Interna-tional Institute for Environment and Development, 1998).

10. Willy Mutunga, *Constitution-Making from the Middle: Civil Society and Transition Politics in Kenya* (Nairobi: Sareat, 1999).

11. Mahmood Mamdani, *Citizen and Subject: Contemporary Africa and the Legacy of Late Colonialism* (Princeton, N.J.: Princeton University Press, 1996).

12. Joel D. Barkan, "The Rise and Fall of a Governance Realm in Kenya," in Hydén and Bratton, eds., *Governance and Politics in Africa*, 167–92.

13. Joel D. Barkan and Frank Holmquist, "Peasant-State Relations and the Social Base of Self-Help in Kenya," *World Politics* 41 (1989); Karuti Kanyinga, "The Social-Political Con-

text of the Growth of NGOs in Kenya," in *Economic Liberalization and Social Change in Africa*, ed. Peter Gibbon (Uppsala: Nordic African Institute, 1993).

14. Kanyinga, "The Social-Political Context." 1993..

15. Mutahi Ngunyi, "Interpreting Political Liberalization in Kenya" (Nairobi: Mimeo, 1995).

16. Karuti Kanyinga, "Civil Society Formations in Kenya: A Growing Role in Development and Democracy," in *Civil Society in the Third Republic*, ed. Duncan Okello (Nairobi: National Council of NGOs, 2004).

17. Mutunga, *Constitution-Making from the Middle*.

CHAPTER 9. STATE AND CIVIL SOCIETY RELATIONS: CONSTRUCTING HUMAN RIGHTS GROUPS FOR SOCIAL CHANGE

1. Larry Diamond, "Rethinking Civil Society: Toward Democratic Consolidation," *Journal of Democracy* 5, 3 (July 1994): 4–17, 5.

2. Robert D. Putnam, "Bowling Alone: America's Declining Social Capital," *Journal of Democracy* 6, 1 (January 1995): 65–78; Putnam, *Making Democracy Work: Civic Traditions in Modern Italy* (Princeton, N.J.: Princeton University Press, 1993).

3. Michael W. Foley and Bob Edwards, "The Paradox of Civil Society," *Journal of Democracy* 7, 3 (July 1996): 38–52, 43.

4. Alexis de Tocqueville, *Democracy in America* (New York: Doubleday, 1969), 193, 524, 192.

5. Nelson Kasfir, "Civil Society and Democracy in Africa: Critical Perspectives," *Journal of Commonwealth & Comparative Politics* 36, 2 (July 1998): 6.

6. Uganda Constitution 1995, Article 20(2), "The rights and freedoms of the individual and groups enshrined in this chapter shall be respected, upheld and promoted by all organs and agencies of the government and by all persons."

7. Foley and Edwards, "The Paradox of Civil Society," 40.

8. Michael Mann, *A Theory of the Modern State* (Cambridge: Cambridge University Press, 1993).

9. Diamond, "Rethinking Civil Society," 7–11.

10. Kasfir, "Civil Society and Democracy," 7.

11. Jeffrey E. Garten, *Globalization Without Tears: A New Social Compact for CEOs* (Boston: Harvard Business School Press, 2002).

CHAPTER 10. GOVERNANCE AND DEMOCRACY IN KENYA: CHALLENGES FOR HUMAN RIGHTS NGOS

1. These organizations comprise what is referred to as civil society. Civil society is defined as that part of society that comprises formal and informal groups outside the state. In this chapter it refers mainly to human rights and democracy lobby groups and nongovernmental organizations.

2. Mutahi Ngunyi, "Transition Without Transformation: Civil Society and the Transi-

tional SeeSaw," Series on Alternative Research in East Africa, http://www.ids.ac.uk/ids/civsoc/final/kenya/kenx.doc.

3. Ibid.

4. The document was the first of its kind ever published through the collective efforts of participating NGOs at various forums. The document was a response to specific experiences by Kenyans over thirty years since independence arising from a defective constitution that permitted bad governance and the lack of accountability. The draft model constitution aimed to enhance constitutional debate in Kenya by providing concrete proposals and paving the way for an inclusive constitution reform process.

5. *Daily Nation*, Monday, May 24, 1999.

6. Audit Report April 2003–March 2004, National Constitutional Conference of Kenya (2004).

7. Rajesh Tandon, "Civil Society Is the First Sector," *Journal of the Society for International Development* 3 (1993): 38–39.

8. Mutahi Ngunyi, "Transition Without Transformation: Civil Society and the Transitional SeeSaw," Series on Alternative Research in East Africa, http//www.ids.ac.uk/ids/civsoc/final/Kenya/kenx.doc.

9. As nations become interdependent through the process of globalization, borders are becoming increasingly irrelevant. This holds true not only for international trade and investment, but also for human rights concerns. Though gross human rights violations often occur within states, from recent trends, under international human rights law, the perpetrators, irrespective of rank, may now be apprehended in any country. This banishes the long reigning fallacy that human rights violations are matters exclusively within the domain of the state in which they are violated. The establishment of ad hoc international criminal tribunals to prosecute authors of genocide in Rwanda and Former Yugoslavia, coupled with the arrest of General Augusto Pinochet for crimes against humanity is abundant evidence of the diminishing role of the state as the ultimate guardian of human rights. The establishment of the International Criminal Court by the Rome Statute on July 17, 1998, is historic. The ICC is the first permanent treaty based court established to promote the rule of law and ensure that the gravest crimes do not go unpunished.

10. K-Hurinet, in existence since 1999, comprises civil society organizations and lobbies committed to protection and promotion of human rights, good governance, democracy, and related objectives. It exists rather loosely without an institutional framework or structure. KHRC serves as the focal point and convener for K-Hurinet. However, efforts to formalize the network are underway.

11. Slim Hugo, "By What Authority? The Legitimacy and Accountability of Non-Governmental Organizations," *Journal of Humanitarian Assistance*, http://www.jha.ac/articles/a082.htm, March 10, 2002.

CHAPTER 13. THE DEATH PENALTY IN EAST AFRICA: LAW AND TRANSNATIONAL ADVOCACY

1. *The State v. T. Makwanyane and M. Mchunu*, Case No. C.C.T/3/94.

2. For a comprehensive treatment of the history and contemporary application of the

death penalty in Africa, see Lilian Manka Chenwi, "Towards the Abolition of the Death Penalty in Africa: A Human Rights Perspective," LL.D. thesis, University of Pretoria, 2005.

3. Roger Hood, *The Death Penalty: A Worldwide Perspective*, 3rd ed. (Oxford: Oxford University Press, 2002). As of 2003, 11 African states had abolished the penalty for all crimes and 30 were retentionist. Lilian Chenwi, "Capital Trials in Africa in the Light of International and Regional Fair Trial Standards," paper presented at First International Conference on the Application of the Death Penalty in Commonwealth Africa, http://www.biicl.org/files/2192_chenwi_capital_trials.pdf.

4. Hands off Cain, www.handsoffcain.org (accessed December 10, 2004).

5. Malawi's President Bakili Muluzi took office in 1994, and there have been no executions since then. In 2004, Muluzi commuted 79 death sentences. President Levy Mwanawasa took office in 2001 in Zambia. In April 2003, he instituted a constitutional review process with abolition of the death penalty as one terms of reference. He ordered review of all capital trials resulting in death sentences, and commuted scores of sentences, including those of 44 soldiers convicted of treason.

6. Amnesty Press Release, http://web.amnesty.org/library/print/ENGAFR490012004 (accessed December 2004).

7. Organic Law No. 8/96 of August 30, 1996; UN Doc. S/RES/955(1994), annex.

8. David Killingray, "Punishment to Fit the Crime? Penal Policy and Practice in British Colonial Africa," in *A History of Prison and Confinement in Africa*, ed. Florence Bernault (Portsmouth, N.H.: Heinemann, 2003), 110.

9. The Murder (Abolition of Death Penalty) Act, 1965, abolished the imposition of death for murder, replacing it with a mandatory life sentence. Another vote in 1969 made the abolition of the death penalty for murder "permanent" in Great Britain.

10. President Mwai Kibaki of Kenya commuted nearly 200 death sentences when he took office and vowed to prevent executions during his presidency.

11. When President Benjamin Mbaka assumed office in 1995 he promised not to apply the penalty. In 2002, responding to legislative concerns over the prolonged incarceration of death row prisoners, President Mkapa commuted the death sentences of about 100 prisoners to life. In Bernault, ed., *A History of Prison and Confinement in Africa*, 110.

12. For a comprehensive discussion of the administration of the death penalty in Uganda, see "Uganda: Challenging the Death Penalty," Report of the International Federation of Human Rights, No. 425/2, October 2005.

13. Statement of Justice Minister Murungi, *Amicus Journal* 7, 1–2 (2003).

14. This proposal cuts back the scope of the death penalty, eliminating the capital sentence for the crimes of robbery with violence, and attempted robbery with violence.

15. http://web.amnesty.org/library/Index/ENGAFR320052005?open&of= ENG-KE N (accessed October 19, 2006).

16. In 2004, the government supported a Constitutional Review Commission's recommendation that the penalty be retained as mandatory for murder, treason, aggravated robbery, kidnapping, and defilement.

17. "Death Penalty in Uganda—Road to Its Abolition?" *Justice Update*, Newsletter of the Foundation for Human Rights Initiative (2004).

18. "Mkapa Never Assented Death Sentence," *The Guardian*, October 11, 2003.

19. Deputy Minister for Home Affairs John Chiligati has stated the penalty could not

be repealed without public support for abolition. "Chiligati: Death Penalty to Stay," *The Guardian*, April 4, 2004. Attorney General Andrew Chenge has registered his support for the penalty. "Death Row: Presidents Save Cons," *East African*, July 28, 2003.

20. See http://www.santegidio.org/pdm/news2002/18_04_02_d.htm.

21. http://www.aegis.com/news/afp/2004/AF041263.html.

22. "Case Study: East Africa," *Amicus Journal* 6, 7 (2003). A warden of Mississippi's infamous Parchman Prison has written a book on how his work led him to oppose the death penalty. Donald A. Caban, *Death at Midnight: The Confession of an Executor* (Boston: Northeastern University Press, 1996).

23. OAU Doc. CAB/Leg/67/3 /Rev. 5. For a general review of the role of the Charter in promoting human rights, see Frans Viljoen, "Application of the African Charter on Human and Peoples' Rights by Domestic Courts in Africa," *JAL* 43 (1999): 1–17; Mirna Adjami, "African Courts, International Law and Comparative Case Law: Chimera or Emerging Human Rights Jurisprudence?" *Michigan Journal of International Law* 24 (2002):103. Article 4 of the Charter provides "Human beings are inviolable. Every human being shall be entitled to respect for his life and the integrity of his person. No one may be arbitrarily deprived of this right." In December 2003, in *Interights et al. (on behalf of Bosch) v. Botswana*, Communication 240/2001, *Seventeenth Annual Activity Report: 2003–2004* (African Commission) the Commission held the death penalty did not violate the prisoner's right to life, and that the Republic of Botswana was not in violation of the Charter, http:www.mmegi.bw/2003/December/Monday8/469942255956.html. However, notwithstanding the result in *Bosch*, the Commission discussed abolition of the death penalty at its 36th Session in 2004, making clear the issue is still very much at the top of the human rights agenda.

24. "Resolution Urging States to Envisage a Moratorium on the Death Penalty, 13th Activity Report of the African Commission on Human and Peoples' Rights," OAU Doc AHG/Dec.153 (XXXVI), Annex IV. http://www.achpr.org/html/directory of resolutions .html.

25. The guidelines can be found at http://www.interights.org.

26. OAU Doc.CAB/LEG/24.9/49 (1990), arts. 5 sec. 3, 30(e). While the Charter does not define a child, the UN Convention on the Rights of the Child does define "every human being below the age of 18 years" as a child.

27. The right to life is protected by Section 71 of the Constitution of Kenya, article 14 of the Constitution of Tanzania, and Article 22(1) of the Constitution of Uganda. The right not to be subjected to cruel, inhuman and degrading punishment or treatment is protected by Section 74(1) of the Constitution of Kenya, article 13(6)(e) of the Constitution of Tanzania, and Article 24 of the Constitution of Uganda. Section 74, Constitution of Kenya; Section 24, Constitution of Uganda; Bill of Rights, Constitution of Tanzania.

28. *Kigula v. Attorney General*. In defense the government has claimed that 57 percent of Ugandans support the penalty. "Uganda: Death Penalty on Trial," Norwegian Council for Africa News, 24 (South Africa 1/19/05, http://www.afrika.do/Detailed/6976.html.

29. *The Uganda Law Society and Jackson Karugaba v. A.G. Uganda*, Constitutional Petition 8 of 2002, Court of Appeal of Uganda.

30. For a useful discussion of the case, see Henry Onoria, "Soldiering and Constitutional Rights in Uganda: The Kotido Military Executions," *East African Journal of Peace and Human Rights* 9, 1 (2003): 87.

31. In the military setting a lengthy list of offenses are punishable by death in Uganda, including causing fire, cowardice, failure to brief, and spreading harmful propaganda.

32. *Mbushuu v. Republic*, [1995] T.L.R. 97, 118 (Tanzania).

33. Bill of Rights, Constitution of Tanzania.

34. *Republic v. Mbushuu*, [1994] T.L.R. 146, 173 (Tanzania High Ct.).

35. Ibid., 156.

36. Ibid., 159

37. *Mbushuu v. Republic*, 111–12.

38. Article 30(2) of the Constitution of Tanzania. In contrast, the Ugandan court has held the right to be free from inhuman treatment or punishment to be non-derogable. *Attorney General v. Abuki* (2001) 1 LRC 63.

39. *Mbushuu v. Republic*, 115–16.

40. See *Woodson v. North Carolina*, 428 U.S. 280 (1976). The Inter-American Commission of Human Rights also rejected the mandatory penalty *in Tracey v. Jamaica*, Report No. 41/100 (Inter-Am. C.H.R. Apr. 13, 2000) and *Hilaire, Constantine and Benjamin et al. v. Trinidad and Tobago*, Ser. C No. 94 (Inter-Am. C.H.R. June 21, 2002), http://www.corteidh .or.cr/seriec_ing/index.html.

41. Section 296 (2) of the Kenya Penal Code provides that any person who commits the felony of robbery armed with any dangerous or offensive weapon or instrument, or . . . in company with one or more other person or persons, or if, at or immediately before or immediately after the time of the robbery he wounds, beats, strikes or uses any other personal violence to any person, . . . shall be sentenced to death. A proposed change in the penal code would eliminate the mandatory sentence for the robbery crimes.

42. Failure to provide legal assistance in these circumstances violates Article 7(1)(c) of the African Charter. The Human Rights Committee has held that "unavailability of legal aid amounts to a violation of article 6 *juncto* article 14 of the [ICCPR]." UN Doc No. CCPR/ C/79/Add.83, 19 November 1997, para 14. See *Daily Nation*, "Lawyers Criticize Death Sentence," December 23, 1999, http://www.nationaudio.com/News/Daily Nation/231299/News/ news_0001.html. See also Kenya: Time for Change, http://www.amnesty.org/ailib/intcam/ kenya/briefing/change.htm.

43. Penal Code Act, Cap 106, §184 (murder), 273(2) (armed robbery), (301(b)(2)(smuggling), and (25(1),(2))(forms of treason)).

44. Uganda: Challenging the Death Penalty, 19, International Federation of Human Rights, October 2005.

45. *Soering v. United Kingdom*, [1989] 11 Eur. Ct. H.R 439; *The State vs. T. Makwanyane and M. Mchunu*, Case No. C.C.T/3/94; *Catholic Commission for Justice and Peace v. AG of Zimbabwe*.

46. The Kenya Human Rights Commission placed the number of death row prisoners at 1,270 in 2002. In its 2003 Report for Kenya, Amnesty International put the figure at 3,200. http://web.amnesty.org/report2004/ken-summary-eng. In an article on October 6, 2004, the *East Standard* newspaper put the number at 1,999. http://www.eastandard.net/archives/ sunday/print/news.php?articleid = 2350.

47. Amnesty put the figure of prisoners under sentence of death at 387 as of August 2004. http://amnesty.org/library/Index/ENGAFR560012005.

48. See *Republic v. Mbushuu*, [1994] T.L.R. 146, 162.

49. Ibid., 163.

50. "Abolish Death Penalty, Prisons Chief Pleads," *The Monitor*, April 14, 2005.

51. "Foes of Death Penalty Making Gradual Gains in Africa," *New York Times*, October 20, 2004.

52. *Justice Update*, Newsletter of the Foundation for Human Rights Initiative 10 (2004).

53. "Resolution Urging States to Envisage a Moratorium on the Death Penalty, 13th Activity Report of the African Commission on Human and People's Rights," OAU Doc. AHG/Dec.153(XXXVI), Annex IV.

54. Polling data in Uganda shows that while 57 percent of those polled favor the death penalty, 42 percent favor abolition. *Uganda: Death Penalty on Trial*, Norwegian Council for Africa, News 24, January 19, 2005, http://www.afrika.no/Detailed/6976.html. In the United States, polls show about 75–80 percent of people polled favor the penalty. Hugo Adam Bedau, "Abolishing the Death Penalty in the United States," in *Capital Punishment: Strategies for Abolition*, ed. Peter Hodgkinson and William A. Schabas (Cambridge: Cambridge University Press, 2004), 203. In the Commonwealth Caribbean, polling suggests that over 80 percent of those polled support capital punishment.

55. Although the distinct trajectory of human rights law is towards abolition, the penalty is not yet barred by customary international law. However, increasingly international instruments prohibit the death penalty. It is not available under the Rome Treaty. It was excluded from the Rwanda and Yugoslavia tribunals, and from the Special Court for Sierra Leone established by the United Nations and the Sierra Leone government.

56. European Community: *Soering v. United Kingdom*, ECHR 1989, Ser A. No. 161; UNHCR: *Pratt and Morgan v. Jamaica*, Communications 210/1986 and 225/1987, UN Doc. A/44/40, 6 April 1989, *Judge v. Canada*, Communication 829/1998, UN Doc CCPR/C/78/D/ 829/1998, 20 October 2003; South Africa: *State v. Makwanyane* CCT/3/94 (1995); *Mohamed v. President of the Republic of South Africa*, CCT 17/01 (2001); Judicial Committee: *Pratt v. Att'y Gen. of Jamaica*, [1994] 2 A.C. 1 (P.C. 1993), [1993] 43 W.I.R. 340; Canada: *United States v. Burns*, [2001] 1 S.C.R. 283; Zimbabwe: *Catholic Commission for Justice and Peace in Zimbabwe v. Attorney General*, Judgment No. S.C. 73/93, 14 Hum Rts. L.J. 323 (1993).

57. See generally Laurence R. Helfer, "Overlegalizing Human Rights: International Relations Theory and the Commonwealth Caribbean Backlash Against Human Rights Regimes," *Columbia Law Review* 102 (2002): 1832.

58. Protocol 6 to the ECHR abolishes the death penalty in times of peace. As of this writing all members of the EU except Turkey had signed Protocol 6. Protocol 13 abolishes the penalty in all circumstances.

59. Prospective member states must ratify Protocol 6 and agree to cease to apply the sanction.

60. See *Guidelines on Human Rights and the Fight Against Terrorism* (adopted July 11, 2002). Guideline X (2) prohibits the death penalty in extradition cases. Article 19 of the Charter of Fundamental Rights of Europe provides that "No one may be removed, expelled, or extradited to a state where there is a serious risk that he or she would be subjected to the death penalty, torture, or other inhuman or degrading treatment or punishment." The Charter has no binding affect, but it is regarded as codifying European human rights norms on capital punishment. See William A. Shabas, *The Abolition of the Death Penalty in International*

Law, 3rd ed. (Cambridge: Cambridge University Press, 2002), 249–50. On extradition policies in Europe and the abolition initiative, see generally Jon Yorke, "Europe's Judicial Inquiry in Extradition Cases: Closing the Door on the Death Penalty," *European Law Review* 29 (2004): 546.

61. In connection with the September 11, 2001, related prosecution of Zaccharias Moussaoui in the United States, France and Germany required assurances that evidence sought by the United States prosecutors would not be used to support a death penalty outcome. See William A. Schabas, "Indirect Abolition: Capital Punishment's Role in Extradition Law and Practice," *Loyola International & Comparative Law Review* 25 (2003): 581, 601.

62. Article 11 of the TEU.

63. Article 49 of the TEU.

64. For an interesting insider's view of the volatile consequences of the death penalty for diplomatic relations between the U.S. and Europe, see Harold Hongju Koh, "Paying 'Decent Respect' to World Opinion on the Death Penalty," *U.C. Davis Law Review* 35 (2002): 1085. One African initiative was the Project on the Application of the Death Penalty in Commonwealth Africa, launched in 2003, sponsored by the British Institute of International and Comparative Law, and funded by the European Commission.

65. Margaret Burnham, "Indigenous Constitutionalism: The Death Penalty and the Case of the Commonwealth Caribbean," *International Journal of Constitutional Law* 3 (2005): 4.

66. For an account of Britain's application of the provisions of the Convention in the colonies, see generally A. W. Brian Simpson, *Human Rights and the End of Empire: Britain and the Genesis of the European Convention* (Oxford: Oxford University Press, 2001).

67. In Jamaica, for example, in 2004 there were four times as many death row inmates per capita as in the United States.

68. The American Charter on Human Rights and the UN human rights treaties provided the substantive basis legal grounds for the petitions to the Inter-American Commission on Human Rights and the UN Human Rights Committee.

69. *Soering v. United Kingdom*, Federal Republic of Germany intervening, 161 Eur. Ct.H.R. (ser.A) 34 (1989). See William A. Schabas, "Soering's Legacy: The Human Rights Committee and the Judicial Committee of the Privy Council Take a Walk down Death Row," *International & Comparative Law Journal* 43 (1994): 913.

70. *Pratt and Morgan v. Attorney General for Jamaica* [1994] 2 A.C. 1.

71. Leonard Birdsong, "Is there a Rush to the Death Penalty in the Caribbean: The Bahamas Says No," *Temp. International & Comparative Law Journal* 13 (1999): 285, 291.

72. Article 6(2) of the International Covenant on Civil and Political Rights provides: In countries which have not abolished the death penalty, sentence of death may be imposed only for the most serious crimes in accordance with the law in force at the time of the commission of the offense and not contrary to the present Covenant.

73. *Reyes v. The Queen* [2002] 2 A.C. 235.

74. *Hilaire, Constantine and Benjamin et al. v. Trinidad and Tobago*, 11.816 Inter-Am. Ct. H.R. 237, 281 ¶103 (2002). As a result of the Inter-American Court's decision 31 convicted prisoners in Trinidad and Tobago were ordered retried.

75. *Lewis v. Att'y Gen. of Jamaica*, [2001] 2 A.C. 50, [2000] 2 W.L.R. 1785.

76. Laurence R. Helfer, "Overlegalizing Human Rights: International Relations Theory

and the Commonwealth Caribbean Backlash Against Human Rights Regimes," *Columbia Law Review* 102 (2002): 1832.

77. In June 2006 the CCJ heard the petition of two Barbados death row prisoners challenging the refusal of the state to delay considering their applications for commutation until final determination of their appeals to international human rights bodies. *Attorney General v. Jeffrey Joseph and Lennox Recardo Boyce,* CCJ Appeal No. CV 002 of 2005.

78. Attorneys Saul Lehrfreund and Parvais Jabbar of the UK firm Simons Muirhead & Burton assisted the Ugandan firm of Katende Ssempebwa & Co in the *Kigula* case. When *Kigula* was decided, the UK lawyers explained that the legal team sought to transpose to East Africa law their firm helped to develop in the Caribbean cases. "UK Lawyers and Ugandan U-Turn on Death Penalty," *Financial Times,* June 20, 2005.

79. Margaret Burnham, "Saving Constitutional Rights from Judicial Scrutiny: The Savings Clause in the Law of the Commonwealth Caribbean," *University of Miami Inter-American Law Review* 36 (2005): 2.

80. J. Oloka-Onyango, "Reinforcing Marginalized Rights in an Age of Globalization: International Mechanisms, Non-State Actors, and the Struggle for Peoples' Rights in Africa," *American University International Law Review* 18 (2003): 851; Nsongurua J. Udombana, "Between Promise and Performance: Revisiting States' Obligations Under the African Human Rights Charter," *Stanford Journal of International Law* 40 (2004): 105.

81. In 2000, Illinois Governor George Ryan ordered a moratorium on executions. In 2003, he commuted the sentences of 167 condemned prisoners to life without parole and pardoned 4 death row prisoners. In 2002, Governor Parris Glendening declared a moratorium on execution in Maryland pending a review of procedures. In *People v. LaValle*, 817 NE 2d 341 (2004), the New York appellate court reversed a capital conviction on the grounds that the deadlock jury instruction of the capital sentence law violated due process.

CHAPTER 14. DEMOCRACY ORGANIZATIONS IN POLITICAL TRANSITIONS: IDASA AND THE NEW SOUTH AFRICA

1. Sue Valentine, "Economy: Justice AND Growth," *Democracy in Action: Monthly Newsletter of the Institute for a Democratic Alternative for South Africa*, Special Edition (May 1990): 1.

2. Alex Boraine, *A Brief History of IDASA, 1987 to 1994: Establishment and Early Years* (Pretoria: Haum, 1994).

3. Magdalena Tham, "An Introduction to IDASA—The Institute for Democracy in South Africa," *Records of Idasa 1987–1999* (National Archive of South Africa, 1999), 1.

4. "IDASA Launched Nationally," *Democracy in Action*, Special Edition (August 1987): 1–2.

5. "Why the Mission to Dakar?" *Democracy in Action*, Special Edition (October 1987): 1.

6. Alex Boraine, "From the Executive Director," *Democracy in Action*, Special Edition (October 1987): 2.

7. Ibid.

8. Marc Dobson, "Historic IDASA Conference—Freedom Charter as Alive and Relevant As Ever," *Democracy in Action*, Special Edition (August 1988): 1–2.

9. Ian Liebenberg, "Options Debate Gets Under Way," *Democracy in Action*, Special Edition (March 1989): 1–4.

10. "IDASA: Taking Up the Challenge of Transition," *Democracy in Action*, Special Edition (June/July 1990): 15.

11. Alex Boraine, "Idasa: The Road Ahead," *Democracy in Action* (August/September 1990): 6–7.

12. Ibid.

13. Alison Curry, "Intolerance: The Beast in All Our Hearts," *Democracy in Action: Journal for the Institute for a Democratic Alternative for South Africa*, 7, 1 (February 1993): 7.

14. "South Africa in Transition," *Democracy in Action* (May 1990): 9.

15. Alex Boraine, "Policing in South Africa in the 1990s: Idasa Conference on Policing in South Africa in the 1990s," IDASA, October 5, 1992.

16. Haddon Klingberg, "Thoughts from a Passing Foreigner," *Democracy in Action* 8, 5 (July/August 1991): 20.

17. Alex Boraine, "What It Means to Be a Leader Now," *Democracy in Action* 6, 6 (October 1992): 3.

18. Fawzia Moodley, "One in Three Wants to 'escape' SA," *Democracy in Action* 7, 7 (December 1993): 23.

19. Alice Coetzee, "Race Is on to Reach Voters," *Democracy in Action* 8, 1 (February 1994): 27.

20. Strom, Marie-Louise, "From Dakar to a Democratic South Africa," *Democracy in Action* (September 1999): 1–2.

21. Sue Valentine, "'Most Complex' Change in the World," *Democracy in Action* 7, 5 (August 1993): 16.

22. Alison Curry, "Voter Education: Tackling the Feverish State of the Nation," *Democracy in Action* 7, 6 (October 1993): 12.

23. Michelle Booth, "Conference Brings Hope for a New Society," *Democracy in Action* 7, 7 (December 1993): 25.

24. Boraine, *A Democratic Alternative*.

25. Levy, Moria, "Idasa Aims to Bridge the Information Gap," *Democracy in Action* 19, 2 (April 1995): 4.

26. Gordhan, Pravin, "Southern Views" *Democracy in Action: Journal for the Institute for a Democratic Alternative for South Africa*, 9, 1 (February 1995): 20.

27. Institute for Democracy in South Africa, "1998 Annual Report": 11.

28. Ibid., 9.

29. Institute for Democracy in South Africa, "Idasa: A Brief Historical Overview," unpublished Idasa Document.

30. Institute for Democracy in South Africa, "Extract from Institute for Democracy in South Africa board minutes," April 1999.

31. Miller, Robin, "Idasa Strategic Review," *Institute for Democracy in South Africa* (September 2004): 1.

32. Institute for Democracy in South Africa, "Idasa Strategic Review," Management Committee Meeting Paper (September 2004).

33. Vicky Mancuso Brehm, "Autonomy or Dependence? North-South NGO Partnerships," International NGO Training and Research Centre (INTRAC) Briefing Paper (Oxford, July 2004): 5.

34. Rick Davies, "Donor Information Demands and NGO Institutional Development," *Journal of International Development* 9, 6 (1997): 613–20.

CONCLUSION. COMING OF AGE: NGOS AND STATE ACCOUNTABILITY IN EAST AFRICA

Epigraph: Kivutha Kibwana, "The Role of Civil Society in Africa's Democratisation and Rebirth," in *Democratisation and Law Reform in Kenya*, ed. Smokin Wanjala and Kivutha Kibwana (Nairobi: Claripress, 1997), 394.

1. William H. Friedland, *Vuta Kamba: The Development of the Trade Unions in Tanganyika* (Stanford, Calif.: Stanford University and Hoover Institution Press, 1969).

2. Mohamed Said, *The Life and Times of Abdulwahid Sykes 1924–1968: The Untold Story of the Muslim Struggle Against British Colonialism in Tanganyika* (London: Minerva Press, 1998), 219.

3. This was in an interview with Susan Geiger held at Kinondoni, Dar es Salaam, in October 1984. See Susan Geiger, "Tanganyikan Nationalism as 'Women's Work': Life Histories, Collective Biography and Changing Historiography," *Journal of African History* 37 (1996): 472. See also Susan Geiger, *TANU Women: Gender and Culture in the Making of Tanganyikan Nationalism, 1955–1965* (Portsmouth, N.H./Oxford/ Nairobi/Dar es Salaam: Heinemann; James Currey; E.A.E.P.; Mkuki na Nyota, 1997), 63, in which Bibi Titi Mohamed claims among other things, having taught Mwalimu Julius Nyerere how to talk to the people.

4. On the various civil society organizations during this period see, inter alia, Sorobea N. Bogonko, *Kenya 1945–1963: A Study in African National Movements* (Nairobi: Kenya Literature Bureau, 1980); Oginga Odinga, *Not Yet Uhuru: An Autobiography* (Nairobi: East African Educational Publishers, 1969); Bildad Kaggia, *Roots of Freedom: 1921–1963* (Nairobi: East African Publishing House, 1975); J. Ojwando Abour, *White Highlands No More* (Nairobi: Pan African Researchers, 1970).

5. See Mutahi G. Ngunyi, "Building Democracy in a Polarised Civil Society: The Transition to Multiparty Democracy in Kenya," in *Law and the Struggle for Democracy in East Africa*, ed. Joseph Oloka-Onyango, Kivutha Kibwana and Chris Maina Peter (Nairobi: Claripress, 1996), 251.

6. See Zarina Patel, *Unquiet: The Life & Times of Makhan Singh* (Nairobi: Zand Graphics Ltd, 2006).

7. See George Gona, *Andrew Mtagwaba Kailembo: The Life and Times of an African Trade Unionist* (Nairobi: Catholic University of Eastern Africa, 2002); Jim Bailey, *Kenya: The National Epic—From the Pages of Drum Magazine* (Nairobi: Kenway, 1993).

8. See G. W. Kanyeihamba, *Constitutional and Political History of Uganda: From 1894 to the Present* (Kampala: Centenary Publishing House, 2002), 40.

9. See Dani Wadada Nabudere, *Imperialism and Revolution in Uganda* (London and Dar es Salaam: Onyx Press and Tanzania Publishing House, 1980), 128.

10. See Mahmood Mamdani, *Politics and Class Formation in Uganda* (Nairobi: Heinemann, 1976), 151.

11. For the effect of this trend on Tanzania, see Goran Hyden, "Party, State, and Civil

Society: Control Versus Openness," in *Beyond Capitalism vs. Socialism in Kenya and Tanzania*, ed. Joel D. Barkan (Nairobi: East African Educational Publishers, 1994), 92.

12. On this dreadful period in which any form of civic organization was highly restricted in Uganda see, inter alia, David Martin, *General Amin* (London: Faber and Faber, 1974); Dani Wadada Nabudere, *Imperialism and Revolution in Uganda* (London: Zed Books, 1980); Tony Avigan and Martha Honey, *War in Uganda: The Legacy of Idi Amin* (Dar es Salaam: Tanzania Publishing House, 1982); Mahmood Mamdani, *Imperialism and Fascism in Uganda* (Nairobi: Heinemann, 1983); Adam Seftel, *Uganda: The Bloodstained Pearl of Africa and Its Struggle for Peace* (Lanseria: Bailey's African Photo Archives Production, 1994).

13. See Juma V. Mwapachu, *Confronting New Realities: Reflections on Tanzania's Radical Transformation* (Dar es Salaam: E & D, 2005), 102.

14. Ibid.

15. On the position of the struggle of the Church against authoritarianism in Kenya, see Gideon Githiga, *The Church as the Bulwark Against Authoritarianism: Development of Church-State Relations in Kenya, With Particular Reference to the Years After Political Independence 1963–1992* (Oxford: Regnum International, 2001).

16. See, for instance, Henry Okullu, *Church and Politics in East Africa* (Nairobi: Uzima Press, 1974); Henry Okullu, *Quest for Justice* (Kisumu: Shalom Publishers and Computer Training Centre, 1997); Martha Wangari Musalia, *Archbishop Manasses Kuria: Strong in the Storms* (Nairobi: Cana Publishing, 2001); Margaret Ogola and Margaret Roche, *Cardinal Otunga: A Gift of Grace* (Nairobi: Pauline Publications Africa, 1999).

17. Among suspicious deaths of people related to faith-based organizations is that of Bishop Alexander Kipsang Muge in August 1990. See Africa Watch, *Kenya: Talking Liberties* (New York: Human Rights Watch, July 1991), 222–24. Bishop Muge is also discussed not in very positive light in Wanyiri Kihoro, *The Price of Freedom: The Story of Political Resistance in Kenya* (Nairobi: Mvule Africa Publishers, 2005), 3. Also unresolved, notwithstanding inviting the Federal Bureau of Investigations, is the death of Father John Anthony Kaiser, an American Mill Hill Missionary. See John Anthony Kaiser, *If I Die* (Nairobi: Cana Publishing, 2003).

18. Yet, it has been noted that the rural areas—at the village level—are the genesis of civil society. See Issa G. Shivji, "Village Democracy: True Root in Civil Society," in *In Search of Freedom and Prosperity: Constitutional Reform in East Africa*, ed. Kivutha Kibwana, Chris Maina Peter, and Joseph Oloka-Onyango (Nairobi: Claripress, 1996), 25.

19. See Robert Rweyemamu, "The Women Who Scared the Men of Power," *East African* 11 (June 9–15, 1997): 9.

20. See "BAWATA Already Deregistered—Tibaijuka: Notice Merely Formal," *The Guardian*, Tanzania, June 7, 1997, 1. See also "Govt Deletes Women Council," *Daily News*, Tanzania, July 2, 1997, 1; "BAWATA Scrapped Since Monday: Set to Lodge an Appeal to the Registrar Within 21 Days," *The Guardian*, Tanzania, July 2, 1997, 1.

21. See the ruling given by Hon. Mr. Justice (rtd.) Chipeta in *Baraza la Wanawake Tanzania (BAWATA) and 5 Others v. Registrar of Societies and 2 Others*, High Court of Tanzania at Dar es Salaam, Miscellaneous Civil Cause No. 27 of 1997.

22. See Issa G. Shivji, "Reflections on NGOs in Tanzania: What We Are, What We Are Not, and What We Ought to Be," Keynote Address at the September 2003 Gender Festival organized by the Tanzania Gender Networking Group of Dar es Salaam, Tanzania, published

in *Development in Practice* 14, 5 (August 2004). This point is picked up and amplified in Kenny Manara, "Why Advocacy Is Good for the Poor," *The African*, Dar es Salaam, April 25, 2006, 18.

23. A good example here is that of the Legal and Human Rights Network (LEGAL-NET) a loose network of six NGOs involved in provision of legal aid in Tanzania [Legal and Human Rights Centre (LHRC); Women Legal Aid Centre (WLAC); Tanzania Women Lawyers Association (TAWLA); Tanganyika Law Society (TLS); Tanzania Media Women Association (TAMWA); and the Legal Aid Committee of the Faculty of Law, University of Dar es Salaam (LAC)]. They voluntarily agreed to forgo TShs. 1.5 billion in financial support from the donor because of the squeeze and excessive interference in their day-to-day operations by the donor. See Chris Maina Peter, "Right of Access to Justice in Tanzania," in *Human Rights Challenges in a Developing Country: Options and Strategies*, ed. Omary Mjenga, Projectus Rwehumbiza, and Simia Ahmadi, 71, 92 (Dar es Salaam: Legal and Human Rights Centre, 2003).

24. For instance former activist lawyers like Kiraitu Murungi and Martha Karua joined the government at cabinet level and were later on joined by Kivutha Kibwana. Other noteworthy appointments include Maina Kiai as Chair of the Kenya Human Rights Commission; Kathurima M'Inoti as Chair of the Law Reform Commission of Kenya; and Raychelle Omamo, the former Law Society of Kenya Chairperson as Ambassador to France. Interestingly, they joined people they have been fighting having been cited in all forms of atrocities such as tribal clashes, Goldenberg scandal etc. See *inter alia, Nairobi Law Monthly* 84 (August 2003); *The Lawyer* 58 (June 2003); *The Lawyer* 90 (February 2006).

25. Act No. 24 of 2002. This Act defines the term NGO widely to include any voluntary grouping of individuals or organization which is autonomous, nonpartisan, non-profit-making which is Organized locally at the grassroots, national or international levels for the purpose of enhancing or Promoting economic, environmental, social or cultural development or Protecting environment, lobbying or advocating on issues of public interest of a group of individuals or organization, and includes a Non-Governmental Organization, established under the auspices of a any religious Organization or faith Propagating organization' trade union, sports club, Political party, or community based Organization; but does not include a trade, union, a social club or a sports club, a political Party, a religious Organization or a community based organization. It is therefore hard for any civil organization to operate outside the law.

26. Section 25 of the Act 24 of 2002.

27. See the Prevention of Terrorism Act, (Act No. 21 of 2002) whose main aim is said to be to provision of comprehensive measures of dealing with terrorism, to prevent and to cooperate with other states in the suppression of terrorism.

28. Chapters 486, 108 of the Laws of Kenya.

29. Patricia Kameri-Mbote, *The Operational Environment and Constraints for NGOs in Kenya: Strategies for Good Policy and Practice* (Geneva: International Environmental Law Research Centre, 2002), 4.

30. On the work of the civil society in rural Kenya particularly in the democratic process see, inter alia, Frederick O. Wanyama, "Civil Society and the Lopsided Democratization Process: The Unfulfilled Expectations of Community-Based Organizations in Rural Kenya," *East African Journal of Human Rights and Democracy* 1, 1 (2003): 43.

31. A government minister once characterized NGOs as a dangerous weed that should be weeded out. See Sunkuli Condemns NGOs," *Daily Nation* (Kenya), July 22, 1999, quoted in Kameri-Mbote, *The Operational Environment and Constraints for NGOs*, 30.

32. Act No. 19 of 1990. This Act has to read together with NGO Coordination Regulations, 1992 (Legal Notice No. 152 of 1992); the NGO Council Code of Conduct 1995 (Legal Notice No. 306 of 1995); and Rules and Regulations of NGOs Council of Kenya approved by the General Assembly of NGOs Council of Kenya, July 15, 1993.

33. Section 2 of the Act defines an NGO as a private voluntary grouping of individuals or associations not operated for profit or for other commercial purposes but which have organized themselves nationally or internationally for the benefit of the public at large and for the promotion of social welfare development, charity or research in the areas inclusive but not restricted to health relief, agricultural, education, industry and supply of amenities and services. The Co-ordination Board is established by Section 3.

34. Section 23 of Act No. 19.

35. This saga is narrated at length in Kameri-MBote, *The Operational Environment and Constraints for NGOs in Kenya: Strategies for Good Policy and Practice*, 14. Also, all documents relating to registration, intention to deregister and deregistration of CLARION, documents by counsel and their memorandum to the High Court and some background materials are all reproduced in Wanjala and Kibwana, *Democratisation and Law Reform in Kenya*, 397.

36. See Karuti Kanyinga, "Civil Society and Democratisation Process in Kenya," in *Yearning for Democracy: Kenya at Dawn of a New Century*, ed. Smokin Wanjala, S. Kichamu Akivaga, and Kivutha Kibwana, 25 (Nairobi: Claripress, 2002).

37. See Africa Watch, Kenya: *Talking Liberties*, esp. chapter 13, which examines the relationship between the Church and the State, 217–236.

38. On the background to NGOs in Uganda and their relationship to political parties see Frederick W. Jjuuko, "Political Parties, NGOs and Civil Society in Uganda," in Oloka-Onyango et al., eds., *Law and the Struggle for Democracy*, 180.

39. On the movement toward this legislation see Human Rights Watch, *Hostile to Democracy: The Movement System and Political Repression in Uganda* (New York: Human Rights Watch, 1999), 88.

40. On this bizarre event see, inter alia, Uganda Human Rights Commission, *The Kanungu Massacre: The Movement for the Restoration of the Ten Commandments of God Indicted* (Kampala: UHRC, 2002); George W. K. L Kasozi, *Assault on the Spying Church in Uganda: The Violation of the Right to Freedom of Religion and Worship* (Maseru, Lesotho: Government Printer, 2001), 155.

41. See Shivji, "Reflections on NGOs in Tanzania," 689.

42. See Mwapachu, *Confronting New Realities*, 103.

CONTRIBUTORS

Margaret A. Burnham is Professor of Law at Northeastern University. Her research interests are in civil rights, human rights, and comparative constitutional law. She began her career at the NAACP Legal Defense Fund. She practiced criminal defense law, represented Angela Davis, served as a state court judge, and was a partner in a firm. She has participated in human rights missions and delegations to thirty countries. In 1991, Nelson Mandela appointed her to a commission that investigated human rights violations charged against the African National Congress. Professor Burnham directs the Northeastern University Program on Civil Rights and Restorative Justice, a resource center that addresses the failure of law enforcement to protect civil rights activists in the United States during the 1950s and 1960s.

Shaila Gupta is a Development Specialist with Emerging Markets Group, an international development consulting in Arlington, Virginia. Ms. Gupta worked in Pretoria with the Institute for Democracy in South Africa as a researcher. Prior to moving to South Africa, Ms. Gupta worked for the District of Columbia as a budget analyst and financial manager. She is a graduate of the Maxwell School of Citizenship at Syracuse University.

Karuti Kanyinga is a Senior Research Fellow at the Institute for Development Studies (IDS), University of Nairobi, Kenya, where he also teaches development theory and development management. He has carried out research and published extensively on governance, democracy, and development in the Eastern Africa region as well as the politics of land rights in Kenya. His articles include "Ethnic Inequalities and Governance of the Public Sector in Kenya," and "The Civil Society and Democratization Process in Kenya." He sits on the Board of the Kenya Human Rights Commission. He has carried out several donor-commissioned studies and assignments on civic and voter education in the Eastern Africa region.

Alycia Kellman is a graduate of Yale College and the University of Witwatersrand in Johannesburg, South Africa. She lived in South Africa for two years and worked as a researcher at the Institute for Democracy in South Africa and the Centre for Human Rights at the University of Pretoria. She is a third-year law student at Georgetown University Law Center.

Wanjiku Miano is a lawyer and an advocate of human rights with extensive experience. She has held various positions with leading NGOs in Kenya. She has previously worked with Kituo Cha Sheria, a pioneering legal aid and human rights organization in Kenya known for innovative public interest litigation and social justice. She has also worked with the Green Belt Movement, an environmental justice and advocacy organization. Until 2006, Ms. Miano served as Executive Director of the Kenya Human Rights Commission, the leading Kenyan human rights NGO popular for its pioneering work in human rights advocacy. She holds a master's degree in human rights law from the University of Notre Dame Law School.

Betty K. Murungi is a feminist lawyer with expertise in international human rights law and transitional justice. She is actively involved in matters of human rights of women, gender, governance, and rule of law, democracy, and constitutional development. Since 1998, she has been a consultant and legal adviser to the Women's Rights Program at Rights and Democracy on gender-related crimes at the International Criminal Tribunal for Rwanda. She serves as the Director of Urgent Action Fund-Africa. In 2005–2006, she was a Visiting Fellow at the Harvard Law School Human Rights Program and was named the 2005 International Advocate for Peace by the Cardozo School of Law. Ms. Murungi serves on the Board of the Kenya Human Rights Commission as Vice Chair. In 2003–2004, she worked closely with UNIFEM in engendering the Sierra Leonean Truth & Reconciliation Commission. She is an advocate of the High Court of Kenya and was awarded by President Mwai Kibaki the national honor of the Moran of the Order of the Burning Spear (MBS) in December 2003 for her work in human rights.

Jacinta K. Muteshi has worked as a consultant and scholar in the field of women's rights and gender equality. She has combined research, teaching, and training in gender studies and has published widely in these areas. In 2006, she was appointed by President Mwai Kibaki of Kenya to the Committee of Eminent Persons to provide a road map for the conclusion of the constitutional review process. She is the Chairperson of the National Commission on Gender and Development in Kenya. Previously, she served as a Director on the Board of the Kenya Human Rights Commission. She is a member of the Board of the Institute for Education and Democracy. Dr. Muteshi has taught locally and abroad: at the University of Toronto and McMaster University in Canada, and at Kenyatta University and United States International University (USIU) in Kenya. She was educated at the State University of New York, McGill University, and the University of Toronto, where she obtained a doctorate in women's studies.

Makau Mutua is Dean and SUNY Distinguished Professor at the State University of New York at Buffalo Law School, where he teaches international human rights, international business transactions, and public international law. He is also the Floyd H. & Hilda L. Hurst Faculty Scholar and Director of the Human Rights Center there. Professor Mutua has been a Visiting Professor at Harvard Law School, the University of Iowa College of Law, the University of Puerto Rico School of Law, and the United Nations University for Peace in Costa Rica. He was educated at the University of Nairobi, the University of Dar es Salaam, and at Harvard Law School, where he obtained a doctorate in juridical science in 1987. Professor Mutua was Co-Chair of the 2000 Annual Meeting of the American Society of International Law (ASIL). He is a member of the Executive Council of the ASIL.

In 2002–2003, while on sabbatical in Kenya, Professor Mutua was appointed by the government of Kenya as Chairman of the Task Force on the Establishment of a Truth, Justice, and Reconciliation Commission. The Task Force recommended a truth commission for Kenya. During the same time, he was a delegate to the National Constitutional Conference, the forum that produced a contested draft constitution for Kenya. He is the author of *Human Rights: A Political and Cultural Critique* (University of Pennsylvania Press). He has written numerous scholarly articles exploring topical subjects in international law, human rights, and religion. He has authored dozens of articles for popular publications such as the *New York Times, Boston Globe, Christian Science Monitor, Daily Nation, East African Standard*, and the *Washington Post*.

Previously, Professor Mutua was Associate Director at the Harvard Law School Human Rights Program. He was also Director of the Africa Project at the Lawyers Committee for Human Rights. He serves as Chairman of the Kenya Human Rights Commission and sits on the boards of several international organizations, including Global Rights, and academic journals, including the *Leiden Journal of International Law*. He is a frequent commentator on politics, human rights, law, and current affairs in the print and electronic media. He has conducted numerous human rights, diplomatic, and rule of law missions to countries in Africa, Latin America, and Europe. He has lectured and spoken at public forums in many parts of the world, including Japan, Brazil, France, and Ethiopia

Willy Mutunga is East Africa's most celebrated human rights pioneer. He was educated at the University of Dar es Salaam and Osgoode Hall Law School in Toronto, where he obtained a doctorate in law. He has mentored scores of leading academics and human rights scholar-activists. An advocate of the High Court of Kenya, Dr. Mutunga taught law at the University of Nairobi from 1974 to 1982 when he was detained by the government of President Daniel arap Moi for being an outspoken advocate of human rights. Dr. Mutunga has been the Secretary General of the Nairobi University Staff Union (USU), Secretary General of the University of Nairobi Academic Staff Association, and a member of the December Twelfth Movement (DTM). He has been an attorney for polit-ical detainees, and served as Chair of the Law Society of Kenya. He is Senior Counsel, the highest rank an attorney can attain in Kenya. He was a founding board member of the Kenya Human Rights Commission, and served as it Vice Chair and Executive Director.

Dr. Mutunga was central to the establishment of Kituo Cha Sheria, Kenya's first public interest legal aid organization. He was a Co-Convener of the Na-tional Convention Assembly (NCA) and its executive arm, the National Con-vention Executive Council (NCEC). He was Co-Chair of the Citizens Coalition for Constitutional Change (4Cs). Dr. Mutunga served as a board member of the Rights and Democracy in Montreal. He is the author of many scholarly articles and publications, including *Constitution-Making from the Middle: Civil Society and Transition Politics in Kenya 1992–1997*, the only comprehensive treat-ment of the Kenyan constitution-making process. Currently, he is Program Of-ficer for Human Rights and Social Justice at the Ford Foundation in Nairobi.

Dani W. Nabudere is Executive Director of Afrika Study Centre and the Mar-cus-Garvey Pan-Afrikan Institute, Mbale, Uganda. He was a member of the Program Committee on Security and International Cooperation of the Social Science Research Council-SSRC of New York under which he undertook a "field building" research activity on human security in pastoral communities in East Africa. He is the Principal Investigator in a Ford Foundation-funded two-year research project on Restorative Justice in five countries—Uganda, Kenya, Tanzania, Rwanda, and Sudan—aimed at developing a synthesis between restor-ative justice and international humanitarian law. Professor Nabudere is pub-lished widely as a legal scholar and critic of liberalism and imperialism. Previously, he was a professor of law at the Faculty of Law, University of Dar es Salaam. He is one of East Africa's most acclaimed academics.

Connie Ngondi-Houghton is a lawyer by training. She was educated at the University of Nairobi and at Yale Law School. She is a leading human rights advocate in Kenya and an advocate of the High Court of Kenya. She has worked as Executive Director of the Kenya chapter of the International Commission of Jurists and has consulted extensively for charities, NGOs, and donors in Kenya, including the Ford Foundation. Her most recent work concentrates on philanthropy in East Africa. She is author, most recently, of *Philanthropy in East Africa.*

Joe Oloka-Onyango is Director of the Human Rights & Peace Centre (HURI-PEC) and former Dean of Law at Makerere University in Uganda. Professor Onyango is a founding director of Kituo Cha Katiba, the Center for Constitutionalism. He has been Visiting Professor at a number of universities, including Harvard Law School, New York University Law School, and the University of Minnesota School of Law. He has also taught in universities in several African states. Professor Oloka-Onyango was a member and Special Rapporteur on Globalization and Human Rights of the United Nations (UN) Sub-Commission on the Promotion and Protection of Human Rights. His areas of teaching interest and research include international human rights law, refugee law, gender and the law, and constitutional law and history. He is one of the most published legal academics in Africa, author and editor of many articles and books, including *Constitutionalism in Africa: Creating Opportunities and Facing Challenges.*

Chris Maina Peter is Professor of Law at the Faculty of Law, University of Dar es Salaam, Tanzania. He holds LL.B. and LL.M. degrees from the University of Dar es Salaam and a doctorate in law from the University of Konstanz in Germany. He teaches public international law, refugee law, and human rights. Professor Peter has been a Visiting Professor at the University of Graz in Austria and University of Hamburg in Germany. He has written and edited several books including *Fundamental Rights and Freedoms in Tanzania*; *Human Rights in Tanzania: Selected Cases and Materials*; and *Human Rights in Africa: A Comparative Study of the African Human and Peoples' Rights Charter and the New Tanzanian Bill of Rights.*

Livingstone Sewanyana is founder and Executive Director of the Foundation for Human Rights Initiative (FHRI), a leading human rights NGO in Uganda. He is a human rights advocate and graduated with distinction in human rights from the University of Essex, United Kingdom. He is the Deputy Secretary General, Penal Reform International, in the United Kingdom. Mr. Sewanyana is founding chair of the Uganda Human Rights Network and serves as Chair of Volunteer Efforts for Development Concerns in Uganda. He has authored numerous articles in leading journals. His book *Human Rights in Uganda* is forthcoming. He is winner of the 2005 Law Society Humanitarian Award and 2006 Young Alumnus Award of the British Uganda Alumni Association.

Sylvia Tamale is a feminist activist and academic based in Kampala, Uganda. She is an Associate Professor of Law and Dean of Law at Makerere University. She holds a bachelor's degree in Law from Makerere University, a master's in law from Harvard Law School, and a Ph.D. in sociology (major) and feminist studies (minor) from the University of Minnesota. Professor Tamale founded and serves as coordinator of the Gender, Law & Sexuality Research Project at the Law Faculty. Her research interests include Third World Women and the Law, Women and Politics, and Gender, Identity and Sexuality. She is author of many publications, including *When Hens Begin to Crow: Gender and Parliamentary Politics in Uganda*. She has won several awards for defending the human rights of marginalized groups such as women, gays and lesbians, and refugees.

L. Muthoni Wanyeki is the Executive Director of the Kenya Human Rights Commission. Kenya's leading human rights NGO. She is a political scientist who works on development communications, gender, and human rights. She has written in these areas. She is the immediate past Executive Director of the African Women's Development and Communication Network (FEMNET), a pan-African membership organization set up in 1988 and based in Nairobi, Kenya. FEMNET works towards African women's development, equality and other human rights through advocacy at the regional and international levels, training on gender analysis and mainstreaming, and communications. She is also a political columnist with the *East African* and serves as a board member and regional advisor with several African and international NGOs.

INDEX

Acknowledgments

Although civil society in East Africa had grown tremendously in the preceding two decades, its key actors rarely come together to critically reflect on the phenomenon. I am grateful to all of them for taking time out of their busy schedules to participate in this project.

I would especially like to recognize several people and institutions without which the book would not have been possible. Willy Mutunga has long been regarded as the father of the human rights movement in Kenya. My earliest and most critical political and academic mentor, he deserves the lion's share of the credit for conceiving the idea and then funding it from his position as Program Officer for Human Rights and Social Justice at the Ford Foundation in Nairobi. At every turn, he encouraged and guided me as I edited the book. At my insistence, he contributed the chapter on feminist masculinity for this book. It is important to point out that the chapter does not reflect the views of the Ford Foundation. It has been my privilege to work with Willy also in many other endeavors, including his stewardship until 2003 of the Kenya Human Rights Commission. I would not be the person I am today without Willy's inspiration and guidance.

I would also like to thank Omotade Aina, head of the Ford Foundation office in Nairobi. He is a towering figure of pan-Africanism and a true postcolonial intellectual. The first African to lead the foundation in Eastern Africa, Tade has more than vindicated the wisdom of that important choice. His leadership within the donor community is well known and greatly appreciated among civil society actors in East Africa. When history is written, it will show that Tade was the critical turning point in transforming donor-donee relationships for the better in the region. His humble approach to this complex relationship has created room for African NGOs to find themselves and pursue the projects that really matter to the region. Tade's unwavering support for this book project is responsible for its realization.

Davinder Lamba, Executive Director at Mazingira, and the staff at Mazingira—Zarina Ishani, Bindu, and Deborah Gathu—were invaluable to this project. They were assisted by two International Law Fellows from the Human Rights Center at the State University of New York at Buffalo Law School, Susan Cimini and Mary Little. This team made everything work in many ways, both large and small.

I would be remiss if I did not thank the yeomanly and excellent work that my research assistant at Buffalo Law School—Lisa Bailey—did on the manuscript. She carefully read through the draft chapters with an editor's mind and checked and corrected multiple citations. I owe her a debt of gratitude. In addition, I would like to thank Erin Tubbs, another research assistant, who also helped with the manuscript. But none of these tasks would have executed without the unflinching support and common sense advice of Sandra Conti, my assistant at the Law School. Sandy is the model workmate—patient, diligent, and hardworking. She is the quintessential professional.

Last, but not least, I owe a big thank you to my family for supporting me through the project. Athena, my spouse, juggled her own demanding career with the ever-challenging task of raising our boys while supporting my work. Her intellectual curiosity and gifts sharpened many an argument in the book. Her support has been priceless. My three boys—Lumumba, Amani, and Mwalimu—had to endure many days without me as I saw this project through. It is their unqualified understanding that has given me some solace. My hope is that they will judge it worth the effort once they have read the book.